CRITICAL PAPERS IN ART
STUBBS'S CALENDAR
BARBER COX

W. M. THACKERAY

AT THE AGE OF ELEVEN

From the Bust by J. Devile in the National Portrait Gallery.

CRITICAL PAPERS IN ART
STUBBS'S CALENDAR
BARBER COX

BY

WILLIAM MAKEPEACE THACKERAY

With Illustrations by the Author and George Cruikshank

London
MACMILLAN AND CO., Limited
NEW YORK : THE MACMILLAN COMPANY
1904

NOTE.

IN preceding editions of Thackeray's Works, the Critical Papers in Art are scattered throughout the numerous volumes. They are now brought together and arranged in chronological order. Of the sixteen articles, three are reprinted for the first time and eight are for the first time included in an edition of Thackeray's Works.

When Thackeray lost his fortune he looked to Art and not to Literature to provide him with the means of living, and, as late as 1837, Edinburgh Reviewer Hayward well remembered seeing him, day after day, engaged in copying pictures in the Louvre, in order to qualify himself for his profession. Indeed, for years he devoted himself to the study of Art, spending his days copying pictures in the gallery or in the studios of Brine or Gros, and his evening in the company of young artists. It was thus that he laid the foundation of his knowledge of pictures and drawings.

'Thackeray was one of the best of art-critics. He had the true instinct and relish, and the nicety and directness, necessary for just as well as high criticism : the white light of his intellect found its way into this as into every region of his work. . . . It would not be easy to imagine better criticisms of art than those from Mr. Thackeray's hand. His art "has its seat in reason," and he is more objective, cool and critical than Mr. Ruskin.' So wrote Dr. John Brown ; and his words have been echoed by many good judges.

On matters artistic again and again Thackeray laid down the law with no uncertain voice. His courage was prodigious. As it was said of Disraeli, even at the beginning of his career, that he attacked men bigger than himself, so it may be noticed that Thackeray made it a rule to tilt against men of recognised position of whose artistic productions he disapproved, and let the smaller fry escape easily enough.

Thackeray's art-criticism was not pleasant reading for the painters of the day. They were not accustomed to such outspoken articles, and their annoyance knew no bounds. 'If you want to know something of the Exhibition, however, read *Fraser's Magazine* for this month [June, 1845]; there Thackeray has a paper [*Picture Gossip*] on the matter, full of fun,' Edward Fitz-Gerald wrote to Frederick Tennyson. 'I met Stone in the street the other day ; he took me by the button, and told me in perfect sincerity and with increasing warmth how, though he loved old Thackeray, yet these yearly out-speakings of his sorely tried him ; not on account of himself (Stone), but on account of some of his friends, Charles Landseer, Maclise, etc. Stone worked himself up to such a pitch under the pressure of forced calmness, that he at last said Thackeray would get himself horsewhipped one day by one of these infuriated Apelleses. At this I, who had partly agreed with Stone that ridicule, though true, need not always be spoken, began to laugh, and told him two could play at that game. These painters cling together and bolster each other up to such a degree that they have really persuaded themselves that any one who ventures to laugh at one of their drawings, exhibited for the express purpose of criticism, insults the whole corps. Thackeray laughs at all this, and goes on in his own way ; writing hard for half-a-day. Reviews and newspapers all the morning ; dining, drinking, and talking of a night ; managing to preserve a fresh colour and perpetual flow of spirits under a wear and tear of thinking and feeding, that would have knocked up all the other men I know two years ago, at least.'

The following is a complete list of Thackeray's Critical Papers in Art :—

(i.) *Strictures on Pictures* (*Fraser's Magazine*, June, 1838), and

(ii.) *A Second Lecture on the Fine Arts* (*Fraser's Magazine*, June, 1839), reprinted in *Miscellanies* (Boston, vol. v., 1870) and in a supplementary volume of the Library edition of Thackeray's Works (vol. xxiii. : *Miscellaneous Essays, etc.*, 1885).

(iii.) *On the French School of Painting* (*Fraser's Magazine*, December, 1839), reprinted in *The Paris Sketch Book* (1840) and in the Library edition of Thackeray's Works (vol. xii. : *The Paris Sketch Book, etc.*, 1868). See vol. vii. of this edition : *The Paris Sketch Book, etc.*

This article also appeared in *The Corsair* (New York, September 28, 1839 ; January 18, 1840) under the title of *Letters from London, Paris, Pekin, Petersburgh, etc. By the Author of ' The Yellowplush Correspondence,' the ' Memoirs of*

Major Gahagan,' etc.—A Ramble in the Picture Galleries. The first instalment was signed 'T. T.'; the second 'M. A. T.' It was reprinted from *The Corsair* in *The Student's Quarter* (1870).

(iv.) A review of *The Humourist. A Collection of Entertaining Tales, Anecdotes, Epigrams, Bon-mots, etc.*, and other books, illustrated by George Cruikshank (*The Westminster Review*, June, 1840), reprinted in book-form under the title of

An | Essay on the Genius | of | George Cruikshank. | With numerous Illustrations of his works. | (From *The Westminster Review*, No. lxvi.) | With additional Etchings. | London : | Henry Hooper, 13 Pall Mall East. | MDCCCXL.

The *Essay* was reprinted, without the Illustrations, in *Miscellanies* (Boston, vol. v., 1870) and in the Library edition of Thackeray's Works (vol. xxii. : *Catherine, etc.*, 1869) ; and, with the illustrations that appeared in *The Westminster Review*, in the cheaper Illustrated edition of Thackeray's Works (vol. xviii. : *The Irish Sketch Book and Critical Reviews*, 1879). It has been reprinted in this volume from the issue in book-form, with all the additional illustrations.

(v.) *A Pictorial Rhapsody* (*Fraser's Magazine*, June, 1840), and

(vi.) *A Pictorial Rhapsody : Concluded* (*Fraser's Magazine*, July, 1840), reprinted in *Miscellanies* (Boston, vol. v., 1870), and in a supplementary volume of the Library edition of Thackeray's Works (vol. xxiii. : *Miscellaneous Essays, etc.*, 1885).

(vii.) *Caricatures and Lithography in Paris* (*The Paris Sketch Book*, 1840), reprinted in the Library edition of Thackeray's Works (vol. xii. : *The Paris Sketch Book, etc.*, 1868). See vol. vii. of this edition : *The Paris Sketch Book, etc.*

(viii.) *On Men and Pictures. À propos of a Walk in the Louvre* (*Fraser's Magazine*, July, 1841), reprinted in *Early and Late Papers* (Boston, 1867), in *Miscellanies* (Boston, vol. v., 1870), and in a supplementary volume of the Library edition of Thackeray's Works (vol. xxiii. : *Miscellaneous Essays, etc.*, 1885).

(ix.) *An Exhibition Gossip* (*Ainsworth's Magazine*, June, 1842), now reprinted for the first time.

(x.) *Letters on the Fine Arts* (*The Pictorial Times*).

No. 1. *The Art Unions* (March 18, 1843).

No. 2. *The Objections against Art Unions* (April 1, 8, 1843).

No. 3. *The Royal Academy* (May 13, 1843).

No. 4. *The Royal Academy.* Second Notice. (May 27, 1843.)

Reprinted in *Sultan Stork, etc.* (1887), and in Thackeray's *Stray Papers*, collected and edited by Mr. Lewis Melville (1901). It is now included for the first time in an edition of Thackeray's Works.

(xi.) *The Water-Colour Exhibition* (*The Pictorial Times*, May 6, 1843), reprinted in Thackeray's *Stray Papers* (1901), and now included for the first time in an edition of Thackeray's Works.

(xii.) *May Gambols; or, Titmarsh in the Picture Galleries* (*Fraser's Magazine*, June, 1844), reprinted in *Miscellanies* (Boston, vol. v., 1870), and in a supplementary volume of the Library edition of Thackeray's works (vol. xxiii. : *Miscellaneous Essays, etc.*, 1885). Now first reprinted in its entirety.

(xiii.) *Picture Gossip* (*Fraser's Magazine*, June, 1845), reprinted in *Early and Late Papers* (Boston, 1867), in *Miscellanies* (Boston, vol. v., 1870), and in a supplementary volume of the Library edition of Thackeray's Works (vol. xxiii. : *Miscellaneous Essays, etc.*, 1885).

(xiv.) Sketches | after | English Landscape Painters. | By L. Marvy. | With Short Notices by W. M. Thackeray. | London. | David Bogue, 86 Fleet Street | [1850].

This volume was subsequently reissued, undated [1851], with a new title-page bearing the name of Griffen and Co. The notices by Thackeray, accompanied by reproductions of the engravings by L. Marvy, are now reprinted for the first time.

(xv.) A review of *Pictures of Life and Character. By John Leech* (*The Quarterly Review*, December, 1854), reprinted in *Early and Late Papers* (Boston, 1867), in *Miscellanies* (Boston, vol. iv., 1869), and in the Library edition of Thackeray's Works (vol. xxii. : *Catherine . . . and Critical Reviews*, 1869).

This paper was the cause of a misunderstanding with the members of the *Punch* staff, because in it he wrote : 'There is no blinking the fact that in *Mr. Punch's* cabinet John Leech is the right-hand man. Fancy a number of *Punch* without Leech's pictures ! What would you give for it ? The learned gentlemen who write the work must feel that without him it were as well left alone.' Anthony Trollope has related that for a week there existed at the *Punch* office a grudge against Thackeray in reference to the awkward question : 'What would you give for your *Punch* without John Leech?' Then he asked the confraternity to dinner —*more Thackerayano*—and the confraternity came.

'Of all the slips of my fatal pen,' Thackeray wrote to 'Professor' Percival Leigh, one of the oldest of *Punch's* contributors and the author of *The Comic Latin Grammar*, 'there's none I regret more than the unlucky half-line which has given pain to such a kind and valued friend as you have been, and I trust will be still to me. I ought never to have said, "*Punch* might as well be left unwritten but for Leech." It was more than my meaning, which is certainly that the drawing is one hundred times more popular than the writing ; but I had no business to write any such thing, and forgot it so much that I was quite surprised when I first heard I had been accused of sneering at *Punch*. I knew when I came back from Paris, and read the line in *The Quarterly Review*, which I had forgotten as utterly as many another speech which I have made and didn't ought. Jerrold has had his fire into me, and, do you know, I feel rather comforted.'

(xvi.) *Cruikshank's Gallery* (*The Times*, May 15, 1863), a notice of an exhibition of Cruikshank's works. It is said that the exhibition was little better than a failure until (anxious to render what help he could to an old friend fallen upon evil days) 'kind Thackeray came with his grave face, and looked through the little gallery, and went off to write one of his charming essays.' This paper is now for the first time reprinted.

Thackeray wrote about Rubens and Hans Hemmelinck in *A Roundabout Journey, Notes of a Week's Holiday* (*The Cornhill Magazine*, November, 1860).

He also wrote of art as it was understood by editors and contributors to Keepsakes and Books of Beauty in *A Word on the Annuals* (*Fraser's Magazine*, December, 1837), *The Annuals* (*The Times*, November 2, 1837), and *Our Annual Execution* (*Fraser's Magazine*, January, 1839). These papers are printed in vol. xii. of this edition : *Critical Papers in Literature*. *Our Annuals* are there reprinted for the first time : *A Word on the Annuals* and *Our Annual Execution* for the first time in England.

STUBBS'S CALENDAR, OR, THE FATAL BOOTS

appeared with twelve Illustrations by George Cruikshank, in

The | Comic | Almanack, | For 1839 : | An Ephemeris in Jest and Earnest, | Containing | 'All things fitting for such a Work.' | By Rigdum Funnidos, Gent. | Adorned with a dozen of 'Right Merry' Cuts, pertaining to the Months, and | an Hieroglyphic, | by George Cruikshank. | London : | Imprinted for Charles Tilt, Bibliopolist, | in Fleet Street.

Stubbs's Calendar was reprinted, without the Illustrations, in *Comic Tales and Sketches* (1841) ; and, under the title of *The*

Fatal Boots, in *Miscellanies* (vol. i.: *Ballads* . . . *The Fatal Boots*, 1856); in the Library edition of Thackeray's Works (vol. xxi.: *Denis Duval* . . . *and Other Stories*, 1869); and also in *Miscellanies* (Boston, vol. iii., 1869). It was reprinted, with the Illustrations, in the Cheaper Illustrated edition of Thackeray's Works (vol. xix.: *The Memoirs of Barry Lyndon* . . . *and The Fatal Boots*, 1879).

Stubbs's Calendar has been set up in this volume from *Comic Tales and Sketches*.

BARBER COX AND THE CUTTING OF HIS COMB

appeared with twelve Illustrations by George Cruikshank, in The | Comic | Almanack, | For 1840 : | An Ephemeris in Jest and Earnest, | Containing | 'All things fitting for such a Work.' | By Rigdum Funnidos, Gent. | Adorned with a dozen of 'Right Merry' Cuts, pertaining to the Months, and | an Hieroglyphic, | by George Cruikshank. | London : | Imprinted for Charles Tilt, Bibliopolist, | in Fleet Street.

Barber Cox and the Cutting of His Comb was reprinted, without the Illustrations, under the title of *Cox's Diary*, in *Miscellanies* (vol. i.: *Ballads* . . . *Cox's Diary*, 1855); in the Library edition of Thackeray's Works (vol. xvi.: *Burlesques* . . . *Cox's Diary*, 1869); and also in *Miscellanies* (Boston, vol. i., 1869). It was reprinted, with the Illustrations, in the Cheaper Illustrated edition of Thackeray's Works (vol. xvii.: *The Memoirs of Mr. Charles J. Yellowplush* . . . *Cox's Diary*, 1879).

L. M.

CONTENTS.

CRITICAL PAPERS IN ART.

* Now first included in an edition of Thackeray's Works.
† Now first reprinted.

STUBBS'S CALENDAR; OR, THE FATAL BOOTS.

BARBER COX, AND THE CUTTING OF HIS COMB.

CRITICAL PAPERS IN ART

STRICTURES ON PICTURES.

A LETTER FROM MICHAEL ANGELO TITMARSH, ESQ., TO MONSIEUR ANATOLE VICTOR ISIDOR HYACINTHE ACHILLE HERCULE DE BRICABRAC, PEINTRE D'HISTOIRE, RUE MOUFFETARD, À PARIS.

Lord's Hotel, New Street, Covent Garden,
Tuesday, May 15.

I PROPOSE to be both learned and pleasant in my remarks upon the exhibitions here ; for I know, my dear Bricabrac, that it is your intention to translate this letter into French, for the benefit of some of your countrymen, who are anxious about the progress of the fine arts—when I say some, I mean all, for, thanks to your government patronage, your magnificent public galleries, and, above all, your delicious sky and sunshine, there is not a scavenger in your nation who has not a feeling for the beauty of Nature, which is, my dear Anatole, neither more nor less than Art.

You know nothing about art in this country—almost as little as we know of French art. One Gustave Planche, who makes visits to London, and writes accounts of pictures in your reviews, is, believe me, an impostor. I do not mean a private impostor, for I know not whether Planche is a real or assumed name, but simply a quack on matters of art. Depend on it, my dear young friend, that there is nobody like Titmarsh : you will learn more about the arts in England from this letter, than from anything in or out of print.

Well then, every year, at the commencement of this blessed month of May, wide open the doors of three picture galleries, in which figure all the works of genius which our brother artists have produced during the whole year. I wish you could see my historical picture of ' Heliogabalus in the ruins of Carthage,' or the full-length of ' Sir Samuel Hicks and his Lady,'—sitting in a garden light, Lady H. reading *The Book of Beauty*, Sir Samuel

[1] [*Fraser's Magazine*, June 1838.]

catching a butterfly, which is settling on a flower-pot. This, however, is all egotism. I am not going to speak of *my* works, which are pretty well known in Paris already, as I flatter myself, but of other artists—some of them men of merit—as myself.

Let us commence, then, with the commencement—the Royal Academy. That is held in one wing of a little building like a gin-shop, which is near St. Martin's Church. In the other wing is our National Gallery. As for the building, you must not take *that* as a specimen of our skill in the fine arts ; come down the Seven Dials, and I will show you many modern structures, of which the architect deserves far higher credit.

But, bad as the place is—a pigmy abortion, in lieu of a noble monument to the greatest school of painting in the greatest country of the modern world (you may be angry, but I'm right in *both* cases)—bad as the outside is, the interior, it must be confessed, is marvellously pretty, and convenient for the reception and exhibition of the pictures it will hold. Since the old pictures have got their new gallery, and their new scouring, one hardly knows them. O, Ferdinand, Ferdinand, that *is* a treat, that National Gallery, and no mistake ! I shall write to you fourteen or fifteen long letters about it some day or other. The apartment devoted to the Academy exhibition is equally commodious : a small room for miniatures and aquarelles, another for architectural drawings, and three saloons for pictures—all very small, but well lighted and neat ; no interminable passage, like your five hundred yards at the Louvre, with a slippery floor, and tiresome straggling cross-lights. Let us buy a catalogue, and walk straight into the gallery, however ;—we have been a long time talking, ' *de omnibus rebus*,' at the door.

Look, my dear Isidor, at the first names in the Catalogue, and thank your stars for being in such good company. Bless us and save us, what a power of knights is here !

> Sir William Beechey.
> Sir Martin Shee.
> Sir David Wilkie.
> Sir Augustus Callcott.
> Sir W. J. Newton.
> Sir Geoffrey Wyattville.
> Sir Francis Chantrey.
> Sir Richard Westmacott.
> Sir Michael Angelo Titmarsh—

not yet, that is ; but I shall be, in course, when our little liege lady—Heaven bless her!—has seen my portrait of Sir Sam and Lady Hicks.

If all these gentlemen in the list of Academicians and Associates are to have titles of some sort or other, I should propose—

1. Baron BRIGGS. (At the very least, he is out and out the best portrait-painter of the set.)
2. DANIEL, PRINCE MACLISE. (His Royal Highness's pictures place him very near to the throne indeed.)
3. Edwin, Earl of Landseer.
4. The Lord Charles Landseer.
5. The Duke of Etty.
6. Archbishop Eastlake.
7. His Majesty KING MULREADY.

King Mulready, I repeat, in double capitals ; for, if this man has not the crowning picture of the exhibition, I am no better than a Dutchman. His picture represents the 'Seven Ages,' as described by a poet whom you have heard of—one Shakespeare, a Warwickshire man : and there they are, all together ; the portly justice, and the quarrelsome soldier ; the lover leaning apart, and whispering sweet things in his pretty mistress's ear ; the baby hanging on her gentle mother's bosom ; the school-boy, rosy and lazy ; the old man, crabbed and stingy ; and the old, old man of all, sans teeth, sans eyes, sans ears, sans everything—but why describe them ? You will find the thing better done in Shakespeare, or possibly translated by some of your Frenchmen. I can't say much about the drawing of this picture, for here and there are some queer-looking limbs ; but—oh, Anatole!—the intention is godlike. Not one of those figures but has a grace and a soul of his own : no conventional copies of the stony antique ; no distorted caricatures, like those of your 'classiques,' David, Girodet, and Co. (the impostors !)—but such expressions as a great poet would draw, who thinks profoundly and truly, and never forgets (he could not if he would) grace and beauty withal. The colour and manner of this noble picture are neither of the Venetian school, nor the Florentine, nor the English, but of the Mulready school. Ah ! my dear Floridor ! I wish that you and I, ere we die, may have erected such a beautiful monument to hallow and perpetuate our names. Our children, my boy, Sebastian Piombo Titmarsh, will see this picture in his old age, hanging by the side of the Raffaelles in our National Gallery. I sometimes fancy, in the presence of such works of genius as this, that my picture of Sir Sam and Lady Hicks is but a magnificent error after all, and that it will die away, and be forgotten.

To this, then, of the whole gallery, I accord the palm, and cannot refrain from making a little sketch, illustrative of my feelings.

TITMARSH PLACING THE LAUREL-WREATH ON THE BROWS OF MULREADY.

I have done everything, you see, very accurately, except Mr. Mulready's face; for, to say truth, I never saw that gentleman, and have no idea of his personal appearance.

Near to 'All the world's a stage' is a charming picture, by Archbishop Eastlake; so denominated by me, because the rank is very respectable, and because there is a certain purity and religious feeling in all Mr. Eastlake does, which eminently entitles him to the honours of the prelacy. In this picture, Gaston de Foix (he whom Titian painted, his mistress buckling on his armour) is parting from his mistress. A fair, peaceful garden is round about them; and here his lady sits and clings to him, as though she would cling for ever. But, look! yonder stands the page, and the horse pawing; and, beyond the wall which binds the quiet garden and flowers, you see the spears and pennons of knights, the banners of King Louis and De Foix, 'the thunderbolt of Italy.' Long shining rows of steel-clad men are marching stately by; and with them must ride Count Gaston—to conquer and die at Ravenna. You can read his history, my dear friend, in Lacretelle, or Brantôme; only, perhaps, not so well expressed as it has just been by me.

Yonder is Sir David Wilkie's grand picture—'Queen Victoria holding her First Council.' A marvellous painting, in which one admires the exquisite richness of the colour, the breadth of light and shadow, the graceful dignity and beauty of the principal figure, and the extraordinary skill with which all the figures have been grouped, so as to produce a grand and simple effect. What can one say more, but admire the artist who has made, out of such unpoetical materials as a table of red cloth, and fifty unoccupied middle-aged gentlemen, a beautiful and interesting picture? Sir David has a charming portrait, too, of Mrs. Maberly, in dark crimson velvet, and delicate white hat and feathers ; a marvel of colour, though somewhat askew in the drawing.

The Earl of Landseer's best picture, to my thinking, is that which represents her majesty's favourite dogs and parrot. He has, in painting, an absolute mastery over

$$\kappa \acute{\upsilon} \nu \epsilon \sigma \sigma \iota \nu$$
$$o \grave{\iota} \omega \nu o \hat{\iota} \sigma \acute{\iota} \ \tau \epsilon \ \pi \hat{a} \sigma \iota \ ;$$

that is, he can paint all manner of birds and beasts as nobody else can. To tell you a secret, I do not think he understands how to paint the great beast, man, quite so well ; or, at least, to do what is the highest quality of an artist, to place *a soul* under the ribs as he draws them. They are, if you like, the most dexterous pictures that ever were painted, but not *great* pictures. I would much rather look at yonder rough Leslie than at all the wonderful painting of parrots or greyhounds, though done to a hair or a feather.

Leslie is the only man in this country who translates Shakespeare into form and colour. Old Shallow and Sir Hugh, Slender and his man Simple, pretty Anne Page and the Merry Wives of Windsor, are here joking with the fat knight ; who, with a monstrous gravity and profound brazen humour, is narrating some tale of his feats with the wild Prince and Poins. Master Brooke is offering a tankard to Master Slender, who will not drink, forsooth.

This picture is executed with the utmost simplicity, and almost rudeness ; but is charming, from its great truth of effect and expression. Wilkie's pictures (in his latter style) seem to begin where Leslie's end ; the former's men and women look *as if the bodies had been taken out of them*, and only the surface left. Lovely as the queen's figure is, for instance, it looks like a spirit, and not a woman ; one may almost see through her into the waistcoat of Lord Lansdowne, and so on through the rest of the transparent heroes and statesmen of the company.

Opposite the queen is another charming performance of Sir David—a bride dressing, amidst a rout of bridesmaids and relations. Some are crying, some are smiling, some are pinning her gown ; a back door is open, and a golden sun shines into a room which contains a venerable-looking bed and tester, probably that in which the dear girl is to—but *parlons d'autres choses*. The colour of this picture is delicious, and the effect faultless : Sir David does everything for a picture nowadays but the *drawing*. Who knows ? Perhaps it is as well left out.

Look yonder, down to the ground, and admire a most beautiful fantastic Ariel.

> On the bat's back do I fly,
> After sunset merrily.

Merry Ariel lies at his ease, and whips with gorgeous peacock's feather his courser, flapping lazy through the golden evening sky. This exquisite little picture is the work of Mr. Severn, an artist who has educated his taste and his hand in the early Roman school. He has not the dash and dexterity of the latter which belongs to some of our painters, but he possesses that solemn earnestness and simplicity of mind and purpose which makes a religion of art, and seems to be accorded only to a few in our profession. I have heard a pious pupil of Mr. Ingres (the head of your academy at Rome) aver stoutly, that, in matters of art, Titian was anti - Christ, and Rubens, Martin Luther. They came with their brilliant colours and dashing worldly notions, upsetting that beautiful system of faith in which art had lived hitherto. Portraits of saints and martyrs, with pure eyes turned heavenward, and (as all true sanctity will) making those pure who came within their reach, now gave way to wicked likenesses of men of blood, or dangerous, devilish sensual portraits of tempting women. Before Titian, a picture was the labour of years. Why did this reformer ever come among us, and show how it might be done in a day ? He drove the good angels away from painters' easels, and called down a host of voluptuous spirits instead, who ever since have held the mastery there.

Only a few artists of our country (none in yours, where the so-called Catholic school is a mere theatrical folly), and some among the Germans, have kept to the true faith, and eschewed the temptations of Titian and his like. Mr. Eastlake is one of these. Who does not recollect his portrait of Miss Bury ? Not a simple woman—the lovely daughter of the authoress of *Love*, *Flirtation*, and other remarkable works,—but a glorified saint. Who does not remember his Saint Sebastian ; his body bare, his eyes cast melancholy down ; his limbs, as yet untouched by the arrows of his persecutors, tied to the fatal tree ? Those two pictures of Mr. Eastlake would merit to hang in a gallery where there were only Raffaelles besides. Mr. Severn is another of the school. I don't know what hidden and indefinable charm there is in his simple pictures; but I never can look at them without a certain emotion of awe—with that thrill of the heart with which one hears country children sing the Old Hundredth, for instance. The singers are rude, perhaps, and the voices shrill; but the melody is still pure and godlike. Some such majestic and pious harmony is there in these pictures of Mr. Severn. Mr. Mulready's mind has lately gained this same kind of inspiration. I know no one else who possesses it, except, perhaps, myself. Without flattery, I may say, that my picture of 'Heliogabalus at Carthage' is *not* in the popular taste, and has about it some faint odour of celestial incense.

Do not, my dear Anatole, consider me too great an ass for persisting upon this point, and exemplifying Mr. Severn's picture of the 'Crusaders catching a first view of Jerusalem' as an instance. Godfrey and Tancred, Raymond and Ademar, Beamond and Rinaldo, with Peter and the Christian host, behold at length the day dawning.

> *E quando il sol gli aridi campi fiede*
>   *Con raggi assai ferventi, e in alto sorge,*
> *Ecco apparir Gerusalem si vede,*
>   *Ecco additar Gerusalem si scorge,*
> *Ecco da mille voci unitamente*
> *Gerusalemme salutar si sente!*

Well, Godfrey and Tancred, Peter, and the rest, look like little wooden dolls; and as for the horses belonging to the crusading cavalry, I have seen better in gingerbread. But, what then? There is a higher ingredient in beauty than mere form; a skilful hand is only the second artistical quality, worthless, my Anatole, without the first, which is a *great heart*. This picture is beautiful, in spite of its defects, as many women are. Mrs. Titmarsh is beautiful, though she weighs nineteen stone.

Being on the subject of religious pictures, what shall I say of Mr. Ward's? Anything so mysteriously hideous was never seen before now; they are worse than all the horrors in your Spanish Gallery at Paris. As Eastlake's are of the Catholic, these may be called of the Muggletonian school of art; monstrous, livid, and dreadful, as the dreams of a man in the scarlet fever. I would much sooner buy a bottled baby with two heads as a pleasing ornament for my cabinet; and should be afraid to sit alone in a room with 'ignorance, envy, and jealousy filling the throat, and widening the mouth of calumny endeavouring to bear down truth!'

Mr. Maclise's picture of 'Christmas' you will find excellently described in the May Number of a periodical of much celebrity among us, called *Fraser's Magazine*. Since the circulation of that miscellany is almost as extensive in Paris as in London, it is needless in this letter to go over beaten ground, and speak at length of the plot of this remarkable picture. There are five hundred merry figures painted on this canvas, gobbling, singing, kissing, carousing. A line of jolly serving-men troop down the hall stairs, and bear the boar's head in procession up to the dais, where sits the good old English gentleman, and his guests and family; a set of mummers and vassals are crowded round a table gorging beef and wassail; a bevy of blooming girls and young men are huddled in a circle, and play at hunt the slipper. Of course, there are plenty of stories told at the huge hall fire, and kissing under the glistening mistletoe-bough. But I wish you could see the wonderful accuracy with which all these figures are drawn, and the extraordinary skill with which the artist has managed to throw into a hundred different faces a hundred different characters and individualities of joy. Every one of these little people are smiling, but each has his own particular smile. As for the colouring of the picture, it is, between ourselves, atrocious; but a man cannot have all the merits at once. Mr. Maclise has for his share humour such as few painters ever possessed, and a power of drawing such as never was possessed by *any other;* no, not by one, from Albert Dürer downwards. His scene from *The Vicar of Wakefield* is equally charming. Moses's shining, grinning face; the little man in red who stands on tiptoe, and painfully scrawls his copy; and the youngest of the family of the Primroses, who learns his letters on his father's knee, are perfect in design and expression. What might not this man do, if he would read and meditate a little, and profit by the works of men whose taste and education were superior to his own.

Mr. Charles Landseer has two *tableaux de genre*, which possess very great merit. His characters are a little too timid, perhaps, as Mr. Maclise's are too bold; but the figures are beautifully drawn, the colouring and effect excellent, and the accessories painted with great faithfulness and skill. 'The Parting Benison' is, perhaps, the most interesting picture of the two.

And now we arrive at Mr. Etty, whose rich luscious pencil has covered a hundred glowing canvases, which every painter must love. I don't know whether the Duke has this year produced anything which one might have expected from a man of his rank and consequence. He is, like great men, lazy, or indifferent, perhaps, about public approbation; and also, like great men, somewhat too luxurious and fond of pleasure. For instance, here is a picture of a sleepy nymph, most richly painted; but tipsy-looking, coarse, and so naked, as to be unfit for appearance among respectable people at an exhibition. You will understand what I mean. There are some figures, without a rag to cover them, which look modest and decent for all that; and others, which may be clothed to the chin, and yet are not fit for modest eyes to gaze on. *Verbum sat*—this naughty 'Somnolency' ought to go to sleep in her night-gown.

But here is a far nobler painting,—the prodigal kneeling down lonely in the stormy evening, and praying to Heaven for pardon. It is a grand and touching picture; and looks as large as if the three-foot canvas had been twenty. His wan, wretched figure, and clasped hands, are lighted up by the sunset; the clouds are livid and heavy; and the wind is howling over the solitary common, and numbing the chill limbs of the poor wanderer. A goat and a boar are looking at him, with horrid obscene eyes. They are the demons of Lust and Gluttony, which have brought him to this sad pass. And there seems no hope, no succour, no Ear for the prayer of this wretched, way-worn, miserable man, who kneels there alone, shuddering. Only above, in the gusty blue sky, you see a glistening, peaceful, silver star, which points to home and hope, as clearly as if the little star were a sign-post, and home at the very next turn of the road.

Away, then, O conscience-stricken prodigal! and you shall find a good father, who loves you; and an elder brother, who hates you—but never mind that; and a dear, kind, stout, old mother, who liked you twice as well as the elder, for all his goodness and psalm-singing, and has a tear and a prayer for you night and morning; and a pair of gentle sisters, maybe; and a poor young thing down in the village, who has never forgotten your walks in the quiet nut-woods, and the bird's nest you brought her, and the big boy you thrashed, because he broke the eggs: he is squire now, the big boy, and would marry her, but she will not have him—not she!—her thoughts are with her dark-eyed, bold-browed, devil-me-care playmate, who swore she should be his little wife—and then went to college—and then came back sick and changed—and then got into debt—and then—But never mind, man! down to her at once. She will pretend to be cold at first, and then shiver and turn red and deadly pale; and then she tumbles into your arms, with a gush of sweet tears, and a pair of rainbows in her soft eyes, welcoming the sunshine back to her bosom again. To her, man!—never fear, miss! Hug him, and kiss him, as though you would draw the heart from his lips.

When she has done, the poor thing falls stone-pale and sobbing

on young Prodigal's shoulder; and he carries her quite gently to
that old bench where he carved her name fourteen years ago, and
steals his arm round her waist, and kisses her hand, and soothes
her.   Then comes out the poor widow, her mother, who is pale
and tearful too, and tries to look cold and unconcerned.   She
kisses her daughter, and leads her trembling into the house.
'You will come to us to-morrow, Tom?' says she, as she takes
his hand at the gate.

To-morrow! To be sure he will; and this very night, too,
after supper with the old people. (Young Squire Prodigal never
sups; and has found out that he must ride into town, to arrange
about a missionary meeting with the Rev. Dr. Slackjaw.) To be
sure, Tom Prodigal will go; the moon will be up, and who knows
but Lucy may be looking at it about twelve o'clock. At one,
back trots the young squire, and he sees two people whispering at a
window; and he gives something very like a curse, as he digs into
the ribs of his mare, and canters, clattering, down the silent road.

Yes—but, in the meantime, there is the old housekeeper, with
'Lord bless us!' and 'Heaven save us!' and 'Who'd have
thought ever again to see his dear face? And master to forget it
all, who swore so dreadful that he would never see him!—as for
missis, she always loved him.' There, I say, is the old housekeeper, logging the fire, airing the sheets, and flapping the feather
beds—for Master Tom's room has never been used this many a
day; and the young ladies have got some flowers for his chimney-
piece, and put back his mother's portrait, which they have had
in their room ever since he went away and forgot it, woe is me!
And old John, the butler, coachman, footman, valet, factotum,
consults with master about supper.

'What can we have?' says master; 'all the shops are shut,
and there's nothing in the house.'

John. — 'No, no more there isn't; only Guernsey's calf.
Butcher kill'd'n yesterday, as your honour knoweth.'

Master.—Come, John, a calf's enough. Tell the cook to *send
us up that.*'

And he gives a hoarse haw! haw! at his wit; and Mrs.
Prodigal smiles too, and says, 'Ah, Tom Prodigal, you were
always a merry fellow!'

Well, John Footman carries down the message to cook, who is
a country wench, and takes people at their word; and what do
you think she sends up?

Top Dish.

Fillet of veal, and bacon on the side-table.

Bottom Dish.

Roast ribs of veal.

In the Middle.

Calves'-head soup (*à la tortue*).
Veal broth.

Between.

Boiled knuckle of veal, and parsley sauce.
Stewed veal, with brown sauce and forcemeat balls.

Entre-mets.

Veal olives (for sauce, see stewed veal).
Veal cutlets (*panées, sauce piquante*).
Ditto (*en papillote*).
Scotch collops.
Fricandeau of veal (*piqué au lard à la chicorée*).
Minced veal.
Blanquet of veal.

Second Course.

Curry of calves'-head.
Sweet-breads.
Calves'-foot jelly.

See, my dear Anatole, what a world of thought can be conjured up out of a few inches of painted canvas.

And now we come to the great and crowning picture of the exhibition, my own historical piece, namely, 'Heliogabalus in the Ruins of Carthage.' In this grand and finished perform—

. . . Mr. Titmarsh's letter stops, unfortunately, here. We found it, at midnight, the 15th-16th May, in a gutter of St. Martin's Lane, whence a young gentleman had been just removed by the police. It is to be presumed that intoxication could be his only cause for choosing such a sleeping-place, at such an hour ; and it had probably commenced as he was writing the above fragment. We made inquiries at Lord's Coffee House, of Mr. Moth (who, from being the active and experienced head-waiter, is now the obliging landlord of that establishment), and were told that a gentleman unknown had dined there at three, and had been ceaselessly occupied in writing and drinking until a quarter to twelve, when he abruptly left the house. Mr. Moth regretted to add, that the stranger had neglected to pay for thirteen glasses of gin and water, half a pint of porter, a bottle of soda-water, and a plate of ham-sandwiches, which he had consumed in the course of the day.

We have paid Mr. Moth (whose very moderate charges and excellent stock of wines and spirits cannot be too highly commended), and shall gladly hand over to Mr. Titmarsh the remaining sum which is his due. Has he any more of his rhapsody?— O. Y.

A SECOND LECTURE ON THE FINE ARTS,
BY MICHAEL ANGELO-TITMARSH, ESQ.[1]

THE EXHIBITIONS.

JACK STRAW'S CASTLE, HAMPSTEAD.

MY DEAR BRICABRAC,

You, of course, remember the letter on the subject of our exhibitions which I addressed to you this time last year. As you are now lying at the Hôtel Dieu, wounded, during the late unsuccessful *émeute* (which I think, my dear friend, is the seventeenth you have been engaged in), and as the letter which I wrote last year was received with unbounded applause by the people here, and caused a sale of three or four editions of this Magazine, I cannot surely, my dear Bricabrac, do better than send you another sheet or two, which may console you under your present bereavement, and at the same time amuse the British public, who now know their friend Titmarsh as well as you in France know that little scamp Thiers.

Well, then, from Jack Straw's Castle, an hotel on Hampstead's breezy heath, which Keats, Wordsworth, Leigh Hunt, F. W. N. Bayley, and others of our choicest spirits, have often patronised, and a heath of which every pool, bramble, furze-bush-with-clothes-hanging-on-it-to-dry, steep, stock, stone, tree, lodging house, and distant gloomy background of London city or bright green stretch of sunshiny Hertfordshire meadows, has been depicted by our noble English landscape painter, Constable, in his own Constabulary way—at Jack Straw's Castle, I say, where I at this present moment am located (not that it matters in the least, but the world is always interested to know where men of genius are accustomed to disport themselves), I cannot do better than look over the heap of picture-gallery-catalogues which I brought with me from London, and communicate to you, my friend in Paris, my remarks thereon.

A man, with five shillings to spare, may at this present

[1] [*Fraser's Magazine*, June 1839.]

15

moment half kill himself with pleasure in London town, and in the neighbourhood of Pall Mall, by going from one picture gallery to another, and examining the beauties and absurdities which are to be found in each. There is first the National Gallery (entrance, nothing) in one wing of the little gin-shop of a building so styled near St. Martin's Church ; in another wing is the exhibition of the Royal Academy (entrance, one shilling ; catalogue, one ditto). After having seen this, you come to the Water-Colour Exhibition in Pall Mall East ; then to the gallery in Suffolk Street ; and, finally, to the New Water-Colour Society in Pall Mall—a pretty room, which formerly used to be a gambling-house, where many a bout of seven's-the-main, and iced champagne, has been had by the dissipated in former days. All these collections (all the modern ones, that is) deserve to be noticed, and contain a deal of good, bad, and indifferent wares, as is the way with all other institutions in this wicked world.

Commençons donc avec le commencement—with the Exhibition of the Royal Academy, which consists, as everybody knows, of thirty-eight knight and esquire academicians, and nineteen simple and ungenteel associates, who have not so much as a shabby Mister before their names. I recollect last year facetiously ranging these gentlemen in rank, according to what I conceived to be their merits—King Mulready, Prince Maclise, Lord Landseer, Archbishop Eastlake (according to the best of my memory, for Jack Straw, strange to say, does not take in *Fraser's Magazine*) and so on. At present, a great number of new-comers, not associates even, ought to be elevated to these aristocratic dignities ; and, perhaps, the order ought to be somewhat changed. There are many more good pictures (here and elsewhere) than there were last year. A great stride has been taken in matters of art, my dear friend. The young painters are stepping forward. Let the old fogies look to it ; let the old Academic Olympians beware, for there are fellows among the rising race who bid fair to oust them from sovereignty. They have not yet arrived at the throne, to be sure, but they are near it. The lads are not so good as the best of the academicians ; but many of the academicians are infinitely worse than the lads, and are old, stupid, and cannot improve, as the younger and more active painters will.

If you are particularly anxious to know what is the best picture in the room, not the biggest (Sir David Wilkie's is the biggest, and exactly contrary to the best) I must request you to turn your attention to a noble riverpiece by J. W. M. Turner, Esq., R.A., 'The Fighting Téméraire'—as grand a painting as ever figured on the walls of any academy, or came from the easel of any painter. The old Téméraire is dragged to her last home by a little, spiteful, diabolical steamer. A mighty red sun, amidst a host of flaring clouds, sinks to rest on one side of the picture, and illumines a river that seems interminable, and a countless navy that fades away into such a wonderful distance as never was painted before. The little demon of a steamer is belching out a volume (why do I say a volume? not a hundred volumes could express it) of foul, lurid, red-hot, malignant smoke, paddling furiously and lashing up the water round about it; while behind it (a cold grey moon looking down on it), slow, sad, and majestic, follows the brave old ship, with death, as it were, written on her, I think, my dear Bricabrac (although, to be sure, your nation would be somewhat offended by such a collection of trophies) that we ought not, in common gratitude, to sacrifice entirely these noble old champions of ours, but that we should have somewhere a museum of their skeletons which our children might visit, and think of the brave deeds which were done in them. The bones of the Agamemnon and the Captain, the Vanguard, the Culloden, and the Victory, ought to be sacred relics, for Englishmen to worship almost. Think of them when alive, and braving the battle and the breeze, they carried Nelson and his heroes victorious by the Cape of St. Vincent, in the dark waters of Aboukir, and through the fatal conflict of Trafalgar. All these things, my dear Bricabrac, are, you will say, absurd, and not to the purpose. Be it so: but Bowbellites as we are, we Cockneys feel our hearts leap up when we recall them to memory; and every clerk in Threadneedle Street feels the strength of a Nelson, when he thinks of the mighty actions performed by him.

It is absurd, you will say (and with a great deal of reason) for Titmarsh, or any other Briton, to grow so politically enthusiastic about a four-foot canvas, representing a ship, a steamer, a river, and a sunset. But herein surely lies the power of the great artist. He makes you see and think of a great deal more than the objects before you; he knows how to soothe or to intoxicate, to fire or to depress, by a few notes, or forms, or colours, of which we cannot trace the effect to the source, but only acknowledge the power. I recollect, some years ago, at the theatre at Weimar, hearing Beethoven's 'Battle of Vittoria,' in which, amidst a storm of glorious music, the air of 'God save the King' was introduced. The very instant it begun, every Englishman in the house was bolt upright, and so stood reverently until the air was played out. Why so? From some such thrill of excitement as makes us glow and rejoice over Mr. Turner and his 'Fighting Téméraire'; which I am sure, when the art of translating colours into music or poetry

C

shall be discovered, will be found to be a magnificent national ode
or piece of music.

I must tell you, however, that Mr. Turner's performances are
for the most part quite incomprehensible to me; and that his
other pictures; which he is pleased to call 'Cicero at his Villa,'
'Agrippina with the ashes of Germanicus,' 'Pluto carrying off
Proserpina,' or what you will, are not a whit more natural, or
less mad, than they used to be in former years, since he has
forsaken nature, or attempted (like your French barbers) to
embellish it. *On n'embellit pas la nature*, my dear Bricabrac;
one may make pert caricatures of it; or mad exaggerations, like
Mr. Turner in his fancy pieces. O ye gods! why will he not
stick to copying her majestical countenance, instead of daubing
it with some absurd antics and fard of her own. Fancy pea-
green skies, crimson-lake trees, and oranges and purple grass—
fancy cataracts, rainbows, suns, moons, and thunderbolts—shake
them well up, with a quantity of gamboge, and you will have
an idea of a fancy picture by Turner. It is worth a shilling
alone to go and see 'Pluto and Proserpina.' Such a landscape!
such figures! such a little red-hot coal-scuttle of a chariot as
Nat Lee sings:—

> Methought I saw a hieroglyphic bat
> Skim o'er the surface of a slipshod hat;
> While, to increase the tumult of the skies
> A damned potato o'er the whirlwind flies.

If you can understand these lines, you can understand one of
Turner's landscapes; and I recommend them to him as a pretty
subject for a piece for next year.

Etty has a picture on the same subject as Turner's 'Pluto
carrying off Proserpina'; and if one may complain that in the
latter the figures are not indicated, one cannot at least lay this
fault to Mr. Etty's door. His figures *are* drawn, and a deuced
deal *too much* drawn. A great, large curtain of fig-leaves should
be hung over every one of this artist's pictures, and the world
should pass on, content to know that there are some glorious
colours painted beneath. His colour, indeed, is sublime: I
doubt if Titian ever knew how to paint flesh better—but his
taste! Not David nor Girodet ever offended propriety so —
scarcely even Peter Paul himself, by whose side, as a colourist
and a magnificent heroic painter, Mr. Etty is sometimes worthy
to stand. I wish he would take Ariosto in hand, and give us a
series of designs from him. His hand would be the very one
for those deep luscious landscapes, and fiery scenes of love and

battle. Besides 'Proserpine,' Mr. Etty has two more pictures, 'Endymion,' with a dirty, affected, beautiful, slatternly Diana, and a portrait of the 'Lady-Mayoress of York'; which is a curiosity in its way. The line of her ladyship's eyes and mouth (it is a front face) are made to meet at a point in a marabon feather which she wears in her turban, and close to her cheek-bone; while the expression of the whole countenance is so fierce, that you would imagine it a Lady Macbeth, and not a lady-mayoress. The picture has, nevertheless, some very fine painting about it— as which of Mr. Etty's pieces has not?

The artists say there is very fine painting too, in Sir David Wilkie's great 'Sir David Baird'; for my part, I think very little. You see a great quantity of brown paint; in this is a great flashing of torches, feather, and bayonets. You see in the foreground, huddled up in a rich heap of corpses and drapery, Tippoo Sahib; and swaggering over him on a step waving a sword, for no earthly purpose, and wearing a red jacket and buckskins, the figure of Sir David Baird. The picture is poor, feeble, theatrical; and I would just as soon have Mr. Hart's great canvas of 'Lady Jane Grey' (which is worth exactly twopence halfpenny) as Sir David's poor picture of 'Seringapatam.' Some of Sir David's portraits are worse even than his historical compositions—they seem to be painted with snuff and tallow grease; the faces are merely indicated and without individuality; the forms only half-drawn, and almost always wrong. What has come to the hand that painted 'The Blind Fiddler,' and 'The Chelsea Pensioners'? Who would have thought that such a portrait as that of 'Master Robert Donne,' or the composition entitled 'The Grandfather,' could ever have come from the author of 'The Rent Day' and 'The Reading of the Will'? If it be but a contrast to this feeble, flimsy, transparent figure of Master Donne, the spectator cannot do better than cast his eyes upwards, and look at Mr. Linnell's excellent portrait of 'Mr. Robert Peel.' It is real, substantial nature, carefully and honestly painted and without any flashy tricks of art. It may seem ungracious in 'us youth' thus to fall foul of our betters; but if Sir David has taught us to like good pictures, by painting them formerly, we cannot help criticising if he paints bad ones now; and bad they most surely are.

From the censure, however, must be excepted the picture of 'Grace before Meat,' which, a little misty and feeble, perhaps, in drawing and substance, in colour, feeling, composition, and expression, is exquisite. The eye loves to repose upon this picture, and the heart to brood over it afterwards. When, as I said before, lines and colours come to be translated into sounds, this picture, I have no doubt, will turn out to be a sweet and touching hymn tune, with rude notes of cheerful voices, and peal of soft, melodious organ, such as one hears stealing over the meadows on sunshiny Sabbath days, while waves under cloudless blue the peaceful golden corn. Some such feeling of exquisite pleasure and content is to be had, too, from Mr. Eastlake's picture of 'Our Lord and the little Children.' You never saw such tender white faces, and solemn eyes, and sweet forms of mothers round their little ones bending gracefully. These pictures come straight to the heart, and then all criticism and calculation vanishes at once,—for the artist has attained his great end, which is, to strike far deeper than the sight; and we have no business to quarrel about defects in form and colour, which are but little parts of the great painter's skill.

Look, for instance, at another piece of Mr. Eastlake's called, somewhat affectedly, ' La Svegliarina.' The defects of the painter, which one does not condescend to notice when he is filled with a great idea, become visible instantly when he is only occupied with a small one ; and you see that the hand is too scrupulous and finikin, the drawing weak, the flesh chalky and unreal. The very same objections exist to the other picture, but the subject and the genius overcame them.

Passing from Mr. Eastlake's pictures to those of a greater genius, though in a different line,—look at Mr. Leslie's little pieces. Can anything be more simple—almost rude—than their manner, and more complete in their effect upon the spectator ? The very soul of comedy is in them ; there is no coarseness, no exaggeration ; but they gladden the eye, and the merriment which they excite cannot possibly be more pure, gentlemanlike, or delightful. Mr. Maclise has humour, too, and vast powers of expressing it ; but whisky is not more different from rich burgundy than his fun from Mr. Leslie's. To our thinking Leslie's little head of ' Sancho' is worth the whole picture from *Gil Blas*, which hangs by it. In point of workmanship, this is, perhaps, the best picture that Mr. Maclise ever painted ; the colour is far better than that usually employed by him, and the representation of objects carried to such an extent as we do believe was never reached before. There is a poached egg, which one could swallow ; a trout, that beats all the trout that was ever seen ; a copper pan, scoured so clean that you might see your face in it ; a green blind, through which the sun comes ; and a wall, with the sun shining on it, that De Hooghe could not surpass. This young man has the greatest power of hand that was ever had, perhaps, by any painter in any time or country. What does he want? Polish, I think; thought, and cultivation. His great picture of 'King Richard and Robin Hood' is a wonder of dexterity of hand; but coarse, I think, and inefficient in humour. His models repeat themselves too continually. Allen-a-Dale, the harper, is the very counterpart of Gil Blas; and Robin Hood is only Apollo with whiskers; the same grin, the same display of grinders,—the same coarse, luscious mouth, belongs to both. In the large picture, everybody grins, and shews his whole *râtelier;* and you look at them, and say, 'These people seem all very jolly.' Leslie's characters do not laugh themselves, but they make *you* laugh; and this is where the experienced American artist beats the dashing young Irish one. We shall say nothing of the colour of Mr. Maclise's large picture; some part appears to us to be excellent, and the whole piece, as far as execution goes, is worthy of his amazing talents, and high reputation. Mr. Maclise has but one portrait, it is, perhaps, the best in the exhibition; sober in colour, wonderful for truth, effect, and power of drawing.

In speaking of portraits there is never much to say; and they are fewer, and for the most part more indifferent than usual. Mr. Pickersgill has a good one, a gentleman in a green chair; and one or two outrageously bad. Mr. Philips's 'Doctor Shephard' is a finely painted head and picture; his Lady Dunraven and her son, as poor, ill-drawn, and ill-coloured a performance as can possibly be. Mr. Wood has a pretty head; Mr. Stone a good portrait of a very noble-looking lady, the Hon. Mrs. Blackwood; Mr. Bewick a good one; and there are, of course, many others whose names might be mentioned with praise or censure, but whom we will, if you please, pass over altogether.

The great advance of the year is in the small historical compositions, of which there are many that deserve honourable mention. Redgrave's 'Return of Olivia to the Vicar' has some very pretty painting and feeling in it; 'Quentin Matsys,' by the same artist, is tolerably good. D. Cowper's 'Othello relating his Adventures,' really beautiful; as is Cope's 'Belgian Family.' All these are painted with grace, feeling, and delicacy; as is E. M. Ward's 'Cimabue and Giotto' (there is in Tiepolo's etchings the selfsame composition, by the way) and Herbert's elegant picture of the 'Brides of Venice.' Mr. Severn's composition from the *Ancient Mariner* is a noble performance; and the figure of the angel with raised arm awful and beautiful too. It does good to see such figures in pictures as those and the above, invented and drawn— for they belong, as we take it, to the best school of art, of which one is glad to see the daily spread among our young painters.

Mr. Charles Landseer's 'Pillage of a Jew's House' is a very well and carefully painted picture, containing a great many figures, and good points; but we are not going to praise it; it wants vigour, to our taste, and what you call *actualité*. The people stretch their arms and turn their eyes the proper way, but as if they were in a tableau, and paid for standing there; one longs to see them all in motion, and naturally employed.

I feel, I confess, a kind of delight in finding out Mr. Edwin Landseer in a bad picture; for the man paints so wonderfully well, that one is angry that he does not paint better, which he might with half his talent, and without half his facility. 'Van Amburgh and the Lions' *is* a bad picture, and no mistake; dexterous, of course, but flat and washy: the drawing even of the animals is careless; that of the man bad, though the head is very like, and very smartly painted. Then there are other dog-and-man portraits; 'Miss Peel with Fido,' for instance. Fido is wonderful, and so are the sponges, and hair-brushes, and looking-glass, prepared for the dog's bath; and the drawing of the child's face, as far as the lines and expression go, is very good; but the face is covered with flesh-coloured paint, and not flesh, and the child looks like a wonderful doll, or imitation child, and not a real young lady, daughter of a gentleman who was prime minister last week (by the bye, my dear Bricabrac, did you ever read of such a pretty Whig game as that, and such a nice *coup d'état?*). There, again, is the beautiful little Princess of Cambridge, with a dog, and a piece of biscuit: the dog and the biscuit are just perfection; but the princess is no such thing,—only a beautiful apology for a princess, like that which Princess Penelope *didn't* send the other day to the lord-mayor of London.

We have to thank you (and not our Academy, which has hung the picture in a most scurvy way) for Mr. Scheffer's 'Prêche Protestante.' This fine composition has been thrust down on the ground, and trampled under foot, as it were, by a great number of worthless academics; but it merits one of the very best places in the gallery; and I mention it to hint an idea to your worship, which only could come from a great mind like that of Titmarsh, —to have, namely, some day, a great European congress of paintings, which might be exhibited at one place,—Paris, say, as the most central; or, better still, travel about, under the care of trusty superintendents, as they might, without fear of injury. I think such a circuit would do much to make the brethren known to one another, and we should hear quickly of much manly emulation, and stout training for the contest. If you will mention this to Louis Philippe the next time you see that *roi citoyen*

(mention it soon,—for, egad ! the next *émeute* may be successful ;
and who knows when it will happen ?)—if you will mention this
at the Tuileries, *we* will take care of St. James's ; for I suppose
that you know, in spite of the Whigs, her most sacred majesty
reads every word of *Fraser's Magazine*, and will be as sure to see
this on the first of next month, as Lord Melbourne will be to dine
with her on that day.

But let us return to our muttons. I think there are few more
of the oil pictures about which it is necessary to speak ; and
besides them, there are a host of miniatures, difficult to expiate
upon, but pleasing to behold. There are Chalon's ogling beauties,
half-a-dozen of them ; and the skill with which their silks and
satins are dashed in by the painter is a marvel to the beholder.
There are Ross's heads, that to be seen must be seen through a
microscope. There is Saunders, who runs the best of the
miniature men very hard ; and Thorburn, with Newton, Robert-
son, Rochard, and a host of others, and, finally, there is the
sculpture-room, containing many pieces of clay and marble, and,
to my notions, but two good things, a sleeping child (ridiculously
called the Lady Susan Somebody) by Westmacott ; and the bust
of Miss Stuart, by Macdonald ; never was anything on earth more
exquisitely lovely.

These things seen, take your stick from the porter at the hall
door, cut it, and go to fresh picture galleries ; but ere you go,
just by way of contrast, and to soothe your mind after the glare
and bustle of the modern collection, take half an hour's repose in
the National Gallery ; where, before the 'Bacchus and Ariadne,'
you may see what the magic of colour is ; before 'Christ and
Lazarus,' what is majestic, solemn grace and awful beauty ; and
before the new 'St. Catharine' what is the real divinity of art.
O, Eastlake and Turner !—O, Maclise and Mulready ! you are all
very nice men ; but what are you to the men of old ?

Issuing then from the National Gallery—you may step over to
Farrance's by the way, if you like, and sip an ice, or bolt a
couple of dozen forcemeat balls in a basin of mock turtle-soup—
issuing, I say, from the National Gallery, and after refreshing
yourself or not, as your purse or appetite permits, you arrive
speedily at the Water-Colour Exhibition, and cannot do better
than enter. I know nothing more cheerful or sparkling than the
first *coup d'œil* of this little gallery. In the first place, you never
can enter it without finding four or five pretty women, that's a
fact ; pretty women with pretty pink bonnets peeping at pretty
pictures, and with sweet whispers vowing that Mrs. Seyffarth is

a dear, delicious painter and that her style is 'so soft'; and that Miss Sharpe paints every bit as well as her sister; and that Mr. Jean Paul Frederick Richter draws the loveliest things, to be sure, that ever were seen. Well, very likely the ladies are right, and it would be impolite to argue the matter; but I wish Mrs. Seyffarth's gentlemen and ladies were not so dreadfully handsome, with such white pillars of necks, such long eyes and lashes and such dabs of carmine at the mouth and nostrils. I wish Miss Sharpe would not paint Scripture subjects, and Mr. Richter great goggle-eyed, red-cheeked, simpering wenches, whose ogling has become odious from its repetition. However, the ladies like it, and, of course, must have their way.

If you want to see *real* nature, now, real expression, real startling home poetry, look at every one of Hunt's heads. Hogarth never painted anything better than these figures, taken singly. That man rushing away frightened from the beer-barrel, is a noble head of terror; that Miss Jemima Crow, whose whole body is a grin, regards you with an ogle that all the race of Richters could never hope to imitate. Look at yonder card-players; they have a penny pack of the devil's hooks, and one has just laid down the king of trumps! I defy you to look at him without laughing, or to examine the wondrous puzzled face of his adversary without longing to hug the greasy rogue. Come hither, Mr. Maclise, and see what genuine comedy is; you who can paint better than all the Hunts and Leslies, and yet not near so well. If I were the Duke of Devonshire, I would have a couple of Hunts in every room in all my houses; if I had the blue devils (and even their graces are, I suppose, occasionally so troubled) I would but cast my eyes upon these grand, good-humoured pictures, and defy care. Who does not recollect 'Before and After the Mutton Pie,' the two pictures of that wondrous boy? Where Mr. Hunt finds his models, I cannot tell; they are the very flower of the British youth; each of them is as good as 'Sancho'; blessed is he that has his portfolio full of them.

There is no need to mention to you the charming landscapes of Cox, Copley Fielding, De Wint, Gastineau, and the rest. A new painter, somewhat in the style of Harding, is Mr. Callow; and better, I think, than his master or original, whose colours are too gaudy, to my taste, and effects too glaringly theatrical.

Mr. Cattermole has, among others, two very fine drawings, a large one, the most finished and the best coloured of any which have been exhibited by this fine artist; and a smaller one, 'The Portrait,' which is charming. The portrait is that of Jane Seymour, or Anne Boleyn; and Henry the VIIIth is the person examining it, with the cardinal at his side, the painter before him, and one or two attendants. The picture seems to me a perfect masterpiece, very simply coloured and composed, but delicious in effect and tone, and telling the story to a wonder. It is much more gratifying, I think, to let a painter tell his own story in this way, than to bind him down to a scene of *Ivanhoe* or Uncle Toby ; or worse still, to an illustration of some wretched story in some wretched fribble Annual. Wo to the painter who falls into the hands of Mr. Charles Heath (I speak, of course, not of Mr. Heath personally, but in a Pickwickian sense—of Mr. Heath the Annual-monger) ; he ruins the young artist, sucks his brains out, emasculates his genius so as to make it fit company for the purchasers of Annuals. Take, for instance, that unfortunate young man, Mr. Corbould, who gave great promise two years since, painted a pretty picture last year, and now—he has been in the hands of the Annual-mongers, and has left well nigh all his vigour behind him. Numerous Zuleikhas and Lalla Rookhs, which are hanging about the walls of the Academy and the New Water-Colour Gallery, give lamentable proofs of this : such handsome Turks and leering sultanas ; such Moors, with straight noses and pretty curled beards ! Away, Mr. Corbould ! away while it is yet time, out of the hands of these sickly, heartless Annual syrens ! and ten years hence, when you have painted a good, vigorous, healthy picture, bestow the tear of gratitude upon Titmarsh, who tore you from the lap of your crimson-silk-and-gilt-edged Armida.

Mr. Cattermole has a couple, we will not say of imitators, but of friends, who admire his works very much ; these are, Mr. Nash, and Mr. Lake Price ; the former paints furniture and old houses, the latter old houses and furniture, and both very pretty. No harm can be said of these miniature scene-painters ; on the contrary, Mr. Price's ' Gallery at Hardwicke ' is really remarkably dexterous ; and the chairs, tables, curtains, and pictures are nicked off with extraordinary neatness and sharpness—and then ? why then, no more is to be said. Cobalt, sepia, and a sable pencil, will do a deal of work, to be sure : and very pretty it is, too, when done ; and as for finding fault with it, that nobody will and can ; but an artist wants something more than sepia, cobalt, and sable pencils, and the knowledge how to use them. What do you think, my dear Bricabrac of a little *genius ?—that's* the picture-painter, depend on it.

Being on the subject of water-colours, we may as well step into the New Water-Colour Exhibition : not so good as the old, but very good. You will see here a large drawing by Mr. Corbould of a tournament, which will shew at once how clever that young artist is, and how weak and *maniéré*. You will see some charming un-affected English landscapes by Mr. Sims ; and a capital Spanish Girl by Hicks, of which the flesh-painting cannot be too much approved. It is done without the heavy white, with which water-colour artists are now wont to belabour their pictures ; and is, therefore, frankly and clearly painted, as all transparent water-colour drawing must be. The same praise of clearness, boldness, and depth of tone must be given to Mr. Absolon, who uses no white, and only just so much stippling as is necessary ; his picture has the force of oil, and we should be glad to see his manner more followed.

Mr. Haghe's 'Town Hall of Courtray' has attracted, and deservedly, a great deal of notice. It is a very fine and masterly architectural drawing, rich and sombre in effect, the figure intro-duced being very nearly as good as the rest of the picture. Mr. Haghe, we suppose, will be called to the upper house of water-colour painters, who might well be anxious to receive into their ranks many persons belonging to the new society. We hope, however, the latter will be faithful to themselves ; there is plenty of room for two galleries, and the public must, ere long, learn to appreciate the merits of the new one. Having spoken a word in favour of Mr. Johnston's pleasing and quaintly coloured South American sketches, we have but to bend our steps to Suffolk Street, and draw this discourse to a close.

Here is a very fine picture, indeed, by Mr. Hurlstone, 'Olympia attacked by Bourbon's Soldiers in Saint Peter's, and flying to the Cross.' Seen from the further room, this picture is grand in effect and colour, and the rush of the armed men towards the girl, finely and vigorously expressed. The head of Olympia has been called too calm by the critics ; it seems to me most beautiful, and the action of the figure springing forward and flinging its arms round the cross, nobly conceived and executed. There is a good deal of fine Titianic painting in the soldiers' figures (Oh, that Mr. Hurl-stone would throw away his lamp-black !), and the background of the church is fine, vast, and gloomy. This is the best historical picture to be seen anywhere this year ; perhaps the worst is the one which stands at the other end of the room, and which strikes upon the eye as if it were an immense water-colour sketch, of a feeble picture by President West. Speaking of historical paint-ings, I forgot to mention a large and fine picture by Mr. Dyce, the 'Separation of Edwy and Elgiva' ; somewhat crude and odd in colour, with a good deal of exaggeration in the countenances of the figures, but having grandeur in it, and unmistakable genius ;

there is a figure of an old woman seated, which would pass muster very well in a group of Sebastian Piombo.

A capitally painted head by Mr. Stone, called the 'Sword-bearer,' almost as fresh, bright, and vigorous as a Vandyke, is the portrait, we believe, of a brother-artist, the clever actor Mr. M'Ian. The latter's picture of 'Sir Tristram in the Cave' deserves especial remark and praise; and is really as fine a dramatic composition as one will often see. The figures of the knight and the lady asleep in the foreground, are novel, striking, and beautifully easy. The advance of the old king, who comes upon the lovers; the look of the hideous dwarf, who finds them out; and behind, the line of spears that are seen glancing over the rocks, and indicating the march of the unseen troops, are all very well conceived and arranged. The piece deserves engraving; it is wild, poetic, and original. To how many pictures, nowadays, can one apply the two last terms?

There are some more new pictures, in the midst of a great quantity of trash, that deserve notice. Mr. D. Cowper is always good; Mr. Stewart's 'Grandfather' contains two excellent like-nesses, and is a pleasing little picture. Mr. Hurlstone's 'Italian Boy,' and 'Girl with a Dog,' are excellent; and, in this pleasant mood, for fear of falling into an angry fit on coming to look further into the gallery, it will be as well to conclude. Wishing many remembrances to Mrs. Bricabrac, and better luck to you in the next *émeute*, I beg here to bid you farewell, and entreat you to accept the assurances of my distinguished consideration.

M. A. T.

Au Citoyen Brutus Napoléon Bricabrac, *Réfugié d'Avril, Blessé de Mai, Condamné de Juin, Decoré de Juillet, etc., etc. Hôtel Dieu, à Paris.*

AN ESSAY ON THE GENIUS OF GEORGE CRUIKSHANK.[1]

GEORGE CRUIKSHANK'S WORKS.

1. *The Humourist.* A Collection of Entertaining Tales, Anecdotes, Epigrams, Bon Mots, etc. J. Robins and Co. London, 1819.
2. *The Political House that Jack Built.* With Thirteen Cuts ; Forty-seventh Edition. William Hone. 1819.
3. *The Queen's Matrimonial Ladder ;* a National Toy, with Fourteen Step Scenes and Illustrations in Verse, and Eighteen other Cuts. Forty-fourth Edition. W. Hone. 1820.
4. *' Non mi ricordo.'* With Cuts. Thirty-first Edition. William Hone. 1820.
5. *Doll Tear Sheet, alias the Countess ' Je ne me rappelle pas,'* a match for *' Non mi ricordo.'* With Cuts by George Cruikshank. John Fairburn. 1820.
6. *The Political Showman.* With Twenty-four Cuts. Twenty-first Edition. William Hone. 1821.
7. *Life in London ; or, The Day and Night Scenes of Jerry Hawthorn, Esq., Corinthian Tom, and Bob Logic in their Rambles through the Metropolis.* By Pierce Egan, with Coloured Plates by G. and R. Cruikshank. Sherwood. London, 1821.
8. *A Slap at Slop and the Bridge Street Gang.* With Twenty-seven Cuts. William Hone. 1822.
9. *Life in Paris ; or, The Rambles of Dick Wildfire, etc.* Illustrated by George Cruikshank. London, 1822.
10. *Italian Tales of Humour, Gallantry and Romance.* Selected and translated from the Italian. With Sixteen Illustrative Drawings by George Cruikshank. Charles Baldwyn. 8vo, London, 1824. J. Robins. 1840,
11. *Tales of Irish Life.* Illustrative of the Manners, Customs, and Condition of the People. With Designs by George Cruikshank. J. Robins. London, 2 vols., 1824.

[1] [*The Westminster Review*, June 1840.]

12. *Points of Humour (Pieces partly original and partly selected).* Illustrated by a Series of Plates Drawn and Engraved by George Cruikshank. Parts 1 and 2. C. Baldwyn. London, 1824.

13. *Peter Schlemihl.* A New Translation from the German, 8vo. Whittaker. London, 1824.

14. *Popular German Stories.* Translated from the *Kinder- und Haus-Maerchen,* collected by M. M. Grimm from oral tradition. James Robins and Co. London, 1825.

15. *The Universal Songster, or, Museum of Mirth.* With Illustrations by George Cruikshank. Fairburn. London, 1825.

16. *Mornings at Bow Street.* With Illustrations by George Cruikshank. Wheatley and Adlard. London, 1825.

17. *More Mornings at Bow Street.* With Twenty-five Illustrations by George Cruikshank. J. Robins and Co. London, 1827.

18. *Hans of Iceland.* A Tale. With Four highly-finished Etchings by George Cruikshank. Price, 7s. 6d. J. Robins.

19. *Greenwich Hospital. A Series of Naval Sketches descriptive of the Life of a Man of War's Man.* By an Old Sailor. With Illustrations by George Cruikshank. J. Robins and Co. London, 1826.

20. *Three Courses and a Dessert.* With Decorations by George Cruikshank. Vizetelly and Co. London, 1830.

21. *Tales of Other Days.* With Illustrations by George Cruikshank. Effingham Wilson. London, 1830.

22. *The Gentleman in Black.* With Illustrations by George Cruikshank. William Kidd. London, 1831. Daly, 1840.

23. *Tom Thumb; and Bombastes Furioso.* Illustrated by George Cruikshank. Reprinted in Thomas's Burlesque Drama. Thomas. London.

24. *Sunday in London.* Illustrated in Fourteen Cuts by George Cruikshank, and a few words by a friend of his, with a copy of Sir Andrew Agnew's Bill. E. Wilson. London, 1833. Darton and Clark, 1840.

25. *Mirth and Morality. A Collection of Original Tales by Carlton Bruce.* Embellished with Engravings by George Cruikshank. Tegg. London, 1835.

26. *The Comic Almanac,* from 1835 to 1840 ; containing Seventy-two Plates on Steel, two vols. 17s. bound. C. Tilt.

27. *The Loving Ballad of Lord Bateman.* With Twelve Humorous Plates, neatly bound in cloth; price 2s. C. Tilt.

28. *My Sketch Book;* containing Two Hundred Groups. Cloth, 15s. plain ; 21s. coloured. C. Tilt.

29. *More Hints on Etiquette.* With Humorous Cuts, 2s. 6d. C. Tilt.

30. *The Comic Alphabet.* Twenty-four Plates. 2s. 6d. plain ; 4s. coloured. C. Tilt.

31. *Scraps and Sketches.* In four Parts, 8s. each. C. Tilt.

32. *Illustrations of Phrenology.* 8s. C. Tilt.

33. *Illustrations of Time.* 8s. C. Tilt.

34. *Demonology and Witchcraft.* In Twelve Plates. 2s. sewed. C. Tilt.

35. *Illustrations of the English Novelists;* containing Humorous Scenes from *Humphrey Clinker, Roderick Random, Peregrine Pickle, Tom Jones, Joseph Andrews, Vicar of Wakefield,* etc., etc. Forty-one Plates, with Descriptive Extracts, 7s. cloth. C. Tilt.

36. *The Bee and the Wasp.* A Comic Tale. Four Plates, 1s. C. Tilt.

37. *Hood's 'Epping Hunt.'* Six Engravings by G. Cruikshank. New and Cheap Edition. Price, 1s. 6d. C. Tilt.

38. *Cowper's 'John Gilpin'* ; with Six Engravings. Price, 1s. C. Tilt.

39. *Punch and Judy.* With Illustrations by George Cruikshank. Septimus Prowitt. London, 1828.

40. *Bentley's Miscellany.* Vols. I. to VI. Richard Bentley. London.

41. *Memoirs of Joseph Grimaldi.* Edited by Boz, with Illustrations by George Cruikshank. 2 vols. 8vo. R. Bentley. London, 1838.

42. *Oliver Twist, or, the Parish Boy's Progress.* By 'Boz.' 3 vols. R. Bentley. London, 1838.

43. *Minor Morals for Young People.* By John Bowring. With Illustrations by George Cruikshank. Parts I., II., and III. W. Tait. Edinburgh, 1839.

44. *Sketches by Boz.* Illustrated by George Cruikshank. 8vo. Chapman and Hall. London, 1839.

45. *Jack Sheppard; a Romance.* By W. H. Ainsworth, Esq. With Twenty-seven Illustrations by George Cruikshank. R. Bentley. 8vo. London, 1840.

46. *The Tower of London; an Historical Romance.* By W. H. Ainsworth. With Illustrations on Steel and Wood by G. Cruikshank. Parts I. to V. Richard Bentley. London, 8vo. 1840.

MAY—OLD MAY DAY

P. 31

GEORGE CRUIKSHANK.

ACCUSATIONS of ingratitude, and just accusations no doubt, are made against every inhabitant of this wicked world, and the fact is, that a man who is ceaselessly engaged in its trouble and turmoil, borne hither and thither upon the fierce waves of the crowd, bustling, shifting, struggling to keep himself somewhat above water—fighting for reputation, or more likely for bread, and ceaselessly occupied to-day with plans for appeasing the eternal appetite of inevitable hunger to-morrow—a man in such straits has hardly time to think of anything but himself, and, as in a sinking ship, must make his own rush for the boats, and fight, struggle, and trample for safety. In the midst of such a combat as this, the 'ingenuous arts, which prevent the ferocity of the manners, and act upon them as an emollient' (as the philosophic bard remarks in the Latin Grammar) are likely to be jostled to death, and then forgotten. The world will allow no such compromises between it and that which does not belong to it—no two gods must we serve ; but (as one has seen in some old portraits) the horrible glazed eyes of Necessity are always fixed upon you ; fly away as you will, black Care sits behind you, and with his ceaseless gloomy croaking drowns the voice of all more cheerful companions. Happy he whose fortune has placed him where there is calm and plenty, and who has the wisdom not to give up his quiet in quest of visionary gain.

Here is, no doubt, the reason why a man, after the period of his boyhood, or first youth, makes so few friends. Want and ambition (new acquaintances which are introduced to him along with his beard) thrust away all other society from him. Some old friends remain, it is true, but these are become as a habit—a part of your selfishness—and, for new ones, they are selfish as you are ; neither member of the new partnership has the capital of affection and kindly feeling, or can even afford the time that is requisite for the establishment of the new firm. Damp and chill the shades of the prison-house begin to close round us, and that 'vision splendid' which has accompanied our steps in our journey daily farther from the east, fades away and dies into the light of common day.

And what a common day ! what a foggy, dull, shivering apology for light is this kind of muddy twilight through which we are about to tramp and flounder for the rest of our existence, wandering farther and farther from the beauty and freshness and from the kindly gushing springs of clear gladness that made all around us green in our youth! One wanders and gropes in a slough of stock-jobbing, one sinks or rises in a storm of politics, and in either case it is as good to fall as to rise—to mount a bubble on the crest of the wave, as to sink a stone to the bottom.

The reader who has seen the name affixed to the head of this article did scarcely expect to be entertained with a declamation upon ingratitude, youth and the vanity of human pursuits, which may seem at first sight to have little to do with the subject in hand. But (although we reserve the privilege of discoursing upon whatever subject shall suit us, and by no means admit the public has any right to ask in our sentences for any meaning, or any connexion whatever) it happens that, in this particular instance, there is an undoubted connexion. In Susan's case, as recorded by Wordsworth, what connexion had the corner of Wood Street with a mountain ascending, a vision of trees, and a nest by the Dove? Why should the song of a thrush cause bright volumes of vapour to glide through Lothbury and a river to flow on through the vale of Cheapside? As she stood at that corner of Wood Street, a mop and a pail in her hand most likely, she heard the bird singing, and straightway began pining and yearning for the days of her youth, forgetting the proper business of the pail and mop. Even so we are moved by the sight of some of Mr. Cruikshank's works— the '*busen fühlt sich jugendlich erschüttert*,' the '*schwankende Gestalten*' of youth flit before one again—Cruikshank's thrush begins to pipe and carol, as in the days of boyhood; hence misty moralities, reflections, and sad and pleasant remembrances arise. He is the friend of the young especially. Have we not read all the story-books that his wonderful pencil has illustrated? Did we not forego tarts, in order to buy his 'Breaking-up,' or his 'Fashionable Monstrosities,' of the year eighteen hundred and something? Have we not before us, at this very moment, a print —one of the admirable 'Illustrations of Phrenology'—which entire work was purchased by a joint stock company of boys, each drawing lots afterwards for the separate prints, and taking his choice in rotation? The writer of this, too, had the honour of drawing the first lot, and seized immediately upon 'Philoprogenitiveness'—a marvellous print (our copy is not at all improved by being coloured, which operation we performed on it ourselves) —a marvellous print, indeed,—full of ingenuity and fine jovial humour. A father, possessor of an enormous nose and family, is surrounded by the latter, who are, some of them, embracing the former. The composition writhes and twists about like the

Kermes of Rubens. No less than seven little men and women in
night-caps, in frocks, in bibs, in breeches, are clambering about
the head, knees, and arms of the man with the nose; their
noses, too, are preternaturally developed—the twins in the cradle
have noses of the most considerable kind : the second daughter,
who is watching them ; the youngest but two, who sits squalling
in a certain wicker chair ; the eldest son, who is yawning; the
eldest daughter, who is preparing with the gravy of two mutton
chops a savory dish of Yorkshire pudding for eighteen persons ;
the youths who are examining her operations (one a literary gentleman, in a remarkably neat night-cap and pinafore, who has just
had his finger in the pudding) ; the genius who is at work on the
slate, and the two honest lads who are hugging the good-humoured
washerwoman, their mother—all, all, save this worthy woman,
have noses of the largest size. Not handsome certainly are they,
and yet everybody must be charmed with the picture. It is full of
grotesque beauty. The artist has at the back of his own skull,
we are certain, a huge bump of philoprogenitiveness. He loves
children in his heart ; every one of those he has drawn is perfectly
happy, and jovial, and affectionate, and innocent as possible. He
makes them with large noses, but he loves them, and you always
find something kind in the midst of his humour, and the ugliness
redeemed by a sly touch of beauty. The smiling mother reconciles
one with all the hideous family ; they have all something of the
mother in them—something kind, and generous, and tender.

Knight's, in Sweeting's Alley; Fairburn's, in a court off Ludgate
Hill ; Hone's, in Fleet Street—bright, enchanted palaces, which
George Cruikshank used to people with grinning, fantastical imps,
and merry, harmless sprites—where are they ? Fairburn's shop
knows him no more ; not only has Knight disappeared from
Sweeting's Alley, but, as we are given to understand, Sweeting's
Alley has disappeared from the face of the globe—Slop, the
atrocious Castlereagh, the sainted Caroline (in a tight pelisse,
with feathers in her head), the 'Dandy of sixty' who used to
glance at us from Hone's friendly windows—where are they ?
Mr. Cruikshank may have drawn a thousand better things since
the days when these were ; but they are to us a thousand times
more pleasing than anything else he has done. How we used to
believe in them ? to stray miles out of the way on holidays, in
order to ponder for an hour before that delightful window in
Sweeting's Alley! in walks through Fleet Street, to vanish abruptly
down Fairburn's passage, and there make one at his 'charming
gratis' exhibition. There used to be a crowd round the window
in those days of grinning, good-natured mechanics, who spelt the

songs, and spoke them out for the benefit of the company, and who received the points of humour with a general sympathising roar. Where are these people now? You never hear any laughing at H.B.; his pictures are a great deal too genteel for that—polite points of wit, which strike one as exceedingly clever and pretty, and cause one to smile in a quiet, gentlemanlike kind of way.

There must be no smiling with Cruikshank. A man who does not laugh outright is a dullard, and has no heart; even the old Dandy of sixty must have laughed at his own wondrous grotesque image, as they say Louis Philippe did, who saw all the caricatures that were made of himself. And there are some of Cruikshank's designs which have the blessed faculty of creating laughter as often as you see them. As Diggory says in the play, who is bidden by his master not to laugh while waiting at table —'Don't tell the story of Grouse in the Gun-room, master, or I can't help laughing.' Repeat that history ever so often, and at the proper moment, honest Diggory is sure to explode. Every man, no doubt, who loves Cruikshank has his Grouse in the Gun-room. There is a fellow in the 'Points of Humour' who is offering to eat up a certain little general, that has made us happy any time these sixteen years; his huge mouth is a perpetual well of laughter—buckets full of fun can be drawn from it. We have formed no such friendships as that boyish one of the man with the mouth. But though, in our eyes, Mr. Cruikshank reached his *apogée* some eighteen years since, it must not be imagined that such is really the case. Eighteen sets of children have since then learned to love and admire him, and may many more of their successors be brought up in the same delightful faith. It is not the artist who fails, but the men who grow cold—the men, from whom the illusions (why illusions? realities) of youth disappear one by one; who have no leisure to be happy, no blessed holidays, but only fresh cares at Midsummer and Christmas, being the inevitable seasons which bring us bills instead of pleasures. Tom, who comes bounding home from school, has the doctor's account in his trunk, and his father goes to sleep at the pantomime to which he takes him. *Pater infelix*, you too have laughed at clown, and the magic wand of spangled harlequin; what delightful enchantment did it wave around you, in the golden days 'when George the Third was king!' But our clown lies in his grave; and our harlequin, Ellar, prince of how many enchanted islands, was he not at Bow Street the other day, at Bow Street, in his dirty, tattered, faded motley—seized as a law-breaker, for acting at a penny theatre, after having well-nigh starved in the streets, where nobody would listen to his old guitar.

No one gave a shilling to bless him, not one of us who owe him so much.

We know not if Mr. Cruikshank will be very well pleased at finding his name in such company as that of Clown and Harlequin, but he, like them, is certainly the children's friend. His drawings abound in feeling for these little ones, and hideous, as in the course of his duty, he is from time to time compelled to design them, he never sketches one without a certain pity for it, and imparting to the figure a certain grotesque grace. In happy school-boys he revels ; plum-pudding and holidays his needle has engraved over and over again ;—there is a design in one of the Comic Almanacs of some young gentlemen who are employed in administering to a schoolfellow the correction of the pump, which is as graceful and elegant as a drawing of Stothard. Dull books about children George Cruikshank makes bright with illustrations —there is one published by the ingenious and opulent Mr. Tegg, of Cheapside, from which we should have been charmed to steal a few wood-cuts. It is entitled ' Mirth and Morality,' the mirth being, for the most part, on the side of the designer—the morality, unexceptionable certainly, the author's capital. Here are then, to these moralities, a smiling train of mirths supplied by George Cruikshank—see yonder little fellows butterfly-hunting across a common ! Such a light, brisk, airy, gentleman-like drawing was never made upon such a theme. Who, cries the author,

> Who has not chased the butterfly
>   And crushed its slender legs and wings,
> And heaved a moralising sigh ;
>   Alas ! how frail are human things ?

A very unexceptionable morality truly, but it would have puzzled another than George Cruikshank to make mirth out of it as he has done. Away, surely not on the wings of these verses, Cruikshank's imagination begins to soar ; and he makes us three darling little men on a green common, backed by old farm-houses, somewhere about May. A great mixture of blue and clouds in the air, a strong fresh breeze stirring, Tom's jacket flapping in the same, in order to bring down the insect queen or king of spring that is fluttering above him,—he renders all this with a few strokes on a little block of wood not two inches square, upon which one may gaze for hours, so merry and life-like a scene does it present. What a charming creative power is this, what a privilege—to be a god, and create little worlds upon paper, and whole generations of smiling, jovial men, women, and children half-inch high, whose portraits are carried abroad, and have the faculty of making us monsters of six feet curious and happy in our turn. Now, who would imagine that an artist could make anything of such a subject as this? The writer begins by stating—

> I love to go back to the days of my youth,
> And to reckon my joys to the letter,
> And to count o'er the friends that I have in the world,
>   Ay, *and those who are gone to a better*.

This brings him to the consideration of his uncle. 'Of all the men I have ever known,' says he, 'my uncle united the greatest degree of cheerfulness with the sobriety of manhood. Though a man when I was a boy, he was yet one of the most agreeable companions I ever possessed. . . . He embarked for America, and nearly twenty years passed by before he came back again ; . . . but oh, how altered !—he was in every sense of the word an old man, his body and mind were enfeebled, and second childishness had come upon him. How often have I bent over him, vainly endeavouring to recal to his memory the scenes we had shared together ; and how frequently, with an aching heart, have I gazed on his vacant and lustreless eye while he has amused himself in clapping his hands and singing with a quavering voice a verse of a psalm.' Alas! such are the consequences of long residences in America, and of old age even in uncles! Well, the point of this morality is, that the uncle one day in the morning of life vowed that he would catch his two nephews and tie them together, ay, and actually did so, for all the efforts the rogues made to run away from him ; but he was so fatigued that he declared he never would make the attempt again, whereupon the nephew remarks, —'Often since then, when engaged in enterprises beyond my strength, have I called to mind the determination of my uncle.'

Does it not seem impossible to make a picture out of this? And yet George Cruikshank has produced a charming design, in which the uncles and nephews are so prettily portrayed that one is reconciled to their existence, with all their moralities. Many more of the mirths in this little book are excellent, especially a great figure of a parson entering church on horseback,—an enormous parson truly, calm, unconscious, unwieldy. As Zeuxis had a bevy of virgins in order to make his famous picture—his express virgin, a clerical host must have passed under Cruikshank's eyes before he sketched this little, enormous parson of parsons.

Being on the subject of children's books, how shall we enough praise the delightful German nursery tales, and Cruikshank's illustrations of them ? We coupled his name with pantomime awhile since, and sure never pantomimes were more charming

than these. Of all the artists that ever drew, from Michael
Angelo upwards, and downwards, Cruikshank was the man to
illustrate these tales, and give them just the proper admixture of
the grotesque, the wonderful, and the graceful. May all Mother
Bunch's collection be similarly indebted to him ; may *Jack the
Giant Killer*, may *Tom Thumb*, may *Puss in Boots* be one
day revivified by his pencil. Is not Whittington sitting yet on
Highgate Hill, and poor Cinderella (in that sweetest of all fairy
stories) still pining in her lonely chimney-nook ? A man who has
a true affection for these delightful companions of his youth is
bound to be grateful to them if he can, and we pray Mr. Cruikshank to remember them.

It is folly to say that this or that kind of humour is too good
for the public, that only a chosen few can relish it. The best
humour that we know of has been as eagerly received by the
public as by the most delicate connoisseur. There is hardly a
man in England who can read but will laugh at Falstaff and the
humour of Joseph Andrews ; and honest Mr. Pickwick's story
can be felt and loved by any person above the age of six. Some
may have a keener enjoyment of it than others, but all the world
can be merry over it, and is always ready to welcome it. The
best criterion of good-humour is success, and what a share of this
has Mr. Cruikshank had ! how many millions of mortals has he
made happy ! We have heard very profound persons talk philosophically of the marvellous and mysterious manner in which he
has suited himself to the time—*fait vibrer la fibre populaire* (as
Napoleon boasted of himself), supplied a peculiar want felt at a
peculiar period, the simple secret of which is, as we take it, that
he, living amongst the public, has with them a general wide-
hearted sympathy, that he laughs at what they laugh at, that he
has a kindly spirit of enjoyment, with not a morsel of mysticism
in his composition ; that he pities and loves the poor, and jokes
at the follies of the great, and that he addresses all in a perfectly
sincere and manly way. To be greatly successful as a professional
humourist, as in any other calling, a man must be quite honest,
and show that his heart is in his work. A bad preacher will get
admiration and a hearing with this point in his favour, where a
man of three times his acquirements will only find indifference
and coldness. Is any man more remarkable than our artist for
telling the truth after his own manner ? Hogarth's honesty of
purpose was as conspicuous in an earlier time, and we fancy that
Gilray would have been far more successful and more powerful
but for that unhappy bribe, which turned the whole course of his
humour into an unnatural channel. Cruikshank would not for

any bribe say what he did not think, or lend his aid to sneer down anything meritorious, or to praise anything or person that deserves censure. When he levelled his wit against the Regent, and did his very prettiest for the Princess, he most certainly believed, along with the great body of the people whom he represents, that the Princess was the most spotless, pure-mannered darling of a Princess that ever married a heartless debauchée of a Prince Royal. Did not millions believe with him, and noble and learned lords take their oaths to her Royal Highness's innocence? Cruikshank would not stand by and see a woman ill-used, and so struck in for her rescue, he and the people belabouring with all their might the party who were making the attack, and determining, from pure sympathy and indignation, that the woman must be innocent because her husband treated her so foully.

To be sure we have never heard so much from Mr. Cruikshank's own lips, but any man who will examine these odd drawings, which first made him famous, will see what an honest, hearty hatred the champion of woman has for all who abuse her, and will admire the energy with which he flings his wood-blocks at all who side against her. Canning, Castlereagh, Bexley, Sidmouth, he is at them, one and all ; and as for the Prince, up to what a whipping-post of ridicule did he tie that unfortunate old man. And do not let squeamish Tories cry out about disloyalty ; if the crown does wrong, the crown must be corrected by the nation, out of respect, of course, for the crown. In those days, and by those people who so bitterly attacked the son, no word was ever breathed against the father, simply because he was a good husband, and a sober, thrifty, pious, orderly man.

This attack upon the Prince Regent we believe to have been Mr. Cruikshank's only effort as a party politician. Some early manifestoes against Napoleon we find, it is true, done in the regular John Bull style, with the Gilray model for the little upstart Corsican ; but as soon as the Emperor had yielded to stern fortune our artist's heart relented (as Béranger's did on the other side of the water), and many of our readers will doubtless recollect a fine drawing of 'Louis XVIII. trying on Napoleon's boots,' which did not certainly fit the gouty son of Saint Louis. Such satirical hits as these, however, must not be considered as political, or as anything more than the expression of the artist's national British idea of Frenchmen.

It must be confessed that for that great nation Mr. Cruikshank entertains a considerable contempt. Let the reader examine the *Life in Paris*, or the five hundred designs in which Frenchmen are introduced, and he will find them almost invariably thin, with ludicrous spindle-shanks, pigtails, outstretched hands, shrugging shoulders, and queer hair and moustachios. He has the British idea of a Frenchman, and if he does not believe that the inhabitants of France are for the most part dancing-masters and barbers, yet takes care to depict such in preference, and would not speak too well of them. It is curious how these traditions endure. In France, at the present moment, the Englishman on the stage is the caricatured Englishman at the time of the war, with a shock red head, a long white coat, and invariable gaiters. Those who wish to study this subject should peruse Monsieur Paul de Kock's histories of Lord *Boulingrog* and Lady *Crockmilove*. On the other hand, the old *émigré* has taken his station amongst us, and we doubt if a good British Gallery would understand that such and such a character *was* a Frenchman unless he appeared in the ancient traditional costume.

A curious book, called *Life in Paris*, published in 1822, contains a number of the artist's plates in the aquatint style; and though we believe he had never been in that capital, the designs have a great deal of life in them, and pass muster very well. We had thoughts of giving a few copies of French heads from this book and others, which would amply show Mr. Cruikshank's anti-Gallican spirit. A villainous race of shoulder-shrugging mortals are his Frenchmen indeed. And the heroes of the tale, a certain Mr. Dick Wildfire, Squire Jenkins, and Captain O'Shuffleton, are made to show the true British superiority on every occasion when Britons and French are brought together. This book was one among the many that the designer's genius has caused to be popular; the plates are not carefully executed, but, being coloured, have a pleasant, lively look. The same style was adopted in the once famous book called *Tom and Jerry, or, Life in London*, which must have had a word of notice here, for, although by no means Mr. Cruikshank's best work, his reputation was extraordinarily raised by it. Tom and Jerry were as popular twenty years since as Mr. Pickwick and Sam Weller now are; and often have we wished, while reading the biographies of the latter celebrated personages, that they had been described as well by Mr. Cruikshank's pencil as by Mr. Dickens's pen.

As for *Tom and Jerry*, to show the mutability of human affairs and the evanescent nature of reputation, we have been to the British Museum and no less than five circulating libraries in quest of the book, and *Life in London*, alas, is not to be found at any one of them. We can only, therefore, speak of the work from recollection, but have still a very clear remembrance of the leather gaiters of Jerry Hawthorn, the green spectacles of Logic, and the hooked nose of Corinthian Tom. They were the schoolboys' delight ; and in the days when the work appeared we firmly believed the three heroes aboved named to be types of the most elegant, fashionable young fellows the town afforded, and thought their occupations and amusements were those of all high-bred English gentlemen. Tom knocking down the watchman at Temple Bar ; Tom and Jerry dancing at Almack's ; or flirting in the saloon at the theatre ; at the night-houses, after the play ; at Tom Cribb's, examining the silver cup then in the possession of that champion ; at Bob Logic's chambers, where, if we mistake not, 'Corinthian Kate' was at a cabinet piano, singing a song ; ambling gallantly in Rotten Row, or examining the poor fellow at Newgate who was having his chains knocked off before hanging ; all these scenes remain indelibly engraved upon the mind, and so far we are independent of all the circulating libraries in London.

As to the literary contents of the book, they have passed sheer away. It was, most likely, not particularly refined ; nay, the chances are that it was absolutely vulgar. But it must have had some merit of its own, that is clear ; it must have given striking descriptions of life in some part or other of London, for all London read it, and went to see it in its dramatic shape. The artist, it is said, wished to close the career of the three heroes by bringing them all to ruin, but the writer, or publishers, would not allow any such melancholy subjects to dash the merriment of the public, and we believe Tom, Jerry, and Logic were married off at the end of the tale, as if they had been the most moral personages in the world. There is some goodness in this pity which authors and the public are disposed to show towards certain agreeable, disreputable characters of romance. Who would mar the prospects of honest Roderick Random, or Charles Surface, or Tom Jones ? only a very stern moralist indeed. And in regard of Jerry Hawthorn and that hero without a surname, Corinthian Tom, Mr. Cruikshank, we make little doubt, was glad in his heart that he was not allowed to have his own way.

Soon after the *Tom and Jerry* and the *Life in Paris*, Mr. Cruikshank produced a much more elaborate set of prints, in a work which was called *Points of Humour*. These 'Points' were selected from various comic works, and did not, we believe, extend beyond a couple of numbers, containing about a score of copperplates. The collector of humorous designs cannot fail to have them in his portfolio, for they contain some of the very best efforts of Mr. Cruikshank's genius, and though not quite so highly laboured as some of his later productions, are none the worse, in our opinion, for their comparative want of finish. All the effects are perfectly given, and the expression as good as it could be in the most delicate engraving upon steel. The artist's style, too, was then completely formed ; and, for our parts, we should say that we preferred his manner of 1825 to any other which he has adopted since. The first picture, which is called 'The Point of Honour,' illustrates the old story of the officer who, on being accused of cowardice for refusing to fight a duel, came among his brother officers and flung a lighted grenade down upon the floor, before which his comrades fled ignominiously. This design is capital, and the outward rush of heroes, walking, trampling, twisting, scuffling at the door, is in the best style of the grotesque. You see but the back of most of these gentlemen, into which, nevertheless, the artist has managed to throw an expression of ludicrous agony that one could scarcely have expected to find in such a part of the human figure. The next plate is not less good. It represents a couple who, having been found one night tipsy, and lying in the same gutter, were, by a charitable though misguided gentleman, supposed to be man and wife, and put comfortably to bed together. The morning came ; fancy the surprise of this interesting pair when they awoke and discovered their situation. Fancy the manner, too, in which Cruikshank has depicted them, to which words cannot do justice. It is needless to state that this fortuitous and temporary union was followed by one more lasting and sentimental, and that these two worthy persons were married, and lived happily ever after.

We should like to go through every one of these prints. There is the jolly miller, who, returning home at night, calls upon his wife to get him a supper, and falls too upon rashers of bacon and ale. How he gormandises, that jolly miller ! rasher after rasher, how they pass away frizzling and smoking from the gridiron down that immense grinning gulf of a mouth. Poor wife ! how she pines and frets at that untimely hour of midnight to be obliged to fry, fry, fry perpetually, and minister to the monster's appetite. And yonder in the clock, what agonised face is that we see ? By heavens, it is the squire of the parish. What business has he there ? Let us not ask. Suffice it to say that he has, in the hurry of the moment, left upstairs his br--, his—psha ! a part of his dress, in short, with a number of bank-notes in the pockets. Look in the next page, and you will see the ferocious, bacon-devouring ruffian of a miller is actually causing this garment to be carried through the village and cried by the town-crier. And we blush to be obliged to say that the demoralised miller never offered to return the bank-notes, although he was so mighty scrupulous in endeavouring to find an owner for the corduroy portfolio in which he had found them.

Passing from this painful subject we come, we regret to state, to a series of prints representing personages not a whit more moral. Burns's famous *Jolly Beggars* have all had their portraits drawn by Cruikshank. There is the lovely 'hempen widow,' quite as interesting and romantic as the famous Mrs. Sheppard, who has at the lamented demise of her husband adopted the very same consolation.

> My curse upon them every one,
> They've hanged my braw John Highlandman ;
> .   .   .   .
> And now a widow I must mourn
> Departed joys that ne'er return ;
> No comfort but a hearty can
> When I think on John Highlandman.

Sweet 'raucle carlin,' she has none of the sentimentality of the English highwayman's lady ; but being wooed by a tinker and

> A pigmy scraper wi' his fiddle,
> Wha us'd at trystes and fairs to driddle,

prefers the practical to the merely musical man. The tinker sings with a noble candour, worthy of a fellow of his strength of body and station in life—

> My bonnie lass, I work in brass,
> A tinker is my station ;
> I've travell'd round all Christian ground
> In this my occupation :
> I've ta'en the gold, I've been enroll'd
> In many a noble squadron ;
> But vain they search'd when off I march'd
> To go an' clout the cauldron.

It was his ruling passion. What was military glory to him, forsooth ? He had the greatest contempt for it, and loved freedom and his copper kettle a thousand times better—a kind of hardware Diogenes. Of fiddling he has no better opinion. The picture represents the 'sturdy caird' taking 'poor gut-scraper' by the beard,—drawing his 'roosty rapier,' and swearing to 'speet him like a pliver' unless he would relinquish the bonnie lassie for ever—

> Wi' ghastly e'e, poor tweedle-dee
> Upon his hunkers bended,
> An' pray'd for grace wi' ruefu' face,
> An' so the quarrel ended.

Hark how the tinker apostrophises the violinist, stating to the widow at the same time the advantages which she might expect from an alliance with himself :—

> Despise that shrimp, that withered imp,
>   Wi' a' his noise and caperin,
> And take a share with those that bear
>   The budget an' the apron !
> And by that stoup, my faith an' houpe,
>   An' by that dear Kilbaigie,
> If e'er ye want, or meet wi' scant,
>   May I ne'er weet my craigie.

Cruikshank's caird is a noble creature ; his face and figure show him to be fully capable of doing and saying all that is above written of him.

In the second part, the old tale of *The Three Hunchbacked Fiddlers* is illustrated with equal felicity. The famous classical dinners and duel in *Peregrine Pickle* are also excellent in their way ; and the connoisseur of prints and etchings may see in the latter plate, and in another in this volume, how great the artist's mechanical skill is as an etcher. The distant view of the city in the duel, and of a market-place in *The Quack Doctor*, are delightful specimens of the artist's skill in depicting buildings and backgrounds. They are touched with a grace, truth, and dexterity of workmanship that leave nothing to desire. We have before mentioned the man with the mouth which appears in this number, and should be glad to give a little vignette emblematical of gout and indigestion, in which the artist has shown all the fancy of Callot. Little demons, with long saws for noses, are making dreadful incisions into the toes of the unhappy sufferer ; some are bringing pans of hot coals to keep the wounded member warm ; a huge, solemn nightmare sits on the invalid's chest, staring solemnly into his eyes ; a monster, with a pair of drumsticks, is banging a devil's tattoo on his forehead ; and a pair of imps are nailing great tenpenny nails into his hands to make his happiness complete.

But, though not able to seize upon all we wish, we have been able to provide a tolerably large Cruikshank gallery for the reader's amusement, and must hasten to show off our wares. Like the worthy who figures below, there is such a choice of pleasures here, that we are puzzled with which to begin.

The Cruikshank collector will recognise this old friend as coming from the late Mr. Clark's excellent work, *Three Courses*

George Cruikshank

AUGUST—'SIC OMNES'

P. 45.

PHILOPROGENITIVENESS

THE ELECTION FOR BEADLE.

THE PARISH ENGINE.

SCOTLAND YARD.

George Cruikshank

THE STREETS—MORNING.

P. 50.

and a Dessert.   The work was published at a time when the rage
for comic stories was not so great as it since has been, and Messrs.
Clark and Cruikshank only sold their hundreds where Messrs.

Dickens and Phiz dispose of their thousands.   But if our recommendation can in any way influence the reader, we would enjoin
him to have a copy of the *Three Courses*, that contains some of
the best designs of our artist, and some of the most amusing tales
in our language.   The invention of the pictures, for which Mr.

Clark takes credit to himself, says a great deal for his wit and
fancy.   Can we, for instance, praise too highly the man who
invented this wonderful oyster?

Examine him well; his beard, his pearl, his little round stomach, and his sweet smile. Only oysters know how to smile in this way; cool, gentle, waggish, and yet inexpressibly innocent and winning. Dando himself must have allowed such an artless native to go free, and consigned him to the glassy, cool, translucent wave again.

In writing upon such subjects as these with which we have been furnished, it can hardly be expected that we should follow any fixed plan and order—we must therefore take such advantage

as we may, and seize upon our subject when and wherever we can lay hold of him.

For Jews, sailors, Irishmen, Hessian boots, little boys, beadles, policemen, tall Life-guardsmen, charity children, pumps, dustmen, very short pantaloons, dandies in spectacles, and ladies with aquiline noses, remarkably taper waists and wonderfully long ringlets, Mr. Cruikshank has a special predilection. The tribe of Israelites he has studied with amazing gusto; witness the Jew in Mr. Ainsworth's *Jack Sheppard*, and the immortal Fagin of *Oliver Twist*. Whereabouts lies the comic *vis* in these persons and things? Why should a beadle be comic, and his opposite a charity boy? Why should a tall Life-guardsman have something in him essentially absurd? Why are short breeches more ridiculous than long? What is there particularly jocose about a pump, and wherefore does a long nose always provoke the beholder to laughter? These points may be metaphysically elucidated by those who list. It is probable that Mr. Cruikshank could not give an accurate definition of that which is ridiculous in these objects, but his instinct has told him that fun lurks in them, and cold must be the heart that can pass by the pantaloons of his charity boys, the Hessian boots of his dandies, and the fan-tail hats of his dustmen, without respectful wonder.

We can submit to public notice a complete little gallery of dustmen. Here is, in the first place, the professional dustman,

who, having in the enthusiastic exercise of his delightful trade, laid hands upon property not strictly his own, is pursued, we presume, by the right owner, from whom he flies as fast as his crooked shanks will carry him.

What a curious picture it is—the horrid rickety houses in some dingy suburb of London, the grinning cobbler, the smothered butcher, the very trees which are covered with dust—it is fine to look at the different expressions of the two interesting fugitives. The fiery charioteer who belabours yonder poor donkey has still a glance for his brother on foot, on whom punishment is about to descend. And not a little curious is it to think of the creative power of the man who has arranged this little tale of low life. How logically it is conducted, how cleverly each one of the accessories is made to contribute to the effect of the whole. What a deal of thought and humour has the artist expended on this

little block of wood ; a large picture might have been painted out
of the very same materials, which Mr. Cruikshank, out of his
wondrous fund of merriment and observation, can afford to throw
away upon a drawing not two inches long.   From the practical
dustmen we pass to those purely poetical.   Here are three of them
who rise on clouds of their own raising, the very genii of the
sack and shovel.

Is there no one to write a sonnet to these ?—and yet a whole
poem was written about Peter Bell the Waggoner, a character by
no means so poetic.

And lastly, we have the dustman in love, the honest fellow is
on the spectator's right hand, and having seen a young beauty
stepping out of a gin-shop on a Sunday morning, is pressing
eagerly his suit.

Gin has furnished many subjects to Mr. Cruikshank, who
labours in his own sound and hearty way to teach his countrymen
the dangers of that drink.   In the *Sketch-Book* is a plate upon the
subject, remarkable for fancy and beauty of design ; it is called the
'Gin Juggernaut,' and represents a hideous moving palace, with a
reeking still at the roof and vast gin-barrels for wheels, under
which unhappy millions are crushed to death.   An immense black
cloud of desolation covers over the country through which the gin
monster had passed, dimly looming through the darkness whereof
you see an agreeable prospect of gibbets with men dangling, burnt
houses, etc.   The vast cloud comes sweeping on in the wake of
this horrible body-crusher ; and you see, by way of contrast, a
distant, smiling, sunshiny tract of old English country, where gin
as yet is not known.   The allegory is as good, as earnest, and as
fanciful as one of John Bunyan's, and we have often fancied there
was a similarity between the men.

The reader will examine the work called *My Sketch-Book* with not a little amusement, and may gather from it, as we fancy, a good deal of information regarding the character of the individual man, George Cruikshank. What points strike his eye as a painter; what move his anger or admiration as a moralist; what classes he seems most especially disposed to observe, and what to ridicule. There are quacks of all kinds, to whom he has a mortal hatred; quack dandies, who assume under his pencil, perhaps in his eye, the most grotesque appearance possible—their hats grow larger, their legs infinitely more crooked and lean; the tassels of

their canes swell out to a most preposterous size; the tails of their coats dwindle away, and finish where coat tails generally begin. Let us lay a wager that Cruikshank, a man of the people if ever there was one, heartily hates and despises these supercilious, swaggering young gentlemen; and his contempt is not a whit the less laudable because there may *tant soit peu* of prejudice in it. It is right and wholesome to scorn dandies, as Nelson said it was to hate Frenchmen; in which sentiment (as we have before said) George Cruikshank undoubtedly shares. Look at this fellow from the *Sunday in London*.[1]

Monsieur the Chief is instructing a kitchen-maid how to compound some rascally French kickshaw or the other—a pretty

[1] The following lines — ever fresh — by the author of *Headlong Hall*,

scoundrel truly with what an air he wears that night-cap of his, and shrugs his lank shoulders, and chatters, and ogles, and grins; they are all the same, these mounseers; look at those other two fellows — *morbleu!* one is putting his dirty fingers into the saucepan; there are frogs cooking in it, no doubt; and see, just over some other dish of abomination, another dirty rascal is taking

published years ago in the *Globe and Traveller*, are an excellent comment on several of the cuts from the *Sunday in London* :—

I

The poor man's sins are glaring;
In the face of ghostly warning
  He is caught in the fact
  Of an overt act,
Buying greens on Sunday morning.

II

The rich man's sins are hidden
In the pomp of wealth and station,
  And escape the sight
  Of the children of light,
Who are wise in their generation.

III

The rich man has a kitchen,
And cooks to dress his dinner;
  The poor who would roast
  To the baker's must post,
And thus becomes a sinner.

IV

The rich man's painted windows
Hide the concerts of the quality;
  The poor can but share
  A crack'd fiddle in the air,
Which offends all sound morality.

V

The rich man has a cellar,
And a ready butler by him;
  The poor must steer
  For his pint of beer
Where the saint can't choose but spy him.

VI

The rich man is invisible
In the crowd of his gay society;
  But the poor man's delight
  Is a sore in the sight,
And a stench in the nose of piety.

snuff! Never mind, the sauce won't be hurt by a few ingredients, more or less. Three such fellows as these are not worth one Englishman, that's clear. See, there is one in the very midst of them, the great burly fellow with the beef, he could beat all three in five minutes. We cannot be certain that such was the process going on in Mr. Cruikshank's mind when he made the

— "Ignorance is bliss" —

design; but some feelings of the sort were no doubt entertained by him.

Against dandy footmen he is particularly severe. He hates idlers, pretenders, boasters, and punishes these fellows as best he may. Who does not recollect the famous picture, 'What is Taxes, Thomas?' What is taxes indeed; well may that vast, over-fed, lounging flunky ask the question of his associate Thomas, and yet not well, for all that Thomas says in reply is, 'I don't know.' '*O beati plushicolæ*,' what a charming state of ignorance is yours! In the *Sketch-Book* many footmen make their appearance; one is a huge fat Hercules of a Portman Square porter, who calmly surveys another poor fellow, a porter likewise, but out of livery, who comes staggering forward with a box that Hercules might lift with his little finger. Will Hercules do so? not he. The giant can carry nothing heavier than a cocked-hat note on a silver tray, and his labours are to walk from his sentry-box to door, and from the door back to his sentry-box, and to read the Sunday paper, and to poke the hall fire twice or thrice, and to make five meals a day. Such a fellow does Cruikshank hate and scorn worse even than a Frenchman.

'MISERABLE SINNERS!'

The man's master, too, comes in for no small share of our artist's wrath. See, here is a company of them at church, who humbly designate themselves 'Miserable sinners!'

Miserable sinners indeed! O what floods of turtle-soup; what tons of turbot and lobster-sauce must have been sacrificed to make those sinners properly miserable. My lady there, with the ermine tippet and dragging feather, can we not see that she lives in Portland Place, and is the wife of an East India Director? She has been to the Opera over-night (indeed her husband, on her right, with his fat hand dangling over the pew-door, is at this minute thinking of Mademoiselle Leocadie, whom he saw behind the scenes)—she has been at the Opera over-night, which with a trifle of supper afterwards—a white and brown soup, a lobster salad, some woodcocks, and a little champagne—sent her to bed quite comfortable.   At half-past eight her maid brings her chocolate in bed, at ten she has fresh eggs and muffins, with, perhaps, a half-hundred of prawns for breakfast, and so can get over the day and the sermon till lunch-time pretty well.   What an odour of musk and bergamot exhales from the pew !—how it is wadded and stuffed, and spangled over with brass nails ! what hassocks are there for those who are not too fat to kneel ! what a flustering and flapping of gilt prayer-books ; and what a pious whirring of bible-leaves one hears all over the church, as the doctor blandly gives out the text !   To be miserable at this rate

you must, at the very least, have four thousand a year ; and many persons are there so enamoured of grief and sin, that they would willingly take the risk of the misery to have a life-interest in the consols that accompany it, quite careless about consequences, and sceptical as to the notion that a day is at hand when you must fulfil *your share of the bargain.*

Our artist loves to joke at a soldier ; in whose livery there appears to him to be something almost as ridiculous as in the uniform of the gentleman of the shoulder-knot.   Tall life-guards-men and fierce grenadiers figure in many of his designs, and almost always in a ridiculous way.   Here again we have the honest popular English feeling which jeers at pomp or pretension of all kinds, and is especially jealous of all display of military authority.   ' Raw Recruit,' ' ditto dressed,' ditto ' served up,' as we see them in the *Sketch-Book*, are so many satires upon the army : Hodge with his ribbons flaunting in his hat, or with red coat and musket, drilled stiff and pompous, or that last, minus leg and arm, tottering about on crutches, do not fill our English artist with the enthusiasm that follows the soldier in every other part of Europe. Jeanjean, the conscript in France, is laughed

Tell Tale —

at, to be sure, but then it is because he is a bad soldier ; when he comes to have a huge pair of moustachios and the *croix d'honneur* to *briller* on his *poitrine cicatrisée*, Jeanjean becomes a member of a class that is more respected than any other in the French nation. The veteran soldier inspires our people with no such awe—we hold that democratic weapon the fist in much more honour than the sabre and bayonet, and laugh at a man tricked out in scarlet and pipe-clay. Look at this regiment of

heroes 'marching to divine service,' to the tune of 'The British
Grenadiers.'

There they march in state, and a pretty contempt our artist
shows for all their grimcracks and trumpery.   He has drawn a

perfectly English scene—the little blackguard boys are playing
pranks round about the men, and shouting 'heads up, soldier,'
'eyes right, lobster,' as little British urchins will do.   Did one

ever hear the like sentiments expressed in France? Shade of
Napoleon, we insult you by asking the question. In England,
however, see how different the case is: and designedly or un-
designedly, the artist has opened to us a piece of his mind. Look
in the crowd—the only person who admires the soldiers is the
poor idiot, whose pocket a rogue is picking. Here is another
picture, in which the sentiment is much the same, only, as in
the former drawing we see Englishmen laughing at the troops
of the line, here are Irishmen giggling at the militia.

We have said that our artist has a great love for the drolleries
of the Green Island. Would any one doubt what was the
country of the merry fellows depicted in the following group?

Place me amid O'Rourkes, O'Tooles,
The ragged, royal race of Tara;
Or place me where Dick Martin rules
The pathless wilds of Connemara.

We know not if Mr. Cruikshank has ever had any such good
luck as to see the Irish in Ireland itself, but he certainly has
obtained a knowledge of their looks, as if the country had been
all his life familiar to him. Could Mr. O'Connell himself desire
anything more national than the following scene, or could Father
Matthew have a better text to preach upon?

There is not a broken nose in the room that is not thoroughly
Irish. Here we have a couple of compositions treated in a
graver manner, as characteristic too as the other.

And with one more little Hibernian specimen we must bid
farewell to Ireland altogether, having many other pictures in

our gallery that deserve particular notice ; and we give this, not
so much for the comical look of poor Teague, who has been

pursued and beaten by the witch's stick, but in order to point
the singular neatness of the workmanship, and the pretty, fanciful,

little glimpse of landscape that the artist has introduced in the background.

Mr. Cruikshank has a fine eye for such homely landscapes, and renders them with great delicacy and taste. Old villages, farm-yards, groups of stack, queer chimneys, churches, gable-

ended cottages, Elizabethan mansion-houses, and other old English scenes, he depicts with evident enthusiasm.

Famous books in their day were Cruikshank's *John Gilpin*

and *Epping Hunt*; for though our artist does not draw horses very scientifically—to use a phrase of the *atelier*—he feels them very keenly; and his queer animals, after one is used to them, answer quite as well as better. Neither is he very happy in trees, and such rustical produce; or rather, we should say, he is very original, his trees being decidedly of his own make and composition, not imitated from any master. Here is a notable instance.

οἴη περ φύλλων γενεή, τοίη δε καὶ ἵππων : Trees or horse-flesh, which is the worst? it is impossible to say which is the most villainous.

But what then? Suppose yonder horned animal near the postchaise has not a very bovine look, it matters not the least. Can a man be supposed to imitate everything? We know what the noblest study of mankind is, and to this Mr. Cruikshank has confined himself. Look at that postillion; the people in the

F

broken-down chaise are roaring after him; he is as deaf as the post by which he passes. Suppose all the accessories were away, could not one swear that the man was stone-deaf, beyond the reach of trumpet? What is the peculiar character in a deaf man's physiognomy?—can any person define it satisfactorily in words?—not in pages, and Mr. Cruikshank has expressed it on a piece of paper not so big as the tenth part of your thumb-nail. The horses of *John Gilpin* are much more of the equestrian order, and, as here, the artist has only his favourite suburban buildings to draw; not a word is to be said against his design. The inn and old buildings in this cut are charmingly designed, and nothing can be more prettily or playfully touched.

At Edmonton his loving wife
    From the balcony spied
Her tender husband, wond'ring much
    To see how he did ride.

'Stop, stop, John Gilpin! Here's the house!'
    They all at once did cry;
'The dinner waits, and we are tired—
    Said Gilpin—'So am I!'

Six gentlemen upon the road
   Thus seeing Gilpin fly,
With post-boy scamp'ring in the rear,
   They raised the hue and cry :—

'Stop thief ! stop thief !—a highwayman !'
   Not one of them was mute ;
And all and each that passed that way
   Did join in the pursuit.

And now the turnpike gates again
   Flew open in short space ;
The toll-men thinking, as before,
   That Gilpin rode a race.

The rush, and shouting, and clatter are here excellently depicted by the artist ; and we, who have been scoffing at his manner of designing animals, must here make a special exception in favour of the hens and chickens ; each has a different action and is curiously natural.

Happy are children of all ages who have such a ballad and such pictures as this in store for them ! It is a comfort to think that wood-cuts never wear out, and that the book still may be had at Mr. Tilt's for a shilling, for those who can command that sum of money.

In *The Epping Hunt*, which we owe to the facetious pen of

Mr. Hood, our artist has not been so successful. There is here too much horsemanship and not enough incident for him; but

the portrait of Roundings the huntsman is an excellent sketch, and a couple of the designs contain great humour. The first represents the cockney hero, who 'like a bird, was singing out while sitting on a tree.'

And in the second the natural order is reversed. The stag having taken heart, is hunting the huntsman, and the Cheapside Nimrod is most ignominiously running away.

The Easter Hunt, we are told, is no more; and as the *Quarterly Review* recommends the British public to purchase Mr. Catlin's pictures, as they form the only record of an interest-

ing race now rapidly passing away, in like manner we should exhort all our friends to purchase Mr. Cruikshank's designs of *another* interesting race, that is run already and for the last time.

Besides these, we must mention, in the line of our duty, the notable tragedies of *Tom Thumb* and *Bombastes Furioso*, both of which have appeared with many illustrations by Mr. Cruikshank. The 'brave army' of Bombastes exhibits a terrific display of brutal force, which must shock the sensibilities of an English radical. And we can well understand the caution of the general, who bids this *soldatesque effrénée* to begone, and not to kick up such a row.

Such a troop of lawless ruffians let loose upon a populous city would play sad havoc in it; and we fancy the massacres of

Birmingham renewed, or at least of Badajoz, which, though not
quite so dreadful, if we may believe his Grace the Duke of
Wellington, as the former scenes of slaughter, were nevertheless
severe enough; but we must not venture upon any ill-timed
pleasantries in presence of the disturbed King Arthur, and the
awful ghost of Gaffer Thumb.

We are thus carried at once into the supernatural, and here
we find Cruikshank reigning supreme. He has invented in his
time a little comic pandemonium, peopled with the most droll,
good-natured fiends possible. We have before us Chamisso's

Peter Schlemihl, with Cruikshank's designs translated into
German, and gaining nothing by the change. The *Kinder- und
Haus-Maerchen* of Grimm are likewise ornamented with a frontis-
piece, copied from that one which appeared to the amusing
version of the English work. The books on Phrenology and
Time have been imitated by the same nation, and even in France,
whither reputation travels more slowly than to any country except
China, we have seen copies of the works of George Cruikshank.

He in return has complimented the French by illustrating a
couple of lives of Napoleon, and the *Life in Paris* before
mentioned. He has also made designs for Victor Hugo's *Hans
of Iceland*. Strange, wild etchings were those, on a strange,
mad subject; not so good in our notion as the designs for the

German books, the peculiar humour of which latter seemed to suit the artist exactly. There is a mixture of the awful and the ridiculous in these, which perpetually excites and keeps awake the reader's attention; the German writer and the English artist seem to have an entire faith in their subject. The reader, no doubt, remembers the awful passage in *Peter Schlemihl* where the little gentleman purchases the shadow of that hero—' " Have the kindness, noble sir, to examine and try this bag." He put

his hand into his pocket, and drew thence a tolerably large bag of Cordovan leather, to which a couple of thongs were fixed. I took it from him, and immediately counted ten gold pieces, and ten more, and ten more, and still other ten, whereupon I held out my hand to him. Done, said I, it is a bargain; you shall have my shadow for your bag. The bargain was concluded : he knelt down before me, and I saw him with a wonderful neatness take my shadow from head to foot, lightly lift it up from the grass, roll and fold it up neatly, and at last pocket it. He then rose up, bowed to me once more, and walked away again, disappearing behind the rose-bushes. I don't know, but I thought I heard him laughing a little. I, however, kept fast hold of the bag. Everything around me was bright in the sun, and as yet I gave no thought to what I had done.'

This marvellous event, narrated by Peter with such a faithful, circumstantial detail, is painted by Cruikshank in the most wonderful poetic way, with that happy mixture of the real and supernatural that makes the narrative so curious, and like truth. The sun is shining with the utmost brilliancy in a great quiet park or garden ; there is a palace in the background ; and a statue basking in the sun quite lonely and melancholy ; there is a sun-dial, on which is a deep shadow, and in the front stands Peter Schlemihl, bag in hand, the old gentleman is down on his knees to him, and has just lifted off the ground the *shadow of one leg ;* he is going to fold it back neatly as one does the tails of a coat, and will stow it, without any creases or crumples, along with the other black garments that lie in that immense pocket of his. Cruikshank has designed all this as if he had a very serious belief in the story ; he laughs, to be sure, but one fancies that he is a little frightened in his heart, in spite of all his fun and joking.

The German tales we have mentioned before. ' The Prince riding on the Fox,' ' Hans in Luck,' ' The Fiddler and his Goose,' ' Heads off,' are all drawings which, albeit not before us now, nor seen for ten years, remain indelibly fixed on the memory—— ' *heisst du etwa Rumpelstilzchen* ? ' There sits the queen on her throne, surrounded by grinning beef-eaters, and little Rumpelstilts-kin stamps his foot through the floor in the excess of his tremendous despair. In one of these German tales, if we remember rightly, there is an account of a little orphan who is carried away by a pitying fairy for a term of seven years, and passing that period of sweet apprenticeship among the imps and sprites of fairyland. Has our artist been among the same company, and brought back their portraits in his sketch-book ? He is the only designer fairyland has had. Callot's imps, for all their strangeness, are only of the earth earthy. Fuseli's fairies belong to the infernal regions ; they are monstrous, lurid, and hideously melancholy. Mr. Cruikshank alone has had a true insight into the character of the ' little people.' They are some-thing like men and women, and yet not flesh and blood ; they are laughing and mischievous, but why we know not. Mr. Cruikshank, however, has had some dream or the other, or else a natural mysterious instinct (as the *Seherin* of Prevorst had for beholding ghosts) or else some preternatural fairy revelation, which has made him acquainted with the looks and ways of the fantastical subjects of Oberon and Titania.

We have, unfortunately, no fairy portraits in the gallery which we have been enabled to provide for the public; but, on the other hand, can descend lower than fairyland, and have procured some fine specimens of devils. One has already been raised, and the reader has seen him tempting a fat Dutch burgomaster, in ancient gloomy market-place, such as George Cruikshank can draw as well as Mr. Prout, Mr. Nash, or any man living. Here is our friend once more; our friend the burgomaster, in a highly excited state, and running as hard as his great legs will carry him, with our mutual enemy at his tail.

What are the bets? Will that long-legged bondholder of a devil come up with the honest Dutchman? It serves him right, why did he put his name to stamped paper? And yet we should not wonder that some lucky chance will turn up in burgomaster's favour, and that his infernal creditor will lose his labour; for one so proverbially cunning as yonder tall individual with the saucer eyes, it must be confessed that he has been very often out-witted.

There is, for instance, the case of 'The Gentleman in Black,' which has been illustrated by our artist. A young French gentle-man, by name M. Desonge, who having expended his patrimony in a variety of taverns and gaming-houses, was one day pondering upon the exhausted state of his finances; and utterly at a loss to think how he should provide means for future support, ex-claimed, very naturally, 'What the devil shall I do?' He had no sooner spoken, when a GENTLEMAN IN BLACK made his appearance, whose authentic portrait Mr. Cruikshank has had the honour to paint. This gentleman produced a black-edged book out of a black bag, some black-edged papers tied up with black crape, and sitting down familiarly opposite M. Desonge, began conversing with him on the state of his affairs.

It is needless to state what was the result of the interview. M. Desonge was induced by the gentleman to sign his name to one of the black-edged papers, and found himself at the close of the conversation to be possessed of an unlimited command of capital. This arrangement completed, the Gentleman in Black posted (in an extraordinarily rapid manner) from Paris to London, there found a young English merchant in exactly the same

situation in which M. Desonge had been, and concluded a bargain with the Briton of exactly the same nature.

The book goes on to relate how these young men spent the money so miraculously handed over to them, and how both, when the period drew near that was to witness the performance of *their* part of the bargain, grew melancholy, wretched, nay, so absolutely dishonourable as to seek for every means of breaking through their agreement. The Englishman living in a country where the lawyers are more astute than any other lawyers in the world, took advice of a Mr. Bagsby, of Lyon's Inn, whose name, as we cannot find it in the 'Law List,' we presume to be fictitious. Who

could it be that was a match for the devil? Lord ——— very
likely; we shall not give his name, but let every reader of this
Review fill up the blank according to his own fancy, and on
comparing it with the copy purchased by his neighbours, he will
find that fifteen out of twenty have written down the same
honoured name.

Well, the Gentleman in Black was anxious for the fulfilment of
his bond. The parties met at Mr. Bagsby's chambers, to consult,
the Black Gentleman foolishly thinking that he could act as his
own counsel and fearing no attorney alive. But mark the

superiority of British law, and see how the black pettifogger was
defeated.

Mr. Bagsby simply stated that he would take the case into
Chancery, and his antagonist, utterly humiliated and defeated,
refused to move a step farther in the matter.

And now the French gentleman, M. Desonge, hearing of his
friend's escape, became anxious to be free from his own rash
engagements. He employed the same counsel who had been
successful in the former instance, but the Gentleman in Black
was a great deal wiser by this time, and whether M. Desonge
escaped, or whether he is now in that extensive place which is

Gentlemen — It was a very fine Oyster; the Court awards you a shell each.

paved with good intentions, we shall not say. Those who are anxious to know had better purchase the book of Mr. Daly, of Leicester Square, wherein all these interesting matters are duly set down. We have one more diabolical picture in our budget, engraved by Mr. Thompson, the same dexterous artist who has rendered the former *diableries* so well.

We may mention Mr. Thompson's name as among the first of the engravers to whom Cruikshank's designs have been entrusted ; and next to him (if we may be allowed to make such arbitrary distinctions) we may place Mr. Williams ; and the reader is not possibly aware of the immense difficulties to be overcome in the

rendering of these little sketches, which, traced by the designer in a few hours, require weeks' labour from the engraver. Mr. Cruikshank has not been educated in the regular schools of drawing, very luckily for him, as we think, and consequently has had to make a manner for himself, which is quite unlike that of any other draughtsman. There is nothing in the least mechanical about it ; to produce his particular effects he uses his own particular lines, which are queer, free, fantastical, and must be followed in all their infinite twists and vagaries by the careful tool of the engraver. Look at these three lovely smiling heads for instance.

Let us examine them, not so much for the jovial humour and wonderful variety of feature exhibited in these darling counte-nances, as for the engraver's part of the work. See the infinite

delicate cross lines and hatchings which he is obliged to render ;
let him go, not a hair's breadth, but the hundredth part of a
hair's breadth, beyond the given line, and the *feeling* of it is
ruined.   He receives these little dots and specks, and fantastical
quirks of the pencil, and cuts away with a little knife round each
nor too much nor too little.   Antonio's pound of flesh did not
puzzle the Jew so much ; and so well does the engraver succeed
at last, that we never remember to have met with a single artist
who did not vow that the wood-cutter had utterly ruined his
design.

Of Messrs. Thompson and Williams we have spoken as the
first engravers in point of rank ; however, the regulations of
professional precedence are certainly very difficult, and the rest of

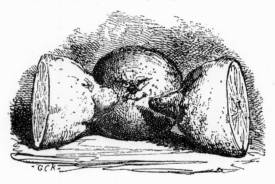

their brethren we shall not endeavour to class.   Why should the
artists who executed the cuts of the admirable ' Three Courses '
yield the pas to any one ?   If the reader will turn back to the
second cut in p. 64, he will agree with us that it is a very
brilliant and faithful imitation of the artist's manner, and admire
the pretty glimpse of landscape and the manner in which it is
rendered ; the oyster cut is likewise very delicately engraved, and
indeed we should be puzzled, were there no signatures, to assign
the prize at all.

Here, for instance, is an engraving by Mr. Landells, nearly as
good in our opinion as the very best woodcut that ever was made
after Cruikshank, and curiously happy in rendering the artist's
peculiar manner : this cut does not come from the facetious
publications which we have consulted, and from which we have
borrowed ; but is a contribution by Mr. Cruikshank to an elaborate
and splendid botanical work upon the Orchidaceæ of Mexico, by

Mr. Bateman. Mr. Bateman dispatched some extremely choice roots of this valuable plant to a friend in England, who, on the arrival of the case, consigned it to his gardener to unpack. A great deal of anxiety with regard to the contents was manifested by all concerned, but on the lid of the box being removed, there issued from it three or four fine specimens of the enormous Blatta beetle that had been preying upon the plants during the voyage; against these the gardeners, the grooms, the porters, and the porter's children issued forth in arms, and which the artist has immortalised, as we see.

We have spoken of the admirable way in which Mr. Cruikshank has depicted Irish character and Cockney character; here is

English country character quite as faithfully delineated in the person of the stout porteress and her children, and of yonder ' Chawbacon' with the shovel, on whose face is written ' Zummerzetsheer.' Is it hypercriticism to say that the gardener on the ground is a Scotchman? there is a well-known Scotch gentleman in London who must surely have stretched for the portrait. Chawbacon appears in another plate, or else Chawbacon's brother. He has come up to Lunnon, and is looking about him at raaces.

How distinct are these rustics from those whom we have just been examining! They hang about the purlieus of the metropolis; Brook Green, Epsom, Greenwich, Ascot, Goodwood, are their haunts. They visit London professionally once a year, and that is at the time of Bartholomew fair. How one may speculate upon the different degrees of rascality, as exhibited in each face of the thimblerigging trio, and form little histories for these worthies, charming Newgate romances, such as have been of late the fashion! Is any man so blind that he cannot see the exact face that is writhing under the thimblerigged hero's hat? Like Timanthes of old, our artist expresses great passions without the aid of the human countenance. Here is another specimen.

SPIRITS OF WINE.

Is there any need of having a face after this? 'Come on,' says Claret-bottle, a dashing, genteel fellow, with his hat on one ear, 'come on, has any man a mind to tap me?' Claret-bottle is a little screwed (as one may see by his legs), but full of gaiety and courage; not so that stout, apoplectic Bottle-of-rum, who has staggered against the wall, and has his hand upon his liver; the fellow hurts himself with smoking, that is clear, and is as sick as sick can be. See, Port is making away from the storm, and Double X. is as flat as ditch-water. Against these, awful in their white robes, the sober watchmen come.

Our artist then can cover up faces, and yet show them quite clearly, as in the thimblerig group; or he can do without faces altogether, as we see above; or he can, at a pinch, provide a countenance for a gentleman out of any given object, as we see here a beautiful Irish physiognomy being moulded upon a keg of whiskey; or here, where a jolly English countenance froths out of a pot of ale (the spirit of brave Toby Philpot come

G

back to reanimate his clay). Not to recognise in this fungus the physiognomy of that mushroom peer, Lord ——, would argue

oneself unknown. Finally, if he is at a loss, he can make a living head, body, and legs out of steel or tortoise-shell, as in the case of

JANUARY—LAST YEAR'S BILLS.

this vivacious pair of spectacles, that are jockeying the nose of Caddy Cuddle.

Of late years Mr. Cruikshank has busied himself very much

with steel engraving, and the consequences of that lucky invention have been, that his plates are now sold by thousands, where they could only be produced by hundreds before. He has made many a bookseller's and author's fortune (we trust that in so doing he

may not have neglected his own). Twelve admirable plates, furnished yearly to that facetious little publication, the *Comic Almanac*, have gained for it a sale, as we hear, of nearly twenty thousand copies. The idea of the work was novel; there was, in the first number especially, a great deal of comic power, and

Cruikshank's designs were so admirable, that the *Almanac* at once became a vast favourite with the public, and has so remained ever since.

Besides the twelve plates, this *Almanac* contains a prophetic wood-cut, accompanying an awful Blarneyhum Astrologicum that appears in this and other Almanacs. Here is one that hints in pretty clear terms that with the Reform of Municipal Corporations the ruin of the great Lord Mayor of London is at hand.

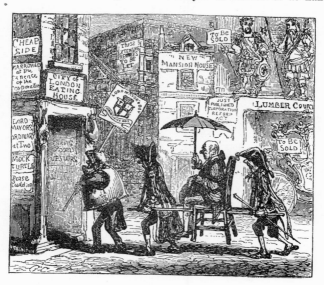

See his lordship here, he is meekly going to dine at an eight-penny ordinary,—his giants in pawn, his men in armour, dwindled to 'one poor knight,' his carriage to be sold, his stalwart aldermen vanished, his sheriffs, alas! and alas! in gaol! Another design shows that Rigdum, if a true, is also a moral and instructive prophet. Behold John Bull asleep, or rather in a vision; the cunning demon, Speculation, blowing a thousand bright bubbles about him.

Meanwhile the rooks are busy at his fob, a knave has cut a cruel hole in his pocket, a rattlesnake has coiled safe round his feet, and will in a trice swallow Bull, chair, money, and all; the rats are at his corn-bags, (as if, poor devil, he had corn to spare), his faithful dog is bolting his leg of mutton, nay, a thief has gotten hold of his very candle, and there, by way of moral, is his ale-pot, which looks and winks in his face, and seems to say, O

Bull, all this is froth, and a cruel satirical picture of a certain rustic who had a goose that laid certain golden eggs, which goose the rustic slew in expectation of finding all the eggs at once.

This is goose and sage too, to borrow the pun of 'learned Doctor Gill'; but we shrewdly suspect that Mr. Cruikshank is becoming a little conservative in his notions.

We love these pictures so, that it is hard to part us, and we still fondly endeavour to hold on, but this wild word, farewell, must be spoken by the best friends at last, and so good-bye, brave wood-cuts : we feel quite a sadness in coming to the last of our collection.   A word or two more have we to say, but no more pretty pictures,—take your last look of the wood-cuts then, for not one more will appear after this page,—not one more with which the pleased traveller may comfort his eye—a smiling oasis in a desert of text.   What could we have done without these excellent merry pictures ?   Reader and reviewer would have been tired of listening long since and would have been comfortably asleep.

In the earlier numbers of the *Comic Almanac* all the manners and customs of Londoners that would afford food for fun were noted down ; and if during the last two years the mysterious personage who, under the title of ' Rigdum Funnidos,' compiles this ephemeris, has been compelled to resort to romantic tales, we must suppose that he did so because the great metropolis was exhausted, and it was necessary to discover new worlds in the cloud land of fancy.   The character of Mr. Stubbs, who made his appearance in the Almanac for 1839,[1] had, we think, great merit, although his adventures were somewhat of too tragical a description to provoke pure laughter.   The publishers have allowed us to give a reprint of that admirable design before mentioned, in which Master Stubbs is represented under the school-pump, to which place of punishment his associates have brought him.   In the following naive way the worthy gentleman describes his own mishap :—

' This did very well, but still I was dissatisfied.   I wanted *a*

[1] *Stubbs's Calendar ; or, The Fatal Boots* [by W. M. Thackeray], appeared in The *Comic Almanac* for 1839, with illustrations by George Cruikshank.

pair of boots. Three boys in the school had boots—I was mad to have them too.

'But my papa, when I wrote to him, would not hear of it; and three pounds, the price of a pair, was too large a sum for my mother to take from the house-keeping, or for me to pay, in the present impoverished state of my exchequer; but the desire for the boots was so strong, that have them I must at any rate.

'There was a German bootmaker who had just set up in our town in those days, who afterwards made his fortune in London. I determined to have the boots from him, and did not despair, before the end of a year or two, either to leave the school, when I should not mind his dunning me, or to screw the money from mamma, and so pay him.

'So I called upon this man—Stiffelkind was his name—and he took my measure for a pair.

'"You are a vary yong gentleman to wear dop-boots," said the shoemaker.

'"I suppose, fellow," says I, "that is my business and not yours. Either make the boots or not—but when you speak to a man of my rank, speak respectfully!" and I poured out a number of oaths, in order to impress him with a notion of my respectability.

'They had the desired effect. "Stay, sir," says he. "I have a nice littel pair of dop-boots dat I tink will jost do for you." And he produced, sure enough, the most elegant things I ever saw. "Dey were made," said he, "for de Honorable Mr. Stiffney, of de Gards, but were too small."

'"Ah, indeed!" said I. "Stiffney is a relation of mine. And what, you scoundrel, will you have the impudence to ask for these things?" He replied, "Three pounds."

'"Well," said I, "they are confoundedly dear, but as you will have a long time to wait for your money, why, I shall have my revenge, you see." The man looked alarmed, and began a speech : "Sare,—I cannot let dem go vidout——" but a bright thought struck me, and I interrupted—"Sir! don't sir me. Take off the boots, fellow, and, harkye, when you speak to a nobleman, don't say Sir."

'"A hundert tousand pardons, my Lort," says he : "if I had known you were a lort, I vood never have called you Sir. Vat name shall I put down in my books?"

'"Name?—Oh! why, LORD CORNWALLIS, to be sure," said I, as I walked off in the boots.

'"And vat shall I do vid my Lort's shoes?"

'"Keep them until I send for them," said I. And giving him

MARCH—SHOWERY.

P. 89.

a patronising bow, I walked out of the shop, as the German
tied up my shoes in paper.

.   .   .   .   .

'This story I would not have told, but that my whole life
turned upon these accursed boots. I walked back to school as
proud as a peacock, and easily succeeded in satisfying the boys as
to the manner in which I came by my new ornaments.

'Well, one fatal Monday morning—the blackest of all black·
Mondays that ever I knew,—as we were all of us playing between
school-hours, I saw a posse of boys round a stranger, who seemed
to be looking out for one of us. A sudden trembling seized me—I
knew it was Stiffelkind. What had brought him here? He talked
loud, and seemed angry. So I rushed into the schoolroom, and,
burying my head between my hands, began reading for dear life.

'"I vant Lort Cornvallis," said the horrid bootmaker. "His
Lortship belongs, I know, to dis honourable school, for I saw him
vid de boys at church yesterday."

'"Lord who?"

'"Vy, Lort Cornvallis, to be sure—a very fat young nobleman,
vid red hair : he squints a little, and svears dreadfully."

'"There's no Lord Cornwallis here," said one ; and there was
a pause.

'"Stop ! I have it," says that odious Bunting.   "*It must be
Stubbs !*" And "Stubbs ! Stubbs !" every one cried out, while I
was so busy at my book as not to hear a word.

'At last, two of the biggest chaps rushed into the schoolroom,
and seizing each an arm, ran me into the playground—bolt up
against the shoemaker.

'"Dis is my man—I beg your Lortship's pardon," says he, "I
have brought your Lortship's shoes, vich you left.   See, dey have
been in dis parcel ever since you vent away in my boots."

'"Shoes, fellow !" says I, "I never saw your face before"—for
I knew there was nothing for it but brazening it out.   "Upon the
honour of a gentleman !" said I, turning round to the boys.   They
hesitated ; and if the trick had turned in my favour, fifty of them
would have seized hold of Stiffelkind and drubbed him soundly.

'"Stop !" says Bunting (hang him !).   "Let's see the shoes.
If they fit him, why, then, the cobbler's right."   They did fit me ;
and not only that, but the name of STUBBS was written in them
at full length.

'"Vat !" said Stiffelkind.   "Is he not a lort ?   So help me
Himmel, I never did vonce tink of looking at de shoes, which
have been lying, ever since, in dis piece of brown paper."   And
then, gathering anger as he went on, thundered out so much of his

George Cruikshank.

MAY—BEATING THE BOUNDS.

abuse at me, in his German-English, that the boys roared with laughter. Swishtail came in in the midst of the disturbance, and asked what the noise meant.

'"It's only Lord Cornwallis, sir," said the boys, "battling with his shoemaker about the price of a pair of top-boots."

'"O sir," said I, "it was only in fun that I called myself Lord Cornwallis."

'"In fun!—Where are the boots? And you, sir, give me your bill." My beautiful boots were brought; and Stiffelkind produced his bill. "Lord Cornwallis to Samuel Stiffelkind, for a pair of boots—four guineas."

'"You have been fool enough, sir," says the doctor, looking very stern, "to let this boy impose upon you as a lord; and knave enough to charge him double the value of the article you sold him. Take back the boots, sir! I won't pay a penny of your bill; nor can you get a penny. As for you, sir, you miserable swindler and cheat, I shall not flog you as I did before, but I shall send you home: you are not fit to be the companion of honest boys."

'"*Suppose we duck him* before he goes?" piped out a very small voice. The doctor grinned significantly, and left the schoolroom; and the boys knew by this they might have their will. They seized me, and carried me to the playground pump: they pumped upon me until I was half dead; and the monster, Stiffelkind, stood looking on for the half-hour the operation lasted.'

If the pictures which we are enabled to give at the conclusion of this notice are not quite so brilliant and clear as they were on the first appearance in the *Almanac*, the critic must be pleased to remember that we have been compelled to transfer to stone, having no other means of adapting them to the size of this review. When we recollect, too, that twenty thousand impressions were previously taken from the steels, the public will not be disposed to judge of the engravings in their present condition, but will see what they must have been when first they issued from the hands of the artist.[1] One or two have withstood the transfer operation very well, especially the pleasant plate of 'beating the bounds' (how

[1] À propos of the 'Holiday at the Public Offices'—(a delightful picture of real life)—we are reminded of the diary kept by a certain clerk in a certain public office eastward of Cornhill, whose daily duties began with a good breakfast provided for him whilst the monopoly of the China trade lasted.

> From 10 till 11—ate a breakfast for seven,
> From 11 till noon,—to begin, 'twas too soon.
> From 12 till 1—asked what's to be done?
> From 1 till 2—found nothing to do.
> From 2 till 3—began to foresee
> That from 3 till 4 would be a great bore

NOVEMBER—LAW LIFE ASSURANCE.

P. 93.

kindly and good-humoured it is !) and the 'scene in court,' from last year's *Almanac*, in which the celebrated Mr. Mulligan appears in the act of addressing the bench in favour of his client, the famous Tuggeridge Coxe Tuggeridge.

'Standing here, (says the orator) on the pedestal of secred Themis (we follow the peculiar mode of spelling that is adopted in the *Almanac*), seeing around me the ornyments of a profission I rispect, a vinnerable judge, an enlightened jury—the netion's glory, the counthry's cheap defendther, the poor man's priceless palladium, how must I thremble, my Lard, how must the blush of modesty befew my cheeks (somebody in court made an allusion to cheeks in the court, which caused a dreadful roar of laughter, and when order was established Mr. Mulligan continued) : My Lard, I heed them not, I come from a counthry accustomed to opprission, and as that counthry, yes, my Lard, that Ireland (do not laugh, I am proud of it) is ever, in spite of her tyrants, green, lovely, and beautiful ; in like manner my client's cause will rise superior to the malignant imbecility, I repeat, me Lard, the MALIGNANT IMBECILITY of those who would thrample it down, and in whose teeth, in my client's name, in my counthry's, aye, and in my own, I with folded arrums hurl a scornful and eternal defiance ! '

We should be glad to devote a few pages to the *Illustrations of Time*, the *Scraps and Sketches*, and the *Illustrations of Phrenology*, which are among the most famous of our artist's publications ; but it is very difficult to find new terms of praise, as find them one must, when reviewing Mr. Cruikshank's publica-tions, and more difficult still (as the reader of this notice will no doubt have perceived for himself long since) to translate his designs into words, and go to the printer's box for a description of all that fun and humour which the artist can produce by a few skilful turns of his needle. A famous article upon the *Illustrations of Time* appeared some dozen years since in *Blackwood's Magazine*, of which the conductors have always been great admirers of our artist, as became men of humour and genius. To these grand qualities do not let it be supposed that we are laying claim, but, thank Heaven, Cruikshank's humour is so good and benevolent that any man must love it, and on this score we may speak as well as another.

Then there are the *Greenwich Hospital* designs, which must not be passed over. *Greenwich Hospital* is a hearty, good-natured book, in the Tom Dibdin school, treating of the virtues of British tars, in approved nautical language. They maul Frenchmen and

Spaniards, they go out in brigs and take frigates, they relieve women in distress, and are yard-arm and yard-arming, athwart-hawsing, marlinspiking, binnacling, and helm's-a-leeing, as honest seamen invariably do in novels, on the stage, and doubtless on board ship. This we cannot take upon us to say, but the artist, like a true Englishman, as he is, loves dearly these brave guardians of Old England, and chronicles their rare or fanciful exploits with the greatest good-will. Let any one look at the noble head of Nelson, in *The Family Library*, and they will, we are sure, think with us that the designer must have felt and loved what he drew. There are to this abridgment of Southey's admirable book many more cuts after Cruikshank ; and about a dozen pieces by the same hand will be found in a work equally popular, Lockhart's excellent *Life of Napoleon*. Among these the retreat from Moscow is very fine ; the Mamlouks most vigorous, furious, and barbarous as they should be. At the end of these three volumes Mr. Cruikshank's contributions to *The Family Library* seem suddenly to have ceased ; the work, which was then the property of Mr. Murray, has since that period passed into the hands of Mr. Tegg, whose shop seems to be the bourne to which most books travel—the fatal retreat of the unfortunate brave. Mr. Tegg, like death, will never give up his prey. We implored of him a loan of the precious wood-blocks that are buried in his warehouses ; but no, Tegg was inexorable, and such of Mr. Cruikshank's charming little children as have found their way to him, have not been permitted to take a holiday with many of their brethren whose guardians are not so severe.

Let us offer our thanks to Messrs. Whitehead, Tilt, Robins, Darton and Clark, Thomas and Daly, proprietors of the Cruikshank cuts, who have lent us of their store. Only one man has imitated Mr. Tegg, and he, we are sorry to say, is no other than George Cruikshank himself, who, although besought by humble ambassadors, pestered by printers'-devils and penny post letters, did resolutely refuse to have any share in the blowing of his own trumpet, and showed our messengers to the door.

Our stock of plate has also been increased by the kindness of Messrs. Chapman and Hall, who have lent us some of the designs for the Boz sketches, not the worst among Mr. Dickens's books, as we think, and containing some of the best of Mr. Cruikshank's designs.

We are not at all disposed to undervalue the works and genius of Mr. Dickens, and we are sure that he would admit as readily as any man the wonderful assistance that he has derived from the artist who has given us the portraits of his ideal personages, and

made them familiar to all the world. Once seen, these figures
remain impressed on the memory, which otherwise would have
had no hold upon them, and the Jew, and Bumble, and the heroes
and heroines of the Boz sketches, become personal acquaintances
with each of us. O that Hogarth could have illustrated Fielding
in the same way! and fixed down on paper those grand figures
of Parson Adams, and Squire Allworthy, and the great Jonathan
Wild.

With regard to the modern romance of *Jack Sheppard*, in
which the latter personage makes a second appearance, it seems
to us that Mr. Cruikshank really created the tale, and that Mr.
Ainsworth, as it were, only put words to it. Let any reader of
the novel think over it for a while, now that it is some months
since he has perused and laid it down—let him think, and tell
us what he remembers of the tale? George Cruikshank's pictures
—always George Cruikshank's pictures. The storm in the Thames,
for instance; all the author's laboured description of that event
has passed clean away—we have only before the mind's eye the
fine plates of Cruikshank. The poor wretch cowering under the
bridge arch, as the waves come rushing in, and the boats are
whirling away in the drift of the great swollen black waters; and
let any man look at that second plate of the murder on the
Thames, and he must acknowledge how much more brilliant the
artist's description is than the writer's, and what a real genius for
the terrible as well as for the ridiculous the former has; how
awful is the gloom of the old bridge, a few lights glimmering from
the houses here and there, but not so as to be reflected on the
water at all, which is too turbid and raging; a great heavy rack
of clouds goes sweeping over the bridge, and men with flaring
torches, the murderers, are borne away with the stream.

The author requires many pages to describe the fury of the
storm, which Mr. Cruikshank has represented in one. First, he
has to prepare you with the something inexpressibly melancholy
in sailing on a dark night upon the Thames; 'the ripple of the
water,' 'the darkling current,' 'the indistinctively seen craft,'
'the solemn shadows,' and other phenomena visible on rivers at
night are detailed, 'with not unskilful rhetoric,' in order to bring
the reader into a proper frame of mind for the deeper gloom and
horror which is to ensue. Then follow pages of description.
'As Rowland sprang to the helm, and gave the signal for pursuit,
a war like a volley of ordnance was heard aloft, and the wind
again burst its bondage. A moment before the surface of the
stream was as black as ink. It was now whitening, hissing, and
seething, like an enormous cauldron. The blast once more swept

over the agitated river, whirled off the sheets of foam, scattered them far and wide in rain drops, and left the raging torrent blacker than before. Destruction everywhere marked the course of the gale. Steeples toppled and towers reeled beneath its fury. All was darkness, horror, confusion, ruin. Men fled from their tottering habitations and returned to them, scared by greater danger. The end of the world seemed at hand. . . . The hurricane had now reached its climax. The blast shrieked, as if exulting in its wrathful mission. Stunning and continuous, the din seemed almost to take away the power of hearing. He who had faced the gale *would have been instantly stifled,*' etc., etc. See with what a tremendous war of words (and good loud words too ; Mr. Ainsworth's description is a good and spirited one) the author is obliged to pour in upon the reader before he can effect his purpose upon the latter, and inspire him with a proper terror. The painter does it at a glance, and old Wood's dilemma in the midst of that tremendous storm, with the little infant at his bosom, is remembered afterwards, not from the words, but from the visible image of them that the artist has left us.

It would not, perhaps, be out of place to glance through the whole of the *Jack Sheppard* plates, which are among the most finished and the most successful of Mr. Cruikshank's performances, and say a word or two concerning them. Let us begin with finding fault with No. 1. 'Mr. Wood offers to adopt little Jack Sheppard.' A poor print, on a poor subject ; the figure of the woman is not as carefully designed as it might be, and the expression of the eyes (not an uncommon fault with our artist) much caricatured. The print is cut up, to use the artist's phrase, by the numbers of accessories which the engraver has thought proper, after the author's elaborate description, elaborately to reproduce. The plate of 'Wild discovering Darrell in the loft' is admirable—ghastly, terrible, and the treatment of it extraordinarily skilful, minute, and bold. The intricacies of the tile-work, and the mysterious twinkling of light among the beams, are excellently felt and rendered, and one sees here, as in the two next plates of the storm and murder, what a fine eye the artist has, what a skilful hand and what a sympathy for the wild and dreadful. As a mere imitation of nature, the clouds, and the bridge in the murder picture may be examined by painters who make far higher pretensions than Mr. Cruikshank. In point of workmanship they are equally good, the manner quite unaffected, the effect produced without any violent contrast, the whole scene evidently well and philosophically arranged in the artist's brain, before he began to put it upon copper.

H

The famous drawing of 'Jack carving the name on the beam,' which has been transferred to half the play-bills in town, is overloaded with accessories, as the first plate; but they are much better arranged than in the last-named engraving and do not injure the effect of the principal figure. Remark, too, the conscientiousness of the artist, and that shrewd pervading idea of form which is one of his principal characteristics. Jack is surrounded by all sorts of implements of his profession; he stands on a regular carpenter's table, away in the shadow under it lie shavings and a couple of carpenter's hampers. The glue-pot, the mallet, the chisel-handle, the planes, the saws, the hone with its cover, and the other paraphernalia are all represented with extraordinary accuracy and forethought. The man's mind has retained the exact *drawing* of all these minute objects (unconsciously perhaps to himself), but we can see with what keen eyes he must go through the world, and what a fund of facts (as such a knowledge of the shape of objects is in his profession) this keen student of nature has stored away in his brain. In the next plate, where Jack is escaping from his mistress, the figure of that lady, one of the deepest of the βαθυκόλποι, strikes us as disagreeable and unrefined; that of Winifred is, on the contrary, very pretty and graceful; and Jack's puzzled, slinking look must not be forgotten. All the accessories are good, and the apartment has a snug, cosy air, which is not remarkable, except that it shows how faithfully the designer has performed his work, and how curiously he has entered into all the particulars of the subject.

Master Thames Darrell, the handsome young man of the book, is, in Mr. Cruikshank's portraits of him, no favourite of ours. The lad seems to wish to make up for the natural insignificance of his face by frowning on all occasions most portentously.

This figure, borrowed from the compositor's desk, will give a notion of what we mean. Wild's face is too violent for the great man of history (if we may call Fielding history), but this is in consonance with the ranting, frowning, braggadocio character that Mr. Ainsworth has given him.

The 'Interior of Willesden Church' is excellent as a composition, and a piece of artistical workmanship; the groups well arranged, and the figure of Mrs. Sheppard looking round alarmed, as her son is robbing the dandy Kneebone, is charming, simple,

George Cruikshank.

JUNE—HOLIDAY AT THE PUBLIC OFFICES

and unaffected. Not so 'Mrs. Sheppard ill in bed,' whose face
is screwed up to an expression vastly too tragic. The little
glimpse of the church seen through the open door of the room is
very beautiful and poetical; it is in such small hints that an
artist especially excels; they are the morals which he loves to
append to his stories, and are always appropriate and welcome.
The boozing ken is not to our liking; Mrs. Sheppard is there with
her horrified eyebrows again. Why this exaggeration — is it
necessary for the public? We think not, or if they require such
excitement, let our artist, like a true painter as he is, teach them
better things.[1]

The 'Escape from Willesden cage' is excellent, the 'Burglary
in Wood's house,' has not less merit; 'Mrs. Sheppard in Bedlam,'
a ghastly picture, indeed, is finely conceived, but not, as we fancy,
so carefully executed; it would be better for a little more careful
drawing in the female figure.

'Jack sitting for his picture' is a very pleasing group, and
savours of the manner of Hogarth, who is introduced in the
company. The 'Murder of Trenchard' must be noticed too as
remarkable for the effect a terrible vigour which the artist has
given to the scene. The 'Willesden Churchyard' has great merit
too, but the gems of the book are the little vignettes illustrating
the escape from Newgate. Here, too, much anatomical care of
drawing is not required; the figures are so small that the outline
and attitude need only to be indicated, and the designer has produced a series of figures quite remarkable for reality and poetry
too. There are no less than ten of Jack's feats so described by
Mr. Cruikshank (let us say a word here in praise of the excellent
manner in which the author has carried us through the adventure).
Here is Jack clattering up the chimney, now peering into the
lonely red room, now opening 'the door between the red
room and the chapel.' What a wild, fierce, scared look he
has, the young ruffian, as cautiously he steps in, holding tight
his bar of iron. You can see by his face how his heart is beating!
If any one were there! but no! And this is a very fine charac-

---

[1] A gentleman (whose wit is so celebrated that one should be very cautious
in repeating his stories) gave the writer a good illustration of the philosophy
of exaggeration. Mr. —— was once behind the scenes at the Opera when the
scene-shifters were preparing for the ballet. Flora was to sleep under a bush,
whereon were growing a number of roses, and amidst which was fluttering a
gay covey of butterflies. In size the roses exceeded the most expansive sun-
flowers, and the butterflies were as large as cocked-hats;—the scene-shifter
explained to Mr. ——, who asked the reason why everything was so magnified,
that the galleries could never see the objects unless they were enormously
exaggerated. How many of our writers and designers work for the galleries?

teristic of the prints, the extreme *loneliness* of them all.   Not a soul is there to disturb him—woe to him who should—and Jack drives in the chapel gate, and shatters down the passage door, and there you have him on the leads, up he goes, it is but a spring of a few feet from the blanket, and he is gone—*abiit, evasit, erupit*.   Mr. Wild must catch him again if he can.

We must not forget to mention *Oliver Twist*, and Mr. Cruikshank's famous designs to that work.[1]   The sausage scene at Fagin's.   Nancy seizing the boy ; that capital piece of humour, Mr. Bumble's courtship, which is even better in Cruikshank's version than in Boz's exquisite account of the interview ; Sikes's farewell to the dog ; and the Jew—the dreadful Jew—that Cruikshank drew !   What a fine touching picture of melancholy desolation is that of Sikes and the dog !   The poor cur is not too well drawn, the landscape is stiff and formal ; but in this case the faults, if faults they be, of execution rather add to than diminish the effect of the picture : it has a strange, wild, dreary, broken-hearted look ; we fancy we see the landscape as it must have appeared to Sikes, when ghastly and with bloodshot eyes he looked at it.   As for the Jew in the dungeon, let us say nothing of it—what can we say to describe it ?   What a fine homely poet is the man who can produce this little world of mirth or woe for us !   Does he elaborate his effects by slow process of thoughts, or do they come to him by instinct ?   Does the painter ever arrange in his brain an image so complete, that he afterwards can copy it exactly on the canvas, or does the hand work in spite of him ?

A great deal of this random work of course every artist has done in his time, many men produce effects of which they never dreamed, and strike off excellencies, hap-hazard, which gain for them reputation ; but a fine quality in Mr. Cruikshank, the quality of his success, as we have said before, is the extraordinary earnestness and good faith with which he executes all he attempts —the ludicrous, the polite, the low, the terrible.   In the second of these he often, in our fancy, fails, his figures lacking elegance and descending to caricature ; but there is something fine in this too ; it is good that he should fail ; that he should have these honest *naïve* notions regarding the *beau monde*, the characteristics of which a namby-pamby tea-party painter could hit off far better than he.   He is a great deal too downright and manly to appreciate the flimsy delicacies of small society—you cannot expect

---

[1] Or his new work, *The Tower of London*, which promises even to surpass Mr. Cruikshank's former productions.

a lion to roar you like any sucking dove, or frisk about a drawing-
room like a lady's little spaniel.

If then, in the course of his life and business, he has been
occasionally obliged to imitate the ways of such small animals,
he has done so, let us say it at once, clumsily, and like as a lion
should.   Many artists, we hear, hold his works rather cheap ;
they prate about bad drawing, want of scientific knowledge ;—
they would have something vastly more neat, regular, anatomical.

Not one of the whole band most likely but can paint an
academy figure better than himself ; nay, or a portrait of an
alderman's lady and family of children.   But look down the list
of the painters and tell us who are they ?   How many among
these men are poets, makers, possessing the faculty to create, the
greatest among the gifts with which Providence has endowed the
mind of man ?   Say how many there are, count up what they
have done, and see what in the course of some nine-and-twenty
years has been done by this indefatigable man.

What amazing energetic fecundity do we find in him !   As a
boy he began to fight for bread, has been hungry (twice a day, we
trust) ever since, and has been obliged to sell his wit for his bread
week by week.   And his wit, sterling gold as it is, will find no
such purchasers as the fashionable painter's thin pinchbeck, who
can live comfortably for six weeks, when paid for and painting a
portrait, and fancies his mind prodigiously occupied all the while.
There was an artist in Paris, an artist hair-dresser, who used to
be fatigued and take restoratives after inventing a new coiffure.
By no such gentle operation of head-dressing has Cruikshank
lived ; time was (we are told so in print) when for a picture
with thirty heads in it he was paid three guineas—a poor week's
pittance truly, and a dire week's labour.   We make no doubt
that the same labour would at present bring him twenty times
the sum, but whether it be ill-paid or well, what labour has Mr.
Cruikshank's been !   Week by week, for thirty years, to produce
something new ; some smiling offspring of painful labour, quite
independent and distinct from its ten thousand jovial brethren ;
in what hours of sorrow and ill-health to be told by the world
' Make us laugh, or you starve—Give us fresh fun ; we have eaten
up the old and are hungry.'   And all this has he been obliged to
do—to wring laughter day by day, sometimes, perhaps, out of
want, often certainly from ill-health or depression—to keep the
fire of his brain perpetually alight, for the greedy public will give
it no leisure to cool.   This he has done and done well.   He has
told a thousand truths in as many strange and fascinating ways ;
he has given a thousand new and pleasant thoughts to millions of

JUNE

George Cruikshank

people ; he has never used his wit dishonestly ; he has never, in all the exuberance of his frolicsome humour, caused a single painful or guilty blush ; how little do we think of the extraordinary power of this man, and how ungrateful we are to him !

Here, as we are come round to the charge of ingratitude, the starting-post from which we set out, perhaps we had better conclude. The reader will perhaps wonder at the high-flown tone in which we speak of the services and merits of an individual, whom he considers a humble scraper on steel, that is wonderfully popular already. But none of us remember all the benefits we owe him ; they have come one by one, one driving out the memory of the other ; it is only when we come to examine them altogether as the writer has done, who has a pile of books on the table before him [1]—a heap of personal kindnesses from George Cruikshank (not presents, if you please, for we bought, borrowed, or stole every one of them), that we feel what we owe him. Look at one of Mr. Cruikshank's works, and we pronounce him an excellent humourist. Look at all, his reputation is increased by a kind of geometrical progression ; as a whole diamond is a hundred times more valuable than the hundred splinters into which it might be broken would be. A fine rough English diamond is this about which we have been writing.

[1] The long list of Mr. Cruikshank's works which heads this article is, we fear, far from complete, though we have tried hard to make it so.

A PICTORIAL RHAPSODY.[1]

By MICHAEL ANGELO TITMARSH.

With an Introductory Letter to Mr. Yorke.

My dear Yorke,

Do you remember the orders which you gave me at the close of our dinner last week at the Clarendon?—that dinner which you always provide upon my arrival in town from my country-seat; knowing full well that Titmarsh before he works must dine, and when he dines must dine well? Do you, I say, remember the remarks which you addressed to me? Probably not; for that third bottle of Clos-Vougeot had evidently done your business, and you were too tipsy, even to pay the bill.

Well, let bills be bills, and what care we? There is Mr. James Fraser, our employer, master, publisher, purse-bearer, and friend, who has such a pleasure in paying that it is a pity to balk him; and I never saw a man look more happy than he when he lugged out four five-pound notes to pay for that dinner of ours. What a scene it was! You asleep with your head in a dish of melted raspberry-ice; Mr. Fraser calm, beneficent, majestic, counting out the thirteens to the waiters; the Doctor and Mr. John Abraham Heraud, singing, '*Suoni la tromba intrepida*,' each clutching the other's hand, and waving a punch-ladle or a dessert-knife in the unemployed paw, and the rest of us joining in chorus when they came to '*gridando liberta*.'—But I am wandering from the point; the address which you delivered to me on drinking my health was in substance this:

'Mr. Michael Angelo Titmarsh, the splendid feast of which you have partaken, and the celebrated company of individuals whom you see around you, will show you in what estimation myself and Mr. Fraser hold your talents,—not that the latter point is of any consequence, as I am the sole editor of the Magazine. Sir, you have been called to the metropolis from a very distant part of the country, your coach-hire and personal expenses have

[1] [*Fraser's Magazine*, June 1840.]

been defrayed, you have been provided with a suit of clothes that *ought* to become you, for they have been for at least six months the wonder of the town while exhibited on my own person ; and you may well fancy that all these charges have not been incurred on our parts, without an expectation of some corresponding return from you. You are a devilish bad painter, sir ; but never mind, Hazlitt was another, and old Peter Pindar was a miserable dauber ; Mr. Alexander Pope, who wrote several pretty poems, was always busy with brush and palette, and made sad work of them. You, then, in common with these before-named illustrations, as my friend, Lady Morgan, calls them (Sir Charles returned thanks), are a wretched artist ; but a tolerable critic—nay, a good critic—nay, let me say to your face, the best critic, the clearest, the soundest, the gayest, the most eloquent, the most pathetic, and, above all, the most honest critic, in matters of art that is to be found in her majesty's dominions. And, therefore, Mr. Titmarsh, for we must give the deuce his due, you have been brought from your cottage near John O'Groat's or Land's End,— I forget which,—therefore you have been summoned to London at the present season.

'Sir, there are at this moment no less than five public exhibitions of pictures in the metropolis ; and it will be your duty carefully to examine every one of them during your residence here, and bring us a full and accurate report upon all the pieces exhibited which are remarkable for goodness, badness, or mediocrity.'

I here got up ; and, laying my hand on my satin waistcoat, looked up to heaven, and said, 'Sir, I——'

'Sit down, sir, and keep your eternal wagging jaws quiet ! Waiter ! whenever that person attempts to speak, have the goodness to fill his mouth with olives or a damson cheese.—To proceed. Sir, and you, gentlemen, and you, O intelligent public of Great Britain ! (for I know that every word I say is in some way carried to you) you must all be aware, I say, how wickedly,— how foully, basely, meanly—how, in a word, with-every-deteriorating-adverb that ends in *ly*—in *ly*, gentlemen (here Mr. Yorke looked round, and myself and Mr. Fraser, rather alarmed lest we should have let slip a pun, began to raise a low, faint laugh)— you have all of you seen how the world has been imposed upon by persons calling themselves critics, who, in daily, weekly, monthly prints, protrude their nonsense upon the town. What are these men ? Are they educated to be painters ?—No ! Have they a taste for painting ?—No ! I know of newspapers in this town, gentlemen, which send their reporters indifferently to a police-office or a picture-gallery, and expect them to describe

Correggio or a fire in Fleet Street with equal fidelity. And, alas! it must be confessed that our matter-of-fact public of England is itself but a dull appreciator of the arts, and is too easily persuaded by the dull critics who lay down their stupid laws.

'But we cannot expect, Mr. Titmarsh, to do any good to our beloved public by telling them merely that their instructors are impostors. Abuse is no argument, foul words admit of no pretence (you may have remarked that I never use them myself, but always employ the arts of gentlemanly persuasion), and we must endeavour to create a reform amongst the nations by simply preaching a purer and higher doctrine. Go you among the picture-galleries, as you have done in former years, and prattle on at your best rate; don't philosophise, or define, or talk big, for I will cut out every line of such stuff, but speak in a simple, natural way,—without fear, and without favour.

'Mark that latter word "favour" well; for you are a great deal too tender in your nature, and too profuse of compliments. Favour, sir, is the curse of the critical trade; and you will observe how a spirit of *camaraderie and* partizanship prevails in matters of art especially. The picture-critics, as I have remarked, are eminently dull—dull and loud; perfectly ignorant upon all subjects connected with art, never able to guess at the name of an artist without a catalogue and a number, quite unknowing whether a picture be well or ill drawn, well or ill painted; they must prate, nevertheless, about light and shade, warm and cool colour, keeping, chiaroscuro, and such other terms, from the Painters' Cant Dictionary, as they hear bandied about among the brethren of the brush.

'You will observe that such a critic has ordinarily his one or two idols that he worships; the one or two painters, namely, into whose studios he has free access, and from whose opinions he forms his own. There is Dash, for instance, of the Star newspaper; now and anon you hear him discourse of the fine arts, and you may take your affidavit that he has just issued from Blank's *atelier:* all Blank's opinions he utters—utters and garbles, of course; all his likings are founded on Blank's dicta, and all his dislikings: 'tis probable that Blank has a rival, one Asterisk, living over the way. In Dash's eye Asterisk is the lowest of creatures. At every fresh exhibition you read how "Mr. Blank has transcended his already transcendent reputation;" "Myriads are thronging round his glorious canvases;" "Billions have been trampled to death while rushing to examine his grand portrait of Lady Smigsmag;" "His picture of Sir Claude Calipash is a gorgeous representation of aldermanic dignity, and high chivalric grace!" As for Asterisk, you are told, "Mr. Asterisk has two or three pictures—pretty, but weak, repetitions of his old faces and subjects in his old namby-pamby style. The committee, we hear, rejected most of his pictures : the committee are very compassionate. How *dared* they reject Mr. Blank's stupendous historical picture of So-and-so ? " '

(Here, my dear sir, I am sorry to say that there was a general snore heard from the guests round the table, which rather disturbed the flow of your rhetoric. You swallowed down two or three pints of burgundy, however, and continued.)

'But I must conclude. Michael Angelo Titmarsh, you know your duty. You are an honest man (loud cheers, the people had awakened during the pause). You must go forth determined to tell the truth, the whole truth, and nothing but the truth ; as far as you, a fallible creature (cries of " No, no ! ") know it. If you see a good picture, were it the work of your bitterest enemy —and you have hundreds—praise it.'

'I will,' gasped I.

'Hold your tongue, sir, and don't be interrupting me with your perpetual orations ! If you see a bad picture, were it the work of your dearest associate, your brother, the friend of your bosom, your benefactor—cut, slash, slaughter him without mercy. Strip off humbug, sir, though it cover your best boon-companion. Praise merit, though it belong to your fiercest foe, your rival in the affections of your mistress, the man from whom you have borrowed money, or taken a beating in private ! '

'Mr. Yorke,' said I, clenching my fists and starting up, 'this passes endurance, were you not intox— ; ' but two waiters here seized and held me down, luckily for you.

'Peace, Titmarsh (said you) ; 'twas but raillery. Be honest, my friend, is all that I would say ; and if you write a decent article on the Exhibitions, Mr. Fraser will pay you handsomely for your trouble ; and, in order that you may have every facility for visiting the picture-galleries, I myself will give you a small sum in hand. Here are ten shillings. Five Exhibitions, five shillings ; catalogues, four. You will have twelve pence for yourself, to take refreshments in the intervals.'

I held out my hand, for my anger had quite disappeared.

'Mr. Fraser,' said you, 'give the fellow half a sovereign ; and, for Heaven's sake, teach him to be silent when a gentleman is speaking ! '

What passed subsequently need not be stated here, but the above account of your speech is a pretty correct one ; and, in pursuance of your orders, I busied myself with the Exhibitions on the following day. The result of my labours will be found in the accompanying report. I have the honour, sir, of laying it at your feet, and of subscribing myself,

With the profoundest respect and devotion, Sir,

Your very faithful and obedient Servant,

MICHAEL ANGELO TITMARSH.

Moreland's Coffee-House,
Dean Street, Soho.

ΡΑΨΩΔΙΑ ἠ ΓΡΑΜΜΑ Α΄.

THE ROYAL ACADEMY.

Had the author of the following paragraphs the pen of a Sir Walter Scott or a Lady Morgan, he would write something excessively brilliant and witty about the first day of the Exhibition, and of the company which crowd the rooms upon that occasion. On Friday the queen comes (Heaven bless her majesty !) attended by her courtiers and train ; and deigns, with royal eyes, to examine the works of her Royal Academicians. Her, as we are given to understand, the President receives, bowing profoundly, awe-stricken ; his gold chain dangles from his presidential bosom, and sweet smiles of respectful courtesy light up his venerable face. Walking by her majesty's side, he explains to her the wonders of the show. 'That, may it please your majesty, is a picture representing yourself, painted by the good knight, Sir Francis Wilkie : deign to remark how the robes seem as if they were cut out of British oak, and the figure is as wooden as the figure-head of one of your majesty's men-of-war. Opposite is your majesty's royal consort, by Mr. Patten. We have the honour to possess two more pairs of Pattens in this Academy — ha, ha ! Round about you will see some of my own poor works of art. Yonder is Mr. Landseer's portrait of your majesty's own cockatoo, with a brace of Havadavats. Please your royal highness to look at the bit of biscuit ; no baker could have done it more natural. Fair maid of honour, look at that lump of sugar ; couldn't one take an affidavit, now, that it cost elevenpence a pound ? Isn't it sweet ? I know only one thing sweeter, and that's your ladyship's lovely face !'

In such lively conversation might we fancy a bland president discoursing. The queen should make august replies ; the lovely, smiling maids of honour should utter remarks becoming their innocence and station (turning away very red from that corner of the apartment where hung certain Venuses and Andromedas, painted by William Etty, Esquire) ; the gallant prince, a lordly, handsome, gallant gentleman, with a slight foreign accent, should curl the dark mustache that adorns his comely lip, and say, ' *Potztausend !* but dat bigure of First loaf by Herr von Mulready *ist wunderschön !* ' and courtly chamberlains, prim gold-sticks, and sly polonaises of the court, should take their due share in the gay scene, and deliver their portions of the dialogue of the little drama.

All this, I say, might be done in a very sprightly, neat way, were poor Titmarsh an Ainsworth or a Lady Morgan ; and the scene might be ended smartly with the knighting of one of the Academicians by her majesty on the spot. As thus :—' The royal party had stood for three-and-twenty minutes in mute admiration before that tremendous picture by Mr. Maclise, representing the banquet in the hall of Dunsinane. " Gory shadow of Banquo," said Lady Almeria to Lady Wilhelmina, " how hideous thou art ! " " Hideous ! hideous yourself, marry ! " replied the arch and lovely Wilhelmina. " By my halidome ! " whispered the seneschal to the venerable prime minister, Lord Melborough—" by cock and pie, sir count, but it seems me that yon Scottish kerne, Macbeth, hath a shrewd look of terror ! " " And a marvellous unkempt beard," answered the earl ; " and a huge mouth gaping wide for very terror, and a hand palsied with fear." " Hoot awa, mon ! " cried an old Scots general, " but the chield Macbeth (I'm descanded from him leeneally in the saxty-ninth generation) knew hoo to wield a gude claymore ! " " His hand looks as if it had dropped a hot potato ! " whispered a roguish page, and the little knave's remark caused a titter to run through the courtly circle, and brought a smile upon the cheek of the President of the Academy ; who, sooth to say, had been twiddling his chain of office between his finger and thumb, somewhat jealous of the praise bestowed upon his young rival.

' " My lord of Wellington," said her majesty, " lend me your sword." The veteran, smiling, drew forth that trenchant sabre,— that spotless blade of battle that had flashed victorious on the plains of far Assaye, in the breach of storm-girt Badajoz, in the mighty and supreme combat of Waterloo ! A tear stood in the hero's eye as he fell on his gartered knee ; and, holding the blade between his finger and thumb, he presented the hilt to his liege lady. " Take it, madam," said he ; " sheathe it in this old breast, if you will, for my heart and sword are my sovereign's. Take it, madam, and be not angry if there is blood upon the steel—'tis the blood of the enemies of my country ! " The queen took it ; and, as the young and delicate creature waved that tremendous war-sword, a gentleman near her remarked, that surely never lighted on the earth a more delightful vision. "Where is Mr. Maclise?" said her majesty. The blushing painter stepped forward. "Kneel! kneel!" whispered fifty voices; and frightened, he did as they ordered him. "Sure she's not going to cut my head off?" he cried to the good knights Sir Augustus Callcott and Sir Isaac Newton, who were standing. "Your name, sir?" said the Ladye of England. "Sure you know it's Maclise!" cried the son of Erin. "Your Christian name?" shrieked Sir Martin Shee, in agony. "Christian name, is it? Oh, then it's Daniel Malcolm, your majesty, and much at your service!" She waved the sword majestically over his head, and said, "Rise up, Sir Malcolm Maclise!"

    .   .   .   .

'The ceremony was concluded, the brilliant *cortège* moved away, the royal caroches received the illustrious party, the heralds cried, "*Largesse, Largesse!*" and flung silver pennies among the shouting crowds in Trafalgar Square; and when the last man-at-arms that accompanied the royal train had disappeared, the loud *vivas* of the crowd were heard no more, the shrill song of the silver clarions had died away, his brother painters congratulated the newly-dubbed chevalier, and retired to partake of a slight collation of bread and cheese and porter in the keeper's apartments.'

Were we, I say, inclined to be romantic, did we dare to be imaginative, such a scene might be depicted with considerable effect; but, as it is, we must not allow poor fancy to get the better of reason, and declare that to write anything of the sort would be perfectly uncalled for and absurd. Let it simply be stated that, on the Friday, her majesty comes and goes. On the Saturday the Academicians have a private view for the great personages; the lords of the empire and their ladies, the editors of the newspapers and their friends; and, after they have seen as much as possible, about seven o'clock the Academicians give a grand feed to their friends and patrons.

In the arrangement of this banquet let us say roundly that *Messieurs de l'Académie* are vastly too aristocratic. Why were *we* not asked? The dinner is said to be done by Gunter; and, though the soup and fish are notoriously cold and uncomfortable, we are by no means squeamish, and would pass over this gross piece of neglect. We long, too, to hear a bishop say grace, and to sit cheek by jowl with a duke or two. Besides, we could make some return; a good joke is worth a plate full of turtle; a smart, brisk pun is quite as valuable as a bottle of champagne; a neat anecdote deserves a slice of venison, with plenty of fat and currant jelly, and so on. On such principles of barter we might be disposed

to treat. But a plague on this ribaldry and beating about the
bush ! let us leave the plates, and come at once to the pictures.

* * *

Once or twice before, in the columns of this Magazine, we have
imparted to the public our notions about Greek art, and its
manifold deadly errors. The contemplation of such specimens of it
as we possess hath always, to tell the truth, left us in a state
of unpleasant wonderment and perplexity. It carries corporeal
beauty to a pitch of painful perfection, and deifies the body and
bones truly ; but, by dint of sheer beauty, it leaves humanity
altogether inhuman—quite heartless and passionless. Look at
Apollo the divine : there is no blood in his marble veins, no
warmth in his bosom, no fire or speculation in his dull, awful eyes.
Laocoon writhes and twists in an anguish that never can, in the
breast of any spectator, create the smallest degree of pity. Diana,

> ' *La chasseresse*
> *Blanche, au sein virginal,*
> *Qui presse*
> *Quelque cerf matinal* ' [1]—

may run from this till doomsday ; and we feel no desire to join the
cold, passionless huntress in her ghostly chase. Such monsters of
beauty are quite out of the reach of human sympathy ; they were
purposely (by the poor benighted heathens who followed this error,
and strove to make their error as grand as possible) placed beyond
it. They seemed to think that human joy and sorrow, passion and
love, were mean and contemptible in themselves. Their gods were
to be calm, and share in no such feelings. How much grander is
the character of the Christian school, which teaches that love is
the most beautiful of all things, and the first and highest element
of beauty in art !

I don't know, madam, whether I make myself clearly understood
in saying so much ; but if you will have the kindness to look at a
certain little picture by Mr. Eastlake in this gallery, you will see
to what the observation applies, and that out of a homely subject,
and a few simple figures not at all wonderful for excessive beauty
or grandeur, the artist can make something infinitely more beautiful
than Medicean Venuses, and sublimer than Pythian Apollos.
Happy are you, Charles Lock Eastlake, Esquire, R.A. ! I think
you have in your breast some of that sacred fire that lighted the
bosom of Raphael Sanctius, Esquire, of Urbino, he being a young
man,—a holy kind of Sabbath repose—a calm that comes not of
feeling, but of the overflowing of it—a tender, yearning sympathy

[1] Alfred de Musset.

and love for God's beautiful world and creatures. Impelled by such a delightful sentiment, the gentle spirit of him in whom it dwells (like the angels of old, who first taught us to receive the doctrine that love was the key to the world) breathes always peace on earth and good-will towards men. And though the privilege of enjoying this happy frame of mind is accorded to the humblest as well as the most gifted genius, yet the latter must remember that the intellect can exercise itself in no higher way than in the practice of this kind of adoration and gratitude. The great artist who is the priest of nature is consecrated especially to this service of praise; and though it may have no direct relation to religious subjects, the view of a picture of the highest order does always, like the view of stars in a calm night, or a fair quiet landscape in sunshine, fill the mind with an inexpressible content and gratitude towards the Maker who has created such beautiful things for our use.

And as the poet has told us how, not out of a wide landscape merely, or a sublime expanse of glittering stars, but of any very humble thing, we may gather the same delightful reflections (as out of a small flower, that brings us 'thoughts that do often lie too deep for tears')—in like manner we do not want grand pictures and elaborate yards of canvas so to affect us, as the lover of drawing must have felt in looking at the Raphael designs lately exhibited in London. These were little faint scraps, mostly from the artist's pencil—small groups, unfinished single figures, just indicated; but the divine elements of beauty were as strong in them as in the grandest pieces: and there were many little sketches, not half an inch high, which charmed and affected one like the violet did Wordsworth; and left one in that unspeakable, complacent, grateful condition which, as I have been endeavouring to state, is the highest aim of the art.

And if I might be allowed to give a hint to amateurs concerning pictures and their merit, I would say look to have your *heart* touched by them. The best paintings address themselves to the best feelings of it; and a great many very clever pictures do not touch it at all. Skill and handling are great parts of a painter's trade, but heart is the first; this is God's direct gift to him, and cannot be got in any academy, or under any master. Look about, therefore, for pictures, be they large or small, finished well or ill, landscapes, portraits, figure-pieces, pen-and-ink sketches, or what not, that contain sentiment and great ideas. He who possesses these will be sure to express them more or less well. Never mind about the manner. He who possesses them not may draw and colour to perfection, and yet do no artist. As for telling you

I

what sentiment is, and what it is not, wherein lies the secret of the sublime, there, madam, we must stop altogether ; only if, after reading Burke *On the Sublime*, you will find yourself exactly as wise as you were before. I cannot tell why a landscape by Claude or Constable should be more beautiful—it is certainly not more dexterous—than a landscape by Mr. —— or Mr. ——. I cannot tell why Raphael should be superior to Mr. Benjamin Haydon (a fact which one person in the world may be perhaps inclined to doubt) ; or why Vedrai Carino, in *Don Juan*, should be more charming to me than ' *Suoni la tromba*,' before mentioned. The latter has twice as much drumming, trumpeting, and thundering in it. All these points are quite undefinable and inexplicable (I never read a metaphysical account of them that did not seem sheer dulness and nonsense) ; but we can have no doubt about them. And thus we come to Charles Lock Eastlake, Esquire, from whom we started about a page since ; during which we have laid down, first, that sentiment is the first quality of a picture ; second, that to say whether this sentiment exists or no rests with the individual entirely, the sentiment not being capable of any sort of definition. Charles Lock Eastlake, Esquire, possesses, to my thinking, this undefinable arch-quality of sentiment to a very high degree. And, besides him, let us mention William Mulready, Esquire, Cope, Boxall, Redgrave, Herbert (the two latter don't show so much of it this year as formerly), and Richmond.

Mr. Eastlake's picture is as pure as a Sabbath-hymn sung by the voices of children. He has taken a very simple subject— hardly any subject at all ; but such suggestive points are the best, perhaps, that a painter can take ; for with the illustration of a given subject out of a history or romance, when one has seen it, one has commonly seen all, whereas such a piece as this, which Mr. Eastlake calls ' The Salutation of the Aged Friar,' brings the spectator to a delightful peaceful state of mind, and gives him matter to ponder upon long after. The story of this piece is simply this :—A group of innocent, happy-looking Italian peasants are approaching a couple of friars ; a boy has stepped forward with a little flower, which he presents to the elder of these, and the old monk is giving him his blessing.

Now, it would be very easy to find fault with this picture, and complain of excessive redness in the shadows, excessive whiteness in the linen, of repetition in the faces—the smallest child is the very counterpart of one in the ' Christ and the Little Children ' by the same artist last year—the women are not only copies of women before painted by Mr. Eastlake, but absolutely copies of one another ; the drawing lacks vigour, the flesh-tints variety, (they seem to be produced, by the most careful stippling, with a brilliant composition of lake and burnt sienna, cooled off as they come to the edges with a little blue.)   But though, in the writer's judgment, there are in the picture every one of these faults, the merits of the performance incomparably exceed them, and these are of the purely sentimental and intellectual kind.   What a tender grace and purity in the female heads !   If Mr. Eastlake repeats his model often, at least he has been very lucky in finding or making her : indeed, I don't know in any painter, ancient or modern, such a charming character of female beauty.   The countenances of the monks are full of unction ; the children, with their mild-beaming eyes, are fresh with recollections of heaven. There is no affectation of middle-age mannerism, such as silly German and silly Frenchmen are wont to call Catholic art ; and the picture is truly Catholic in consequence, having about it what the hymn calls ' solemn mirth,' and giving the spectator the utmost possible pleasure in viewing it.   Now, if we might suggest to Mr. Lane, the lithographer, how he might confer a vast benefit upon the public, we would entreat him to make several large copies of pictures of this class, executing them with that admirable grace and fidelity which are the characteristics of all his copies. Let these be coloured accurately, as they might be, at a small charge, and poor people for a few guineas might speedily make for themselves delightful picture-galleries.   The colour adds amazingly to the charm of these pictures, and attracts the eye to them. And they are such placid, pious companions for a man's study, that the continual presence of them could not fail to purify his taste and his heart.

I am not here arguing, let it be remembered, that Mr. Eastlake is absolute perfection ; and will concede to those who find fault with him that his works are deficient in power, however remarkable for grace.   Be it so.   But, then, let us admire his skill in choosing such subjects as are best suited to his style of thinking, and least likely to shew his faults.   In the pieces ordinarily painted by him, grace and tender feeling are the chief requisites ; and I don't recollect a work of his in which he has aimed at other qualities.   One more picture besides the old Friar has Mr. Eastlake, a portrait of that beautiful Miss Bury, whom our readers must recollect in the old house, in a black mantle, a red gown, with long golden hair waving over her shoulders, and a lily in her hand.   The picture was engraved afterwards in one of the Annuals ; and was one of the most delightful works that ever came from Mr. Eastlake's pencil.   I can't say as much for the present portrait ; the picture wants relief, and is very odd and heavy in

colour. The handsome lady looks as if she wanted her stays.
O beautiful lily-bearer of six years since! you should not have
appeared like a mortal after having once shone upon us as an
angel.

And now we are come to the man whom we delight to honour,
Mr. Mulready, who has three pictures in the Exhibition that are
all charming in their way. The first ('Fair Time,' 116) was
painted, it is said, more than a score of years since; and the
observer may look into it with some payment for his curiosity,
for it contains specimens of the artist's old and new manner.
The picture in its first state is somewhat in the Wilkie style of
that day (O for the Wilkie style of that day!), having many
greys, and imitating closely the Dutchmen. Since then the
painter has been touching up the figures in the foreground with
his new and favourite lurid orange-colour; and you may see how
this is stippled in upon the faces and hands, and borrow, perhaps,
a hint or two regarding the Mulreadian secret.

What is the meaning of this strange colour?—these glowing,
burning crimsons, and intense blues, and greens more green than
the first budding leaves of spring, or the mignonette-pots in a
Cockney's window at Brixton. But don't fancy that we are joking
or about to joke at Mr. Mulready. These gaudy prismatic colours
are wonderfully captivating to the eye; and, amidst a host of
pictures, it cannot fail to settle on a Mulready in preference to
all. But, for consistency's sake, a protest must be put in against
the colour; it is pleasant, but wrong; we never saw it in nature
—not even when looking through an orange-coloured glass. This
point being settled, then, and our minds eased, let us look at the
design and conception of 'First Love'; and pray, sir, where in
the whole works of modern artists will you find anything more
exquisitely beautiful? I don't know what that young fellow, so
solemn, so tender, is whispering into the ear of that dear girl (she
is only fifteen now, but, *sapristi*, how beautiful she will be about
three years hence!), who is folding a pair of slim arms round a
little baby, and making believe to nurse it, as they three are
standing one glowing summer day under some trees by a stile.
I don't know, I say, what they are saying; nor, if I could hear,
would I tell—'tis a secret, madam. Recollect the words that
the captain whispered in your ear that afternoon in the shrubbery.
Your heart throbs, your cheek flushes; the sweet sound of those
words tells clear upon your ear, and you say, 'Oh, Mr. Titmarsh,
how can you?' Be not afraid, madam—never, never will I peach;
but sing, in the words of a poet who is occasionally quoted in the
House of Commons—

' *Est et fideli tuta silentio*
Merces.   Vetabo qui Cereris sacrum
Vulgarit arcanæ, sub iisdem
Sit trabibus, fragilemve mecum
Solvat phaselum.'

Which may be interpreted (with the slight alteration of the name
of Ceres for that of a much more agreeable goddess)—

Be happy, and thy counsel keep,
  'Tis thus the bard adviseth thee ;
Remember that the silent lip
  In silence shall rewarded be.
And fly the wretch who dares to strip
  Love of its sacred mystery.
My loyal legs I would not stretch
  Beneath the same mahogany ;
Nor trust myself in Chelsea Reach,
  In punt or skiff, with such as he.
The villain who would kiss and peach,
  I hold him for mine enemy !

But, to return to our muttons, I would not give a fig for the taste
of the individual who does not see the exquisite beauty of this
little group.   Our artist has more passion than the before-lauded
Mr. Eastlake, but quite as much delicacy and tenderness ; and
they seem to me to possess the poetry of picture-making more
than any other of their brethren.

By the way, what is this insane yell that has been raised
throughout the public press about Mr. Mulready's other performance, the postage cover, and why are the sages so bitter against
it ?   *The Times* says it is disgraceful and ludicrous ; the elegant
writers of *The Weekly Dispatch* vow it is ludicrous and disgraceful ; the same sweet song is echoed by papers, Radical and
Conservative, in London and the provinces, all the literary gentlemen being alive and smarting under the insult to the arts of the
country.   Honest gentlemen of the press, be not so thin-skinned !
Take my word for it, there is no cause for such vehement anger
—no good opportunity here for you to shew off that exquisite
knowledge of the fine arts for which you are so celebrated throughout the world.   Gentlemen, the drawing of which you complain
is *not* bad.   The commonest engravers, who would be ashamed to
produce such a design, will tell you, if they know anything of
their business, that they could not make a better in a hurry.
Every man who knows what drawing is will acknowledge that
some of these little groups are charmingly drawn ; and I will

trouble your commonest engravers to design the Chinese group, the American, or the West Indian, in a manner more graceful and more characteristic than that of the much‑bespattered post envelope.

I am not holding up the whole affair as a masterpiece—*pas si bête*. The 'triumphant hallegory of Britannia ruling the waves,' as Mathews used to call it, is a little stale, certainly, nowadays; but what would you have? How is the sublime to be elicited from such a subject? Let some of the common engravers, in their leisure moments, since the thing is so easy, make a better design, or the literary men who are so indignant invent one. The government, no doubt, is not bound heart and soul to Mr. Mulready, and is willing to hear reason. *Fiat justitia, ruat cœlum:* though all the world shall turn on thee, O government, in this instance Titmarsh shall stand by thee—ay, and without any hope of reward. To be sure, if my Lord Normanby absolutely insists—but that is neither here nor there. I repeat, the Post Office envelope is not bad, *quoad* design. That very lion, which some of the men of the press (the Daniels!) have been crying out about, is finely, carefully, and characteristically sketched; those elephants I am sure were closely studied, before the artist in a few lines laid them down on his wood‑block; and as for the persons who are to imitate the engraving so exactly, let them try. It has been done by the best wood‑engraver in Europe. Ask any man in the profession if Mr. Thompson is not at the head of it? He has bestowed on it a vast deal of time, and skill, and labour; and all who know the difficulties of wood‑engraving—of outline wood‑engraving—and of rendering faithfully a design so very minute as this, will smile at the sages who declare that all the world could forge it. There was one provincial paper which declared, in a style peculiarly elegant, that a man 'with a block of wood and a *bread‑and‑cheese* knife could easily imitate the envelope;' which remark, for its profound truth and sagacity, the London journals copied. For shame, gentlemen! Do you think you show your knowledge by adopting such opinions as these, or prove your taste by clothing yourselves in the second‑hand garments of the rustic who talks about bread and cheese? Try, Tyrotomos, upon whatever block thou choosest to practise; or be wise, and with appropriate bread‑and‑cheese knife cut only bread and cheese. Of bread, white and brown, of cheese, old, new, mouldy, toasted, the writer of *The Double‑Gloster Journal, The Stilton Examiner, The Cheddar Champion, and North Wiltshire Intelligencer*, may possibly be a competent critic, and (with mouth replete with the delicious condiment) may no doubt eloquently speak. But let us be cautious before we agree to and admiringly adopt his opinions upon matters of art. Mr. Thompson is the first wood-engraver in our country—Mr. Mulready one of the best painters in our or any school : it is hard that such men are to be assailed in such language, and by such a critic !

This artist's picture of an interior is remarkable for the same exaggerated colour, and for the same excellences. The landscape seen from the window is beautifully solemn, and very finely painted, in the clear bright manner of Van Dyck and Cranach, and the early German school.

Mr. Richmond's picture of ' Our Lord after the Resurrection ' deserves a much better place than it has in the little, dingy, newly-discovered octagon closet ; and leaves us to regret that he should occupy himself so much with water-colour portraits, and so little with compositions in oil. This picture is beautifully conceived, and very finely and carefully drawn and painted. One of the apostles is copied from Raphael, and the more is the pity : a man who could execute two such grand figures as the other two in the picture need surely borrow from no one. A water-colour group, by the same artist (547. ' The Children of Colonel Lindsay '), contains two charming figures of a young lady and a little boy, painted with great care and precision of design and colour, with great purity of sentiment, and without the least affectation. Let our aristocracy send their wives and children (the handsomest wives and children in the world) to be painted by this gentleman, and those who are like him. Miss Lindsay, with her plain red dress and modest looks, is surely a thousand times more captivating than those dangerous smiling Delilahs in her neighbourhood, whom Mr. Chalon has painted. We must not be understood to undervalue this latter gentleman, however ; his drawings are miracles of dexterity ; every year they seem to be more skilful and more brilliant. Such satins and lace, such diamond rings and charming little lap-dogs, were never painted before,—not by Watteau, the first master of the *genre*,—and Lancret, who was scarcely his inferior. A miniature on ivory by Mr. Chalon, among the thousand prim, pretty little pictures of the same class which all the ladies crowd about, is remarkable for its brilliancy of colour and charming freedom of handling ; as is an oil sketch of masquerading figures, by the same painter, for the curious coarseness of the painting.

Before we leave the high-class pictures, we must mention Mr. Boxall's beautiful ' Hope,' which is exquisitely refined and delicate in sentiment, colour, and execution. Placed close beneath one of Turner's magnificent tornadoes of colour, it loses none of its own beauty. As Uhland writes of a certain king and queen who are seated in state side by side—

Der Turner *furchtbar prächtig wie blut'ger Nordlichtschein*
Der Boxall *süss und milde, als blickte Vollmond drein.*

Which signifies in English, that

As beams the moon so gentle near the sun, that blood-red burner,
So shineth William Boxall by Joseph Mallord Turner.

In another part of the room, and contrasting their quiet grace in the same way with Mr. Turner's glaring colours, are a couple of delightful pictures by Mr. Cope, with mottoes that will explain their subjects. 'Help thy father in his age, and despise him not when thou art in thy full strength;' and 'Reject not the affliction of the afflicted, neither turn away thy face from a poor man.' The latter of these pictures is especially beautiful, and the figure of the female charity as graceful and delicate as may be. I wish I could say a great deal in praise of Mr. Cope's large altar-piece : it is a very meritorious performance ; but here praise stops, and such praise is worth exactly nothing. A large picture must either be splendid, or else naught. This 'Crucifixion' has a great deal of vigour, feeling, grace ; BUT,—the but is fatal ; all minor praises are drowned in it. Recollect, however, Mr. Cope, that Titmarsh, who writes this, is only giving his private opinion ; that he is mortal ; that it is barely possible that he should be in the wrong ; and with this confession, which I am compelled (for fear you might overlook the circumstance) to make, you will, I dare say, console yourself, and do well. But men must gird themselves, and go through long trainings, before they can execute such gigantic works as altar-pieces. Handel, doubtless, wrote many little pleasing melodies before he pealed out the 'Hallelujah' chorus ; and so painters will do well to try their powers, and, if possible, measure and understand them, before they use them. There is Mr. Hart, for instance, who took in an evil hour to the making of great pictures ; in the present Exhibition is a decently small one ; but the artist has over-stretched himself in the former attempts ; as one hears of gentlemen on the rack, the limbs are stretched one or two inches by the process, and the patient comes away by so much the taller ; but he can't *walk* near so well as before, and all his strength is stretched out of him.

Let this be a solemn hint to a clever young painter, Mr Elmore, who has painted a clever picture of 'The Murder of Saint Thomas à Becket,' for Mr. Daniel O'Connell. Come off your rack, Mr. Elmore, or you will hurt yourself. Much better is it to paint small subjects, for some time at least, '*Non cuivis contingit adire Corinthum*,' as the proverb says; but there is a number of pleasant villages in this world besides, where we may snugly take up our quarters. By the way, what is the meaning of Tom à Becket's black cassock under his canonicals? Would John Tuam celebrate mass in such a dress? A painter should be as careful about his costumes as an historian about his dates, or he plays the deuce with his composition.

Now, in this matter of costume, nobody can be more scrupulous than Mr. Charles Landseer, whose picture of Nell Gwynn is painted with admirable effect, and honest scrupulousness. It is very good in colour, very gay in spirits (perhaps too refined,—for Nelly never was such a hypocrite as to look as modest as that); but the gentlemen and ladies do not look as if they were accustomed to their dresses, for all their correctness, and had put them on for the first time. Indeed, this is a very small fault, and the merits of the picture are very great; every one of the accessories is curiously well painted,—some of the figures very spirited (the drawer is excellent); and the picture one of the most agreeable in the whole gallery. Mr. Redgrave has another costume picture, of a rather old subject, from *The Rambler*. A poor girl comes to be companion to Mr. and Mrs. Courtly, who are at piquet; their servants are bringing in tea, and the master and mistress are looking at the new-comer with a great deal of easy scorn. The poor girl is charming; Mrs. Courtly not quite genteel, but with a wonderful quilted petticoat; Courtly looks as if he were not accustomed to his clothes; the servants are very good; and as for the properties, as they would be called on the stage, these are almost too good-painted, with a daguerreotypical minuteness, that gives this and Mr. Redgrave's other picture of 'Paracelsus' a finnikin air, if we may use such a disrespectful term. Both performances, however, contain very high merit of expression and sentiment; and are of such a character as we seldom saw in our schools twenty years ago.

There is a large picture by a Scotch artist, Mr. Duncan, representing 'The Entry of Charles Edward into Edinburgh,' which runs a little into caricature, but contains a vast deal of character and merit; and which, above all, in the article of costume, shews much study and taste. Mr. Duncan seems to have formed his style upon Mr. Allan and Mr. Wilkie—I beg his pardon—Sir David. The former has a pleasing brown picture likewise on the subject of the Pretender. The latter's maid of Saragossa and Spaniard at the gun, any one may see habited as Irish peasants superintending 'A Whisky Still,' in the middle room, No. 252.

This picture, I say, any one may see and admire who pleases ; to me it seems all rags, and duds, and a strange, straggling, misty composition. There are fine things, of course ; for how can Sir David help to paint fine things ? In the 'Benvenuto' there is superb colour, with a rich management of lakes especially, which has been borrowed from no master that we know of. The queen is as bad a likeness and picture as we have seen for many a day. 'Mrs. Ferguson of Raith,' a magnificent picture indeed, as grand in effect as a Rubens or Titian, and having a style of its own. The little sketch from Allan Ramsay is delightful ; and the noble-man and hounds (with the exception of his own clumsy vermilion robe), as fine as the fellow-sized portrait mentioned before. Allan Ramsay has given a pretty subject, and brought us a pretty picture from another painter, Mr. A. Johnston, who has illustrated those pleasant quaint lines,—

> Last morning I was gay, and early out ;
> Upon a dyke I leaned, glow'ring about.
> I saw my Meg come linken o'er the lea ;
> I saw my Meg, but Meggy saw na me.

And here let us mention with praise two small pictures in a style somewhat similar, — 'The Recruit,' and 'Herman and Dorothea,' by Mr. Poole. The former of these little pieces is very touching and beautiful. There is among the present exhibitioners no lack of this kind of talent ; and we could point out many pictures that are equally remarkable for grace and agreeable feeling. Mr. Stone's 'Annot Lyle' should not be passed over,—a pretty picture, very well painted ; the female head of great beauty and expression.

Now, if we want to praise performances showing a great deal of power and vigour, rather than grace and delicacy, there are Mr. Etty's 'Andromeda' and 'Venus.' In the former, the dim figure of advancing Perseus galloping on his airy charger is very fine and ghostly ; in the latter, the body of the Venus, and indeed the whole picture, is a perfect miracle of colour. Titian may have painted Italian flesh equally well : but he never, I think, could surpass the skill of Mr. Etty. The trunk of this voluptuous Venus is the most astonishing representation of beautiful English flesh and blood, painted in the grandest and broadest style. It is said that the Academy at Edinburgh has a room full of Etty's pictures : they could not do better in England than follow the example ; but perhaps the paintings had better be kept *for the Academy only*, —for the *profanum vulgus* are scarcely fitted to comprehend their peculiar beauties. A prettily drawn, graceful, nude figure, is 'Bathsheba,' by Mr. Fisher, of the street and city of Cork.

The other great man of Cork is Daniel Maclise by name ; and if in the riot of fancy he hath by playful Titmarsh been raised to the honour of knighthood, it is certain that here Titmarsh is a true prophet, and that the sovereign will so elevate him, one day or other, to sit with other cavaliers at the Academic round table. As for his pictures,—why, as for his pictures, madam, these are to be carefully reviewed in the next number of this Magazine ; for the present notice has noticed scarcely anybody, and yet stretched to an inordinate length. 'Macbeth' is not to be hurried off under six pages ; and, for this June number, Mr. Fraser vows that he has no such room to spare.

We have said how Mr. Turner's pictures blaze about the rooms : it is not a little curious to hear how artists and the public differ in their judgments concerning them ; the enthusiastic wonder of the first-named, the blank surprise and incredulity of the latter. 'The new moon : or, I've lost my boat ; you shan't have your hoop,' is the ingenious title of one,—a very beautiful picture, too, of a long shining sea-sand, lighted from the upper part of the canvas by the above-named luminary of night, and from the left-hand corner by a wonderful wary boy in a red jacket —the best painted figure that we ever knew painted by Joseph Mallord Turner, Esquire.

He and Mr. Ward vie with each other in mottoes for their pictures. Ward's epigraph to the S——'s nest is wondrous poetic.

277.   The S——'s Nest.   S. Ward, R.A.

> Say they that happiness lives with the great,
> On gorgeous trappings mixt with pomp and state ?
> More frequent found upon the simple plain,
> In poorest garb, with Julia, Jess, or Jane ;
> In sport or slumber, as it likes her best,
> Where'er she *lays* she finds it a S——'s nest.

Ay, and a S——'s eggs, too, as one would fancy, were great geniuses not above grammar. Mark the line, too,

> On gorgeous trappings *mixt* with pomp and state,

and construe the whole of this sensible passage.

Not less sublime is Mr. Ward's fellow academician.

230.   'Slavers throwing overboard the Dead and Dying : Typhon coming on.'   J. M. W. Turner, R.A.

Aloft all hands, strike the topmasts and belay !
Yon angry setting sun and fierce-edged clouds
Declare the Typhon's coming.
Before it sweeps your decks, throw overboard
The dead and dying,—ne'er heed their chains.
Hope, Hope, fallacious Hope
Where is thy market now ?

MS. Fallacies of Hope.

Fallacies of Hope, indeed : to a pretty mart has she brought her pigs ! How should Hope be hooked on to the slaver ? By the anchor, to be sure, which accounts for it. As for the picture, the R.A.'s rays are indeed terrific ; and the slaver throwing its cargo overboard is the most tremendous piece of colour that ever was seen ; it sets the corner of the room in which it hangs into a flame. Is the picture sublime or ridiculous ? Indeed I don't know which. Rocks of gamboge are marked down upon the canvas ; flakes of white laid on with a trowel ; bladders of vermilion madly spirted here and there. Yonder is the slaver rocking in the midst of a flashing foam of white-lead. The sun glares down upon a horrible sea of emerald and purple, into which chocolate-coloured slaves are plunged, and chains that will not sink ; and round these are floundering such a race of fishes as never was seen since the *sæculum Pyrrhæ ;* gasping dolphins redder than the reddest herrings ; horrid spreading polypi, like huge, slimy, poached eggs, in which hapless niggers plunge and disappear. Ye gods, what a 'middle passage !' How Mr. Fowell Buxton must shudder ! What would they say to this in Exeter Hall ? If Wilberforce's statue downstairs were to be confronted with this picture, the stony old gentleman would spring off his chair, and fly away in terror !

And here, as we are speaking of the slave-trade, let us say a word in welcome to a French artist, Monsieur Biard, and his admirable picture. Let the friends of the negro forthwith buy this canvas, and cause a plate to be taken from it. It is the best, most striking, most pathetic lecture against the trade that ever was delivered. The picture is as fine as Hogarth ; and the artist, who, as we have heard, right or wrong, has only of late years adopted the profession of painting, and was formerly in the French navy, has evidently drawn a great deal of his materials from life and personal observation. The scene is laid upon the African coast. King Tom or King Boy has come with troops of slaves down the Quorra, and sits in the midst of his chiefs and mistresses (one a fair creature, not much darker than a copper tea-kettle), bargaining with a French dealer. What a horrible callous brutality there is in the scoundrel's face, as he lolls over his greasy ledger, and makes his calculations. A number of his crew are about him ; their boats close at hand, in which they are stowing their cargo. See the poor wretches, men and women, collared together, drooping down. There is one poor thing, just parted from her child. On the ground in front lies a stalwart negro ; one connoisseur is handling his chest, to try his wind ; another has opened his mouth, and examines his teeth, to know his age and soundness. Yonder is a poor woman kneeling before one of the Frenchmen. Her shoulder is fizzing under the hot iron with which he brands her ; she is looking up, shuddering and wild, yet quite mild and patient ; it breaks your heart to look at her. I never saw anything so exquisitely pathetic as that face. God bless you, Monsieur Biard, for painting it ! It stirs the heart more than a hundred thousand tracts, reports, or sermons : it must convert every man who has seen it. You British government, who have given twenty millions towards the good end of freeing this hapless people, give yet a couple of thousand more to the French painter, and don't let his work go out of the country, now that it is here. Let it hang along with the Hogarths in the National Gallery ; it is as good as the best of them. Or, there is Mr. Thomas Babington Macaulay, who has a family interest in the matter, and does not know how to spend all the money he brought home from India ; let the right honourable gentleman look to it. Down with your dust, right honourable sir ; give Monsieur Biard a couple of thousand for his picture of the negroes, and it will be the best black act you ever did in your life ; and don't go for to be angry at the suggestion, or fancy we are taking liberties. What is said is said from one public man to another, in a Pickwickian sense, *de puissance en puissance*,—from Titmarsh, in his critical *cathedra*, to your father's eminent son, rich with the spoils of Ind, and wielding the bolts of war.

What a marvellous power is this of the painter's ! how each great man can excite us at his will ! what a weapon he has, if he knows how to wield it ! Look for a while at Mr. Etty's pictures, and away you rush, your 'eyes on fire,' drunken with the luscious colours that are poured out for you on the liberal canvas, and warm with the sight of the beautiful syrens that appear on it. You fly from this (and full time too,) and plunge into a green, shady landscape of Lee or Creswick, and follow a quiet stream babbling beneath whispering trees, and chequered with cool shade and golden sunshine ; or you set the world—nay, the Thames and the ocean—on fire with that incendiary Turner ; or you laugh with honest, kind-hearted Webster, and his troops of merry children ; or you fall a-weeping with Monsieur Biard for his poor blacks ; or you go and consult the priests of the place, Eastlake, Mulready, Boxall, Cope, and the like, and straightway your mind is carried off in an ecstasy,—happy, thrilling hymns sound in your ears melodious, — sweet thankfulness fills your bosom. How much instruction and happiness have we gained from these men, and how grateful should we be to them !

It is well that Mr. Titmarsh stopped here, and I shall take special care to examine any further remarks which he may think fit to send. Four-fifths of this would have been cancelled, had the printed sheets fallen sooner into our hands. The story about the Clarendon is an absurd fiction ; no dinner ever took place there. I never fell asleep in a plate of raspberry ice ; and though I certainly did recommend this person to do justice by the painters, making him a speech to that effect, my opinions were infinitely better expressed, and I would repeat them, were it not so late in the month.—O. Y.

A PICTORIAL RHAPSODY: CONCLUDED.[1]

AND FOLLOWED BY A REMARKABLE STATEMENT OF FACTS BY
MRS. BARBARA.

AND now, in pursuance of the promise recorded in the last number
of this Magazine, and for the performance of which the public
has ever since been in breathless expectation, it hath become
Titmarsh's duty to note down his opinions of the remaining
pictures in the Academy exhibition ; and to criticise such other
pieces as the other galleries may show.

In the first place, then, with regard to Mr. Maclise, it becomes
us to say our say ; and as *The Observer* newspaper, which,
though under the express patronage of the royal family, devotes
by far the noblest part of its eloquence to the consideration of
dramatic subjects, and to the discussion of the gains, losses, and
theatrical conduct of managers,— as, I say, *The Observer* newspaper, whenever Madame Vestris or Mr. Yates adopts any plan
that concurs with the notions of the paper in question, does not
fail to say that Madame Vestris or Mr. Yates have been induced
so to reform in consequence of *The Observer's* particular suggestion ;
in like manner, Titmarsh is fully convinced, that all the painters
in this town have their eyes incessantly fixed upon his criticisms,
and that all the wise ones regulate their opinions by his.

In the language of *The Observer*, then, Mr. Maclise has done
wisely to adopt our suggestions with regard to the moral treatment of his pictures, and has made a great advance in his art.
Of his four pictures, let us dismiss the scene from *Gil Blas* at
once.   Coming from a second-rate man, it would be well enough :
it is well drawn, grouped, lighted, shadowed, and the people all
grin very comically, as people do in pictures called comic ; but
the soul of fun is wanting, as I take it,— the merry, brisk, good-
humoured spirit which in Le Sage's text so charms the reader.

' Olivia and Malvolio ' is, on the contrary, one of the best and
most spiritual performances of the artist.   Nothing can be more

[1] [*Fraser's Magazine*, July, 1840.]

elegant than the tender, languid melancholy of Olivia, nor more
poetical than the general treatment of the picture.   The long
clipped alleys and quaint gardens, the peacocks trailing through
the walks, and vases basking in the sun, are finely painted and
conceived.   Examine the picture at a little distance, and the
ensemble of the composition and colour is extraordinarily pleasing.
The details, too, are, as usual, wonderful for their accuracy.
Here are flower-beds, and a tree above Olivia's head of which
every leaf is painted, and painted with such skill, as not in the
least to injure the general effect of the picture.   Mr. Maclise has
a daguerreotypic eye, and a feeling of form stronger, I do believe,
than has ever been possessed by any painter before him.

Look at the portrait of Mr. Dickens,—well arranged as a
picture, good in colour, and light, and shadow, and as a likeness
perfectly amazing ; a looking-glass could not render a better fac-
simile.   Here we have the real identical man Dickens : the artist
must have understood the inward Boz as well as the outward
before he made this admirable representation of him.   What
cheerful intelligence there is about the man's eyes and large forehead !   The mouth is too large and full, too eager and active,
perhaps ; the smile is very sweet and generous.   If Monsieur de
Balzac, that voluminous physiognomist, could examine this head,
he would, no doubt, interpret every tone and wrinkle in it : the
nose firm, and well placed ; the nostrils wide and full, as are the
nostrils of all men of genius (this is Monsieur Balzac's maxim).
The past and the future, says Jean Paul, are written in every
countenance.   I think we may promise ourselves a brilliant future
from this one.   There seems no flagging as yet in it, no sense of
fatigue, or consciousness of decaying power.   Long mayest thou,
O Boz ! reign over thy comic kingdom ; long may we pay tribute,
whether of threepence weekly or of a shilling monthly, it matters
not.   Mighty prince ! at thy imperial feet, Titmarsh, humblest
of thy servants, offers his vows of loyalty and his humble tribute
of praise.

And now (as soon as we are off our knees, and have done paying court to sovereign Boz) it behoves us to say a word or two
concerning the picture of ' Macbeth,' which occupies such a conspicuous place in the Academy gallery.   Well, then, this picture
of ' Macbeth ' has been, to our notion, a great deal too much
praised and abused : only Titmarsh understands the golden mean,
as is acknowledged by all who read his criticisms.   Here is a
very fine masterly picture, no doubt, full of beauties, and showing
extraordinary power ; but not a masterpiece, as I humbly take it,
—not a picture to move the beholder as much as many perform-

ances that do not display half the power that is here exhibited.
I don't pretend to lay down any absolute laws on the sublime
(the reader will remember how the ancient satirist hath accused
John Dennis of madness, for his vehement preaching of such rules).
No, no ; Michael Angelo T. is not quite so impertinent as that ;
but the public and the artist will not mind being told, without
any previous definitions, that this picture is not of the highest
order : the ' Malvolio ' is far more spiritual and suggestive, if we
may so speak ; it tells not only its own tale very charmingly, but
creates for the beholder a very pleasant, melancholy train of
thought, as every good picture does in its kind, from a six-inch
canvas by Hobbema or Ruysdael up to a thousand-foot wall of
Michael Angelo.   If you read over the banquet-scene in words, it
leaves an impression far more dreadful and lively.   On the stage,
it has always seemed to us to fail ; and though out of a trap-door
in the middle of it Mr. Cooper is seen to rise very solemnly,—his
face covered with white, and a dreadful gash of vermilion across
his neck ; though he nods and waggles his head about in a very
quiet, ghostlike manner ; yet, strange to say, neither this scene,
nor this great actor, has ever frightened us, as they both should,
as the former does when we read it at home.   The fact is, that it
is quite out of Mr. Cooper's power to look ghostly enough, or,
perhaps, to soar along with us to that sublime height to which
our imagination is continually carrying us.

> *Len.* May it please your highness, sit ?
> [*The Ghost of* BANQUO *rises, and sits in* MACBETH's *place.*]
> *Macb.* Here had we now our country's honour roof'd,
> Were the grac'd person of our Banquo present ;
> Who may I rather challenge for unkindness
> Than pity for mischance.
> *Rosse.* His absence, sir,
> Lays blame upon his promise.   Please it your highness
> To grace us with your royal company ?
> *Macb.* The table's full.
> *Len.* Here's a place reserv'd, sir.
> *Macb.* Where ?
> *Len.* Here, my lord.   What is't that moves your highness ?
> *Macb.* Which of you have done this ?
> *Lords.* What, my good lord ?
> *Macb.* Thou canst not say I did it.   Never shake
> Thy gory locks at me.
> *Rosse.* Gentlemen, arise ; his highness is not well.
> *Lady M.* Sit, worthy friends ; my lord is often thus,
> And hath been from his youth.   Pray you, keep seat ;

The fit is momentary ; upon a thought
He will again be well.   If much you note him,
You shall offend him, and extend his passion.
Feed, and regard him not.—Are you a man ?

Macb. Ay, and a bold one, that dare look on that
Which might appal the devil.

Lady M.   O proper stuff !
This is the very painting of your fear ;
This is the air-drawn dagger which you said
Led you to Duncan.   Oh, these flaws and starts
(Impostors to true fear) would well become
A woman's story, at a winter's fire,
Authoris'd by her grandam.   Shame itself !
Why do you make such faces ?   When all's done,
You look but on a stool.

Macb. Pr'ythee, see there !—Behold !—Look !—Lo !   How say you ?
Why, what care I ?   If thou canst nod, speak too.
If charnel-houses and our graves must send
Those that we bury back, our monuments
Shall be the maws of kites.

                                        [*Ghost disappears.*

Lady M.   What !   Quite unmann'd in folly ?
Macb. If I stand here, I saw him.
Lady M.   Fie, for shame !
Macb. Blood hath been shed ere now, i' the olden time,
Ere human statute purg'd the gentle weal ;
Ay, and since too, murders have been perform'd
Too terrible for the ear.   The times have been
That, when the brains were out, the man would die,
And there an end ; but now they rise again,
With twenty mortal murders on their crowns,
And push us from our stools.   This is more strange
Than such a murder is.

Lady M.   My worthy lord,
Your noble friends do lack you.

Macb.   I do forget.
Do not muse at me, my most worthy friends :
I have a strange infirmity, which is nothing
To those that know me.   Come, love and health to all ;
Then I'll sit down.   Give me some wine—fill full :
I drink to the general joy of the whole table,

                    Ghost rises.

And to our dear friend Banquo, whom we miss :
Would he were here !   To all, and him, we thirst,
And all to all.

Lords.   Our duties, and the pledge.

Macb. Avaunt! and quit my sight! Let the earth hide thee!
Thy bones are marrowless—thy blood is cold;
Thou hast no speculation in those eyes
Which thou dost glare with!

Lady M.   Think of this, good peers,
But as a thing of custom: 'tis no other;
Only it spoils the pleasure of the time.

Macb. What man dare, I dare:
Approach thou like the rugged Russian bear,
The arm'd rhinoceros, or the Hyrcan tiger,—
Take any shape but that, and my firm nerves
Shall never tremble: or be alive again,
And dare me to the desert with thy sword;
If trembling I inhibit thee, protest me
The baby of a girl. Hence, horrible shadow!

[*Ghost disappears.*

Unreal mockery, hence! Why, so; being gone,
I am a man again. Pray you, sit still.

Lady M. You have displac'd the mirth, broke the good meeting,
With most admir'd disorder.

A large part of this vast picture Mr. Maclise has painted very
finely. The lords are all there in gloomy state, fierce stalwart
men in steel; the variety of attitude and light in which the
different groups are placed, the wonderful knowledge and firm-
ness with which each individual figure and feature are placed
down upon the canvas will be understood and admired by the
public, but by the artist still more, who knows the difficulty of
these things, which seem so easy, which are so easy, no doubt, to
a man with Mr. Maclise's extraordinary gifts. How fine is yonder
group at the farthest table, lighted up by the reflected light from
the armour of one of them! The effect, as far as we know, is
entirely new; the figures drawn with exquisite minuteness and
clearness, not in the least interrupting the general harmony of the
picture. Look at the two women standing near Lady Macbeth's
throne, and those beautiful little hands of one of them placed over
the state-chair: the science, workmanship, feeling, in these figures
are alike wonderful. The face, bust, and attitude of Lady Macbeth are grandly designed; the figures to her right, with looks of
stern doubt and wonder, are nobly designed and arranged. The
main figure of Macbeth, I confess, does not please; nor the object
which has occasioned the frightful convulsive attitude in which he
stands. He sees not the ghost of Banquo, but a huge, indistinct,
gory shadow, which seems to shake its bloody locks, and frown

upon him.   Through this shade, intercepted only by its lurid
transparency, you see the figures of the guests ; they are looking
towards it, and *through* it.   The skill with which this point is
made is unquestionable ; there is something there, and nothing.
The spectators feel this as well as the painted actors of the scene :
there are times when, in looking at the picture, one loses sight of
the shade altogether, and begins to wonder with Rosse, Lenox,
and the rest.

The idea, then, so far as it goes, is as excellently worked out
as it is daringly conceived.   But is it a just one ?   I think not.
I should say it was a grim piece of comedy rather than tragedy.
One is puzzled by this piece of *diablerie*,—not deeply affected
and awe-stricken, as in the midst of such heroical characters and
circumstances one should be.

> Avaunt ! and quit my sight !   Let the earth hide thee !
> Thy bones are marrowless—thy blood is cold ;
> Thou hast no speculation in those eyes
> Which thou dost glare with.

Before the poet's eyes, at least, the figure of the ghost stood
complete—an actual visible body, with the life gone out of it ; an
image far more grand and dreadful than the painter's fantastical
shadow, because more simple.   The shadow is an awful object,—
granted ; but the most sublime, beautiful, fearful sight in all
nature is, surely, the face of a man ; wonderful in all its expressions of grief or joy, daring or endurance, thought, hope, love, or
pain.   How Shakespeare painted all these ; with what careful
thought and brooding were all his imaginary creatures made !

I believe we have mentioned the best figure-pieces in the
exhibition ; for, alas ! the 'Milton and his Daughters' of Sir
Augustus Calcott, although one of the biggest canvases in the
gallery, is by no means one of the best ; and one may regret that
this most *spirituel* of landscape-painters should have forsaken his
old style to follow figure-drawing.   Mr. Hollins has a picture of
'Benvenuto Cellini showing a Trinket to a Lady.'   A subject of
absorbing interest and passionate excitement, painted in a corresponding manner.   A prim lady sits smiling in a chair, by a
table, on which is a very neat, regular table-cloth, drawn at right
angles with the picture-frame ; parallel with the table is a chest
of drawers, secrétaire, cabinet, or *bahut.*   Near this stands a
waiting-maid, smiling archly ; and in front you behold young
Benvenuto, spick and span in his very best clothes and silk
stockings, looking—as Benvenuto never did in his life.   Of some
parts of this picture, the colour and workmanship is very pretty ;

but was there ever such a niminypiminy subject treated in such a niminypiminy way? We can remember this gentleman's picture of 'Margaret at the Spinning-wheel,' last year, and should be glad to see and laud others that were equally pretty. Mr. Lauder has, in the same room, a pleasing picture from Walter Scott, 'The Glee-Maiden'; and a large sketch, likewise from Scott, by a French artist (who has been celebrated in this Magazine as the author of the picture 'The Sinking of the Vengeur'), is fine in effect and composition.

If Mr. Herbert's picture of 'Travellers taking Refreshment at a Convent Gate' has not produced much sensation, it is because it is feeble in tone, not very striking in subject, and placed somewhat too high. There is a great deal of beauty and delicacy in all the figures; and though lost here, amidst the glare and bustle of the Academy, will be an excellent picture for the cabinet, where its quiet graces and merits will be better seen.

Mr. Webster's 'Punch,' before alluded to, deserves a great deal of praise. The landscape is beautiful, the group of little figures assembled to view the show are delightfully gay and pretty. Mr. Webster has the bump of philoprogenitiveness (as some ninny says of George Cruikshank in *The Westminster Review* [1]); and all mothers of large families, young ladies who hope to be so one day or the other, and honest papas, are observed to examine this picture with much smiling interest. It is full of sunshine and innocent playful good-humour : all Punch's audience are on the grin. John, the squire's footman, is looking on with a protecting air ; the old village folk are looking on, grinning with the very youngest ; boys are scampering over the common, in order to be in time for the show ; Punchman is tootooing on the pipes, and banging away on the drum ; potboy has consigned to the earth his precious cargo, and the head of every tankard of liquor is wasting its frothy fragrance in the air ; in like manner, the pieman permits his wares to get cold ; nursery-maids, school-boys, happy children in go-carts, are employed in a similar way : indeed, a delightful little rustic comedy.

In respect of portraits, the prettiest, as I fancy, after Wilkie's splendid picture of Mrs. Ferguson, is one by Mr. Grant, of a lady with a scarf of a greenish colour. The whole picture is of the same tone, and beautifully harmonious ; nor is the lady's face and air the least elegant and charming part of it. The Duke has been painted a vast number of times, such are the penalties of glory ; nor is it possible to conceive anything much worse than that portrait of him in which Col. Gurwood is represented by his

---

[1] [Thackeray here refers to the article written by himself.]

side, in a red velvet waistcoat, offering to his grace certain
despatches.   It is in the style of the famous picture in the Regent
Circus, representing Mr. Coleby the cigarist, an orange, a pine-
apple, a champagne-cork, a little dog, some decanters, and a
yellow bandanna,—all which personages appear to be so excessively important, that the puzzled eyes scarcely know upon which
to settle.   In like manner, in the Wellington-Gurwood testimonial,
the accessories are so numerous, and so brilliantly coloured, that
it is long before one can look up to the countenances of the
colonel and his grace ; which, it is to be presumed, are the main
objects of interest in the piece.   And this plan has been not
unartfully contrived, —for the heads are by no means painted up to
the point of brilliancy which is visible in boots, clocks, bell-pulls,
Turkey carpets, arm-chairs, and other properties here painted.

Now, if the artist of the above picture wishes to know how
properties may be painted with all due minuteness, and yet
conduce to the general effect of the picture, let him examine the
noble little portrait of Lord Cottenham, by Leslie,—the only contribution of this great man to the exhibition.   Here are a number
of accessories introduced, but with that forethought and sense of
propriety which, as I fancy, distinguish all the works of Mr.
Leslie.   They are not here for mere picturesque effect or ornamental huddle ; but are made to tell the story of the piece, and
indicate the character of the dignified personage who fills the
centre of it.   The black brocade drapery of the chancellor's gown
is accurately painted, and falls in that majestic grave way in
which a chancellor's robe *should* fall.   Are not the learned lord's
arms somewhat short and fin-like ?   This is a query which we
put humbly, having never had occasion to remark that part of
his person.

Mr. Briggs has his usual pleasant, well-painted portraits ; and
Mr. Patten a long full-length of Prince Albert that is not admired
by artists, it is said, but a good downright honest *bourgeois*
picture, as we fancy ; or, as a facetious friend remarked, good
plain *roast-and-boiled* painting.   As for the portrait opposite—
that of her majesty, it is a sheer libel upon that pretty gracious
countenance, an act of rebellion for which Sir David should be
put into York gaol.   Parts of the picture are, however, splendidly
painted.   And here, being upon the subject, let us say a word
in praise of those two delightful lithographic heads, after Ross,
which appear in the printshop windows.   Our gracious queen's
head is here most charming ; and that of the prince full of such
manly frankness and benevolence as must make all men cry, 'God
bless him.'   I would much sooner possess a copy of the Ross

miniature of the queen, than a cast from her majesty's bust by Sir Francis Chantrey, which has the place of honour in the sculpture vault.

All Macdonald's busts deserve honourable notice. This lucky sculptor has some beautiful subjects to model, and beautiful and graceful all his marbles are. As much may be said of Mr. M'Dowell's girl,—the only piece of imaginative sculpture in the Academy that has struck us as pleasing. Mr. Behnes, too, should receive many commendations ; an old man's head particularly, that is full of character and goodness ; and ' The Bust of a Lady,' which may be called ' A Lady with a Bust,'—a beautiful bust, indeed, of which the original and the artist have both good reason to be proud. Mr. Bell's virgin is not so pleasing to us in the full size as in the miniature copy of it.

For the matter of landscapes, we confess ourselves to be no very ardent admirers of these performances, clever and dexterous as most of them are. The works of Mr. Stanfield and Mr. Roberts cannot fail to be skilful ; and both of these famous artists show their wonderful power of drawing, as usual. But these skilful pictures have always appeared to us more pleasing in little on the sketching-board than when expanded upon the canvas. A couple of Martin's must be mentioned,—huge, queer, and tawdry to our eyes, but very much admired by the public, who is no bad connoisseur, after all ; and also a fine Castle of Chillon, or Chalon, rudely painted, but very poetical and impressive.

[Here Titmarsh exchanges his check at the door for a valuable gingham umbrella, with a yellow horn-head, representing Lord Brougham or Dr. Syntax, and is soon seen, with his hat very much on one side, swaggering down Pall Mall East, to the Water-Colour Gallery. He flings down eighteenpence in the easiest way, and goes upstairs.]

Accident, or, what is worse, ill-health, has deprived us of the two most skilful professors of the noble art of water-colour painting ; and, without the works of Messrs. Lewis and Cattermole, the gallery looks empty indeed. Those gentlemen are accustomed to supply the picture-lover with the *pièces de résistance* of the feast, with which, being decently satisfied, we can trifle with an old market-place by Prout, or six cows and four pigs by Hill, or a misty Downs by Copley Fielding, with some degree of pleasure. Discontented, then, with the absence of the substantials, it must be confessed that we have been examining the rest of the pictures in no very good-humour. And so, to tell you a secret, I do not care a fig for all the old town-halls in the world, though they be drawn ever so skilfully. How long are we to go on with Venice, Verona, Lago di Soandso, and Ponte di What-d'ye-call-'em? I am weary of gondolas, striped awnings, sailors with red night (or rather day) caps, cobalt distances, and posts in the water. I have seen so many white palaces standing before dark purple skies, so many black towers with gamboge atmospheres behind them, so many masses of rifle-green trees plunged into the deepest shadow, in the midst of sunshiny plains, for no other reason but because dark and light contrast together, that a slight expression of satiety may be permitted to me, and a longing for more simple nature. On a great staring theatre such pictures may do very well—you are obliged there to seek for these startling contrasts ; and by the aid of blue lights, red lights, transparencies, and plenty of drums and appropriate music, the scene thus presented to one captivates the eye, and calls down thunder from the galleries.

But in little quiet rooms, on sheets of paper of a yard square, such monstrous theatrical effects are sadly painful. You don't mistake patches of brickdust for maidens' blushes, or fancy that tinfoil is diamonds, or require to be spoken to with the utmost roar of the lungs. Why, in painting, are we to have monstrous, flaring, Drury Lane tricks and claptraps put in practice, when a quieter style is, as I fancy, so infinitely more charming ?

There is no use in mentioning the names of persons who are guilty of the above crimes ; but let us say who is *not* guilty, and that is D. Cox, upon whose quiet landscapes, moist grass, cool trees, the refreshed eye rests with the utmost pleasure, after it has been perplexed and dazzled elsewhere. May we add an humble wish that this excellent painter will remain out of doors, amidst such quiet scenes as he loves, and not busy himself with Gothicism, middleageism, and the painting of quaint interiors ? There are a dozen artists, of not a tithe of his genius, who can excel him at the architectural work. There is, for instance, Mr. Nash, who is improving yearly, and whose pictures are not only most dexterously sketched, but contain numberless little episodes, in the shape of groups of figures, that are full of grace and feeling. There is Mr. Haghe, too, of the lower house ; but of him anon.

To show how ill and how well a man may paint at the same time, the public may look at a couple of drawings by J. Nash,— one, the interior of a church ; the other, a plain landscape : both of which are executed with excessive, almost childish rudeness, and are yet excellent, as being close copies of the best of all drawing-masters, Nature : and Mr. Barrett, who has lately written a book for students, tells them very sagaciously *not* to copy the manner of any master, however much he may be in the mode.

Some there are, fashionable instructors in the art of water-colouring, of whom, indeed, a man had better not learn at any price ; nay, were they to offer a guinea per lesson, instead of modestly demanding the same, the reader should be counselled not to accept of their instructions.

See in what a different school Mr. Hunt works, and what marvellous effects he produces ! There is a small picture of an interior by him (to which the blue ticket, having the pretty word SOLD written on it, is not fixed) that, as a copy of nature, is a perfect miracle. No De Hooghe was ever better, more airy and sunshiny. And the most extraordinary part of this extraordinary picture is, that the artist has not produced his effect of excessive brilliancy by any violent contrasting darkness ; but the whole picture is light ; the sunshine is in every corner of the room : and this drawing remains unsold, while Dash, and Blank, and Asterisk, have got off all theirs. The large head of the black girl is painted with wonderful power ; in water-colours, we have scarcely seen anything so vigorous. The boys and virgins are, as usual, admir-able ; the lad with the bottle, he reading ballads in the barn, and the red, ragged, brickdust-coloured, brigand-looking fellow, especially good. In a corner is a most astonishing young gentle-man, with a pan of milk : he is stepping forward full into your face ; and has seen something in it which has caused him to spill his milk and look dreadfully frightened. Every man who is worth a fig, as he comes up to this picture bursts out a-laughing —he can't help himself ; you hear a dozen such laughs in the course of your visit. Why does this little drawing so seize hold of the beholder, and cause him to roar ? There is the secret : the painter has got the soul of comedy in him—the undefinable humorous genius. Happy is the man who possesses that drawing : a man must laugh if he were taking his last look at it before being hanged.

Mr. Taylor's flowing pencil has produced several pieces of delightful colour ; but we are led bitterly to deplore the use of that fatal white-lead pot, that is clogging and blackening the pictures of so many of the water-colour painters nowadays. His large picture contains a great deal of this white mud, and has lost, as we fancy, in consequence, much of that liquid, mellow tone for which his works are remarkable. The retreating figures in this picture are beautiful ; the horses are excellently painted, with as much dexterous brilliancy of colour as one sees in the oil pictures of Landseer. If the amateur wants to see how far transparent colour will go, what rich effect may be produced by it, how little necessary it is to plaster drawings with flakes of white, let him examine the background of the design, representing a page asleep on a chair, than which nothing can be more melodious in colour, or more skilfully and naturally painted.

In the beauty gallery which this exhibition usually furnished, there is Mr. Richter, who contributes his usual specimens ; the fair Miss Sharpe, with those languishing-eyed charmers whom the world admires so much ; and still more to our taste, a sweet pretty lady, by Mr. Stone, in a hideous dress, with upper-Benjamin buttons ; a couple of very graceful and delicate heads by Wright ; and one beautiful head, a portrait evidently, by Cristall, that is placed very modestly in a corner near the ground—where such a drawing should be placed, of course, being vigorous, honest, natural, and beautiful. This artist's other drawing—a mysterious subject, representing primæval Scotchmen, rocks, waterfalls, a cataract of bulls, and other strange things, looks like a picture painted in a dream. Near it hangs Mr. Mackenzie's view of St. Denis's Cathedral, that is painted with great carefulness, and is very true to nature. And having examined this, and Mr. Varley's fine gloomy sketches, you shall be no longer detained at this place, but walk on to see what more remains to be seen.

Of the New Water-Colour Society, I think it may be asserted that their gallery contains neither such good nor such bad drawings as may be seen in the senior exhibition ; unless, indeed, we except Mr. Haghe, a gentleman who in architectural subjects has a marvellous skill, and whose work deserves to be studied by all persons who follow the trade of water-colouring. This gentleman appears to have a profound knowledge (or an extraordinary instinct) of his profession as an architectural draughtsman. There are no tricks, no clumsy plastering of white, no painful niggling, nor swaggering affectation of boldness. He seems to understand every single tone and line which he lays down ; and his picture, in my humble judgment, contains some of the very best qualities of which this branch of painting is capable. You cannot produce by any combination of water-colours such effects as may be had from oil, such richness and depth of tone, such pleasing variety of texture, as gums and varnishes will give ; but, on the other hand, there are many beauties peculiar to the art, which the oil-painter cannot arrive at,—such as air, brightness, coolness, and flatness of surface ; points which painters understand and can speak of a great deal better than amateur writers and readers. Why will the practitioners, then, be so ambitious ? Why strive after effects that are only to be got imperfectly at best, and at the expense of qualities far more valuable and pleasing ? There are some aspiring individuals who will strive to play a whole band of music off a guitar, or to perform the broadsword exercise with a rapier,—monstrous attempts, that the moral critic must lift up his voice to reprehend. Valuable instruments are guitars and smallswords in themselves, the one for making pleasant small music, the other for drilling small holes in the human person ; but let the professor of each art do his agreeable duty in his own line, nor strive with his unequal weapons to compete with persons who have greater advantages. Indeed, I have seldom seen the works of a skilful water-colour painter of figures, without regretting that he had not taken to oil, which would allow him to put forth all the vigour of which he was capable. For works, however, like that of Mr. Haghe, which are not finished pictures, but admirable finished sketches, water is best ; and we wish that his brethren followed his manner of using it. Take warning by these remarks, O Mr. Absolon ! Your interiors have been regarded by Titmarsh with much pleasure, and deserve at his hands a great deal of commendation. Mr. Absolon, we take it, has been brought up in a French school—there are many traces of foreign manner in him ; his figures, for instance, are better costumed than those of our common English artists. Look at the little sketch which goes by the laconic title of ' Jump.' Let Mrs. Seyffarth come and look at it before she paints Sir Roger de Coverley's figures again, and she will see what an air of life and authenticity the designer has thrown into his work. Several larger pieces by Mr. Absolon, in which are a face—is it the artist's own, by any chance ?—(We fancy that we have a knack at guessing a portrait of an artist by himself, having designed about five thousand such in our own experience, — ' Portrait of a Painter,' ' A Gentleman in a Vandyke Dress,' ' A Brigand,' ' A Turkish Costume,' and so on : they are somehow always rejected by those cursed Academicians,)—but to return to Absolon, whom we have left hanging up all this time on the branch of a sentence, he has taken hugely to the body-colour system within the last twelve months, and small good has it done him. The accessories of his pictures are painted with much vigour and feeling of colour, are a great deal stronger than heretofore—a great deal too strong for the figures themselves ; and the figures being painted chiefly in transparent colour, will not bear the atmosphere of distemper by which they are surrounded. The picture of ' The Batchelor ' is excellent in point of effect and justness of colour.

Mr. Corbould is a gentleman who must be mentioned with a great deal of praise. His large drawing of the ' Canterbury Pilgrims at the Tabard ' is very gay and sparkling ; and the artist

shows that he possesses a genuine antiquarian or Walter-Scottish
spirit.   It is a pity that his people are all so uncommon handsome.   It is a pity that his ladies wear such uncommonly low
dresses—they did not wear such (according to the best authorities)
in Chaucer's time ; and even if they did, Mr. Corbould had much
better give them a little more cloth, which costs nothing, and
would spare much painful blushing to modest men like—never
mind whom.   But this is a moral truth : nothing is so easy to
see in a painter as a certain inclination towards naughtiness, which
we press-Josephs are bound to cry fie at.   Cover them up, Mr.
Corbould—muslin is the word ; but of this no more.   Where the
painter departs from his line of beauty, his faces have considerable
humour and character.   The whole of the pilgrim group, as he
has depicted it, is exceedingly picturesque.   It might be painted
with a little more strength, and a good deal less finical trifling
with the pencil ; but of these manual errors the painter will no
doubt get the better as his practice and experience increase.

Here is a large and interesting picture by Mr. Warren, of the
Pasha of Egypt in the middle of the Nubian desert, surrounded
by pipe-bearers and camels, and taking his cup of coffee.   There
is much character both in the figures and scenery.   A slight
sketch by the same artist, ' The King in Thule,' is very pretty, and
would make a very good picture.

Mr. Bright is an artist of whom we do not before remember to
have heard.   His pictures are chiefly effects of sunset and moonlight ; of too *criarde* a colour as regards sun and moon, but pretty
and skilful in other points, and of a style that strikes us as almost
new.   The manner of a French artist, M. Collignon, somewhat
resembles that of Mr. Bright.   The cool parts of his pictures are
excellent ; but he has dangerous dealings with gamboge and
orange, pigments with the use of which a painter is bound to be
uncommonly cautious.   Look at Mr. Turner, who has taken to
them until they have driven him quite wild.   If there be any
Emperor of the Painters, he should issue 'a special edict' against
the gamboge-dealers :—'tis a deleterious drug.   ' Hasten, hasten,'
Mr. Bright ; ' obey with trembling,' and have a care of gamboge
henceforth.

For the rest of the artists at this place, it may be said that Mr.
Hicks has not been quite so active this year as formerly ; Mr.
Boys has some delightful drawings in his style of art ; and for the
curious there is, moreover, a second-hand Cattermole, a sham
Prout, a pseudo Bently, and a small double of Cox, whose works
are to be seen in various parts of the room.   Miss Corbould has a
pretty picture.   Mr. Duncan's drawings exhibit considerable skill

and fidelity to nature. And here we must close our list of the juniors, whose exhibition is very well worth the shilling which all must pay who would enter their pretty gallery.

We have been through a number of picture galleries, and cannot do better than go and visit a gentleman who has a gallery of his own, containing only one picture. We mean Mr. Danby, with his 'Deluge,' now visible in Piccadilly. Every person in London will no doubt go and see this ; artists, because the treatment and effect of the picture are extraordinarily skilful and broad ; and the rest of the world, who cannot fail of being deeply moved by the awful tragedy which is here laid before them. The work is full of the strongest dramatic interest ; a vast performance, grandly treated, and telling in a wonderful way its solemn awful tale. Mr. Danby has given a curious description of it to our hand ; and from this the reader will be able to understand what is the design and treatment of the piece.

The general idea of the picture is founded on a supposition that a comet, which appears in the centre at the top, is the immediate cause of the deluge, and that it illuminates the scene with a bright phosphoric light, which overpowers the setting sun, already obscured by falling rain. On the left of the spectator, in the distance, are a few domes of a city still appearing above the waters, from which the inhabitants have flown to the highest rocks within their reach in the vicinity, but where they are soon overtaken by the rising flood. On the right the mountains are deluged with water, which falls from the heavens condensed into solid masses in the form of tremendous water-spouts ; and, as they descend over precipices, they carry with them immense fragments of the mountains.

The situation of the spectator is supposed to be on a height, beneath a higher range of mountains, a part of which is seen on the right of the picture, declining in shelving precipices towards the plain, to which in perspective it runs. Immediately before him, in the nearest part of the scene, is a small ravine, which separates him from a towering mass of splinter-broken rocks (which form a rude and barren middle distance), beyond whose summits the country declines less wildly to the plain, where is situated, near the horizon on the left, a grand antediluvian city.

Composition and Effect of the Picture.

Through turgid clouds and whirling columns of falling rain, the struggling sun, as though in tears, throws his last fond look upon the dying world ; setting never to rise more to the teeming inhabitants of the city. Wrapped in his crimson mantle, and shrouded in the black and mystic curtains of the mourning skies, he sinks behind the once-proud dome, whose golden sculptured front so long had glittered in his noontide blaze.

The blooming plain around, rich without cultivation, where once sweet-scented groves of blossoms and fruit luxuriantly twined, now lies deep sunk beneath the raging and swelling ocean,—the great deep! 'whose fountains are broken up.' Wildly the loosened waters rush upon the plain : they spread—they rise—they mount above the city walls, bursting the grand yet little barriers of man ; while fiercely now they rush, in eddying currents, through the depeopled streets. This, the moment, the picture represents.

The Almighty's vengeance is at hand ; who can escape his wrath ? Man is against man ; friendship is no more ; the loveliness of woman, the innocence of childhood, or the low moan of suffering age, no longer gain the sigh of pity or of love ;—fear or rage alone possess the human breast.

The towering rock, which forms the centre middle distance of the picture, is the nearest refuge to the maddening crowd. Blindly, and with giant strength, they scale its splintered sides ; in masses, like the gaining waters, wildly they urge their course upon the side the most accessible. Exhausted at the moment they reach the object of their hope, they sink, while others mount over piles of fellow-men, yet mount they to their death. The top is full, even more than full, while yet they climb and grapple with those above in deadly struggle for a moment's resting-place. Alas ! they see not, that on the narrow surface of the cliff above is piled a horrid rocking mass of human forms, of life and death, where the smothering groan, deep buried, is unheard, and the wild cry of those above is more unheeded.

The ponderous giant, amid the crowd above, presents his matchless shoulders against the increasing mass, his foot and arms against the rock. In vain are women, young and delicate of frame, with their more tender infants, crushed to silence against his broad unyielding muscles. The solid rock gives way, and all the clinging, trembling mass of human life upon it falls precipitately to the whirling flood below.

The waters gain,—resistlessly they rush, bursting each rocky barrier, that for a moment may resist their course, rolling huge fragments of the mountain's side, with forest trees, that crash and snap as twigs in the mighty torrent's force, sinking or rising to the boiling surface of the flood ; the broken trees are swept along, their tops and roots alternately uppermost,—still offering to the drowning man a false and fatal aid.

In the middle of the composition is a group of lately-fallen rocks, which the painter has attempted to express by the trees they have entangled and broken in their fall, occasioned by earthquake, which he supposes to have accompanied the Deluge. These rocks have fallen in such a position as to serve as a species of flight of steps to the crowd who have gained the height, and are now occupied by a few feeble stragglers, that still urge on their weary and useless flight. Here a few incidents of the heart-rending distress of mothers for their darling off-spring, or children for their parents, may appear, as these were with the first, and must remain the last of ties upon the human heart.

In the fore part of the picture, on the left, is a portion of a large tree, which still remains rooted in the earth, but trembles to its fall in the rush of waters : it is supposed to have been a momentary refuge to hundreds of beings, before the waters had gained their present height ; but, from the weight above, the stem has broken midway, and with its struggling, writhing charge, the upper half is swept along the roaring flood.

In the middle of the fore part of the picture, men, women, and children, with a strangling lion, are entangled in the broken trees that are precipitated down the current ; and on the right, floating on a hastily constructed raft, are the lifeless bodies of a giant and a female (crushed by a fallen tree), over whose pallid forms weeps an Angel of Light, who, though not involved in the ruin, may, with a heart of heavenly mould, drop a tear of more than diamond purity and bright-ness over that once divine and glorious human race, once bright as he, and who were still so beautiful, though fallen, that the ' Sons of God saw that the Daughters of Men were fair, and chose from amongst them such as they loved.'

This episode of the angel is the sole part of the picture with which we should be disposed to quarrel ; but the rest, which has been excellently described in the queer, wild words of the artist, is really as grand and magnificent a conception as ever we saw. Why Poussin's famous picture of an inundation has been called ' The Deluge,' I never could understand : it is only a very small and partial deluge. The artist has genius enough, if any artist ever had, to have executed a work far more vast and tremendous ; nor does his picture at the Louvre, nor Turner's deluge, nor Martin's, nor any that we have ever seen, at all stand a competition with this extraordinary performance of Mr. Danby. He has painted *the* picture of ' The Deluge ' ; we have before our eyes still the ark in the midst of the ruin floating calm and lonely, the great black cataracts of water pouring down, the mad rush of the miserable people clambering up the rocks ;—nothing can be finer than the way in which the artist has painted the picture in all its innumerable details, and we hope to hear that his room will be hourly crowded, and his great labour and genius rewarded in some degree.

Let us take some rest after beholding this picture, and what

place is cooler and more quiet thán the Suffolk Street Gallery?
If not remarkable for any pictures of extraordinary merit, it is at
least to be praised as a place singularly favourable to meditation.
It is a sweet, calm solitude, lighted from the top with convenient
blinds to keep out the sun. If you have an assignation, bid your
mistress to come hither, there is only a dumb secretary in the
room; and sitting, like the man in *The Arabian Nights*, perpetually before a great book, in which he pores. This would be a
grand place to hatch a conspiracy, to avoid a dun, to write an epic
poem. Something ails the place! What is it?—what keeps the
people away, and gives the money-taker in his box a gloomy, lonely
sinecure? Alas, and alas! not even Mr. Haydon's 'Samson
Agonistes' is strong enough to pull the people in.

And yet this picture is worth going to see. You may here
take occasion to remark the truth of Mr. Yorke's astute remark
about another celebrated artist, and see how bad a painter is this
great *writer* of historical paintings, Mr. Haydon. There is an
account in some of the late papers—from America, of course—of
a remarkably fat boy, three years old, five feet six high, with a
fine bass voice, and a handsome beard and whiskers. Much such
a hero is this Samson,—a great red chubby-cheeked monster,
looking at you with the most earnest, mild, dull eyes in the world,
and twisting about a brace of ropes, as he comes sprawling forwards.
Sprawling backwards is a Delilah—such a Delilah, with such an arm,
with such a dress, on such a sofa, with such a set of ruffians
behind her! The picture is perfectly amazing? Is this the
author of the 'Judgment of Solomon?'—the restorer or setter up
of the great style of painting in this country? The drawing of the
figures is not only faulty, but bad and careless as can be. It
never was or could be in nature; and, such as it is, the drawing is
executed in a mannner so loose and slovenly, that one wonders to
behold it. Is this the way in which a *chef d'école* condescends to
send forth a picture to the public? Would he have his scholars
finish no more and draw no better? Look at a picture of 'Milton
and his Daughters,' the same subject which Sir A. Callcott has
treated in the Academy, which painters will insist upon treating,
so profoundly interesting does it seem to be. Mr. Haydon's
'Milton' is playing on the organ, and turning his blind eyes towards the public with an expression that is absolutely laughable.
A buxom wench in huge gigot sleeves stands behind the chair,
another is at a table writing. The draperies of the ladies are
mere smears of colour; in the foreground lies a black cat or dog,
a smudge of lamp-black, in which the painter has not condescended
to draw a figure. The chair of the poetical organ-player is a

similar lump of red and brown ; nor is the conception of the picture, to our thinking, one whit better than the execution. If this be the true style of art, there is another great work of the kind at the Saracen's Head, Snow Hill, which had better be purchased for the National Gallery.

Mr. Hurlstone has, as usual, chosen this retired spot to exhibit a very great number of pictures. There is much good in almost all of these. The children especially are painted with great truth and sweetness of expression, but we never shall be able to reconcile ourselves to the extraordinary dirtiness of the colour. Here are ladies' dresses which look as if they had served for May-day, and arms and shoulders such as might have belonged to Cinderella. Once in a way the artist shows he can paint a clean face, such an one is that of a child in the little room ; it is charming, if the artist did but know it, how much more charming for being clean! A very good picture of a subject somewhat similar to those which Mr. Hurlstone loves to paint, is Mr. Buckner's 'Peasants of Sora in the Regno di Napoli.' The artist has seen the works of Leopold Robert, and profited evidently by the study of them.

Not far from this is a performance embellished with a brace of poetical quotations, by Mr. Stewart :

> Lo ! on the strand the Indian mother kneels,
> And to the fervid skies her prayers prefers,
> That her gone cherub may inhabit there.
> —*Anon.*

> Lo ! yon Brahmin mother kneeling
>   By the sacred river's verge ;
> Mark her deep impassioned feeling
>   Wailing forth her infant's dirge !
>
> She has watched it, when the dawning
>   Found her by the Ganges' side ;
> Until now, advancing morning,
>   Rolls along its swelling tide.
>
> Onward rolls, but quick returning,
>   Sweeps her cherished charge away ;
> And that scene her bosom burning,
>   She hath knelt her down to pray.

And the picture, it must honestly be confessed, is worthy of the poetry. Some portraits by the same artist are executed in a much more satisfactory manner.

Concerning other artists whose works appear in this gallery, we should speak favourably of Mr. O'Neill, who has two pretty pictures, of a couple of animal pieces, 'A Pony and Cows,' by Mr. Sosi, and of a pretty picture by Mr. Elmore, a vast deal better than his great Becket performance before alluded to. Mr. Tomkins has some skilful street-scenes ; and Mr. Holland, a large, raw, clever picture, of Milan Cathedral. And so farewell to this quiet spot, and let us take a peep at the British Gallery, where a whole room is devoted to the exhibition of Mr. Hilton, the late Academician.

A man's sketches and his pictures should never be exhibited together ; the sketches invariably kill the pictures ; are far more vigorous, masterly, and effective. Some of those hanging here, chiefly subjects from Spencer, are excellent, indeed ; and fine in drawing, colour, and composition. The decision and spirit of the sketch disappear continually in the finished piece, as any one may see in examining the design for 'Comus,' and the large picture afterwards, the 'Two Amphitrites,' and many others. Were the sketches, however, removed, the beholder would be glad to admit the great feeling and grace of the pictures, and the kindly poetical spirit which distinguishes the works of the master. Besides the Hiltons, the picture-lover has here an opportunity of seeing a fine Virgin by Julio Romano, and a most noble one by Sebastian del Piombo, than which I never saw anything more majestically beautiful. The simpering beauties of some of the Virgins of the Raphael school, many painters are successful in imitating. See, O ye painters ! how in Michael Angelo strength and beauty are here combined, wonderful chastity and grace, humility, and a grandeur almost divine. The critic must have a care as he talks of these pictures, however, for his words straightway begin to grow turgid and pompous ; and, lo ! at the end of his lines, the picture is not a whit better described than before.

And now having devoted space enough to the discussion of the merits of these different galleries and painters, I am come to the important part of this paper—viz. to my Essay on the State of the Fine Arts in this Kingdom, my Proposals for the General Improvement of Public Taste, and my Plan for the Education of Young Artists.

In the first place, I propose that government should endow a college for painters, where they may receive the benefits of a good literary education, without which artists will never prosper. I propose that lectures should be read, examinations held, and prizes and exhibitions given to students ; that professorships should be instituted, and—and a president or lord rector appointed, with a baronetcy, a house, and a couple of thousand a year.   This place, of course, will be offered to Michael Angelo Tit——

. . . . .

Mr. Titmarsh's paper came to us exactly as the reader here sees it.   His contribution had been paid for in advance, and we regret exceedingly that the public should be deprived of what seemed to be the most valuable part of it.   He has never been heard of since the first day of June.   He was seen on that day pacing Waterloo Bridge for two hours ; but whether he plunged into the river, or took advantage of the steam-boat and went down it only, we cannot state.

Why this article was incomplete, the following document will, perhaps, show.   It is the work of the waiter at Morland's Hotel, where the eccentric and unhappy gentleman resided.

STATEMENT BY MRS. BARBARA.

' On the evening of the 30th of May, Anay Domino 1840, Mr. Mike Titmash came into our house in a wonderful state of delarium, drest in a new coat, a new bloo satting hankysher, a new wite at, and polisht jipannd boots, all of which he'd bot sins he went out after dinner ; nor did he bring any of his old cloves back with him, though he'd often said, " Barbara," says he to me, " when Mr. Frasier pays me my money, and I git new ones, you shall have these as your requisites : " that was his very words, thof I must confess I don't understand the same.

' He'd had dinner and coughy before he went ; and we all cumjectured that he'd been somewhere particklar, for I heer'd him barging with a cabman from Hollywell Street, of which he said the fair was only hatepence ; but being ableeged to pay a shilling, he cust and swoar horrybill.

' He came in, ordered some supper, laft and joakt with the gents in the parlor, and showed them a deal of money, which some of the gentlemen was so good as to purpose to borry of him.

' They talked about literaryture and the fine harts (which is both much used by our gentlemen) ; and Mr. Mike was very merry.   Specially he sung them a song, which he ancored hisself for twenty minutes ; and ordered a bole of our punch, which is chocked against his skor to this very day.

' About twelve o'clock he went to bed, very comfortable and quiet, only he cooldnt stand on his legs very well, and cooldnt speak much, excep, " Frasier for ever ! "   " All of a York ! " [1] and

<hr>

[1] [The pseudonym of Dr. Maginn, the editor of *Fraser's Magazine*, was Oliver Yorke.]

some such nonsense, which neither me nor George nor Mrs. Stoaks could understand.

' " What's the matter ? " says Mrs. Stokes, " Barbara," says she to me, " has he taken anythin ? " says she.

' " Law bless you, mum ! " says I (I always says, Law bless you), " as I am a Christen woman, and hope to be married, he's had nothin out of common."

' " What had he for dinner ? " says she, as if she didn't know.

' " There was biled salmon," says I, " and a half-crown lobster in soss (bless us if he left so much as a clor or tisspunful !), boil pork and peace puddn, and a secknd course of beef steak and onions, cole plumpuddn, maccarony, and afterwards cheese and sallat."

' " I don't mean that," says she. " What was his liquors, or bavyrage ? "

' " Two Guineas's stouts ; old madeira, one pint ; port, half a ditto ; four tumlers of niggus ; and three cole brandy and water, and sigars."

' " He is a good fellow," says Mrs. Stokes, " and spends his money freely, that I declare."

' " I wish he'd ony *pay* it," says I to Mrs. Stokes, says I. " He's lived in our house any time these fourteen years and never ——"

' " Hush your imperence ! " says Mrs. Stokes ; " he's a gentleman, and pays when he pleases. He's not one of your common sort. Did he have any tea ? "

' " No," says I, " not a drop ; ony coughy and muffns. I told you so—three on 'em ; and growled preciously, too, because there was no more. But I wasn't a-going to fetch him any more, he whose money we'd never ——"

' " Barbara," says Mrs. Stokes, " leave the room—do. You're always a-suspecting every gentleman. Well, what did he have at supper ? "

' " You know," says I, " pickled salmon—that chap's a reglar devil at salmon (those were my very words)—cold pork, and cold peace puddn agin ; toasted chease this time ; and such a lot of hale and rum-punch as I never saw—nine glasses of heach, I do believe, as I am an honest woman."

' " Barbara," says mistress, " that's not the question. *Did he mix his liquors*, Barbara ? That's the pint."

' " No," says I, " Mrs. Stokes ; that indeed he didn't." And so we agread that he couldnt posbly be affected by drink, and that something wunderfie must have hapned to him, to send him to bad so quear like.

' Nex morning I took him his tea in bed (on the 4th flore

back, No. 104 was his number); and says he to me, "Barbara," says he, "you find me in sperrits."

'"Find you in sperrits! I believe we do," says I; "we've found you in 'em these fifteen year. I wish you'd find us in *money*," says I; and laft, too, for I thought it was a good un.

'"Pooh!" says he, "my dear, that's not what I mean. You find me in spirits bycause my exlent publisher, Mr. Frasier, of Regent Street, paid me handsum for a remarkable harticle I wrote in his Magazine. He gives twice as much as the other publishers," says he; "though, if he didn't, I'd write for him just the same—rayther more, I'm so fond of him."

'"How much has he gave you?" says I; "because I hope you'll pay us."

'"Oh," says he, after a bit, "a lot of money. Here, you, you darling," says he (he did; upon my word, he did), "go and git me change for a five-pound note."

'And when he got up and had his brekfast, and been out, he changed another five-pound note; and after lunch, another five-pound note; and when he came in to dine, another five-pound note, to pay the cabman. Well, thought we, he's made of money, and so he seemed; but you shall hear soon how it was that he had all them notes to change.

'After dinner he was a sitten over his punch, when some of our gents came in; and he began to talk and brag to them about his harticle, and what he had for it; and that he was the best cricket[1] in Europe; and how Mr. Murray had begged to be introjuiced to him, and was so pleased with him, and he with Murray; and how he'd been asked to write in *The Quartly Review*, and in bless us knows what; and how, in fact, he was going to carry all London by storm.

'"Have you seen what *The Morning Poast* says of you?" says Frank Flint, one of them hartist chaps as comes to our house.

'"No," says he, "I aint. Barbara, bring some more punch, do you hear? No, I aint; but that's a fashnable paper," says he, "and always takes notice of a fashnable chap like me. What *does* it say?" says he.

'Mr. Flint opened his mouth and grinned very wide; and taking *The Morning Poast* out of his pocket (he was a great friend of Mr. Titmarsh's, and, like a good-naterd friend as he was, had always a kind thing to say or do)—Frank pulls out a *Morning Poast*, I say (which had cost Frank Phippens[2]): "Here

---

[1] Critic, Mrs. Barbara means, an absurd monomania of Mr. Titmarsh.

[2] Fivepence, Mrs. Barbara means.

it is," says he ; " read for yourself ; it will make you quite happy."
And so he began to grin to all the gents like winkin.

' When he red it, Titmarsh's jor dropt all of a sudn : he turned
pupple, and bloo, and violate ; and then, with a mighty effut, he
swigg off his rum and water, and staggered out of the room.

' He looked so ill when he went up stairs to bed, that Mrs.
Stokes insisted upon making him some grool for him to have
warm in bed ; but, Lor bless you ! he threw it in my face when
I went up, and rord and swor so dredfle, that I rann down stairs
quite frightened.

' Nex morning I knockt at his dor at nine—no anser.

' At ten, tried agin—never a word.

' At eleven, twelve, one, two, up we went, with a fresh cup of
hot tea every time.   His dor was lockt, and not one sillibaly
could we get.

' At for we began to think he'd suasided hisself ; and having
called in the policemen, bust open the dor.

' And then we beheld a pretty spactycle !   Fancy him in his
gor, his throat cut from hear to hear, his white night-gownd all
over blood, his beautiful face all pale with hagny !—well, no such
thing.   Fancy him hanging from the bedpost by one of his pore
dear garters !—well, no such thing.   Agin, fancy him flung out of
the window, and dasht into ten billium peaces on the minionet-
potts in the fust floar ; or else a naked, melumcolly corpse, laying
on the hairy spikes !—not in the least.   He wasn't dead, nor he
wasn't the least unwell, nor he wasn't asleep neither—he only
wasn't there ; and from that day we have heard nothen about
him.   He left on his table the following note as follows :—

' *1st June*, 1840.   *Midnight.*

' MRS. STOKES, — I am attached to you by the most disinterested
friendship.   I have patronised your house for fourteen years, and it was
my intention to have paid you a part of your bill, but *The Morning Post*
newspaper has destroyed that blessed hope for ever.

' Before you receive this I shall be—*ask not where ;* my mind shudders
to think where !   You will carry the papers directed to Regent Street
to that address, and perhaps you will receive in return a handsome sum
of money ; but if the bud of my youth is blighted, the promise of a long
and happy career suddenly and cruelly cut short, an affectionate family
deprived of its support and ornament, say that *The Morning Post* has
done this by its savage criticism upon me the last this day.

' FAREWELL.'

' This is hall he said.   From that day to this we have never
seen the poor fellow—we have never heerd of him—we have never

known anythink about him. Being halarmed, Mrs. Stoks had-vertized him in the papers ; but not wishing to vex his family, we called him by another name, and put hour address diffrent too. Hall was of no use ; and I can't tell you what a pang I felt in my busum when, on going to get change for the five-pound notes he'd given me at the public-house in Hoxford Street, the lan'lord laft when he saw them ; and said, says he, " Do you know, Mrs. Barbara, that a queer gent came in here with five sovrings one day, has a glass of hale, and haskes me to change his sovrings for a note ? which I did. Then in about two hours he came back with five more sovrings, gets another note and another glass of hale, and so goes on four times in one blessed day ! It's my beleaf that he had only five pound, and wanted you to suppose that he was worth twenty, for you've got all his notes, I see ! "

' And so the poor fellow had no money with him after all ! I do pity him, I do, from my hart ; and I do hate that wicked *Morning Post* for so treating such a kind, sweet, good-nater'd gentleman !   (*Signed*)   BARBARA.

' *Morland's Hotel,* 15 *Jewin,* 1840.'

This is conclusive. Our departed friend had many faults, but he is gone, and we will not discuss them now. It appears that, on the 1st of June, *The Morning Post* published a criticism upon him, accusing him of ignorance, bad taste, and gross partiality.[1] His gentle and susceptible spirit could not brook the rebuke ; he was not angry ; he did not retort ; but *his heart broke !*

Peace to his ashes ! A couple of volumes of his works, we see by our advertisements, are about immediately to appear.[2]

---

[1] [' Among other papers in the Magazine is what is called *A Pictorial Rhapsody* upon the Royal Academy, in which great personal favouritism and general bad taste in the criticism is boldly and unscrupulously indulged. The absurdities of this notice are plenty, and *parmi les autres* the writer defends Mulready and the postage cover.'—*The Morning Post,* June 1, 1840.]

[2] [*The Paris Sketch-Book.*]

ON MEN AND PICTURES.[1]

À PROPOS OF A WALK IN THE LOUVRE.

Paris, June 1841.

In the days of my youth I knew a young fellow that I shall here call Tidbody, and who, born in a provincial town of respectable parents, had been considered by the drawing-master of the place, and, indeed, by the principal tea-parties there, as a great genius in the painting line, and one that was sure to make his fortune.

When he had made portraits of his grandmother, of the house-dog, of the door-knocker, of the church and parson of the place, and had copied, *tant bien que mal*, the most of the prints that were to be found in the various houses of the village, Harry Tidbody was voted to be very nearly perfect ; and his honest parents laid out their little savings in sending the lad to Rome and Paris.

I saw him in the latter town in the year '32, before an immense easel, perched upon a high stool, and copying with perfect complacency a Correggio in the gallery, which he thought he had imitated to a nicety. No misgivings ever entered into the man's mind that he was making an ass of himself ; he never once paused to consider that his copy was as much like the Correggio as my nose is like the Apollo's. But he rose early of mornings, and scrubbed away all day with his macgilps and varnishes ; he worked away through cold and through sunshine ; when other men were warming their fingers at the stoves, or wisely lounging on the Boulevard, he worked away, and thought he was cultivating art in the purest fashion, and smiled with easy scorn upon those who took the world more easily than he. Tidbody drunk water with his meals—if meals those miserable scraps of bread and cheese, or bread and sausage, could be called, which he lined his lean stomach with ; and voted those persons godless gluttons who recreated themselves with brandy and beef. He rose up at daybreak, and worked away with bladder and brush ; he passed all night at life-academies, designing life-guardsmen with chalk and stump ; he never was

[1] [*Fraser's Magazine*, July, 1841.]

known to take any other recreation ; and in ten years he had spent as much time over his drawing as another man spends in thirty. At the end of his second year of academical studies, Harry Tidbody could draw exactly as well as he could eight years after. He had visited Florence, and Rome, and Venice, in the interval ; but there he was as he had begun, without one single farther idea, and not an inch nearer the goal at which he aimed.

One day, at the Life-Academy in St. Martin's Lane, I saw before me the back of a shock head of hair and a pair of ragged elbows, belonging to a man in a certain pompous attitude which I thought I recognised ; and when the model retired behind his curtain to take his ten minutes' repose, the man belonging to the back in question turned round a little, and took out an old snuffy cotton handkerchief and wiped his forehead and lank cheekbones, that were moist with the vast mental and bodily exertions of the night. Harry Tidbody was the man in question. In ten years he had spent at least three thousand nights in copying the model. When abroad perhaps, he had passed the Sunday evenings too in the same rigorous and dismal pastime. He had piles upon piles of grey paper at his lodgings, covered with worthless nudities in black and white chalk.

At the end of the evening we shook hands, and I asked him how the arts flourished. The poor fellow, with a kind of dismal humour that formed a part of his character, twirled round upon the iron heels of his old patched Blucher boots, and showed me his figure for answer. Such a lean, long, ragged, fantastical-looking personage, it would be hard to match out of the drawing schools.

'Tit, my boy,' said he, when he had finished his pirouette, 'you may see that the arts have not fattened me as yet ; and between ourselves I make by my profession something considerably less than a thousand a year. But, mind you I am not discouraged ; my whole soul is in my calling ; I can't do anything else if I would : and I will be a painter, or die in the attempt.'

Tidbody is not dead, I am happy to say, but has a snug place in the Excise of eighty pounds a year, and now only exercises the pencil as an amateur. If his story has been told here at some length, the ingenious reader may fancy that there is some reason for it. In the first place, there is so little to say about the present exhibition at Paris, that your humble servant does not know how to fill his pages without some digressions ; and, secondly, the Tidbodian episode has a certain moral in it, without which it never would have been related, and which is good for all artists to read.

It came to my mind upon examining a picture of sixty feet by forty (indeed, it cannot be much smaller) which takes up a good

deal of room in the large room of the Louvre.   But of this picture
anon.   Let us come to the general considerations.

Why the deuce will men make light of that golden gift of
mediocrity which for the most part they possess, and strive so
absurdly at the sublime ?   What is it that makes a fortune in this
world but energetic mediocrity ?   What is it that is so respected
and prosperous as good, honest, emphatic, blundering dulness,
bellowing commonplaces with its great healthy lungs, kicking and
struggling with its big feet and fists, and bringing an awe-stricken
public down on its knees before it ?   Think, my good sir, of the
people who occupy your attention and the world's.   Who are they?
Upon your honour and conscience now, are they not persons with
thews and sinews like your own, only they use them with somewhat more activity—with a voice like yours, only they shout a
little louder—with the average portion of brains, in fact, but
working them more ?   But this kind of disbelief in heroes is very
offensive to the world, it must be confessed.   There, now, is *The
Times* newspaper, which the other day rated your humble servant
for publishing an account of one of the great humbugs of modern
days, viz. the late funeral of Napoleon [1]—which rated me, I say, and
talked in its own grave, roaring way, about the flippancy and
conceit of Titmarsh.

O, you thundering old *Times !*   Napoleon's funeral was a
humbug, and your constant reader said so.   The people engaged in
it were humbugs, and this your Michael Angelo hinted at.   There
may be irreverence in this, and the process of humbug-hunting may
end rather awkwardly for some people.   But, surely there is no
conceit.   The shamming of modesty is the most pert conceit of all,
the *precieuse* affectation of deference where you don't feel it, the
sneaking acquiescence in lies.   It is very hard that a man may
not tell the truth as he fancies it, without being accused of conceit:
but so the world wags.   As has already been prettily shown in
that before-mentioned little book about Napoleon, that is still to
be had of the publisher's, there is a ballad in the volume, which,
if properly studied, will be alone worth two-and-sixpence to any
man.

Well, the funeral of Napoleon *was* a humbug ; and being so,
what was a man to call it ?   What do we call a rose ?   Is it
disrespectful to the pretty flower to call it by its own innocent
name ?   And, in like manner, are we bound, out of respect for
society, to speak of humbug only in a circumlocutory way—to call
it something else, as they say some Indian people do their devil—

[1] *The Second Funeral of Napoleon : in three Letters to Miss Smith of
London ; and The Chronicle of the Drum.   By Mr. M. A. Titmarsh.*

to wrap it up in riddles and charades ?   Nothing is easier.   Take,
for instance, the following couple of sonnets on the subject :—

> The glad spring sun shone yesterday, as Mr.
>   M. Titmarsh wandered with his favourite lassie
> By silver Seine, among the meadows grassy
> Meadows, like mail-coach guards new clad at Easter.
> Fair was the sight 'twixt Neuilly and Passy :
> And green the field and bright the river's glister.
>
> The birds sang salutations to the spring ;
>   Already buds and leaves from branches burst :
>   'The surly winter time hath done its worst,'
> Said Michael : 'lo, the bees are on the wing !'
> Then on the ground his lazy limbs did fling.
>   Meanwhile the bees pass'd by him with my *first*.
>   My *second* dare I to your notice bring,
> Or name to delicate ears that animal accurst ?

> To all our earthly family of fools
>   My *whole*, resistless despot, gives the law—
>   Humble and great, we kneel to it with awe ;
> O'er camp and court, the senate and the schools,
> Our grand invisible Lama sits and rules,
>   By ministers that are its men of straw.
>
> Sir Robert utters it in place of wit,
>   And straight the Opposition shouts 'Hear, hear !'
>   And oh ! but all the Whiggish benches cheer
> When great Lord John retorts it as is fit.
> In you, my *Press* [1] each day throughout the year,
>   On vast broad sheets we find its praises writ.
>   O wondrous are the columns that you rear,
> And sweet the morning hymns you roar in praise of it !

Sacred word ! it is kept out of the dictionaries, as if the great
compilers of those publications were afraid to utter it.   Well, then,

---

[1] The reader can easily accommodate this line to the name of his favourite
paper.   Thus :—

In you, my $\left\{ \begin{matrix} Times \\ Post \end{matrix} \right\}$ each day throughout the year.

Or :

In you, my $\left\{ \begin{matrix} Herald \\ 'Tiser \end{matrix} \right\}$ daily through the year.

Or, in France :—

In you, my *Galignani's Messengere ;*

a capital paper, because you have there the very cream of all the others.   In
the last line, for 'morning' you can read 'evening,' or 'weekly,' as circumstances prompt.

the funeral of Napoleon was a humbug, as Titmarsh wrote ; and a still better proof that it was a humbug was this, that nobody bought Titmarsh's book, and of the 10,000 copies made ready by the publisher not above 3000 went off. It was a humbug, and an exploded humbug. Peace be to it ! *Parlons d'autres choses ;* and let us begin to discourse about the pictures without further shilly-shally.

I must confess, with a great deal of shame, that I love to go to the picture gallery of a Sunday after church, on purpose to see the thousand happy people of the working sort amusing them-selves—not very wickedly, as I fancy—in the only day in the week on which they have their freedom. Genteel people, who can amuse themselves every day throughout the year, do not frequent the Louvre on a Sunday. You can't see the pictures well, and are pushed and elbowed by all sorts of low-bred creatures. Yesterday, there were at the very least two hundred common soldiers in the place—little vulgar ruffians, with red breeches and three halfpence a-day, examining the pictures in company with fifteen hundred grisettes, two thousand liberated shop-boys, eighteen hundred and forty-one artist-apprentices, half a dozen of livery servants, and many scores of fellows with caps, and jackets, and copper-coloured countenances, and gold ear-rings, and large ugly hands, that are hammering, or weaving, or filing, all the week. *Fi, donc !* what a thing it is to have a taste for low company ! Every man of decent breeding ought to have been in the Bois de Boulogne, in white kid gloves and on horse-back, or on hack-back at least. How the dandies just now went prancing and curvetting down the Champs Elysees making their horses jump as they passed the carriages, with their japanned boots glittering in the sunshine !

The fountains were flashing and foaming, as if they too were in their best for Sunday ; the trees are covered all over with little, twinkling, bright green sprouts ; numberless exhibitions of Punch and the Fantoccini are going on beneath them ; and jugglers and balancers are entertaining the people with their pranks. I met two fellows the other day, one with a barrel organ, and the other with a beard, a turban, a red jacket, and a pair of dirty, short, spangled, white trousers, who were cursing each other in the purest St. Giles's English ; and if I had had impudence or generosity enough, I should have liked to make up their quarrel over a chopine of Strasbourg beer, and hear the histories of either. Think of these fellows quitting our beloved country, and their homes in some calm nook of Field Lane or Seven Dials, and toiling over to France with their music and their jiggling-traps, to balance

cart-wheels and swallow knives for the amusement of our natural
enemies. They are very likely at work at this minute, with
grinning *bonnes* and conscripts staring at their skill. It is pleasant
to walk by and see the nurses and the children so uproariously
happy. Yonder is one who has got a halfpenny to give to the
beggar at the crossing ; several are riding gravely in little carriages
drawn by goats. Ah, truly, the sunshine is a fine thing ; and
one loves to see the little people and the poor basking in it, as
well as the great in their fine carriages, or their prancing cock-
tailed horses.

In the midst of sights of this kind, you pass on a fine Sunday
afternoon down the Elysian Fields and the Tuileries until you
reach the before-mentioned low-bred crowd rushing into the Louvre.

Well, then, the pictures of this exhibition are to be numbered
by thousands, and these thousands contain the ordinary number of
chefs d'œuvre ; that is to say, there may be a couple of works of
genius, half a dozen very clever performances, a hundred or so of
good ones, fifteen hundred very decent good or bad pictures, and the
remainder atrocious. What a comfort it is, as I have often
thought, that they are not all masterpieces, and that there is a good
stock of mediocrity in this world, and that we only light upon
genius now and then, at rare angel intervals, handed round like
tokay at dessert, in a few houses, and in very small quantities only !
Fancy how sick one would grow of it, if one had no other drink !

Now, in this exhibition there are, of course, a certain number of
persons who make believe that they are handing you round tokay
—giving you the real imperial stuff, with the seal of genius
stamped on the cork. There are numbers of ambitious pictures,
in other words, chiefly upon sacred subjects, and in what is called
a severe style of art.

The severe style of art consists in drawing your figures in the
first place very big and very neat, in which there is no harm ; and
in dressing them chiefly in stiff, crisp, old-fashioned draperies,
such as one sees in the illuminated missals and the old masters.
The old masters, no doubt, copied the habits of the people about
them ; and it has always appeared as absurd to me to imitate
these antique costumes, and to dress up saints and virgins after the
fashion of the fifteenth century, as it would be to adorn them with
hoops and red-heels such as our grandmothers wore : and to make
a Magdalen, for instance, taking off her patches, or an angel in
powder and a hoop.

It is, or used to be, the custom at the theatres for the gravedigger in *Hamlet* always to wear fifteen or sixteen waistcoats of
which he leisurely divested himself, the audience roaring at each

change of raiment. Do the Denmark gravediggers always wear
fifteen waistcoats ? Let any body answer who has visited the
country.   But the probability is that the custom on the stage is a
very ancient one, and that the public would not be satisfied at a
departure from the legend. As in the matter of gravediggers, so
it is with angels : they have—and Heaven knows why—a regular
costume, which every ' serious ' painter follows ; and which has a
great deal more to do with serious art than people at first may
imagine.   They have large white wings, that fill up a quarter of
the picture in which they have the good fortune to be ; they have
white gowns that fall round their feet in pretty fantastical
draperies ; they have fillets round their brows, and their hair
combed and neatly pomatumed down the middle ; and if they have
not a sword, have an elegant portable harp of a certain angelic
shape.   Large rims of gold leaf they have round their heads always ;
a pretty business it would be if such adjuncts were to be left out.

Now, suppose the legend ordered that every gravedigger should
be represented with a gold leaf halo round his head, and every
angel with fifteen waistcoats, artists would have followed serious
art just as they do now most probably, and looked with scorn at
the miserable creature who ventured to scoff at the waistcoats.   Ten to one but a certain newspaper would have called
a man flippant who did not respect the waistcoats—would have
said that he was irreverent for not worshipping the waistcoats.[1]   But why talk of it ?   The fact is I have rather a desire
to set up for a martyr, like my neighbours in the literary trade ;
it is not a little comforting to undergo such persecutions courage-
ously.   ' O Socrate ! je boirai la cigue avec toi ! ' as David said
to Robespierre. You too were accused of blasphemy in your
time ; and the world has been treating us poor literary gents in
the same way ever since.   There, now, is Bulw——

But to return to the painters. In the matter of canvas cover-
ing, the French artists are a great deal more audacious than ours ;
and I have known a man starve all the winter through, without
fire and without beef, in order that he might have the honour of
filling five-and-twenty feet square of canvas with some favourite
subject of his.

It is curious to look through the collection, and see how for
the most part the men draw their ideas.   There are caricatures
of the late and early style of Raphael ; there are caricatures of

---

[1] Last year, when our friend published some article in this Magazine, he
seemed to be agitated almost to madness by a criticism, and a very just one
too, which appeared in *The Morning Post*.   At present he is similarly affected
by some strictures on a defunct work of his.

Masaccio ; there is a picture painted in the very pyramidical form, and in the manner of Andrea del Sarto ; there is a Holy Family, the exact counterpart of Leonardo da Vinci ; and, finally, there is Achille Deveria—it is no use to give the names and numbers of the other artists who are not known in England—there is Achille Deveria, who, having nothing else to caricature, has caricatured a painted window, and designed a Charity, of which all the outlines are half an inch thick.

Then there are numberless caricatures in colour as in form. There is a Violet Entombment—a crimson one, a green one ; a light emerald and gamboge Eve ; all huge pictures, with talent enough in their composition, but remarkable for this strange mad love of extravagance, which belongs to the nation. Titian and the Venetians have loved to paint lurid skies and sunsets of purple and gold : here, in consequence, is a piebald picture of crimson and yellow, laid on in streaks from the top to the bottom.

Who has not heard a great, comfortable, big-chested man, with bands round a sleek double chin, and fat white cushion-squeezers of hands, and large red whiskers and a soft roaring voice, the delight of a congregation, preaching for an hour with all the appearance and twice the emphasis of piety, and leading audiences captive ? And who has not seen a humble individual, who is quite confused to be conducted down the aisle by the big beadle with his silver staff (the stalwart ' drum-major ecclesiastic ') ; and when in his pulpit, saying his say in the simplest manner possible, uttering what are very likely commonplaces, without a single rhetorical grace or emphasis ?

The great, comfortable, red-whiskered, roaring cushion-thumper, is most probably the favourite with the public. But there are some persons who, nevertheless, prefer to listen to the man of timid, mild commonplaces, because the simple words he speaks come from *his* heart, and so find a way directly to yours ; where, if perhaps you can't find belief for them, you still are sure to receive them with respect and sympathy.

There are many such professors at the easel as well as the pulpit ; and you see many painters with a great vigour and dexterity, and no sincerity of heart ; some with little dexterity, but plenty of sincerity ; some one or two in a million who have both these qualities, and thus become the great men of their art. I think there are instances of the two former kinds in this present exhibition of the Louvre. There are fellows who have covered great swaggering canvases with all the attitudes and externals of piety ; and some few whose humble pictures cause no stir, and remain in quiet nooks, where one finds them, and straightway acknowledges the simple, kindly appeal, which they make.

Of such an order is the picture entitled ' La Prière,' by M. Trimolet. A man and his wife are kneeling at an old-fashioned praying desk, and the woman clasps a little sickly-looking child in her arms, and all three are praying as earnestly as their simple hearts will let them. The man is a limner or painter of missals, by trade, as we fancy. One of his works lies upon the praying desk, and it is evident that he can paint no more that day, for the sun is just set behind the old-fashioned roofs of the houses in the narrow street of the old city where he lives. Indeed, I have had a great deal of pleasure in looking at this little quiet painting, and in the course of half a dozen visits that I have paid to it, have become perfectly acquainted with all the circumstances of the life of the honest missal illuminator and his wife, here praying at the end of their day's work in the calm summer evening.

Very likely M. Trimolet has quite a different history for his little personages, and so has everybody else who examines the picture. But what of that? There is the privilege of pictures. A man does not know all that lies in his picture, any more than he understands all the character of his children. Directly one or the other makes its appearance in the world, it has its own private existence, independent of the progenitor. And in respect of works of art, if the same piece inspire one man with joy, that fills another with compassion, what are we to say of it, but that it has sundry properties of its own which its author even does not understand? The fact is, pictures 'are as they seem to all,' as Mr. Alfred Tennyson sings in the first volume of his poems.

Some of this character of holiness and devotion that I fancy I see in M. Trimolet's pictures is likewise observable in a piece of Madame Juillerat, representing Saint Elizabeth, of Hungary, leading a little beggar boy into her house, where the holy dame of Hungary will, no doubt, make him comfortable with a good plate of victuals. A couple of young ladies follow behind the princess, with demure looks, and garlands in their hair, that hangs straight on their shoulders, as one sees it in the old illuminations. The whole picture has a pleasant, mystic, innocent look; and one is all the better for regarding it. What a fine instinct or task it was in the old missal illuminators to be so particular in the painting of the minor parts of their pictures! the precise manner in which the flowers and leaves, birds and branches, are painted, give an air of truth and simplicity to the whole performance, and make nature, as it were, an accomplice and actor in the scene going on. For instance, you may look at a landscape with certain feelings of pleasure; but if you have pulled a rose, and are smelling it, and if of a sudden a blackbird in a bush hard by begins to sing and chirrup, your feeling of pleasure is very much enhanced most likely; the senses with which you examine the scene become brightened as it were, and the scene itself becomes more agreeable to you. It is not the same place as it was before you smelt the rose, or before the blackbird began to sing. Now, in Madame Juillerat's picture of the Saint of Hungary and the hungry boy, if the flowers on the young ladies' heads had been omitted, or not painted with their pleasing minuteness and circumstantiality, I fancy that the effect of the piece would have been by no means the same. Another artist of the mystical school, Monsieur Servan, has employed the same adjuncts in a similarly successful manner. One of his pictures represents St. Augustin meditating in a garden; a great cluster of rose-bushes, hollyhocks, and other plants, are in the foreground, most accurately delineated; and a fine rich landscape and river stretch behind the saint, round whom the flowers seem to keep up a mysterious waving and whispering that fill one with a sweet, pleasing, indescribable kind of awe—a great perfection in this style of painting.

In M. Aguado's gallery there is an early Raphael (which all the world declares to be a copy, but no matter). This piece only represents two young people walking hand in hand in a garden, and looking at you with a kind of 'solemn mirth' (the expression of old Sternhold and Hopkins has always struck me as very fine). A meadow is behind them, at the end of which is a cottage, and by which flows a river, environed by certain very prim-looking trees; and that is all. Well, it is impossible for any person who has a sentiment for the art to look at this picture without feeling indescribably moved and pleased by it. It acts upon you—how? How does a beautiful, pious, tender air of Mozart act upon you? What is there in it that should make you happy and gentle, and fill you with all sorts of good thoughts and kindly feelings? I fear that what Doctor Thumpcushion says at church is correct, and that the indulgences are only carnal, and of the earth earthy; but the sensual effort in this case carries one quite away from the earth, and up to something that is very like heaven.

Now the writer of this has already been severely reprehended for saying that Raphael at thirty had lost that delightful innocence and purity which rendered the works of Raphael of twenty so divine; and perhaps it may be the critic's fault, and not the painter's (I'm not proud, and will allow that even a magazine

M

critic may be mistaken). Perhaps by the greatest stretch of the perhaps, it may be that Raphael was every whit as divine at thirty as at eighteen; and that the very quaintnesses and imperfections of manner observable in his early works are the reasons why they appear so singularly pleasing to me. At least among painters of the present day, I feel myself more disposed to recognise spiritual beauties in those whose powers of execution are manifestly incomplete, than in artists whose hands are skilful and manner formed. Thus there are scores of large pictures here, hanging in the Louvre, that represent subjects taken from Holy Writ, or from the lives of the saints—pictures skilfully enough painted and intended to be religious, that have not the slightest effect upon me, no more than Doctor Thumpcushion's loudest and glibbest sermon.

Here is No. 1475, for instance—a 'Holy Family,' painted in the antique manner, and with all the accessories before spoken of, viz. large flowers, fresh roses, and white stately lilies; curling tendrils of vines forming fantastical canopies for the heads of the sacred personages, and rings of gold-leaf drawn neatly round the same. Here is the Virgin, with long, stiff, prim draperies of blue, red, and white; and old Saint Anne in a sober dress, seated gravely at her side; and Saint Joseph in a becoming attitude; and all very cleverly treated, and pleasing to the eye. But though this picture is twice as well painted as any of those before mentioned, it does not touch my heart in the least; nor do any of the rest of the sacred pieces. Opposite the 'Holy Family' is a great 'Martyrdom of Polycarp,' and the Catalogue tells you how the executioners first tried to burn the saint; but the fire went out, and the executioners were knocked down; then a soldier struck the saint with a sword, and so killed him. The legends recount numerous miracles of this sort, which I confess have not any very edifying effect upon me. Saints are clapped into boiling oil, which immediately turns cool; or their heads are chopped off, and their blood turns to milk; and so on. One can't understand why these continual delays and disappointments take place, especially as the martyr is always killed at the end; so that it would be best at once to put him out of his pain. For this reason, possibly the execution of Saint Polycarp did not properly affect the writer of this notice.

M. Laemlein has a good picture of the 'Waking of Adam,' so royally described by Milton—a picture full of gladness, vigour, and sunshine. There is a very fine figure of a weeping woman in a picture of the 'Death of the Virgin'; and the Virgin falling in M. Steuben's picture of 'Our Saviour going to Execution' is very pathetic. The mention of this gentleman brings us to what is called the *bourgeois* style of art, of which he is one of the chief professors. He excels in depicting a certain kind of sentiment, and in the vulgar, which is often too the true, pathetic.

Steuben has painted many scores of Napoleons ; and his picture of Napoleon this year brings numbers of admiring people round it. The Emperor is sitted on a sofa, reading dispatches ; and the little King of Rome, in a white muslin frock, with his hair beautifully curled, slumbers on his papa's knee. What a contrast ! the conqueror of the world, the stern warrior, the great giver of laws and ruler of nations, he dare not move because the little baby is asleep ; and he would not disturb him for all the kingdoms he knows so well how to conquer. This is not art, if you please ; but it is pleasant to see fat, good-natured mothers and grandmothers clustered round this picture, and looking at it with solemn eyes. The same painter has an Esmeralda dancing and frisking in her night-gown, and playing the tambourine to her goat, capering likewise. This picture is so delightfully bad, the little gipsy has such a killing ogle, that all the world admires it. M. Steuben should send it to London, where it would be sure of a gigantic success.

M. Grenier has a piece much looked at, in the *bourgeois* line. Some rogues of gipsies, or mountebanks, have kidnapped a fine fat child, and are stripping it of its pretty clothes ; and poor baby is crying.; and the gipsy-woman holding up her finger, and threatening ; and the he-mountebank is lying on a bank, smoking his pipe,—the callous monster ! Preciously they will ill-treat that dear little darling, if justice do not overtake them,—if, ay, *if*. But, thank Heaven : there in the corner come the police and they will have that pipe-smoking scoundrel off to the galleys before five minutes are over.

1056. A picture of the galleys. Two galley-slaves before you, and the piece is called, ' A Crime and a Fault.' The poor ' Fault ' is sitting on a stone, looking very repentant and unhappy indeed. The great ' Crime ' stands grinning you in the face, smoking his pipe. The ruffian ! That pipe seems to be a great mark of callosity in ruffians. I heard one man whisper to another, as they were looking at these galley-slaves, ' *They are portraits,*' and very much affected his companion seemed by the information.

Of a similar virtuous interest is 705, by M. Finart. ' A family of African Colonists carried off by Abd-el-Kader.' There is the poor male colonist without a single thing on but a rope round his wrists. His silver skin is dabbled with his golden blood, and he looks up to heaven as the Arabs are poking him on with the tips of their horrid spears. Behind him come his flocks and herds, and other members of his family. In front, principal figure, is his angelic wife, in her night-gown, and in the arms of an odious blackamoor on horseback. Poor thing—poor thing! she is kicking, and struggling and resisting as hard as she possibly can.

485. 'The Two friends.' Debay.

'Deux jeunes femmes se donnent le gage le plus sacré d'une amitié sincère, dans un acte de dévoûment et de reconnaissance.

'L'une d'elles, faible, exténuée d'efforts inutilement tentés pour allaiter, découvre son sein tari, cause du dépérissement de son enfant. Sa douleur est comprise par son amie, à qui la santé permet d'ajouter au bonheur de nourrir son propre enfant, celui de rappeler à la vie le fils mourant de sa compagne.'

M. Debay's pictures are not bad, as most of the others here mentioned as appertaining to the bourgeois class; but, good or bad, I can't but own that I like to see these honest, hearty representations, which work upon good simple feeling in a good downright way; and if not works of art, are certainly works that can do a great deal of good, and make honest people happy. Who is the man that despises melodramas? I swear that T. P. Cooke is a benefactor to mankind. Away with him who has no stomach for such kind of entertainments, where vice is always punished, where virtue always meets its reward; where Mrs. James Vining is always sure to be made comfortable somewhere at the end of the third act; and if O. Smith is lying in agonies of death, in red breeches, on the front of the stage, or has just gone off in a flash of fire down one of the traps, I know it is only make-believe on his part, and believe him to be a good, kind-hearted fellow, that would not do harm to mortal! So much for pictures of the serious melodramatic sort.

M. Biard, whose picture of the 'Slave Trade' made so much noise in London last year—and indeed it is as fine as Hogarth,—has this year many comic pieces, and a series representing the present Majesty of France when Duke of Orleans undergoing various perils by land and by water. There is much good in these pieces; but I mean no disrespect in saying I like the comic ones best. There is one entitled '*Une Distraction.*' A National Guard is amusing himself by catching flies. You can't fail to laugh when you see it. There is '*Le Gros Peche,*' and the biggest of all sins, no less than a drum-major confessing. You can't see the monster's face, which the painter has wisely hidden behind the curtain, as beyond the reach of art; but you see the priest's, and, murder! what a sin it must be that the big tambour has just imparted to him! All the French critics sneer at Biard, as they do at Paul de Kock, for not being artistical enough ; but I do not think these gentlemen need mind the sneer ; they have the millions with them, as Feargus O'Connor says, and they are good judges, after all.

A great comfort it is to think that there is a reasonable prospect that, for the future, very few more battle-pieces will be painted. They have used up all the victories, and Versailles is almost full. So this year, much to my happiness, only a few yards of warlike canvas are exhibited in place of the furlongs which one was called upon to examine in former exhibitions. One retreat from Moscow is there, and one storming of El Gibbet, or El Arish, or some such place, in Africa. In the latter picture, you see a thousand fellows, in loose red pantaloons, rushing up a hill with base heathen Turks on the top, who are firing off guns, carabines, and other pieces of ordnance, at them. All this is very well painted by Monsieur Bollange, and the rush of red breeches has a queer and pleasing appearance. In the Russian piece, you have frozen men and cattle ; mothers embracing their offspring ; grenadiers scowling at the enemy, and especially one fellow standing on a back with his bayonet placed in the attitude for receiving the charge, and actually charged by a whole regiment of Cossacks,— a complete pulk, my dear madam, coming on in three lines, with their lances pointed against this undaunted warrior of France. I believe Monsieur Thiers sat for the portrait, or else the editor of the *Courrier Français*—the two men in this belligerent nation who are the belligerentest. *A propos* of Thiers ; the *Nouvelles a la Main* have a good story of this little sham Napoleon. When the second son of the Duke of Orleans was born (I forget his royal highness's title) news was brought to Monsieur Thiers. He was told the princess was well, and asked the courier who brought the news, '*Comment se portait de Roi de Rome ?*' It may be said, in confidence, that there is not a single word of truth in the story. But what of that? Are not sham stories as good as real ones ? Ask M. Leullier ; who, in spite of all that has been said and written upon a certain sea-fight, has actually this year come forward with his

1311—*Héroisme de l'Equipage du Vaisseau le Vengeur, 4 Juin, 1794.*

'*Après avoir soutenu longtemps un combat acharné contre trois vaisseaux Anglais, le vaisseau le Vengeur avait perdu la moitié de son équipage, le reste était blessé pour la plupart : le second capitaine avait été coupé en deux par un boulet ; le vaisseau était rasé par le feu de l'ennemi, sa mâture abattue, ses flancs criblés par les boulets étaient ouverts de toutes parts : sa cale se remplissait à vu d'œil ; il s'enfonçait dans la mer. Les marins*

*qui restent sur son bord servent la batterie basse jusqu'à ce qu'elle se
trouve au niveau de la mer ; quand elle va disparaître, ils s'élancent dans
la seconde, où ils répètent la même manœuvre ; celle-ci engloutie, ils mon-
tent sur le pont.   Un tronçon de mât d'artimon restait encore debout ;
leurs pavillons en lambeaux y sont cloués ; puis, réunissant instinctive-
ment leurs volentés en une seule pensée, ils veulent périr avec le navire qui
leur a été confié.   Tous, combattants, blessés, mourants se raniment : un
cri immense s'élève, répété sur toutes les parties du tillac : Vive la Répub-
lique ! Vive la France ! . . . Le Vengeur coule . . . les cris continuent ;
tous les bras sont dressés au ciel, et ces braves, préférant la mort à la cap-
tivité, emportent triomphalement leur pavillon dans ce glorieux tombeau.'
—France Maritime.*

I think Mr. Thomas Carlyle is in the occasional habit of calling
lies wind-bags. *This* wind-bag one would have thought exploded
last year ; but no such thing. You *can't* sink it, do what you
will : it always comes bouncing up to the surface again, where it
swims and bobs about gaily for the admiration of all. This lie
the Frenchman will believe ; all the papers talk gravely about
the affair of the *Vengeur*, as if an established fact : and I
heard the matter disposed of by some artists the other day in
a very satisfactory manner. One has always the gratification, in
all French societies where the matter is discussed, of telling the
real story (or if the subject be not discussed, of bringing the
conversation round to it, and then telling the real story), one has
always this gratification, and a great wicked, delightful one it is,—
you make the whole company uncomfortable at once ; you narrate
the history in a calm, good-humoured, dispassionate tone ; and as
you proceed, you see the different personages of the audience looking
uneasily at one another, and bursting out occasionally with a ' *Mais
cependant ;*' but you continue your tale with perfect suavity of
manner, and have the satisfaction of knowing that you have stuck
a dagger into the heart of every single person using it.

Telling, I say, this story to some artists who were examining
M. Leullier's picture, and I trust that many scores of persons
besides were listening to the conversation, one of them replied to
my assertion, that Captain Renaudin's letters were extant, and
that the whole affair was a humbug, in the following way.

' Sir,' said he, ' the sinking of the *Vengeur is* an *established* fact
of history. It is completely proved by the documents of the
time ; and as for the letters of Captain Renaudin of which you
speak, have we not had an example the other day of some
pretended letters of Louis Philippe's which were published in a
newspaper here ? And what, sir, were those letters ? *Forgeries !* '

Q.E.D. Everybody said sansculotte was right; and I have no doubt that if all the *Vengeur's* crew could rise from the dead, and that English cox—or boat-swain, who was last *on board the ship*,[1] of which he and his comrades had possession, and had to swim for his life, could come forward, and swear to the real story, I make no doubt that the Frenchmen would not believe it. Only one I know, my friend Julius, who, ever since the tale has been told to him, has been crying it into all ears and in all societies, and vows he is perfectly hoarse with telling it.

As for M. Leullier's picture, there is really a great deal of good in it. Fellows embracing each other, and holding up hands and eyes to heaven; and in the distance an English ship, with the crew in *red coats*, firing away on the doomed vessel. Possibly, they are only marines whom we see; but as I once beheld several English naval officers in a play habited in top-boots, perhaps the legend in France may be, that the navy, like the army, with us, is caparisoned in scarlet. A good subject for another historical picture would be Cambronne, saying, '*La Garde meurt mais ne se rend pas.*' I have bought a couple of engravings of *Vengeur* and Cambronne, and shall be glad to make a little historical collection of facts similarly authenticated.

Accursed, I say, be all uniform coats of blue or of red; all ye epaulets and sabertaches; all ye guns, shrapnels, and musketoons; all ye silken banners embroidered with bloody reminiscences of successful fights: down—down to the bottomless pit with you all, and let honest men live and love each other without you! What business have I, forsooth, to plume myself because the Duke of Wellington beat the French in Spain and elsewhere; and kindle as I read the tale, and fancy myself of a heroic stock, because my uncle Tom was at the battle of Waterloo, and because we beat Napoleon there? Who are *we*, in the name of Beelzebub? Did we ever fight in our lives? Have we the slightest inclination for fighting and murdering one another? Why are we to go on hating one another from generation to generation, swelling up our little bosoms with absurd national conceit, strutting and crowing over our neighbours, and longing to be at fisticuffs with them again? As Aristotle remarks, in war there are always two parties; and though it often happens that both declare themselves to be victorious, it still is generally the case that one party beats and the other is beaten. The conqueror is thus filled with national pride, and the conquered with national hatred and a desire to do better next time. If he has his revenge and beats his opponent as

---

[1] The writer heard of this man from an English captain in the navy, who had him on board his ship.

desired, these agreeable feelings are reversed, and so Pride and
Hatred continue in *saecula saeculorum*, and ribands and orders are
given away, and great men rise and flourish. 'Remember you are
Britons!' cries our general; 'there is the enemy, and d— 'em,
give 'em the bayonet!' Hurrah! helter skelter, load and fire, cut
and thrust, down they go! '*Soldats! dans ce moment terrible
la France vous regarde! Vive l'Empereur!*' shouts Jacques
Bonhomme, and his sword is through your ribs in a twinkling,
'Children!' roars Feldmarechal Sauerkraut, 'men of Hohenzollern-
sigmaringen! remember the eyes of Vaterland are upon you!' and
murder again is the consequence. Tomahee-tereboo leads on the
Ashantees with the very same war-cry, and they eat all their
prisoners with true patriotic cannibalism.

Thus the great truth is handed down from father to son, that

> A Briton, ⎫
> A Frenchman, ⎪
> An Ashantee, ⎬   is superior to all the rest
> A Hohenzollernsig- ⎪   of the world ;
>   maringenite, etc. ⎭

and by this truth the dullards of the respective nations swear, and
by it statesmen govern.

Let the reader say for himself, does he not believe himself to
be superior to a man of any other country? We can't help it—in
spite of ourselves we do. But if, by changing the name, the fable
applies to yourself, why do you laugh?

> Κυιδ ριδης ; μυτατω νωμινε δη τη
> Φαβλα ναρρατυρ,

as a certain poet says (in a quotation that is pretty well known in
England, and therefore put down here in a new fashion). Why do
you laugh, forsooth? Why do you not laugh? If donkeys' ears
are a matter of laughter, surely we may laugh at them when
growing on our own skulls.

Take a couple of instances from 'actual life' as the fashionable
novel-puffers say.

A little, fat, silly woman, who in no country but this would
ever have pretensions to beauty, has lately set up a circulating
library in our street. She lends the five franc editions of the
English novels, as well as the romances of her own country, and I
have had several of the former works of fiction from her store :
Bulwer's *Night and Morning*, very pleasant, kind-hearted reading ;
Peter Priggins, an astonishing work of slang, that ought to be
translated if but to give Europe an idea of what a gay young

gentleman in England sometimes is ; and other novels never mind what. But to revert to the fat woman.

She sits all day ogling and simpering behind her little counter ; and from the slow, prim precise way in which she lets her silly sentences slip through her mouth, you see at once that she is quite satisfied with them, and expects that every customer should give her an opportunity of uttering a few of them for his benefit. Going there for a book, I always find myself entangled in a quarter of an hour's conversation.

This is carried on in not very bad French on my part ; at least I find that when I say something genteel to the library-woman, she is not at a loss to understand me, and we have passed already many minutes in this kind of intercourse. Two days since, returning *Night and Morning* to the library-lady and demanding the romance of *Peter Priggins*, she offered me instead *Ida*, par M. le Vicomte Darlincourt, which I refused, having already experienced some of his lordship's works ; next she produced *Stella*, *Valida*, *Eloa*, by various French ladies of literary celebrity ; but again I declined, declaring respectfully that however agreeable the society of ladies might be, I found their works a little insipid. The fact is, that after being accustomed to such potent mixtures as the French romancers offer you, the mild compositions of the French romanceresses pall on the palate.[1]

'*Madame*,' says I, to cut the matter short, '*je ne demande qu'un roman Anglais, Peter Priggins ; l'avez-vous ? oui ou non ?*'

'*Ah*,' says the library-woman, '*Monsieur ne comprend pas nôtre langue, c'est dommage.*'

Now one might, at first sight, fancy the above speech an epigram, and not a bad one, on an Englishman's blundering French grammar and pronunciation ; but those who know the library-lady must be aware that she never was guilty of such a thing in her life. It was simply a French bull, resulting from the lady's dulness, and by no means a sarcasm. She uttered the words with a great air of superiority and a prim toss of the head, as much as to say, 'How much cleverer I am than you, you silly foreigner ! and what a fine thing it is in me to know the finest language in the world !' In this way I have heard donkeys of our two countries address foreigners in broken English or French, as if people

[1] In our own country, of course—Mrs. Trollope, Miss Mitford, Miss Pardoe, Mrs. Charles Gore, Miss Edgeworth, Miss Ferrier, Miss Stickney, Miss Barrett, Lady Blessington, Miss Smith, Mrs. Austin, Miss Austin, etc.—form exceptions to this rule ; and glad am I to offer per favour of this note a humble tribute of admiration to those ladies.

who could not understand a language when properly spoken could comprehend it when spoken ill. Why the deuce do people give themselves these impertinent, stupid airs of superiority, and pique themselves upon the great cleverness of speaking their own language ?

Take another instance of this same egregious national conceit. At the English pastry-cook's—(you can't readily find a prettier or more graceful woman than Madame Colombin, nor better plum-cake than she sells)—at Madame Colombin's, yesterday, a huge Briton, with sandy whiskers and a double chin, was swallowing patties and cherry-brandy, and all the while making remarks to a friend similarly employed. They were talking about English and French ships.

'Hang me, Higgins,' says Sandy whiskers, 'if *I'd* ever go into one of their cursed French ships ! I should be afraid of sinking at the very first puff of wind ! '

What Higgins replied does not matter. But think what a number of Sandy whiskerses there are in our nation,—fellows who are proud of this stupid mistrust,—who think it a mark of national spirit to despise French skill, bravery, cookery, seamanship, and what not. Swallow your beef and porter, you great, fat-paunched man ; enjoy your language and your country, as you have been bred to do ; but don't fancy yourself, on account of these inheritances of yours, superior to other people of other ways and language. You have luck, perhaps, if you will, in having such a diet and dwelling place, but no *merit*. . . . And with this little discursive essay upon national prejudices, let us come back to the pictures, and finish our walk through the gallery.

In that agreeable branch of the art for which we have I believe no name, but which the French call *genre*, there are at Paris several eminent professors ; and as upon the French stage the costume pieces are far better produced than with us, so also are French costume-pictures much more accurately and characteristic-ally handled than are such subjects in our own country. You do not see Cimabue and Giotto in the costume of Francis the First, as they appeared (depicted by Mr. Simpson, I think) in the Royal Academy Exhibition of last year ; but the artists go to some trouble for collecting their antiquarian stuff, and paint it pretty scrupulously.

M. Jacquard has some pretty small pictures *de genre ;* a very good one, indeed, of fat ' Monks granting Absolution from Fast-ing ' ; of which the details are finely and accurately painted, a task more easy for a French artist than an English one, for the former's studio (as may be seen by a picture in this exhibition) is generally a magnificent curiosity shop; and for old carvings, screens, crockery, armour, draperies, etc., the painter here has but to look to his own walls, and copy away at his ease. Accordingly Jacquard's monks, especially all the properties of the picture, are admirable. M. Baron has 'The Youth of Ribera,' a merry Spanish beggar-boy, among a crowd of his like, drawing sketches of them under a garden wall. The figures are very prettily thought and grouped; there is a fine terrace and palace, and statues in the background, very rich and luxurious; perhaps too pretty and gay in colours, and too strong in details.

But the king of the painters of small history subjects, is M. Robert Fleury; a great artist indeed, and I trust heartily he may be induced to send one or two of his pieces to London, to show our people what he can do. His mind, judging from his works, is rather of a gloomy turn; and he deals somewhat too much, to my taste, in the horrible. He has this year 'A Scene in the Inquisition.' A man is howling and writhing with his feet over a fire; grim inquisitors are watching over him; and a dreadful executioner, with fierce eyes peering from under a mysterious capuchin, is doggedly sitting over the coals. The picture is downright horror, but admirably and honestly drawn; and in effect rich, sombre, and simple.

'Benvenuto Cellini' is better still; and the critics have lauded the piece as giving a good idea of the fierce, fantastic Florentine sculptor; but I think M. Fleury has taken him in too grim a mood, and made his ferocity too downright. There was always a dash of the ridiculous in the man, even in his most truculent moments; and I fancy that such simple rage as is here represented scarcely characterises him. The fellow never cut a throat without some sense of humour, and here we have him greatly too majestic, to my taste.

'Old Michael Angelo watching over the Sick-bed of his servant Urbino,' is a noble painting; as fine in feeling as in design and colour. One can't but admire in all these the *manliness* of the artist. The picture is painted in a large, rich, massive, vigorous manner; and it is gratifying to see that this great man, after resolute seeking for many years, has found the full use of his hand at last, and can express himself as he would. The picture is fit to hang in the very best gallery in the world; and a century hence will no doubt be worth five times as many crowns as the artist asks or has had for it.

Being on the subject of great pictures, let us here mention—

712. 'Portrait of a Lady,' by Hippolyte Flandrin.

Of this portrait all I can say is, that if you take the best portraits by the best masters—a head of Sebastian, or Michael Angelo, a head of Raphael, or one of those rarer ones of Andrea del Sarto—not one of them, for lofty character and majestic nobleness and simplicity, can surpass this magnificent work.

This seems, doubtless, very exaggerated praise, and people reading it may possibly sneer at the critic who ventures to speak in such a way. To all such I say, Come and see it. You who admire Sir Thomas and the *Books of Beauty* will possibly not admire it ; you who give ten thousand guineas for a blowsy Murillo will not possibly relish M. Flandrin's manner ; but you who love simplicity and greatness come and see how an old lady, with a black mantilla and dark eyes, and grey hair and a few red flowers in her cap, has been painted by M. Flandrin of Lyons. If I were Louis-Philippe, I would send a legion of honour cross, of the biggest sort, to decorate the bosom of the painter who has executed this noble piece.

As for portraits (with the exception of this one, which no man in England can equal, not even Mr. Samuel Lawrence, who is trying to get to this point, but has not reached it yet) our English painters keep the lead still, nor is there much remarkable among the hundreds in the gallery. There are vast numbers of English faces staring at you from the canvases ; and among the miniatures especially one can't help laughing at the continual recurrence of the healthy, vacant, simpering, aristocratic English type. There are black velvets and satins, ladies with birds of paradise, deputies on sofas, and generals and marshals in the midst of smoke and cannon-balls. Nothing can be less to my taste than a pot-bellied, swaggering Marshal Soult, who rests his baton on his stomach, and looks at you in the midst of a dim cloud of war. The Duchess de Nemours is done by M. Winterhalter, and has a place of honour, as becomes a good portrait ; and, above all, such a pretty lady. She is a pretty, smiling, buxom blonde, with plenty of hair, and rather too much hands, not to speak disrespect-fully ; and a slice of lace which goes across the middle of her white satin gown seems to cut the picture very disagreeably in two. There is a beautiful head in a large portrait of a lad of eighteen, painted by himself ; and here may be mentioned two single figures in pastel by an architect, remarkable for earnest, *spirituel* beauty ; likewise two heads in chalk by De Rudder ; most charming sketches, full of delicacy, grace and truth.

The only one of the acknowledged great who has exhibited this year is M. Delacroix, who has a large picture relative to the siege of Constantinople, that looks very like a piece of crumpled tapestry, but that has nevertheless its admirers and its merits, as what work of his has not ?

His two smaller pieces are charming. ' A Jewish Wedding at Tangiers,' is brilliant with light, and merriment ; a particular sort of merriment, that is, that makes you gloomy in the very midst of the hey-day : and his 'Boat' is awful. A score of shipwrecked men are in this boat, on a great, wide, swollen, interminable sea —no hope, no speck of sail—and they are drawing lots which shall be killed and eaten. A burly seaman, with a red beard, has just put his hand into the hat, and is touching his own to the officer. One fellow sits with his hands clasped, and gazing— gazing into the great void before him. By Jupiter, his eyes are unfathomable ! he is looking at miles and miles of lead-coloured, bitter, pitiless brine ! Indeed one can't bear to look at him long ; nor at that poor woman, so sickly and so beautiful, whom they may as well kill at once, or she will save them the trouble of drawing straws ; and give up to their maws that poor, white, faded, delicate, shrivelled carcass. Ah, what a thing it is to be hungry ! Oh, Eugenius Delacroix ! how can you manage with a few paint-bladders, and a dirty brush, and a careless hand, to dash down such savage histories as these, and fill people's minds with thoughts so dreadful ? Ay, there it is ; whenever I go through that part of the gallery where M. Delacroix's picture is, I always turn away now, and look at a fat woman with a parroquet opposite. For what's the use of being uncomfortable ?

Another great picture is one of about four inches square—' The Chess-players' by M. Meissonnier—truly an astonishing piece of workmanship. No silly tricks of effect and abrupt startling shadow and light, but a picture painted with the minuteness and accuracy of a daguerreotype, and as near as possible perfect in its kind. Two men are playing at chess, and the chess-men are no bigger than pin-heads ; every one of them an accurate portrait, with all the light, shadow, roundness, character and colour, belonging to it.

Of the landscapes it is very hard indeed to speak, for professors of landscapes almost all execute their art well ; but few so well as to strike one with especial attention or to produce much remark. Constable has been a great friend to the new landscape-school in France, who have laid aside the slimy weak manner formerly in vogue, and perhaps have adopted in its place a method equally reprehensible—that of plastering their pictures excessively. When you wish to represent a piece of old timber, or a crumbling wall, or the ruts and stones in a road, this impasting method is very successful, but here the skies are trowelled on ; the light vapouring distances are as thick as plum-pudding, the cool clear shadows are mashed-down masses of sienna and indigo. But it is undeniable that by these violent means a certain power is had, and noon-day effects of strong sunshine are often dashingly rendered.

How much pleasanter is it to see a little quiet grey waste of David Cox than the very best and smartest of such works ! Some men from Dusseldorf have sent very fine scientific faithful pictures, that are a little heavy, but still you see that they are portraits drawn respectfully from the great, beautiful, various, divine face of Nature.

In the statue-gallery there is nothing worth talking about ; and so let us make an end of the Louvre, and politely wish a good morning to everybody.

AN EXHIBITION GOSSIP.[1]

By Michael Angelo Titmarsh.

In a Letter to Monsieur Guillaume, Peintre, à son Atelier, Rue de Monsieur, Faubourg St. Germain, Paris.

Dear Guillaume,

Some of the dullest chapters that ever were written in this world—viz., those on *The History of Modern Europe*, by Russell, begin with an address to some imaginary young friend, to whom the Doctor is supposed to communicate his knowledge. 'Dear John,' begins he, quite affectionately, 'I take up my pen to state that the last of the Carlovingians,'—or, 'Dear John, I am happy to inform you, that the aspect of Europe on the accession of Henry VIII. was so and so.' In the same manner, and in your famous *Lettres à Sophie* the history of the heathen gods and goddesses is communicated to some possible young lady; and this simple plan has, no doubt, been adopted because the authors wished to convey their information with the utmost simplicity possible, and in a free, easy, honest, confidential sort of a way.

This, (as usual), dear Guillaume, has nothing to do with the subject in hand; but I have ventured to place a little gossip concerning the Exhibition, under an envelope inscribed with your respectable name, because I have no right to adopt the editorial *we*, and so implicate a host of illustrious authors, who give their names and aid to Mr. Ainsworth's magazine, in opinions that are very likely not worth sixpence; and because that simple upright I, which often seems egotistical and presuming, is, I fancy, less affected and pert than 'we' often is. 'I' is merely an individual; whereas 'we' is clearly somebody else. 'I' merely expresses an opinion; whereas 'we' at once lays down the law.

Pardon, then, the continued use of the personal pronoun, as I am sure, my dear friend, you will; because as you do not understand a word of English, how possibly can you quarrel with my style?

---

[1] [*Ainsworth's Magazine*, June, 1842.]

We have often had great battles together on the subject of our respective schools of art ; and having seen the two Exhibitions, I am glad to be able to say that ours is the best this year, at least ; though, perhaps, for many years past you have had the superiority. We have more good pictures in our 1400, than you in your 3000 ; among the good, we have more *very* good, than you have this year, (none nobler and better than the drawings of M. Decamps) ; and though there are no such large canvases and ambitious subjects as cover the walls of your salon, I think our painters have more first-class pictures in their humble way.

They wisely, I think, avoid those great historical 'parades' which cover so much space in the Louvre. A young man has sometimes a fit of what is called 'historical painting' ; comes out with a great canvas, disposed in the regular six-feet heroical order ; and having probably half ruined himself in the painting of his piece, which nobody (let us be thankful for it !) buys, curses the decayed state of taste in the country, and falls to portrait-painting, or takes small natural subjects, in which the world can sympathise, and with which he is best able to grapple.   We have no government museums like yours to furnish ;—no galleries in chief towns of departments to adorn ;—no painted chapels, requiring fresh supplies of saints and martyrs, which your artists do to order. Art is a matter of private enterprise here, like everything else : and our painters must suit the small rooms of their customers, and supply them with such subjects as are likely to please them. If you were to make me a present of half a cartoon, or a prophet by Michael Angelo, or a Spanish martyrdom, I would turn the picture against the wall.   Such great things are only good for great edifices, and to be seen occasionally ;—we want pleasant pictures, that we can live with—something that shall be lively, pleasing or tender, or sublime, if you will, but only of a moderate-sized sublimity.   Confess, if you had to live in a huge room with ' The Last Judgment ' at one end of it, and ' The Death of Ananias ' at the other, would not you be afraid to remain alone—or, at any rate, long for a comfortable bare wall ?   The world produces, now and then, one of the great daring geniuses who make those tremendous works of art ; but they come only seldom—and Heaven be thanked for it !   We have had one in our country— John Milton by name.   Honestly confess now, was there not a fervour in your youth when you had a plan of an epic, or, at least, of an heroic Michael-Angelesque picture ?   The sublime rage fades as one grows older and cooler ; and so the good, sensible, honest English painters, for the most part, content themselves with doing no more than they can.

But though we have no heroical canvases, it is not to be inferred that we do not cultivate a humbler sort of high art; and you painters of religious subjects know, from the very subjects which you are called upon to draw, that humility may be even more sublime than greatness. For instance, there is in almost everything Mr. Eastlake does (in spite of a little feebleness of hand and primness of mannerism) a purity which is to us quite angelical, so that we can't look at one of his pictures without being touched and purified by it. Mr. Mulready has an art, too, which is not inferior, and though he commonly takes, like the before-mentioned gentleman, some very simple, homely subject to illustrate, manages to affect and delight one, as much as painter can. Mr. Mulready calls his picture 'The Ford'; Mr. Eastlake styles his, 'Sisters.' The 'Sisters' are two young ladies looking over a balcony; 'The Ford' is a stream, through which some boys are carrying a girl; and how is a critic to describe the beauty in such subjects as these? It would be easy to say these pictures are exquisitely drawn, beautifully coloured, and so forth; but that is not the reason of their beauty: on the contrary, any man who has a mind may find fault with the drawing and colouring of both. Well, there is a charm about them seemingly independent of drawing and colouring; and what is it? There's no foot-rule that I know of to measure it; and the very wisest lecturer in art might define and define, and be not a whit nearer the truth. I can't tell you why I like to hear a blackbird sing; it is certainly not so clever as a piping bullfinch.

I always begin with the works of these gentlemen, and look at them oftenest and longest; but that is only a simple expression of individual taste, and by no means an attempt at laying down the law, upon a subject which is quite out of the limits of all legislation. A better critic might possibly (I say 'possibly,' not as regards the correctness of my own opinion, but the unquestionable merit of the two admirable artists above named), another critic will possibly have other objects for admiration, and if such a person were to say, Pause—before you award pre-eminence to this artist or that, pause—for instance, look at these two Leslies, can anything in point of *esprit* and feeling surpass them?—indeed the other critic would give very sound advice. Nothing can be finer than the comedy of the Scene from Twelfth Night, more joyous, frank, manly, laughter-moving;—or more tender, and grave, and *naïf*, than the picture of Queen Catherine and her attendant. The great beauty of these pieces is the total absence of affectation. The figures are in perfectly quiet, simple positions, looking as if they were not the least aware of the spectator's presence, (a rare quality in pictures, as I think, of which little dramas, the actors, like those upon the living stage, have a great love of 'striking an attitude,' and are always on the look-out for the applause of the lookers-on,) whereas Mr. Leslie's excellent little troop of comedians know their art so perfectly, that it becomes the very image of nature, and the best nature, too. Some painters (skilled in the depicting of such knicknacks) over-power their pieces with 'properties'—guitars, old armours, flower-jugs, curtains and what not. The very chairs and tables in the picture of Queen Catherine have a noble, simple arrangement about them ; they look sad and stately, and cast great dreary shadows —they will lighten up a little, doubtless, when the girl begins to sing.

You and I have been in the habit of accusing one of the cleverest painters of the country of want of poetry : no other than Mr. Edwin Landseer, who, with his marvellous power of hand, a sort of aristocrat among painters, has seemed to say—I care for my dog and my gun ; I'm an English country gentleman, and poetry is beneath me. He has made us laugh sometimes, when he is in the mood, with his admirable humour, but has held off as it were from poetic subjects, as a man would do who was address-ing himself in a fine ball-room to a party of fine people, who would stare if any such subjects were broached. I don't care to own that in former years those dogs, those birds, deer, wild-ducks, and so forth, were painted to such a pitch of desperate perfection, as to make me quite angry—elegant, beautiful, well-appointed, perfect models for grace and manner ; they were like some of our English dandies that one sees, and who never can be brought to pass the limits of a certain polite smile, and decorous, sensible insipidity. The more one sees them, the more vexed one grows, for, be hanged to them, there is no earthly fault to find with them. This, to be sure, is begging the question, and you may not be disposed to allow either the correctness of the simile, or that dandies are insipid, or that field-sports, or pictures thereof, can possibly be tedious ; but, at any rate, it is a comfort to see that a man of genius who is a poet *will* be one sometimes, and here are a couple of noble poetical pieces from Mr. Landseer's pencil. The 'Otter and Trout' has something awful about it ; the hunted stag, pant-ing through the water and startling up the wild-fowl, is a beautiful and touching poem. Oh, that these two pictures, and a few more of different English artists, could be carried across the Channel— say when Mr. Partridge's portrait of the Queen goes, to act as a counterpoise to that work !

A few Etties might likewise be put into the same box, and a

few delightful golden landscapes of Callcott. To these I would add Mr. Maclise's 'Hamlet,' about whose faults and merits there have been some loud controversies ; but in every Exhibition for the last five years, if you saw a crowd before a picture, it was sure to be before his ; and with all the faults people found, no one could go away without a sort of wonder at the prodigious talent of this gentleman. Sometimes it was mere wonder ; in the present Exhibition it is wonder and pleasure too ; and his picture of Hamlet is by far the best, to my thinking, that the artist has ever produced. If, for the credit of Old England (and I hereby humbly beg Mr. Maclise to listen to the suggestion) it could be transported to the walls of your *salon*, it would show French artists, who are accustomed to sneer at the drawing of the English school, that we have a man whose power of drawing is greater than that of any artist among you,—of any artist that ever lived, I should like to venture to say. An artist, possessing this vast power of hand, often wastes it—as Paganini did, for instance —in capriccios, and extravagances, and brilliant feats of skill, as if defying the world to come and cope with him. The picture of the play in 'Hamlet' is a great deal more, and is a noble poetic delineation of the awful story. Here I am obliged to repeat, for the tenth time in this letter, how vain it is to attempt to describe such works by means of pen and ink. Fancy Hamlet, ungartered, lying on the ground, looking into the very soul of King Claudius, who writhes under the play of Gonzago. Fancy the Queen, per-plexed and sad, (she does not know of the murder), and poor Ophelia, and Polonius, with his staff, pottering over the tragedy ; and Horatio, and all sorts of knights and ladies, looking wonder-ing on. Fancy, in the little threatre, the King asleep ; a lamp in front casts a huge forked fantastic shadow over the scene—a shadow that looks like a horrible devil in the background that is grinning and aping the murder. Fancy ghastly flickering tapestries of Cain and Abel on the walls, and all this painted with the utmost force, truth and dexterity—fancy all this, and then you will have not the least idea of one of the most startling, wonderful pictures that the English school has ever produced.

Mr. Maclise may be said to be at the head of the young men ; and though you and I, my dear Guillaume, are both old, and while others are perpetually deploring the past, I think it is a consolation to see that the present is better, and to argue that the future will be better still. You did not give up David with-out a pang, and still think Baron Gérard a very wonderful fellow. I can remember once, when Westall seemed really worth looking at, when a huge black exaggeration of Northcote or Opie struck

me as mighty fine, and Mr. West seemed a most worthy President
of our Academy.   Confess now that the race who succeeded them
did better than they ; and indeed the young men, if I may be
permitted to hint such a thing, do better still—not better than
individuals—for Eastlake, Mulready, Etty, Leslie, are exhibitors
of twenty years' standing, and the young men may live a thousand
years and never surpass them ; but a finer taste is more general
among them than existed some thirty years back, and a purer,
humbler, truer love of nature.   Have you seen 'The Deserted
Village' of the 'Etching Club?'   What charming feeling and
purity is there among most of the designs of these young painters,
and what a credit are they to the English school !

The designers of the 'Etching Club' seem to form a little knot
or circle among themselves ; and though the names of Cope,
Redgrave, Herbert, Stone, have hardly reached you as yet in
France, they will be heard of some day even there, where your
clever people, who can appreciate all sorts of art, will not fail to
admire the quiet, thoughtful, pious, delicate feeling which
characterises the works of this charming little school.   All Mr.
Cope's pictures, though somewhat feeble in hand, are beautifully
tender and graceful.   'The Hawthorn Bush, with seats beneath
the shade, for talking age and whispering lovers made,' is a
beautiful picture for colour, sentiment and composition.   The old
people, properly garrulous, talking of old times, or the crops, or
the Doctor's sermon ; the lovers—a charming pair—loving with
all their souls, kind, hearty, and tender.   The Schoolmaster of
one of his other pictures is an excellent awful portrait of Goldsmith's pedagogue.   Mr. Redgrave's 'Cinderella' is very pleasant,
his landscape beautiful.   Mr. Stone's 'Advice' is full of tender
sentiment, and contains some frank, excellent painting ; but how
vapid all such comments appear, and how can you, on the banks
of the Seine, understand from these sort of vague, unsatisfactory
praises, what are the merits or demerits of the pieces spoken
about !

We have here a delightful, *naïf* artist, Mr. Webster by name,
who has taken little boys under his protection, and paints them
in the most charming comic way—in that best sort of comedy
which makes one doubt whether to laugh or to cry.   His largest
picture this year represents two boys bound for school.   Breakfast is hurried over (a horrid early breakfast) ; the trunk is
packed ; papa is pulling on his boots ; there is the coach coming
down the hill, and the guard blowing his pitiless horn.   All the
little girls are gathered round their brothers : the elder is munch-
ing a biscuit, and determined to be a man ; but the younger,

whom the little sister of all has got hold of by the hand, can't bear the parting, and is crying his eyes out.

I quarrel with Mr. Webster for making one laugh at the boy, and giving him a comic face. I say no man who has experienced it, has a right to laugh at such a sorrow. Did you ever, in France, look out for the diligence that was to take you to school, and hear a fatal conducteur blowing his horn as you waited by the hill side—as you waited with the poor mother, turning her eyes away—and slowly got off the old pony, which you were not to see for six months—for a century—for a thousand miserable years again? Oh, that first night at school! those bitter, bitter tears at night, as you lay awake in the silence, poor little lonely boy, yearning after love and home. Life has sorrows enough, God knows, but, I swear, none like that! I was thinking about all this as I looked at Mr. Webster's picture, and behold it turned itself into an avenue of lime-trees, and a certain old stile that led to a stubble-field; and it was evening, about the 14th of September, and after dinner (how that last glass of wine used to choke and burn in the throat!) and presently, a mile off, you heard, horribly distinct, the whirring of the well-known Defiance coach wheels. It was up in a moment—the trunk on the roof; and—bah! from that day I can't bear to see mothers and children parting.

This, to be sure, is beside the subject; but pray let Mr. Webster change the face of his boy.

Letters (except from young ladies to one another) are not allowed to go beyond a certain decent length; hence, though I may have a fancy to speak to you of many score of other good pictures, out of the fourteen hundred here exhibited, there are numbers which we must pass over without any notice whatever. It is hard to pass by Mr. Richmond's beautiful water-colour figures, without a word concerning them; or Mr. Charles Land-seer's capital picture of 'Ladies and Cavaliers'; or not to have at least half a page to spare, in order to make an onslaught upon Mr. Chalon and his ogling beauties : he has a portrait of Mdlle. Rachel, quite curious for its cleverness and unlikeness, and one of the most chaste and refined of our actresses, Mrs. Charles Kean, who is represented as a killing coquette; and so Mr. Kean may be thankful that the portrait does not in the least resemble his lady.

There is scarce any need to say that the oil portrait-painters maintain their usual reputation and excellence : Mr. Briggs, Mr. Pickersgill, Mr. Grant, show some excellent canvases : the latter's ladies are beautiful, and his 'Lord Cardigan' a fine painting and

portrait ; Mr. Briggs' 'Archbishop' is a noble head and picture ;
Mr. Pickersgill has, among others, a full-length of a Navy Captain,
very fine ; Mr. Linnell's portraits are very fine ; and Mr. S.
Lawrence has one (the Attorney-General), excellently drawn, and
fine in character.   This year's picture of her Majesty is intended
for *your* Majesty, Louis Philippe—perhaps the French court might
have had a more favourable representation of the Queen.   There
is only one 'Duke of Wellington' that I have remarked—(indeed
it must be a weary task to the good-natured and simple old
nobleman to give up to artists the use of his brave face, as he is
so often called upon to do)—at present he appears in a group of
red-coated brethren in arms, called the 'Heroes of Waterloo.'
The picture from the quantity of requisite vermilion, was most
difficult to treat, but is cleverly managed, and the likeness very
good.   All the warriors assembled are smiling, to a man ; and in
the background is a picture of Napoleon, who is smiling too—
and this is surely too great a stretch of good-nature.

What can I say of the Napoleon of Mr. Turner, called (with
frightful satire) the 'Exile and the *Rocklimpet*'?   He stands in
the midst of a scarlet tornado, looking at least forty feet high.

Ah ! says the mysterious poet, from whom Mr. Turner loves to
quote,—

> Ah ! thy tent-formed shell is like
> The soldier's nightly bivouac, alone
> Amidst a sea of blood————
> ————*but you can join your comrades.*
>
> FALLACIES OF HOPE.

These remarkable lines entirely explain the meaning of the
picture ; another piece is described by lines from the same poem,
in a metre more regular :—

> The midnight-torch gleam'd o'er the steamer's side
> And merit's corse was yielded to the tide.

When the pictures are re-hung, as sometimes I believe is the
case, it might perhaps be as well to turn these upside down, and
see how they would look *then ;* the Campo Santo of Venice, when
examined closely, is scarcely less mysterious ; at a little distance,
however, it is a most brilliant, airy, and beautiful picture.   O for
the old days, before Mr. Turner had lighted on 'The Fallacies,' and
could see like other people !

Other landscape-painters, not so romantic, are, as usual, excellent.   You know Mr. Stanfield and Mr. Roberts, in France, as
well as I do : I wish one day you could see the beauty, fresh
English landscapes of Lee and Creswick, where you can almost see

the dew on the fresh grass, and trace the ripple of the water, and the whispering in the foliage of the cool wholesome wind.

There is not an inch more room in the paper ; and a great deal that was to be said about the Water-colour Societies and Suffolk Street must remain unsaid for ever and ever. But I wish you could see a drawing by Miss Setchel, in the Junior Water-colour Society, and a dozen by Mr. Absolon, which are delightful in grace and expression, and in tender, pathetic humour.

M. A. T.

LETTERS ON THE FINE ARTS.[1]

No. 1.—The Art Unions.

From M. A. Titmarsh, Esq., to Sanders McGilp, Esq.

My dear Sanders,

I have always had the highest confidence in your judgment, and am therefore pretty certain that your picture is one of vast merit. The value, you say, is two hundred guineas, and you have, I hope, with laudable prudence, induced your relatives, your grandmother, your confiding aunts, the tradesmen with whom you have little accounts, and the friends with whom you are occasionally kind enough to go and dine, to subscribe to the Art Union, in hopes that one or other of them may gain the principal prize, when your taste as well as their friendship (and where can friendship be better bestowed?) will induce them to purchase your work. To your relatives affection alone would dictate the acquisition of your picture; to your tradesmen you offer, if possible, a still stronger inducement. 'I owe you £40,' you can say to Mr. Snip, your respected tailor: 'I cannot pay those £40; but gain the first prize, and you have my picture for two hundred guineas, which, in reality, is worth five hundred, plus the payment of your bill, the amount of which you can deduct from the sum due to myself.' Thus Mr. Snip gets

A picture (valued at 500 guineas) .	. £525	0	0
The payment of his bill . .	. 40	0	0
And costs of Writ . . .	. 2	2	0
	£567	2	0

in return for a single sovereign subscribed to the Union.

The advantage of Art Unions has never before, I believe, been considered in this light; and if every artist would but go round to his tradesmen and represent to them the truth as here laid down, no doubt great numbers of additional patrons would be found for the noble art you practise.

[1] [*The Pictorial Times*, March 18, 1843.

How many a man, for instance, has not one, but half-a-dozen tailors in the category in which I have placed Mr. Snip. Well, let them all subscribe;—the more the merrier. ' If one win, gentlemen,' you say, ' remember I am in a condition to pay all the rest their accounts.' And thus is an interest for Art brought home to the bosoms and boards of six deserving families.

Is, or is not, the principle a good one ? Are, or are not, tradesmen to be paid ? Are, or are not, artists to be well-clothed ? And would, or would not, the diffusion of their divine science enlarge the heart and soften the rude manners of the million ? What, on this head, does Hesiod observe ? The Teian bard nobly remarks,—

Ινγεννας διδικισσε φιδηλιτερ αρτης,
Ημολλιτ μωρης νεκ σινιτ εσσε φερως.

And if the principle *be* a good one, I say it should be universal. Say (as an encouragement) to the collector who comes for your rate, ' I'll pay you if you take a ticket in the *Art Union!* ' Remark to your butcher, in a pleasant way, ' Mr. Brisket, I desire from you, for your own advantage, one stake more.'

' From the loin, or where ? ' says he.

' No,' say you, laughingly interrupting him, ' a stake in the *Art Union.*'

And point out to your washerwoman what an ennobling and glorious thing it would be—a holy effluence, a bright and beaming radiance woven into the dark chain of her existence,—(or other words of might and poesy suited to her capacity), point out —I say, what a pleasure it would be to her to be able to exclaim, ' I wash Mr. McGilp's shirts—and look ! one of his five hundred guinea master-pieces hangs yonder, over my mangle.'

It is in his power, it is in anybody's power. The very Malay sweeper who shivers at the corner of your street, and acts as your model, may easily save money enough to take a ticket, and have his portrait, as Othello, to decorate his humble place of abode.

You may fancy, my friend, that there is some caricature in this, and possibly you are right. You will never stoop to Mr. Snip in the manner pointed out by me ; you are above entreating your washerwoman, cutting jokes with your butcher, or cajoling the respectable gentleman who calls for your contributions once a quarter. Art, say you, is above paltry speculation and mean ideas of gain. An artist never stoops to intrigue, nor chaffers for money. He is the priest of nature, called to worship at her glorious altar, by special vocation ; one chosen out of the million, and called up to the high places ; in short, you will make a speech, crammed with fine words, proving your disinterestedness, and the awful poetical nature of your calling.

Psha! my good friend, let us have no more of this stale talk. You are a tradesman as well as my lord on the woolsack, or Mr. Smith selling figs, or General Sones breathing freely and at his ease in an atmosphere of cannon-balls. You each do your duty in your calling, and according to your genius, but you want to be paid for what you do. You want the best pay, and the greatest share of reputation you can get. You will do nothing dishonest in the pursuit of your trade; but will you not yield a little 'to the exigencies of the public service'? General Sones, though he may have his own opinion of the Chinese war, will attack mandarins without mercy; my Lord Chancellor has pleaded many a queer cause before he reposed on yonder woolsack; Smith has had recourse to many little harmless tricks to get a sale for his figs and treacle; and you (as I take it) are not a whit better than they. Did you ever paint a lady handsomer in her portrait than nature made her? Did you ever, when your immense genius panted to be at work on some vast historical piece, crush your aspirations so far as to sit down and depict a plain gentleman in a buff waistcoat and a watch-chain, for the sake of the twenty guineas which were to be elicited from his ample pepper-and-salt pantaloons? You have done all this, and were quite right in doing it, too. How else are the little McGilps to get their dinners, or your lady the means of discharging her weekly bills?

And now you will begin, I trust, to perceive that the ridicule cast upon the Art Union system in the first sentences of this letter is not in reality so very severe; it is the sort of sneering language which the enemies of those establishments are in the habit of indulging in, though expressed as high, no doubt you will think in a far more satiric and witty manner than most of the anti-Unionists have at command.

Hear, for instance, *The Athenæum.* 'So early,' says that journal, 'as 1837, we put on record our opinion that the Art Union would and must of necessity tend to the still further degradation of Art. Any man,' we observed, 'who purchases pictures may be presumed to have a love for, and this will in the end generate a knowledge of, Art. But there will be many subscribers who desire only a little gambling—to risk a pound for the sake of winning a hundred—and who would quite as soon join in a raffle for a horse, or a snuff-box, or a pipe of port wine, as for a picture. The motive of the subscriber is of no consequence, so long as others have to dispose of the money; but the Art Union proposes that each subscriber 'shall select for himself.' Now, is it not certain that such patronage must tend to degrade Art? The scheme may be beneficial to the lowest class of artists, but utterly ruinous to Art itself. When every individual, be he *whom* he may, is allowed to follow his own judgment in the disposal of his prize-money, the best results can be but an irresponsible indulgence of individual whim and caprice—the worst and certain in the degradation of Art. Men who paint to live, instead of working with all their power, be it more or less, up to the best and highest judgments, must solicit the sweet voices of the uninformed, the chance prize-holders and therefore purchasers of the Art Unions.'

So writes *The Athenæum*, and you will at once perceive the truth of my previous assertion:—1. That *The Athenæum's* arguments resemble those employed at the commencement of this letter. 2. That the arguments at the beginning of this letter are far more cleverly and wickedly put.

Let us now proceed to demolish the one and the other, and we will, if you please, take the dicta of *The Athenæum* in the first place into consideration.

'Every man (says *The Athenæum*) who purchases pictures, may be presumed to have a love for, and this will in the end generate a knowledge of, Art.'

'But this Art Union is joined by many for the sake of gambling, and who would *quite as soon* join in a raffle for a horse, or a snuff-box, or a pipe of port wine, as for a picture.'

Why quite as soon? A man who wants a pipe of port wine does not, we presume, raffle for a horse; or being eagerly desirous of a snuff-mull, he does not raffle for a pipe of port wine. There are certainly in the world many 'uninformed' persons, as the insinuating *Athenæum* remarks; let us say at once there are fools, but not such tremendous fools as our misanthropic contemporary would discover. No, no. A man raffles for a horse, because the dealers or the knackers will give him a price for it, or because his wife wishes to be driven out in a gig, or because he has a mind to cut a dash in the ring. A man raffles for a gold snuff-box, because he is fond of Macabaw, or because he likes to sport such a box after dinner, or because he wishes to make it a present to Mr. Boys when he brings out any more of his relatives' lithographs, or for some other simple and equally apparent reason. And so for a pipe of port wine, a man risks his money in order to gain it, because he likes port wine, or because he can sell it, or because he wishes to present a few dozens to a friend. I wish, for my part, I had a friend who desired to dispose of either of the three articles; but that is a mere personal ejaculation, and nothing to the point.

The point is that a man bids money for a horse, because he wants it ; for a picture, because he would like to have a picture. Common charity must admit so much good sense in the world. Well, then, it is granted that a man joins in a raffle for a set of pictures because he is interested in pictures ; that is, *he may be presumed to have a love for Art*. And a love for Art, in the end, says *The Athenæum, will generate a knowledge of Art*. Amen. In that case the excellence of Art Unions is established at once.

But no, says the philosopher who argues every week from under the columns of the temple of Minerva ; this love which generates knowledge is only conceded to men who purchase pictures, not to those who raffle for them ! Is not this a little hard ? How much income tax must a man pay in order to have a decent love of Art ; a love that shall be potent enough to become the father of a future knowledge ?

I may say, without exaggeration, that Sir Robert Peel is richer than I am ; but does it follow that he loves Art better ? It may be, or not ; but at least the right honourable baronet's income does not establish the superiority of his taste. Let any gentleman go into a pastry-cook's, and eat raspberry tarts ; ten to one, pressed against the window of the shop you will see the blue nose of a penniless urchin, who is looking at the good things with all his might. Would one say that Dives, because he eats the tarts, loved them better than the little Lazarus who yearned after them ? No, even *The Athenæum* would not say that ; the cruel, cruel *Athenæum*.

Now, suppose that round that shop-window, and allured by the same charming prospect which has brought their comrade thither, other little Lazaruses should assemble : they love tarts ; they are penniless ; but still not altogether without coin. Say they have a farthing apiece ; and clubbing together their wealth, or poverty rather, these rascally young gamblers made a lottery in the cap of one of them, and what is the consequence ? the winner of the prize steps in and takes a raspberry tart from the very same tray at which great Dives himself has been gormandising. It is gambling, certainly ; but I suspect the pastry-cook (considering its result) will look upon the crime rather justly—she might never have sold her wares but for that TART UNION.

I shall resume this subject next week with philosophical considerations upon Polytechnic Societies, upon the lunar prospectus (or that of Mr. Moon), and upon the puerile distribution (or that of Mr. Boys).

Meanwhile, dear McGilp, I remain,
Your very humble servant,
MICHAEL ANGELO TITMARSH.

No. 2.—The Objections against Art Unions.[1]

M. A. Titmarsh, Esq., to Sanders McGilp, Esq.

My dear Sanders,

The Tart Union alluded to last week has been appreciated; and I am given to understand that several young gentlemen about Covent Garden and the foundation colleges in the City (where the youthful students wear leather breeches and green coats, and caps famous for their similarity in shape to the muffin) have put the scheme into practice, and are very eager in borrowing or begging farthings for the pastry-cook's interest and their own.

That the scheme will benefit the former is clear; and should any of them be inclined, by way of gratitude, to forward to the office of the paper a *proof plate* of their tarts, there are several juvenile persons about the premises who will gladly give an opinion of their merits.

One of the union or distribution schemes mentioned in our last has forwarded proofs of its claims to public favour, proofs of its puffs, we would say, but that is a pun, and the truth must be told, let what will come of it, and we are now solemnly met, my brave McGilp, to discuss it. The fact is that the goodness or badness of the prints in question does not, at least for the sake of the argument, matter a fig. Suppose a man (by means of the electrotype, of course) were enabled to produce a series of copies of Mr. Catnach's ballads, and charge a guinea, two guineas—a thousand pounds; three farthings, for whitey-brown proofs of the same. He is quite free to do so. Nobody need buy unless they like. Or suppose he could (always by means of the electrotype) produce India paper proof plates of all the cartoons, and sell them for a halfpenny? He is quite as much at liberty to do the one as the other; and I do believe that the reason of fair dealing and moderate prices in the world has been not so much the honesty as the selfishness of our nature. We sell cheap, because no one will buy else. We are honest because no one *will* trust us unless they *can* trust us.

In a doubtful commerce with few concurrents and uncertain gains, men do not unfrequently cheat. But competition hustles roguery pretty quickly out of the market; the swaggering, swindling, lying imposter has no chance against the burly good sense of the public.

And I must confess, for my part, that if a man has a thirty-

guinea watch to raffle for, and thirty persons are willing to
subscribe so much amongst them, and try the chance of winning
it, I see no much greater harm in this 'union' than in many
other speculations where (of course) chances exist of losing or
winning.   But to moralise on the Art Union case because of this
harmless peddling with guineas, and to say that it provokes a
spirit of gambling, is too hard.   Is it altogether sinful to play a
rubber of whist at shilling points ?   Does it imply an abominable
desire of gain and a frightful perversion in the individual who
bets half-a-crown on the rubber ?   Are we basely cast down
because we lose, or brutally exultant because we win half-a-score
of shillings ?   If it be a deadly sin, heaven help our grandfathers
and grandmothers, who played cards every night of their lives,
and must be anything but comfortable now.   But let us hope
that with regard to the criminality of the proceeding *The
Athenæum* is wrong.   Many of us have tried a raffle at Margate,
and slept no worse for it.   Once, at school, I drew lots with two
other boys, and the prize was a flogging ; and it does not much
matter which of us won ; but the others were not very sorry
about it, depend on that.   No ; let this harmless little sin pass.
As long as it provokes no very evil passions, as long as the
pleasure of winning is great, and the pain of losing small, let
gentlemen and ladies have their sport, and bet their bet, and our
moralists not altogether despair.   You cannot say that the Art
Union supporters are actuated by a violent or unwholesome love
of gambling ; they don't injure their properties by the subscription
of their guinea ; they don't absent themselves from home, contract
dissipated habits, bring their wives and families to ruin.   They
give a guinea, and are not much the better or the worse for the
outlay.   This is an encouragement of lotteries, *The Athenæum*
may say, presently ; but indeed the objection is not worth a fig.

The old lotteries were undisguised robberies.   The Art Unions
are none.   The old lotteries lived upon atrocious lies and puffs,
encouraged silly people with exaggerated notions of gain.   The
Art Union offers but to purchase pictures with the aggregate of
your money, and to distribute the pictures so bought.   There are
no falsehoods told, and no absurd lying baits held out.   A country
book-club is a lottery, a wicked gambling transaction in which
squires and parsons take a part.   A house or life assurance
is a lottery.   You take the odds there to win in a certain
event ; and may by very strait-laced moralists be accused
of 'gambling,' for so providing against fortune ; but the Parliament has sanctioned this gambling, and the state draws a
considerable profit from it.   An underwriter gambles when he

insures a ship ; calculating that he has a profit on the chances. A man gambles when he buys stock to sell afterwards, or a newspaper, or a house, or any other commodity, upon which profit or loss may accrue. In the latter cases, perhaps, he gambles as he does at whist, knowing himself to be a good player, and trusting to skill and chance for his success. But in the former cases, the underwriter of the ship or house has no security ; it is sheer luck ; dependent on a fire or a gale of wind, with the *pull* of the chances in his favour.

In a commercial country, then, where there is so much authorised gambling for profit, a little gambling for mere amusement's and kindness's sake may be tolerated. Let it be allowed, at any rate, that there is no great criminality in the Art Union species of gambling ; and so quietly pass over the moral objection to the scheme. Then there has been lately mooted in the papers a legal objection ; but that is not a very frightful one. Both of the learned gentlemen who have been consulted and have pronounced for and against Art Unions have allowed that there is no danger of prosecution, and that poor bugbear will frighten honest folks no more.

But the strong objection is that on the part of some artists of the old school, who say that the Art Union system deteriorates Art ; that it sets painters speculating upon fancy pieces, to suit the taste of the prize-holders ; that they think this will be a taking two-hundred guinea subject, or that a neat gaudy piece that will be sure to hook something ; and they paint accordingly.

Now, let any man who has looked at English picture-galleries for the last ten or twenty years be called upon to say from his heart, whether there has not been a great, a noble, improvement ? —whether there is not infinitely more fancy, feeling, poetry, education, among artists as a body now than then ? Good Heavens ! if they do paint what are called *subjects*, what is the harm ? If people do like fancy pieces, where is the great evil ? If I have no fancy to have my own portrait staring me in the face in the dining-room, and would rather have Mr. Stone's 'one particular star,' for instance (and it is a charming picture), am I such a degraded wretch ? This is but cant on the part of humbugs on the one side, and on the other the ultra-ticklishness of too susceptible minds.

What does the charge amount to ? That the artist tries by one means or other to consult the taste of the public. The public is ignorant ; therefore its choice is bad ; therefore the artists paint bad pictures ; therefore the taste grows worse and worse ; therefore the public grows worse and worse ; therefore the public and the artist are degraded by a desperate, helpless, arithmetical progression, out of which, as one fancies, there is no escape.

But look what the real state of the case is, as it has been recited by a weekly paper (*The Age*)—that, too, moans over the degeneracy of its namesake, and prophesies a most pathetic future for Englishmen, because they have been lately seized with a love for illustrated books. First, says *The Age*, came *The Observer*, with its picture of Thurtell's Cottage, then *The Hive*, then *The Mirror*, then this and that, then *The Illustrated London News*, then *The Pictorial Times*. Well, *après?* as the French say. *The Hive* was better than Thurtell's Cottage, *The Mirror* was better than *The Hive*, *The News* better than *The Mirror*, and *The Times* better than *The News*, and (though *The Times* readers may fancy the thing impossible) the day will come when something shall surpass even *The Times*, and so on to the infinity of optimism. And so with pictures as with prints. The public is not used to having the former yet ; but wait awhile and it will take them ; and take them better and better every day. The commercial energy of our hearty country is such that where there is a small demand dealers well know how to raise it to a great one ; and raise fresh wants by fresh supplies ingeniously insinuated and by happy inventions in advance. As to GENIUS, that is not to be spoken of in this way ; but genius is rare ; it comes to us but once in many, many years ; and do you think the genius of painting less likely to flourish in our country because people are buying (by means of these Art Unions) five hundred little fancy pictures per annum, in addition to the ten thousand portraits they bought before ?

As for aristocratic patronage of Art only, let us ask in what state was Art before Art Unions began ? Did artists complain or not ? Did they say that there was no opportunity to cultivate their poetical feelings, and that they must paint portraits to live ? I am sure the people of England are likely to be better patrons of art than the English aristocracy ever were, and that the aristocracy have been tried and *didn't* patronise it ; that they neither knew how to value a picture nor an artist ; what artist ever got so good a place as a tenth-rate lawyer, or as a hundredth-rate soldier, or as a lucky physician, or as an alderman who had made a good speculation, or a country squire who had a borough ? The aristocracy never acknowledged the existence of Art in this country, for they never acknowledged the artist. They were the handsomest men and women in the world, and they had their simpering faces painted, but what have they done for Art to honour it ? No, no ; *they* are not the friends of genius. That day is over ; its friends lie elsewhere ; rude and uncultivated as yet, but hearty, generous, and eager. It may put up with rough fare ; but it can't live in ante-chambers with lackeys, eating my lord's broken meat ; equality is its breath, and *sympathy* the condition of its existence. What sympathy did my lords ever give it ? No ; the law, the sword, the alderman's consols, the doctor's pill, they can stomach ; they can reconcile these to their lordly nature, and infuse them into their august body. But the poet had best come lower. What have their lordships to do with *him ?* He has never been one of their intimates. In the old song of Schiller, Love bids the poet, now that the earth is partitioned among the strong and wealthy, to come to Heaven in his distress, in which there will always be a place for him ; but he has to try the people yet—the weak and poor ; and they whose union makes their strength, depend on it, have a shelter and a welcome for him.

And so (though the taste of the public might be better than it is now, of which there is no question) I think we have every right to hope that it *will* be better. There are a thousand men read and think to-day, for one who read on this same day of April, 1743. The poet and artist is called upon to appeal to the few no longer. His profit and fame are with the many ; and do not let it be thought irreverence to put the profit and fame together. Nobody ever denies the Duke of Wellington's genius, because his Grace receives twenty thousand a year from his country in gratitude for the services by him ; and if the nation should take a fancy to reward poets in the same way, we have similarly no right to quarrel with the verdict.

The dukedoms, twenty-thousands-a-year, Piccadilly-palaces, and the like, are not, however, pleaded for here. Miss Coutts or Mr. Rothschild have the like (or may, no doubt, for the asking), and nobody grudges the wealth, though neither ever were in the battle of Waterloo, that I know of. But let us ask, as the condition of improvement in Art, if not fame and honour, at least sympathy, from the public, for the artist. The refinement of taste will come afterwards ; and as every man a little conversant with the art of painting, or any other art, must know how his judgment improves, and how by degrees he learns to admire justly, so the public will learn to admire more and more justly every day. The sixpenny prints they buy twenty years hence will be better than the six-penny prints now ; the Art Union pictures they select, better than those which frighten the desponding susceptibilities of our philosophers now-a-days. Away with these prophets of ill, these timid old maids of Cassandras, who lift up their crutches, and

o

croak, and cry 'Woe!' It is the nature of the old bodies to despond, but let 'us youth' be not frightened by their prate. If any publisher could find it worth his while to bring out a hundred beautiful engravings for a penny, depend on it Art would not retrograde in the country. If a hundred thousand people chose to subscribe to the Art Unions, the interest for Art would be so much the greater, the encouragement to artists so much the greater; and if you interest the people and encourage the artists, it is absurd to suppose that one or the other would go back.

But this, as you will doubtless observe, has nothing to do with the lunatic prospectus (that of Mr. Moon), or with the puerile distribution (that of Mr. Boys). Let us consider the sham Art Unions another day. What I wish to observe in the above sentences is, that the people are the artist's best friends; that for his reputation and profit he must henceforth, he had best look to them; and rather than work for a class of *patrons*, he had better rely for support on his friends. If you have something that is worth the telling — something for the good of mankind — it is better to take it to a hundred tailors or tinkers than to one duke or two dandies (speaking with perfect respect of both), and as an actor would rather have a hundred people in the pit than but one hearer who had paid ten pounds for a private box, an artist need have no squeamish objections to the same popularity, and will find a more sure and lasting profit in it. Many men of genius will say, 'No; we do not want the applause of the vulgar; give us the opinion of the few.' Who prevents them? They *have* those few as before; but because the artist of a lower walk changes his patron, and, instead of catering for the private boxes, appeals to the pit, there is no harm done. The pit, it is my firm belief, knows just as much about the matter in question as the boxes know; and now you have made Art one of the wants of the public, you will find the providers of the commodity and its purchasers grow more refined in their tastes alike; and the popular critic of a few years hence calling for good pictures, when now bad ones please him.

How should he know better as yet? His betters have taught him to admire Books of Beauty, trashy, flashy coronation pictures, and the like tawdry gimcracks, which please a feeble intellect and a debauched taste. Give him time, and he will learn to like better things.

And for the artist himself, will he not gain by bringing to the public market the article which he was obliged before to prepare for individual patronage? He has made many more sacrifices to the latter than ever he will be called upon to do for the former.

His independence does not suffer by honest barter in the public place, any more than an author's does who takes his wares to the bookseller or newspaper, and asks and gets his price. The writer looks to my lord no longer, but he has found a better and surer friend; and so for Art: I would like to see Art Unions all over England, from London to Little Peddlington: every one of the subscribers become interested in a subject about which he has not thought hitherto, and which was kept as the exclusive privilege of his betters.

The Spectator has an excellent suggestion with regard to Art Unions, I think; which is, that a committee should purchase pictures with the funds of the Union, and that the prize-holder should then choose. Bad pictures would not, probably, be bought in this way; and the threatened degradation of Art would then be averted. Perhaps the majority of the present Unionists, however, would not accede to this plan, and prefer to choose their pictures for themselves. Well: let them keep to the old plan; and let us have another Art Union as the new. The more the better—the more *real* Unions; as for the sham ones, we will discourse of these anon.

Yours, my dear McGilp,

M. A. TITMARSH.

P.S.—I hope your cartoon is in a state of forwardness; we shall see in a month or two what the giants of Art can do. But, meantime, do not neglect your little picture out of *Gil Blas* or *The Vicar of Wakefield* (of course it is out of one or the other). Let those humble intellects which can only understand common feeling and every-day life have, too, their little gentle gratifications. Why should not the poor in spirit be provided for as well as the tremendous geniuses? If a child take a fancy to a penny theatrical print, let him have it; if a workman want a green parrot with a bobbing head to decorate his humble mantel-piece, let us not grudge it to him; and if an immense supereminent intelligence cannot satisfy his poetical craving with anything less sublime than Milton, or less vast than Michael Angelo,—all I can say, for my part, is, that I wish he may get it.

The kind and beneficent Genius of Art has pleasures for all according to their degree; and spreads its harmless happy feast for big and little,—for the Titanic appetite that can't be satisfied with anything less than a roasted elephant, as well as for the small humble cock-robin of an intellect that can sing its little grace and make its meal on a bread-crumb.

No. 3.—THE ROYAL ACADEMY.[1]

MY DEAR McGILP,

I think every succeeding year shows a progress in the English school of painters. They paint from *the heart* more than of old, and less from the old heroic, absurd, incomprehensible unattainable rules. They look at Nature very hard, and match her with the best of their eyes and ability. They do not aim at such great subjects as heretofore, or at subjects which the world is pleased to call great, viz., tales from Hume or Gibbon of royal personages under various circumstances of battle, murder, and sudden death. Lemprière, too, is justly neglected, and Milton has quite given place to *Gil Blas* and *The Vicar of Wakefield*.

The heroic, and peace be with it! has been deposed; and our artists, in place, cultivate the pathetic and the familiar. But a few, very few, worshippers of the old gods remain. There are only two or three specimens in the present exhibition of the grand historic style. There is a huge dim-coloured picture, in the large room, by an Academician, probably; but I have neither the name nor the subject; there is Mr. Haydon's history-piece of 'The Maid of Saragossa'—a great, coarse, vulgar, ill-drawn, ill-painted caricature; and an allegory or two by other artists, in the old-fashioned style.

The younger painters are content to exercise their art on subjects far less exalted: a gentle sentiment, an agreeable, quiet incident, a tea-table tragedy, or a bread-and-butter idyl, suffices for the most part their gentle powers. Nor surely ought one to quarrel at all with this prevalent mode. It is at least natural, which the heroic was not.

Bread and butter can be digested by every man; whereas Prometheus on his rock, or Orestes in his strait-waistcoat, or Hector dragged behind Achilles' car, or Britannia, guarded by Religion and Neptune, welcoming General Tomkins in the Temple of Glory — the ancient, heroic, allegorical subjects — can be supposed deeply to interest very few of the inhabitants of this city or kingdom. We have wisely given up pretending that we were interested in such, and confess a partiality for more simple and homely themes.

The Exhibition rooms are adorned with numberless very pleasing pictures in this quiet taste. Mr. Leslie offers up to our simple household gods a 'Vicar of Wakefield'; Mr. Maclise

---

[1] [*The Pictorial Times,* May 13, 1843.]

presents a 'Gil Blas'; Mr. Redgrave gently depicts the woes of
a governess who is reading a black-edged note, and the soft
sorrows of a country lass going to service; Mr. Stone has the
last appeal of a rustic lover; Mr. Charles Landseer has a party
drinking quietly under the trees; Mr. McNee shows a young
person musing in a quiet nook, and thinking of her love.

All these subjects, it will be observed, are small subjects; but
they are treated, for the most part, with extraordinary skill.   As
for Lady Blarney, in Mr. Leslie's picture, with that wonderful
leer of her wicked, squinting, vacant eyes, she is as good as the
very best Hogarth; her face is the perfection of comedy; and
the honest primrose countenances round about, charming for their
simplicity, and rich kindly humour.   The 'Malade Imaginaire' is
no less excellent; more farcical and exaggerated in the arrangement; but the play is farcical and exaggerated; and the picture,
as the play, is full of jovial, hearty laughter.   No artist possesses
this precious quality of making us laugh kindly so much as Mr.
Leslie.   There is not the least gall or satire in it; only sheer
irresistible good-humour.

Now, in the *tableau* by Mr. Maclise, many of the principal
personages are scowling, or ogling, or grinning and showing their
teeth, with all their might, and yet the spectator, as I fancy, is
by no means so amused as by those more quiet actors in Mr.
Leslie's little comedies.   There is, especially in Mr. Maclise's
company, one young fellow who ought to be hissed, or who
should have humble parts to act, and not be thrust forward in
the chief characters, as he has of late years, with his immense
grinning mouthful of white teeth and knowing, leering eyes.   The
ladies we have seen too, repeatedly, and it must be confessed they
are not of the high comedy sort.   The characters appear to be,
as it were, performing a tableau from *Gil Blas*, not the actual
heroes or heroines of that easy jovial drama.

As for the 'properties' of the piece, to use the dramatic phrase,
they are admirably rich and correct.   The painter's skill in representing them is prodigious.   The plate, the carvings, the wine-
flasks, the poor old melancholy monkey on his perch, the little
parrots, the carpet, are painted with a truth and dexterity quite
marvellous, and equal the most finished productions of the Dutch
schools.   Terbury never painted such a carpet; every bit of
plate is a curiosity of truthful representation.   This extraordinary
power of minute representation is shown in another picture by
Mr. Maclise, 'The Cornish Waterfall,' round which every leaf in
every tree is depicted, and in which the figure of the girl is a
delightful specimen of the artist's graphic power.

Mr. Redgrave's 'Going to Service' is not so well drawn as his pictures of former years. An old lady in an arm-chair, two young sisters embracing each other, a brother very stiff and solemn in a smock frock, and a waggon waiting outside, tell the story of this little domestic comedy. It has a milk-and-watery pathos. The governess has her bread-and-butter by her side, too : but the picture is much better, the girl's figure extremely beautiful and graceful, and the adjuncts of the picture are painted with extreme care and skill.

Mr. Stone's 'Last Appeal' is beautiful. It is evidently the finish of the history of the two young people who are to be seen in the Water-Colour Exhibition. There the girl is smiling and pleased, and there is some hope still for the pale, earnest young man who loves her with all his might. But between the two pictures, between Pall Mall and the Trafalgar Column, sad changes have occurred. The young woman has met a big life-guardsman, probably, who has quite changed her views of things ; and you see that the last appeal is made without any hope for the appellant. The girl hides away her pretty face, and we see that all is over. She likes the poor fellow well enough, but it is only as a brother ; her heart is with the life-guardsman, who is strutting down the lane at this moment, with his laced cap on one ear, cutting the buttercups' heads off with his rattan cane. The whole story is told, without, alas ! the possibility of a mistake, and the young fellow in the grey stockings has nothing to do but to jump down the well, at the side of which he has been making his appeal.

The painting of this picture is excellent ; the amateur will not fail to appreciate the beauty of the drawing, the care, and at the same time freedom, of the execution, and a number of excellences of method which are difficult to be described in print, except in certain technical terms that are quite unsatisfactory to the general reader.

Mr. Charles Landseer's 'Monks of Rubrosi' is the best, perhaps, of his pictures. The scene is extremely cheerful, fresh, and brilliant ; the landscape almost as good as the figures, and these are all good. Two grave-looking, aristocratic fathers of the abbey have been fly-fishing ; a couple of humbler brethren in brown are busy at a hamper of good things ; a gallant young sportsman in green velvet lies on the grass and toasts a pretty lass that is somehow waiting upon their reverences. The picture is not only good, but has the further good quality of being *pleasant ;* and some clever artist will do no harm in condescending so far to suit the general taste. There is no reason, after all, why a man should not humble himself to this extent, and make friends with the public patron.

For instance, take Mr. Poole's picture of 'Solomon Eagle and the Plague of London.' It is exceedingly clever; but who would buy such a piece? Figures writhe over the picture blue and livid with the plague—some are dying in agony—some stupid with pain. You see the dead-cart in the distance; and in the midst stands naked Solomon, with blood-shot eyes and wild maniacal looks, preaching death, woe, and judgment. Where should such a piece hang? It is too gloomy for a hospital, and surely not cheerful enough for a dining-room. It is not a religious picture, that would serve to decorate the walls of a church. A very dismal, gloomy conventicle might, perhaps, be a suitable abode for it; but would it not be better to tempt the public with something more good-humoured?

Of the religious pieces, Mr. Herbert's 'Woman of Samaria' will please many a visitor to the Exhibition, on account of the beauty and dignity of the head of the Saviour. The woman, as I thought, was neither beautiful nor graceful. Mr. Eastlake's 'Hagar' is beautiful as everything else by this accomplished artist; but here, perhaps, the beauty is too great, and the pain not enough. The scene is not represented with its actual agony and despair; but it is, as it were, a sort of limning to remind you of the scene; a piece of mystical poetry with Ishmael and Hagar for the theme. I must confess that Mr. Linnett's 'Supper at Emmaus' did not strike me as the least mystical or poetical, and that Mr. Etty's 'Entombment' was anything but holy and severe. Perhaps the most pious and charming head in the whole Exhibition, is that of the Queen, by Mr. Leslie, in his Coronation picture; it has a delightful modesty and a purity quite angelical.

Mr. Etty's pictures of the heathen sort are delightful; wonderful for a gorgeous flush of colour, such as has belonged, perhaps, to no painter since Rubens. But of these we will discourse next week.

No. 4.—The Royal Academy.[1]   (Second Notice.)

My dear McGilp,

If her Majesty is the purchaser of all the royal pictures by Paris, by Hayter, by Leslie, by Landseer,—of all the royal portraits by these and a score more in and out of the Academy,—there must be a pretty large gallery at Buckingham Palace by this time, and, let it be said with respect, a considerable sameness in the collection.   The royal face is a very handsome one, and especially in the medallion-shape, in gold.   I would like to look at thousands of them every week, for my part, and would never tire in extending my cabinet.

But, confess, my dear Sir, are we not beginning to have enough of royal parade-pictures ?   And are not the humbler classes somewhat tired of them ?   Only the publishers and the grandees, their enlightened patrons, still continue to admire. Dark rooms are still prepared for such ; gas-jets and large sub-scription books artfully laid on and out.   The Court Guide still goes to see Winterhalter's portrait of the Queen ('I wish they may get it,' as the Duchess of —— observes ; the picture is not painted by Winterhalter ; but what do *they* know, whether it be good or bad ?).   The Court Guide still buys huge proofs of her Majesty's marriage, or the Princess's christening, or the real authorised coronation picture (every one of the half-dozen are real authorised coronation pictures), and is content therewith.   Ah ! Heaven bless that elegant aristocracy of England ; that wise, that enlightened, that noble clan of our betters !

The subject of these pictures is worthy of their noble souls,—fit for their vast comprehensions ; and as the poor workman buys his prints of 'The Prodigal Son's Progress,' the young cockney-buck his portrait of Mrs. Honey, or some other beauty with long ringlets and short petticoats, the sporting man his varnished hunting-piece, so the great have their likings, and we judge them by what they admire.

And what an admiration theirs is !   There's her Majesty in state !   What a lovely white satin !   and the velvet, my dear, painted to the very life.   Every single jewel's a portrait, I give you my honour ; and Prince Albert's own star and garter sat to the artist ; the Archbishop's wig is done to a hair ; and was there ever a more wonderful piece of art than that picture of the Duke in his orders and his epaulets, and his white Kerseymere

[1] [*The Pictorial Times*, May 27, 1843.]

pantaloons? Round the sovereign are all the maids of honour; round the maids of honour all the officers of state; round the officers of state all the beefeaters and gentlemen-at-arms; and on these magnificent subjects our painters are continually employed. Noble themes for the exercise of genius! brilliant proofs of enlightened public taste! The court milliners must be proud to think that their works are thus immortalised, and the descendants of our tailors will look at these pieces with a justifiable family pride.

Mr. Leslie has had to chronicle coats and satin-slips in this way, and has represented *his* scene in the drama of the coronation (how many more episodes of the same piece have been represented and by how many more painters, I don't know), and his picture is so finely done, so full of beauty and grandeur, that for once a court picture has been made interesting. I have remarked on the principal figure before,—the exquisite grace and piety represented in the countenance and attitude of the Queen; but the judgment of the quality as far as I have been able to gather it (and it is good to this end to play the spy's part, and overhear the opinions of the genteel personages who come to see the Exhibition)—the genteel judgment is decidedly against the painter, and his portraits are pronounced to be failures, and his pictures quite inferior to many others by others' hands. Let us hope the opinion will be so general, that this charming painter shall never be called upon to paint a court ceremony again. I would rather see honest Mrs. Primrose's portrait by him than that of the loveliest lady of honour; and the depicting of uniforms and lappets and feathers left to those politer artists whose genius is suited to subjects so genteel.

There is no Prince Albert this year, I regret to say; but we have two portraits of her Majesty, in trains, velvets, arm-chairs, etc.—one by the President [1] and one by Mr. Grant—and neither worth a crown-piece. One of the most exquisite and refined little sketches ever seen is the portrait of Lady Lyttelton, by the latter artist; it is a delightful picture of a beautiful and high-bred maiden. Mr. Chalon's aristocracy does not ogle and simper quite so much as in former years; and their ladyships are painted with all the artist's accustomed skill. Mr. Richmond's heads are excellent as usual; and there is a rival to these gentlemen, who has given us a water-colour portrait of the Bishop of Exeter, in which the amiable and candid features of that prelate are depicted with great fidelity and talent. Mr. Carrick's men-miniatures are perhaps the best among those pleasing performances; the likeness

[1] Sir Martin Archer Shee, President of the Royal Academy.

of a former Secretary for Ireland will especially please those who
know his lordship's countenance, and those who do not, by its
resemblance to an eminent comedian whose absence from the stage
all regret.

Mr. Thorburn cultivates more, perhaps, than any other
miniature painter, the poetry of his art. The gallant knights,
Sir Ross and Sir Newton, are as victorious as usual ; and Mr.
Lover's head of Mr. Lever deserves praiseworthy mention ; it will
be looked at with interest by 'Harry Lorrequer's' English
readers, and by those who had the opportunity of seeing him in
the body, and hearing his manly and kind-hearted speech at the
Literary Fund the other day.

Of Mr. Etty's colour pieces what words can give an idea ?
Many lovers of Titian and Rubens will admit that here is an
English painter who almost rivals them in his original way, and
all will admire their magnificent beauty. Mr. Turner, our other
colourist, is harder to be understood. The last time the gentle
reader received a black eye at school and for a moment after the
delivery of the blow, when flashes of blue, yellow, and crimson
lightning blazed before the ball so preternaturally excited, he saw
something not unlike the 'Moses' of Mr. Turner. His picture of
'Cleopatra Meeting Alexander the Great at Moscow the Morning
Before the Deluge' (perhaps this may not be the exact title, but
it will do as well as another) is of the most transcendental sort.
The quotations from the *Fallacies of Hope* continue still in great
force ; as thus :—

> The Ark stood firm on Ararat ; the returning Sun
> Exhaled Earth's humid bubbles, and, emulous of light,
> Reflected her lost forms, each in prismatic guise,
> Hope's harbinger, ephemeral as the summer fly,
> Which rises, flits, expands, and dies.—*Fallacies of Hope.*

The artist has done full justice to these sweet lines.

We are given to understand by *cognoscenti* that the Italian
skies are always of the bluest cobalt ; hence many persons are
dissatisfied with Mr. Stanfield's Italian landscapes, as unfaithful,
because deficient in the proper depth of ultra-marine. On this
subject let proper judges speak ; but others less qualified will
find the pictures beautiful, and more beautiful for their quiet and
calm. Who can praise Mr. Creswick sufficiently ? The 'Welsh
Girl' will, one of these days, fetch a sum of money as great as
ever was given for Hobbema or Ruysdael ; and 'Evening' is an
English Claude. Mr. Lee's fresh country landscapes will find
hundreds of admirers ; and perhaps there are no two prettier

little pictures in the gallery than Mr. Linton's 'Sorrento' and Mr. Jutsum's 'Tintern.'

In walking round the vault in which the sculpture is entombed, I did not see anything especially worthy of mark, except a bust of Count d'Orsay, who has himself broken ground as an artist, and whose genius will one day no doubt make its way. Why have we not our common share of the admirable pictures of Mr. Edwin Landseer? It can't be that a man of his facility has painted but three pictures in a year, and picture-lovers wonder where the rest are?

M. A. TITMARSH.

THE WATER-COLOUR EXHIBITION.[1]

THE Water-Colour Exhibitions this year are quite as gay and pretty as in preceding seasons, though presenting no works of very extraordinary merit. The gentlemen of the New Society are commonly more ambitious than the painters of the old; but their efforts have not this year been quite so successful as in former seasons. Mr. Warren has a pair of large pictures, in which one is sorry to see so much labour and ingenuity have been expended in vain; Mr. Corbould has a large Scripture piece, which is as bad, poor, mannered, and feeble a performance as ever was perpetrated by a clever young painter; Mr. Hayter, always good, is not quite so good as formerly; Mr. Wehnert has a large piece representing Luther preaching, and though the figures look as if they were made of wood, they exhibit some powerful painting and expression; Miss Corbaux has her pretty little, rather caricatured, subject of Cinderella (but, perhaps, the artist is right, and in a fairy tale all the grotesque should be somewhat caricatured); Mr. Absalon has a snow-piece from the eternal *Vicar of Wakefield*—a large picture, and a failure.

On the other hand, and although the artist's practice is very imperfect, and he cannot compete in skill and tricks of pencilling with many an inferior workman, he has some qualities which the inferior workman cannot acquire, labour he ever so—an exceedingly fine sentiment of pure beauty and tender humour. All his little pieces sparkle with this delicate, kindly sentiment; here is a little sketch of a young couple passing over a plank across a brook; you see that they are in love, though they make no big eyes or ogles at each other to express the tender passion, as it is commonly expressed in pictures; then there is a drawing of a farmer coming home from the cornfield, wife and child at the cottage waiting for him, which little stale rustic history is yet told with remarkable grace and sweetness. Finally, there are two designs of Sir Roger de Coverley and the Widow, of which more

[1] [*The Pictorial Times*, May 6, 1843.]

need not be said than that they are as good as if Mr. Leslie
himself had drawn them. Let all Art Union prize-men have a
look at these rough, exquisite little pieces. Perhaps, however, it
is for such slight sketches that water-colours are best adapted;
the larger pieces are wonderful and curious, but not satisfactory,
any more than an overture when played on a guitar, which can
accompany a ballad very sweetly.

Very wisely, as we think, Mr. Cattermole has exhibited this
year a few of those magnificent sketches in which he is unrivalled,
in place of more elaborate pieces, which are not so well suited to
his style or to the material in which he works. Two sketches on
rough brown paper, seemingly, are quite extraordinary for depth
and power of colour; and the large drawing of 'Charles and his
Army after the battle of Newbury' is a magnificent wild composition,
full of power and rich colour, and awful romantic gloom.

Mr. Taylor's 'Vicar of Wakefield' is exceedingly pleasant and
graceful in humour, and exhibits much of the skill of this artist's
brilliant and flowing pencil. The drawings of Mr. Copley Fielding
are, perhaps, even better than in former years. A forest scene
may especially be remarked for its extraordinary vigour and richness of tone. There are only a pair of those delightful boys with
whose society Mr. Hunt is accustomed to amuse us; but there are
some wonderful fruit pieces from his pencil, and some interiors not
quite, we think, so happy.

Mr. Nash's 'Gothic Halls' are drawn with great skill and
truth, not so his meagre composition of 'Milton and his Daughters,'
as unromantic and likewise unreal a piece as heart can desire.
The young ladies' fingers are like shreds of muslin, the old
gentleman's eyes as inane as Farren's in 'Grandfather Whitehead,' or as those of a monk in a certain picture by Mr. Richter,
from the novel of *The Trustee*. Words cannot be found in the
dictionary strong enough to express our sense of this picture of
Father Lawrence, and of a twin abomination from the same
hand, and to illustrate the same romance. On the subject of
'Una and her Lion,' serious though polite remonstrances should
be addressed to Miss Sharpe. Here are represented the biggest
lion, the largest tear, and the yellowist head of hair ever painted;
but, alas! a tear that should be painted big enough to fill a
tablespoon would not be necessarily pathetic: nor is a spun-silk
wig necessarily pathetic: it is not with stage properties that
imagination is manufactured; and in spite of her tear, and her
hair, and her lion, this Una must be set down as the least
romantic of young women.

Mr. S. W. Wright's beauties have that charm of grace and

delicacy for which all the works of this pleasing artist are known ; and Mr. Stone has a charming little drawing of a pair of lovers, with a motto in an outlandish tongue, very difficult of comprehension. But it is clear that the *ragazza* is a *franche coquette*, and the *povero fanciullo* a *dummkopf*, whose example *nosotros* would do well to avoid :—*verbum sap.*

The lover of landscape will find at this exhibition many an agreeable recollection of nature in the drawings of De Wint and Gastineau ; and may take his last look at those gloomy and romantic scenes, which only Varley knew how to paint.

By the way, a gentleman at the New Water-Colour Society has managed to copy the Varley manner very closely.

MICHAEL ANGELO TITMARSH.

MAY GAMBOLS;
OR, TITMARSH IN THE PICTURE GALLERIES.[1]

THE readers of this Miscellany may, perhaps, have remarked that always at the May season and the period of the exhibitions, our eccentric correspondent Titmarsh seems to be seized with a double fit of eccentricity, and to break out into such violent fantastical gambols as might cause us to be alarmed did we not know him to be harmless, and induce us to doubt of his reason but that the fit is generally brief, and passes off after the first excitement occasioned by visiting the picture galleries. It was in one of these fits, some years since, that he announced in this Magazine his own suicide, which we know to be absurd, for he has drawn many hundred guineas from us since — on the same occasion he described his debts and sojourn at a respectable hotel, in which it seems he has never set his foot. But these hallucinations pass away with May, and next month he will, no doubt, be calmer, or, at least, not more absurd than usual. Some disappointments occurring to himself, and the refusal of his great picture of 'Heliogabalus' in the year 1803 (which caused his retirement from practice as a painter) may account for his extreme bitterness against some of the chief artists in this, or any other school or country. Thus we have him in these pages abusing Raphael; in the very last month he fell foul of Rubens, and in the present paper he actually pooh-poohs Sir Martin Shee and some of the Royal Academy. This is too much. '*Caelum ipsum*,' as Horace says, '*petimus stultitiâ.*' But we will quote no more the well-known words of the Epicurean bard.

We only add that we do not feel in the least bound by any one of the opinions here brought forward, from most of which, except where the writer contradicts himself and so saves us the trouble, we cordially dissent; and perhaps the reader had best pass on to the next article, omitting all perusal of this, excepting, of course, the editorial notice of—O. Y.

[1] [*Fraser's Magazine*, June, 1844.]

Jack Straw's Castle, Hampstead, May 25.

This is written in the midst of a general desolation and dis-
couragement of the honest practitioners who dwell in the dingy
first floors about Middlesex Hospital and Soho. The long-haired
ones are tearing their lanky locks ; the velvet-coated sons of
genius are plunged in despair ; the law has ordered the suppression
of Art-Unions, and the wheel of Fortune has suddenly and cruelly
been made to stand still. When the dreadful news came that the
kindly, harmless Art-lottery was to be put an end to, although
Derby-lotteries are advertised in every gin-shop in London, and
every ruffian in the City may gamble at his leisure, the men of
the brush and palette convoked a tumultuous meeting, where,
amidst tears, shrieks, and wrath, the cruelty of their case was
debated. Wyse of Waterford calmly presided over the stormy
bladder-squeezers, the insulted wielders of the knife and maul-
stick. Wyse soothed their angry spirits with words of wisdom
and hope. He stood up in the assembly of the legislators of the
land and pointed out their wrongs. The painters' friend, the
kind old Lansdowne, lifted up his cordial voice among the peers
of England, and asked for protection for the children of Raphael
and Apelles. No one said nay. All pitied the misfortune of the
painters ; even Lord Brougham was stilled into compassion, and
the voice of Vaux was only heard in sobs.

These are days of darkness, but there is hope in the vista ; the
lottery-subscription lies in limbo, but it shall be released there-
from and flourish, exuberantly revivified, in future years. Had
the ruin been consummated, this hand should have withered rather
than have attempted to inscribe jokes concerning it. No.
Fraser is the artists' friend, their mild parent. While his Royal
Highness Prince Albert dines with the Academicians, the rest of
painters, less fortunate, are patronised by her majesty REGINA.

Yes, in spite of the Art-Union accident, there is hope for the
painters. Sir Martin Archer Shee thinks that the Prince's condescension in dining with the Academy will do incalculable benefit
to the art. Henceforth its position is assured in the world. This
august patronage, the president says, evincing the sympathy of
the higher classes, must awaken the interest of the low ; and the
public (the ignorant rogues) will thus learn to appreciate what
they have not cared for hitherto. Interested ! of course they will
be. O Academicians ! ask the public to dinner and you will see
how much interested they will be. We are authorised to state
that next year any person who will send in his name will have a
cover provided ; Trafalgar Square is to be awned in, plates are to

be laid for 250,000, one of the new basins is to be filled with turtle and the other with cold punch. The president and the *élite* are to sit upon Nelson's pillar, while rows of benches, stretching as far as the Union Club, Northumberland House, and St. Martin's Church, will accommodate the vulgar. Mr. Toole is to have a speaking trumpet ; and a twenty-four pounder to be discharged at each toast.

There are other symptoms of awakening interest in the public mind. The readers of newspapers will remark this year that the leaders of public opinion have devoted an unusually large space and print to reviews of the fine arts. They have been employing critics who, though they contradict each other a good deal, are yet evidently better acquainted with the subject than critics of old used to be when gentlemen of the profession were instructed to report on a fire, or an Old Bailey trial, or a Greek play, or an opera, or a boxing match, or a picture gallery, as their turn came. Read now *The Times, The Chronicle, The Post* (especially *The Post*, of which the painting critiques have been very good) and it will be seen that the critic knows his business, and from the length of his articles it may be conjectured that the public is interested in knowing what he has to say. This is all, probably, from the prince having dined at the Academy. The nation did not care for pictures until then—until the nobility taught us ; gracious nobility. Above all, what a compliment to the public !

As one looks round the rooms of the Royal Academy, one cannot but deplore the fate of the poor fellows who have been speculating upon the Art-Unions ; and yet in the act of grief there is a lurking satisfaction. The poor fellows can't sell their pieces ; that is a pity. But why did the poor fellows paint such fiddle-faddle pictures ? They catered for the *bourgeois*, the sly rogues ! they know honest John Bull's taste, and simple admiration of namby-pamby, and so they supplied him with an article that was just likely to suit him. In like manner savages are supplied with glass beads ; children are accommodated with toys and trash, by dexterous speculators who know their market. Well, I am sorry that the painting speculators have had a stop put to their little venture, and that the ugly law against lotteries has stepped in and seized upon the twelve thousand pounds, which was to furnish many a hungry British Raphael with a coat and a beefsteak. Many a Mrs. Raphael, who was looking out for a new dress, or a trip to Margate or Boulogne for the summer, must forego the pleasure, and remain in dingy Newman Street. Many little ones will go back to Turnham Green academies and not carry the amount of last half-year's bill in the trunk ; many a landlord will bully about the non-payment of the rent; and a vast number of frame-makers will look wistfully at their carving and gilding as it returns after the exhibition to Mr. Tinto, Charlotte Street, along with poor Tinto's picture from *The Vicar of Wakefield* that he made sure of selling to an Art-Union prizeman. This is the pathetic side of the question. My heart is tender, and I weep for the honest painters peering dismally at the twelve thousand pounds like hungry boys do at a tart-shop.

But—here stern justice interposes, and the MAN having relented the CRITIC raises his inexorable voice—but, I say, the enemies of Art-Unions have had some reason for their complaints, and I fear it is too true that the effect of those institutions, as far as they have gone hitherto, has not been mightily favourable to the cause of art. One day, by custom, no doubt, the public taste will grow better, and as the man who begins by intoxicating himself with a glass of gin finishes sometimes by easily absorbing a bottle; as the law-student, who at first is tired with a chapter of Blackstone, will presently swallow you down with pleasure a whole volume of Chitty; as EDUCATION, in a word, advances, it is humbly to be hoped that the great and generous British public will not be so easily satisfied as at present, and will ask for a better article for its money.

Meanwhile, their taste being pitiable, the artists supply them with poor stuff—pretty cheap tawdry toys and gimcracks in place of august and beautiful objects of art. It is always the case. I do not mean to say that the literary men are a bit better. Poor fellows of the pen and pencil! We must live. The public likes light literature and we write it. Here am I writing magazine jokes and follies, and why? Because the public like such, will purchase no other. Otherwise, as Mr. Nickisson, and all who are acquainted with M. A. Titmarsh, in private know, my real inclinations would lead me to write works upon mathematics, geology, and chemistry, varying them in my lighter hours with little playful treatises on questions of political economy, epic poems, and essays on the Æolic digamma. So, in fact, these severe rebukes with which I am about to belabour my neighbour must be taken, as they are given, in a humble and friendly spirit; they are not actuated by pride, but by deep sympathy. Just as we read in holy Mr. Newman's life of Saint Stephen Harding, that it was the custom among the godly Cistercian monks (in the good old times, which holy Newman would restore) to assemble every morning in full chapter; and there, after each monk had made his confession, it was free to—nay, it was strictly enjoined on—any other brother to rise and say, 'Brother So-and-so hath not told all his sins; our dear brother has forgotten that yesterday he ate his split-pease with too much gormandise;' or, 'This morning he did indecently rejoice over his water-gruel,' or what not. These real Christians were called upon to inform, not only of themselves, but to be informers over each other; and, the information being given, the brother informed against thanked his brother the informer, and laid himself down on the desk, and was flagellated with gratitude. Sweet friends! be you like the Cistercians! Brother Michael Angelo is going to inform against you. Get ready your garments and prepare for flagellation. Brother Michael Angelo is about to lay on and spare not.

Brother Michael lifts up his voice against the young painters collectively in the first place, afterwards individually, when he will also take leave to tickle them with the wholesome stripes of the flagellum. In the first place, then (and my heart is so tender that, rather than begin the operation, I have been beating about the bush for more than a page, of which page the reader is cordially requested to omit the perusal, as it is not the least to the purpose), I say that the young painters of England, whose uprise this Magazine and this critic were the first to hail, asserting loudly their superiority over the pompous old sham-classical big-wigs of the Academy, the young painters of England *are not doing their duty.* They are going backwards, or rather, they are flinging themselves under the wheels of that great golden Juggernaut of an Art-Union. The thought of the money is leading them astray; they are poets no longer, but money-hunters. They paint down to the level of the public intelligence, rather than seek to elevate the public to them. Why do these great geniuses fail in their duty of instruction? Why, knowing better things, do they serve out such awful twaddle as we have from them. Alas! it is not for art they paint, but for the Art-Union.

The first dear brother I shall take the liberty to request to get ready for operation is brother Charles Landseer. Brother Charles has sinned. He has grievously sinned. And we will begin with this miserable sinner, and administer to him admonition in a friendly, though most fierce and cutting manner.

The subject of brother Charles Landseer's crime is this. The sinner has said to himself, 'The British public likes domestic pieces. They will have nothing *but* domestic pieces. I will give them one, and of a new sort. Suppose I paint a picture that must have a hit. My picture will have every sort of interest. It shall interest the religious public; it shall interest the domestic public; it shall interest the amateur for the cleverness of its

painting ; it shall interest little boys and girls, for I will introduce
no end of animals : camels, monkeys, elephants, and cockatoos ;
it shall interest sentimental young ladies, for I will take care to
have a pretty little episode for them.   I will take the town by
storm, in a word.'   This is what I conceive was passing in
brother Charles Landseer's sinful soul when he conceived and
executed his NOAH'S ARK IN A DOMESTIC POINT OF VIEW.

Noah and his family (with some supplemental young children,
very sweetly painted) are seated in the ark, and a port-hole is
opened, out of which one of the sons is looking at the now
peaceful waters.   The sunshine enters the huge repository of the
life of the world, and the dove has just flôwn in with an olive
branch and nestles in the bosom of one of the daughters of Noah ;
the patriarch and his aged partner are lifting up their venerable
eyes in thankfulness ;   the children stand around, the peaceful
labourer and the brown huntsman each testifying his devotion
after his fashion.   The animals round about participate in the
joyful nature of the scene, their instinct seems to tell them that
the hour of their deliverance is near.

There, the picture is described romantically and in the best of
language.   Now let us proceed to examine the poetry critically
and to see what its claims are.   Well, the ark is a great subject.
The history from which we have our account of it, from a poet,
surely demands a reverend treatment ; a blacksmith roaring from
the desk of a conventicle may treat it familiarly, but an educated
artist ought surely to approach such a theme with respect.   The
point here is only urged æsthetically.   As a matter of *taste*, then
(and the present humble writer has no business to speak on any
other), such a manner of treating the subject is certainly reprehensible.   The ark is vulgarised here and reduced to the
proportions of a Calais steamer.   The passengers are rejoicing :
they are glad to get away.   Their live animals are about them no
more nor less sublime than so many cattle or horses in loose
boxes.   The parrots perched on the hoop yonder have as little
signification as a set of birds in a cage at the Zoological Gardens ;
the very dove becomes neither more nor less than the *pet* of the
pretty girl represented in the centre of the picture.   All the
greatness of the subject is lost ; and, putting the historical nature
of the personages out of the question, they have little more
interest than a group of any emigrants in the hold of a ship, who
rouse and rally at the sound of ' Land ho ! '

Why, if all great themes of poetry are to be treated in this
way, the art would be easy.   We might have Hector shaving
himself before going out to fight Achilles, as undoubtedly the

Trojan hero did; Priam in a cotton nightcap asleep in a four-poster on the night of the sack of Troy, Hecuba, of course, by his side, with curl papers, and her *tour de tête* on the toilet-glass. We might have Dido's maid coming after her mistress in the shower with pattens and an umbrella; or Cleopatra's page guttling the figs in the basket which had brought the asp that killed the mistress of Antony. Absurd trivialities, or pretty trivialities, are nothing to the question; those I have adduced here are absurd, but they are just as poetical as prettiness, not a whit less degrading and commonplace. No painter has a right to treat great historical subjects in such a fashion: and though the public are sure to admire, and young ladies, in raptures, look on at the daring of a dove, and little boys in delight cry, 'Look, papa, at the parroquets!'—'Law, ma, what big trunks the elephants have!' it yet behoves the critic to say this is an unpoetical piece, and severely to reprehend the unhappy perpetrator thereof.

I know brother Charles will appeal. I know it will be pleaded in his favour that the picture is capitally painted, some of the figures very pretty; two, that of the old woman and the boy looking out, quite grand in drawing and colour; the picture charming for its silvery tone and agreeable pleasantry of colour. All this is true. But he has sinned, he has greatly sinned; let him acknowledge his fault in the presence of the chapter, and receive the customary and wholesome reward thereof——

Frater Redgrave is the next malefactor whose sins deserve a reprobation. In the namby-pamby line his errors are very sad. Has he not been already warned in this very miscellany of his propensity to small sentiment? Has he corrected himself of that grievous tendency? No; his weakness grows more and more upon him, and he is now more sinful than ever. One of his pictures is taken from the most startling lyric in our language, the 'Song of the Shirt,' a song as bitter and manly as it is exquisitely soft and tender, a song of which the humour draws tears.[1]

Mr. Redgrave has illustrated everything except the humour, the manliness, and the bitterness of the song. He has only depicted the tender, good-natured part of it. It is impossible to quarrel with the philanthropy of the painter. His shirt-maker sits by her little neat bed, work, working away. You may see how late it is, for the candle is nearly burnt out, the clock (capital poetic notion!) says what o'clock it is, the grey-streaked dawn is rising over the opposite house seen through the cheerless

---

[1] How is it that none of the papers have noticed the astonishing poem by Mr. Hood in the May number of his magazine, to which our language contains no parallel?

M. A. T.

casement, and where (from a light which it has in its window)
you may imagine that another poor shirt-maker is toiling too.
The one before us is pretty, pale and wan; she turns up the
whites of her fine, fatigued eyes to the little ceiling. She is ill,
as the artist has shewn us by a fine stroke of genius—a parcel of
medicine bottles on the mantelpiece! The picture is carefully
and cleverly painted—extremely popular—gazed at with vast
interest by most spectators. Is it, however, a poetical subject?
Yes, Hood has shewn that it can be made one, but by surprising
turns of thought brought to bear upon it, strange, terrible unex-
pected lights of humour which he has flung upon it. And, to
'trump' this tremendous card, Mr. Redgrave gives us this
picture; his points being the clock, which tells the time of day,
the vials which show the poor girl takes physic, and such other
vast labours of intellect!

Mr. Redgrave's other picture, the 'Marriage Morning,' is also
inspired by that milk-and-water of human kindness, the flavour of
which is so insipid to the roast-beef intellect. This is a scene of
a marriage morning; the bride is taking leave of her mamma after
the ceremony, and that amiable lady, reclining in an easy-chair, is
invoking benedictions upon the parting couple, and has a hand of
her daughter and her son-in-law clasped in each of hers. She is
smiling sadly, restraining her natural sorrow, which will break
out so soon as the post-chaise you see through the window, and
on which the footman is piling the nuptial luggage, shall have
driven off to Salt Hill, or Rose Cottage, Richmond, which I
recommend. The bride's father, a venerable, bald-headed gentleman, with a most benignant, though slow-coachish look, is trying
to console poor Anna Maria, the unmarried sister, who is losing
the companion of her youth. Never mind, Anna Maria, my dear,
your turn will come too; there is a young gentleman making a
speech in the parlour to the health of the new-married pair, who,
I lay a wager, will be struck by your fine eyes, and be for serving
you as your sister has been treated. This small fable is worked
out with great care in a picture in which there is much clever and
conscientious painting, from which, however, I must confess I
derive little pleasure. The sentiment and colour of the picture
somehow coincide; the eye rests upon a variety of neat tints of
pale drab, pale green, pale brown, pale puce colour, of a sickly
warmth, not pleasant to the eye. The drawing is feeble, the
expression of the face pretty, but lackadaisical. The penance I
would order Mr. Redgrave should be a pint of port wine to be
taken daily, and a devilled kidney every morning for breakfast
before beginning to paint.

A little of the devil, too, would do Mr. Frank Stone no harm.
He, too, is growing dangerously sentimental. His picture, with
a quotation from Horace, '*Mœcenas atavis edite regibus*,'
represents a sort of game of tender cross-purposes, very difficult
to describe in print. Suppose two lads, Jocky and Tommy, and
two lasses, Jenny and Jessamy. They are placed thus :—

		Tommy.
Jessamy.	Jenny.	Jocky.
	A dog.	

Now Jocky is making love to Jenny in an easy, offhand sort of
way, and though, or, perhaps, *because* he doesn't care for her
much, is evidently delighting the young woman. She looks
round, with a pleased smile on her fresh, plump cheeks, and
turns slightly towards Heaven a sweet little retroussé nose, and
twiddles her fingers (most exquisitely these hands are drawn and
painted, by the way) in the most contented way. But, ah! how
little does she heed Tommy, who, standing behind Jocky, reclining against a porch, is looking and longing for this light-hearted
Jenny. And, oh! why does Tommy cast such sheep's eyes upon
Jenny, when by her side sits *Jessamy*, the tender and romantic,
the dark-eyed and raven-haired being, whose treasures of affection
are flung at heedless Tommy's feet? All the world is interested
in Jessamy; her face is beautiful, her look of despairing love is
so exquisitely tender, that it touches every spectator; and the
ladies are unanimous in wondering how Tommy can throw himself
away upon that simpering Jenny, when such a superior creature
as Jessamy is to be had for the asking. But such is the way of
the world, and Tommy will marry, simply because everybody
tells him not.

Thus far for the sentiment of the picture. The details are very
good; there is too much stippling and show of finish, perhaps, in the
handling, and the painting might have been more substantial and
lost nothing. But the colour is good, the group very well composed, the variety of expression excellent. There is great passion,
as well as charming delicacy, in the disappointed maiden's face;
much fine appreciation of character in the easy, smiling triumph of
the rival; and, although this sentence was commenced with the
express determination of rating Mr. Stone soundly, lo! it is
finished without a word of blame. Well, let's vent our anger on
the dog. That *is* very bad, and seems to have no more bones than

an apple-dumpling. It is only because the artist has been painting disappointed lovers a great deal of late, that one is disposed to
grumble not at the work, but the want of variety of subject.

As a sentimental picture, the best and truest, to my taste, is
that by Mr. Webster, the 'Portraits of Mr. and Mrs. Webster,'
painted to celebrate their fiftieth wedding-day. Such a charming
old couple were never seen. There is delightful grace, sentiment,
and purity in these two gentle, kindly heads ; much more sentiment and grace than even in Mr. Eastlake's 'Heloïse,' a face
which the artist has painted over and over again ; a beautiful
woman, but tiresome, unearthly, unsubstantial, and no more like
Heloïse than like the Duke of Wellington. If the late Mr.
Pope's epistle be correct, Eloisa was a most unmistakable
woman ; this is a substanceless, passionless, solemn, mystical
apparition ; but I doubt if a woman be not the more poetical being
of the two.

Being on the subject of sentimental pictures, Mr. Delaroche's
great 'Holy Family' must be mentioned here ; and, if there is
reason to quarrel with the unsatisfactory nature of English sentiment, in truth it appears that the French are not much better provided with the high poetical quality. This picture has all the
outside of poetry, all the costume of religion, all the prettiness and
primness of the new German dandy-pietistical school. It is an
agreeable compound of Correggio and Raphael with a strong dash
of Overbeck ; it is painted as clean and pretty as a tulip on a
dessert-plate, the lines made out so neatly that none can mistake
them. The drawing good, the female face as pretty and demure
as can be, her drapery of spotless blue, and the man's of approved
red, the infant as pink as strawberries and cream, every leaf of the
tree sweetly drawn, and the trunk of the most delicate dove-
coloured grey. All these merits the picture has ; it is a well-
appointed picture. But is that all ? Is that enough to make a
poet ? There are lines in the Oxford prize poems that are smooth
as Pope's ; and it is notorious that, for colouring, there is no
painting like the Chinese. But I hope the French artists have
better men springing up among them than the president of the
French Academy at Rome.

Biard, the Hogarthian painter, whose slave-trade picture was
so noble, has sent us a couple of pieces, which both, in their way,
deserve merit. The one is an Arabian caravan moving over a
brickdust coloured desert, under a red, arid sky. The picture is
lifelike, and so far poetical that it seems to tell the truth. Then
there is a steam-boat disaster, with every variety of sea-sickness,
laughably painted. Shuddering soldiery, · sprawling dandies,

Englishmen, Savoyards, guitars, lovers, monkeys—a dreadful confusion of qualmish people, whose agonies will put the most
philanthropic observer into good - humour.   Biard's 'Havre
Packet' is much more praiseworthy in my mind than Delaroche's
'Holy Family'; for I deny the merit of failing greatly in pictures,
the great merit is to succeed.   There is no greater error, surely,
than that received dictum of the ambitious, to aim at high
things; it is best to do what you mean to do; better to kill a
crow than to miss an eagle.

As the French artists are sending in their works from across
the water, why, for the honour of England, will not some of our
painters let the Parisians know that here, too, are men whose
genius is worthy of appreciation?   They may be the best draughtsmen in the world, but they have no draughtsman like Maclise,
they have no colourist like Etty, they have no painter like
MULREADY, above all, whose name I beg the printer to place in
the largest capitals, and to surround with a wreath of laurels.
Mr. Mulready was crowned in this Magazine once before.   Here
again he is proclaimed.   It looks like extravagance, or flattery, for
the blushing critic to tell his real mind about the 'Whistonian
Controversy.'

And yet, as the truth must be told, why not say it now at
once?   I believe this to be one of the finest cabinet pictures in
the world.   It seems to me to possess an assemblage of excellences
so rare, to be in drawing so admirable, in expression so fine, in
finish so exquisite, in composition so beautiful, in humour and
beauty of expression so delightful, that I can't but ask where is a
good picture if this be not one.   And, in enumerating all the
above perfections I find I have forgotten the greatest of all, the
colour; it is quite original this—brilliant, rich, astonishingly
luminous and intense.   The pictures of Van Eyck are not more
brilliant in tone than this magnificent combination of blazing reds,
browns, and purples.   I know of no scheme of colour like it, and
heartily trust that time will preserve it; when this little picture, and
some of its fellows, will be purchased as eagerly as a Hemlinck or a
Gerald Douw is bought nowadays.   If Mr. Mulready has a mind
to the Grand Cross of the Legion of Honour, he has but to send
this picture to Paris next year, and, with the recommendation of
Fraser's Magazine, the affair is settled.   Meanwhile it is pleasant to
know that the artist (although his work will fetch ten times as
much money a hundred years hence) has not been ill rewarded, as
times go, for his trouble and genius.

We have another great and original colourist among us, as
luscious as Rubens, as rich almost as Titian, Mr. Etty; and every

year the exhibition sparkles with magnificent little canvases, the works of this indefatigable strenuous admirer of rude Beauty. The form is not quite so sublime as the colour in this artist's paintings; the female figure is often rather too expansively treated, it swells here and there to the proportions of the Caffrarian, rather than the Medicean, Venus; but, in colour, little can be conceived that is more voluptuously beautiful. This year introduces us to one of the artist's noblest compositions, a classical and pictorial *orgy*, as it were,—a magnificent vision of rich colours and beautiful forms;—a grand feast of sensual poetry. The verses from *Comus*, which the painter has taken to illustrate, have the same character—

> All amidst the gardens fair
> Of Hesperus and his daughters three,
> That sing about the golden tree,
> Along the crisped shades and bowers,
> Revels the spruce and jocund spring.
> Beds of hyacinths and roses,
> Where young Adonis oft reposes,
> Waxing well of his deep wound,
> In slumber soft and on the ground
> Sadly sits the Assyrian queen;
> But far above in spangled sheen
> Celestial Cupid, her famed son, advanced,
> Holds his dear Psyche sweet entranced.

It is a dream rather than a reality, the words and images purposely indistinct and incoherent. In the same way the painter has made the beautiful figures sweep before us in a haze of golden sunshine. This picture is one of a series to be painted in fresco, and to decorate the walls of a summer-house in the gardens of Buckingham Palace, for which edifice Mr. Maclise and Mr. Leslie have also made paintings.

That of Mr. Leslie's is too homely, he is a prose painter. His kind, buxom young lass has none of the look of Milton's lady, that charming compound of the saint and the fine lady — that sweet impersonation of the chivalric mythology — an angel, but with her sixteen quarterings—a countess descends from the skies. Leslie's lady has no such high breeding, the Comus above her looks as if he might revel on ale; a rustic seducer with an air of rude, hob-nailed health. Nor are the demons and fantastic figures introduced imaginative enough; they are fellows with masks from Covent Garden. Compare the two figures at the sides of the picture with the two Cupids of Mr. Etty. In the former there is no fancy. The latter are two flowers of poetry; there are no words to characterise those two delicious little figures, no more than to describe a little air of Mozart, which, once heard, remains with you for ever; or a new flower, or a phrase of Keats or Tennyson, which blooms out upon you suddenly, astonishing as much as it pleases. Well, in endeavouring to account for his admiration, the critic pumps for words in vain; if he uses such as he finds, he runs the risk of being considered intolerably pert and affected; silent pleasure, therefore, best beseems him; but this I know, that were my humble recommendations attended to at court, when the pictures are put in the pleasure-house, her sacred majesty, giving a splendid banquet to welcome them and the painters, should touch Mr. Etty on the left shoulder, and say, 'Rise, my knight of the Bath, for painting the left-hand Cupid;" and the Emperor of Russia (being likewise present) should tap him on the right shoulder, exclaiming, 'Rise, my knight of the Eagle, for the left-hand Cupid.'

Mr. Maclise's Comus picture is wonderful for the variety of its design, and has, too, a high poetry of its own. All the figures are here still and solemn as in a tableau; the lady still on her unearthly snaky chair, Sabrina still stooping over her. On one side the brothers, and opposite the solemn attendant spirit; round these interminable groups and vistas of fairy beings, twining in a thousand attitudes of grace, and sparkling white and bloodless against a leaden blue sky. It is the most poetical of the artist's pictures, the most extraordinary exhibition of his proper skill. Is it true that the artists are only to receive three hundred guineas apiece for these noble compositions? Why, a print-seller would give more, and artists should not be allowed to paint simply for the honour of decorating a royal summer-house.

Among the poetical pictures of the Exhibition should be mentioned with especial praise Mr. Cope's delightful 'Charity,' than the female figures in which Raphael scarce painted anything more charmingly beautiful. And Mr. Cope has this merit that his work is no prim imitation of the stiff old Cimabue and Giotto manner, no aping of the crisp draperies and hard outlines of the missal illuminations, without which the religious artist would have us believe religious expression is impossible. It is pleasant after seeing the wretched caricature of the old-world usages which stare us in the face in every quarter of London now—little dumpy Saxon chapels built in raw brick, spick and span *bandbox* churches of the pointed Norman style for Cockneys in zephyr coats to assemble in, new old painted windows of the twelfth century, tessellated pavements of the Byzantine school, gimcrack imitations

of the Golden Legend printed with red letters, and crosses, and
quaint figures stolen out of Norman missals—to find artists aim-
ing at the Beautiful and Pure without thinking it necessary to
resort to these paltry archæological quackeries, which have no
Faith, no Truth, no Life in them; but which give us ceremony
in lieu of reality, and insist on forms as if they were the conditions
of belief.

Lest the reader should misunderstand the cause of this anger,
we beg him to take the trouble to cross Pall Mall to St. James's
Street, where objects of art are likewise exhibited; he will see
the reason of our wrath.   Here are all the ornamental artists
of England sending in their works, and what are they?—All
imitations.   The Alhambra here; the Temple Church there;
here a Gothic Saint; yonder a Saxon altar-rail; farther on a
sprawling rococo of Louis XV.; all worked neatly and cleverly
enough, but with no originality, no honesty of thought.   The
twelfth century revived in Mr. Crockford's bazaar, forsooth! with
examples of every century except our own.   It would be worth
while for some one to write an essay, shewing how astonishingly
Sir Walter Scott [1] has influenced the world; how he changed the
character of novelists, then of historians, whom he brought from
their philosophy to the study of pageantry and costume; how the
artists then began to fall back into the middle ages and the
architects to follow; until now behold we have Mr. Newman and
his congregation of Littlemore marching out with taper and crosier,
and falling down to worship St. Willibald, and St. Winnibald,
and St. Walberga the Saxon virgin.   But Mr. Cope's picture is
leading the reader rather farther than a critique about exhibitions
has any right to divert him, and let us walk soberly back to
Trafalgar Square.

Remark the beautiful figures of the children in Mr. Cope's
picture (276), the fainting one, and the golden-haired infant at the
gate.   It is a noble and touching Scripture illustration.   The
artist's other picture, 'Geneviève,' is not so successful; the faces
seem to have been painted from a dirty palette, the evening tints
of the sky are as smoky as a sunset in St. James's Park; the
composition unpleasant, and not enough to fill the surface of
canvas.

Mr. Herbert's picture of 'The Trial of the Seven Bishops' is
painted with better attention to costume than most English
painters are disposed to pay.   The characters in our artist's

---

[1] Or more properly Goethe.   *Götz von Berlichingen* was the father of the
Scottish romances, and Scott remained constant to that mode, while the
greater artist tried a thousand others.

history-pieces, as indeed on our theatres, do not look commonly accustomed to the dresses which they assume; wear them awkwardly, take liberties of alteration and adjustment, and spoil thereby the truth of the delineation. The French artists, on the canvas or the boards, understand this branch of their art much better. Look at M. Biard's 'Mecca Pilgrims,' how carefully and accurately they are attired; or go to the French play and see Cartigny in a Hogarthian dress. He wears it as though he had been born a hundred years back—looks the old marquess to perfection. In this attention to dress, Mr. Herbert's picture is very praiseworthy; the men are quite at home in their quaint coats and periwigs of James the Second's time; the ladies at ease in their stiff, long-waisted gowns, their fans, and their queer caps and patches. And the picture is pleasing from the extreme brightness and cleanliness of the painting. All looks as neat and fresh as Sam Pepys when he turned out in his new suit, his lady in her satin and brocade. But here the praise must stop. The great concourse of people delineated, the bishops and the jury, the judges and the sheriffs, the halberdiers and the fine ladies, seem very little interested in the transaction in which they are engaged, and look as if they were assembled rather for show than business. Nor, indeed, is the artist much in fault. Painters have not fair-play in these parade pictures. It is only with us that Reform-banquets, or views of the House of Lords at the passing of the Slopperton Railway bill, or Coronation Processions, obtain favour; in which vast numbers of public characters are grouped unreally together, and politics are made to give an interest to art.

Mr. Herbert's picture of 'Sir Thomas Moore and his Daughter watching from the prisoner's room in the Tower four Monks led away to Execution,' is the most elaborate, perhaps, but the very best of this painter's works. It is full of grace, and sentiment, and religious unction. You see that the painter's heart is in the scenes which he represents. The countenances of the two figures are finely conceived; the sorrowful, anxious beauty of the daughter's face, the resigned humility of the martyr at her side, and the accessories or properties of the pious little drama are cleverly and poetically introduced; such as mystic sentences of hope and trust inscribed by former sufferers on the walls, the prisoner's rosary and book of prayers to the Virgin that lie on his bed. These types and emblems of the main story are not obtruded, but serve to increase the interest of the action; just as you hear in a concerted piece of music a single instrument playing its little plaintive part alone, and yet belonging to the whole.

If you want to see a picture where costume is *not* represented, behold Mr. Lauder's 'Claverhouse ordering Morton to Execution.' There sits Claverhouse in the centre in a Kean wig and ringlets, such as was never worn in any age of this world, except at the theatre in 1816, and he scowls with a true melodramatic ferocity; and he lifts a sign-post of a finger towards Morton, who forthwith begins to writhe and struggle into an attitude in the midst of a group of subordinate, cuirassed, buff-coated gentry. Morton is represented in tights, slippers, and a tunic, something after the fashion of Retzch's figures in *Faust* (which are refinements of costumes worn a century and a half before the days when Charles disported at Tillietudlem); and he, too, must proceed to scowl and frown 'with a flashing eye and a distended nostril,' as they say in the novels,—as Gomersal scowls at Widdicomb before the combat between those two chiefs begins; and while they are measuring each other according to the stage wont, from the toe of the yellow boot up to the tip of the stage wig. There is a tragedy heroine in Mr. Lauder's picture striking her attitude too, to complete this scene. It is entirely unnatural, theatrical, of the Davidgian, nay Richardsonian drama, and all such attempts at effect must be reprehended by the stern critic. When such a cool practitioner as Claverhouse ordered a gentleman to be shot, he would not put himself into an attitude; when such a quiet gentleman as Morton received the unpleasant communication in the midst of a company of grenadiers who must overpower him, and of ladies to whom his resistance would be unpleasant, he would act like a man and go out quietly, not stop to rant and fume like a fellow in a booth. I believe it is in Mr. Henningsen's book that there is a story of Zumalacarreguy, Don Carlos's Dundee, who, sitting at table with a Christino prisoner, smoking cigars and playing picquet very quietly, received a communication which he handed over to the Christino. 'Your people,' says he, 'have shot one of my officers, and I have promised reprisals; I am sorry to say, my dear general, that I must execute you in twenty minutes!' And so the two gentlemen finished their game at picquet, and parted company—the one to inspect his lines, the other for the courtyard hard by, where a file of grenadiers was waiting to receive his excellency—with mutual politeness and regret. It was the fortune of war. There was no help for it; no need of ranting and stamping, which would ill become any person of good-breeding.

The Scotch artists have a tragic taste; and we should mention with especial praise Mr. Duncan's picture with the agreeable epigraph, 'She set the bairn on the ground and tied up his head, and straighted his body, and covered him with her plaid, and lay down and wept over him.' The extract is from Walker's *Life of Peden ;* the martyrdom was done on the body of a boy by one of those bloody troopers whom we have seen in Mr. Lauder's picture carrying off poor shrieking Morton. Mr. Duncan's picture is very fine—dark, rich, and deep in sentiment; the woman is painted with some of Rubens' swelling lines (such as may be seen in some of his best Magdalens) and with their rich tones of grey. If a certain extremely heavy Cupid poising in the air by a miracle be the other picture of Mr. Duncan's, it can be only said that his tragedy is better than his lightsome compositions—an arrow from yonder lad would bruise the recipient black and blue.

Another admirable picture of a Scotch artist is 427, 'The Highland Lament,' by Alexander Johnston. It is a shame to put such a picture in such a place. It hangs on the ground almost invisible, while dozens of tawdry portraits are staring at you on the line. Could Mr. Johnston's picture be but seen properly, its great beauty and merit would not fail to strike hundreds of visitors who pass it over now. A Highland piper comes running forward, playing some wild laments on his dismal instrument; the women follow after, wailing and sad; the mournful procession winds over a dismal moor. The picture is as clever for its fine treatment and colour, for the grace and action of the figures, as it is curious as an illustration of national manners.

In speaking of the Scotch painters, the Wilkie-like pictures of Mr. Fraser, with their peculiar *smeary* manner, their richness of tone, and their pleasant effect and humour, should not be passed over; while those of Mr. Geddes and Sir William Allan may be omitted with perfect propriety. The latter represents her majesty and Prince Albert perched on a rock; the former has a figure from Walter Scott, of very little interest to any but the parties concerned.

Among the Irish painters we remark two portraits by Mr. Crowley, representing Mrs. Aikenhead, superior*ess* of the Sisters of Charity in Ireland, who gives a very favourable picture of the Society—for it is impossible to conceive an abbess more comfortable, kind, and healthy-looking; and a portrait of Dr. Murray, Roman Catholic archbishop of Dublin, not a good picture of a fine, benevolent and venerable head. We do not know whether the painter of 149, 'An Irish Peasant awaiting her Husband's return,' Mr. Anthony, is an Irishman; but it is a pretty sad picture, which well characterises the poverty, the affection, and the wretchedness of the poor Irish cabin, and tells sweetly and modestly a plaintive story. The largest work in the exhibition is from the pencil of an Irishman, Mr. Leahy, 'Lady Jane Grey praying before execution.' One cannot but admire the courage of artists who paint great works upon these tragic subjects; great works quite unfitted for any private room, and scarcely suited to any public one. But, large as it is, it may be said (without any playing upon words) that the work grows upon estimation. The painting is hard and incomplete; but the principal figure excellent; the face, especially, is finely painted, and full of great beauty. Also, in the Irish pictures may be included Mr. Solomon Hart's Persian gentleman smoking a *calahan*—a sly hit at the learned sergeant, member for Cork, who has often done the same thing.

Mr. Maclise's little scene from *Undine* does not seem to us German in character, as some of the critics call it, because it is clear and hard in line. What German artist is there who can draw with this astonishing vigour, precision, and variety of attitude? The picture is one of admirable and delightful fancy. The swarms of solemn little fairies crowding round Undine and her somewhat theatrical lover may keep a spectator for hours employed in pleasure and wonder. They look to be the real portraits of the little people, sketched by the painter in some visit to their country. There is, especially on a branch in the top corner of the picture, a conversation going on between a fairy and a squirrel (who is a fairy too) which must have been taken from nature, or Mother Bunch's delightful super-nature. How awful their great glassy blue eyes are! How they peer out from under grass, and out of flowers, and from twigs and branches, and swing off over the tree-top, singing shrill little fairy choruses! We must have the *Fairy Tales* illustrated by this gentleman, that is clear; he is the only person, except Tieck, of Dresden, who knows anything about them. Yes, there *is* some one else; and a word may be introduced here in welcome to the admirable young designer, whose hand has lately been employed to illustrate the columns of our facetious friend (and the friend of everybody) *Punch*. This young artist (who has avowed his name, a very well-known one, that of DOYLE) has poured into *Punch's* columns a series of drawings quite extraordinary for their fancy, their variety, their beauty, and fun. It is the true genius of fairy-land, of burlesque which never loses sight of beauty. Friend *Punch's* very wrapper is quite a marvel in this way, at which we can never look without discovering some new little quip of humour or pleasant frolic of grace.

And if we have had reason to complain of Mr. Leslie's 'Comus' as deficient in poetry, what person is there that will not welcome

'Sancho,' although we have seen him before almost in the same attitude, employed in the same way, recounting his adventures to the kind, smiling duchess, as she sits in state ? There is only the sour old duenna, who refuses to be amused, and nothing has ever amused her these sixty years. But the ladies are all charmed, and tittering with one another ; the black slave who leans against the pillar has gone off in an honest fit of downright laughter. Even the little dog, the wonderful little Blenheim, by the lady's side, would laugh if she could (but, alas ! it is impossible), as the other little dog is said to have done on the singular occasion when 'the cow jumped over the moon.' [1] The glory of dulness is in Sancho's face. I don't believe there is a man in the world—no, not even in the House of Commons—so stupid as that. On the Whig side there is, certainly,—but no, it is best not to make comparisons which fall short of the mark. This is, indeed, the Sancho that Cervantes drew.

Although the editor of this Magazine had made a solemn condition with the writer of this notice that no pictures taken from *The Vicar of Wakefield* or *Gil Blas* should, by any favour or pretence, be noticed in the review ; yet, as the great picture of Mr. Mulready compelled the infraction of the rule, rushing through our resolve by the indomitable force of genius, we must, as the line is broken, present other Vicars, Thornhills, and Olivias, to walk in and promenade themselves in our columns, in spite of the vain placards at the entrance, 'VICARS OF WAKEFIELD NOT ADMITTED.' In the first place, let the Rev. Dr. Primrose and Miss Primrose walk up in Mr. Hollins' company. The vicar is mildly expostulating with his daughter regarding the attentions of Squire Thornhill. He looks mildly, too mild ; she looks ill-humoured, very sulky. Is it about the scolding, or the squire ? The figures are very nicely painted ; but they do not look accustomed (the lady especially) to the dresses they wear. After them come Mrs. Primrose, the Misses, and the young Masters Primrose, presented by Mr. Frith in his pretty picture (491). Squire Thornhill sits at his ease, and recounts his town adventures to the ladies ; the beautiful Olivia is quite lost in love with the slim red-coated dandy ; her sister is listening with respect ; but above all, the old lady and children hearken with wonder. These latter are charming figures, as, indeed, are all in the picture. As for Gil Blas,— but we shall be resolute about *him*. Certain Gil Blas there are in the exhibition eating ollapodridas, and what not. Not a word, however, shall be said regarding any one of them.

[1] *Qualia prospiciens Catulus ferit æthera risu*
Ipsaque trans lunæ cornua Vacca salit.—LUCRETIUS.

Among the figure-pieces Mr. Ward's 'Lafleur' must not be forgotten, which is pleasant, lively, and smartly drawn and painted ; nor Mr. Gilbert's 'Pear-tree Well,' which contains three graceful classical figures, which are rich in effect and colour ; nor Mr. MacInnes' good picture of Luther listening to the sacred ballad (the reformer is shut up in the octagon-room) ; nor a picture of Oliver Goldsmith on his rambles, playing the flute at a peasant's door, in which the colour is very pretty ; the character of the French peasants not French at all, and the poet's figure easy, correct, and well drawn.

Among more serious subjects may be mentioned with praise Mr. Dyce's two fierce figures, representing King Joash shooting the arrow of deliverance, which if the critics call 'French,' because they are well and carefully drawn, Mr. Dyce may be proud of being a Frenchman. Mr. Lauder's 'Wise and Foolish Virgins' is a fine composition ; the colour sombre and mysterious ; some of the figures extremely graceful, and the sentiment of the picture excellent. This is a picture which would infallibly have had a chance of a prize, if the poor, dear Art-Union were free to act.

Mr. Elmore's 'Rienzi addressing the People' is one of the very best pictures in the gallery. It is well and agreeably coloured, bright, pleasing, and airy. A group of people are gathered round the tribune, who addresses them among Roman ruins under a clear blue sky. The grouping is very good ; the figures rich and picturesque in attitude and costume. There is a group in front of a mother and child, who are thinking of anything but Rienzi and liberty ; who, perhaps, ought not to be so prominent, as they take away from the purpose of the picture, but who are beautiful wherever they are. And the picture is further to be remarked for the clear, steady, and honest painting which distinguishes it.

What is to be said of Mr. Poole's 'Moors beleaguered in Valencia?' A clever hideous picture in the very worst taste ; disease and desperation characteristically illustrated. The Spaniards beleaguer the town, and everybody is starving. Mothers with dry breasts unable to nourish infants ; old men, with lean ribs and blood-shot eyes, moaning on the pavement ; brown young skeletons pacing up and down the rampart, some raving, all desperate. Such is the agreeable theme which the painter has taken up. It is worse than last year, when the artist only painted the plague of London. Some *did* recover from that. All these Moors will be dead before another day, and the vultures will fatten on their lean carcasses, and pick out their red-hot eyeballs. Why do young men indulge in these horrors? Young

poets and romancers often do so and fancy they are exhibiting
'power'; whereas nothing is so easy. Any man with mere
instinct can succeed in the brutal in art. The coarse fury of
Zurbaran and Morales is as far below the sweet and beneficent
calm of Murillo as a butcher is beneath a hero. Don't let us
have any more of these hideous exhibitions—these Ghoul festivals.
It may be remembered that Amina in *The Arabian Nights*, who
liked churchyard suppers, could only eat a grain of rice when she
came to natural food. There is a good deal of sly satire in the
apologue which might be applied to many (especially French)
literary and pictorial artists of the convulsionary school.

We must not take leave of the compositions without mentioning
Mr. Landseer's wonderful ' Shoeing ' and ' Stag '; the latter the
most poetical, the former the most dexterous, perhaps, of the
works of this accomplished painter. The latter picture, at a
little distance, expands almost into the size of nature. The
enormous stag by the side of a great blue northern lake stalks
over the snow down to the shore, whither his mate is coming
through the water to join him. Snowy mountains bend round
the lonely landscape, the stars are shining out keenly in the deep
icy blue overhead ; in a word, your teeth begin to chatter as you
look at the picture, and it can't properly be seen without a greatcoat. The donkey and the horse in the shoeing picture are
prodigious imitations of nature ; the blacksmith only becomes
impalpable. There is a charming portrait in the great room by
the same artist in which the same defect may be remarked. A
lady is represented with two dogs in her lap ; the dogs look real ;
the lady a thin unsubstantial vision of a beautiful woman. You
ought to see the landscape through her.

Amongst the landscape-painters, Mr. Stanfield has really painted
this year better than any former year—a difficult matter. The
pictures are admirable, the drawing of the water wonderful, the
look of freshness, and breeze, and motion conveyed with delightful
skill. All Mr. Creswick's pictures will be seen with pleasure,
especially the delicious ' Summer Evening '; the most airy and
clear, and also the most poetical of his landscapes. The fine
' Evening Scene ' of Danby also seems to have the extent and
splendour, and to suggest the solemn feelings of a vast mountain-
scene at sunset. The admirers of Sir Augustus Callcott's soft,
golden landscapes will here find some of his most delightful
pieces. Mr. Roberts has painted his best in his Nile scene, and
his French architectural pieces are of scarce inferior merit. Mr.
Lee, Mr. Witherington, and Mr. Leitch have contributed works,
showing all their well-known qualities and skill. And as for Mr.

Turner, he has out-prodigied almost all former prodigies. He has made a picture with real rain, behind which is real sunshine, and you expect a rainbow every minute. Meanwhile, there comes a train down upon you, really moving at the rate of fifty miles an hour, and which the reader had best make haste to see, lest it should dash out of the picture, and be away up Charing Cross through the wall opposite. All those wonders are performed with means not less wonderful than the effects are. The rain, in the astounding picture called ' Rain—Steam—Speed,' is composed of dabs of dirty putty *slapped* on to the canvas with a trowel ; the sunshine scintillates out of very thick, smeary lumps of chrome yellow. The shadows are produced by cool tones of crimson lake, and quiet glazings of vermilion, although the fire in the steam-engine *looks* as if it were red. I am not prepared to say that it is not painted with cobalt and pea-green. And as for the manner in which the '*Speed*' is done, of that the less said the better,—only it is a positive fact that there is a steam coach going fifty miles an hour. The world has never seen anything like this picture.

In respect of the portraits of the Exhibition, if Royal Academicians will take the word of *The Morning Post, The Morning Chronicle, The Spectator*, and, far above all, of *Fraser's Magazine*, they will pause a little before they hang such a noble portrait as that of W. Conyngham, Esq., by Samuel Lawrence, away out of sight, while some of their own paltry canvases meet the spectator nose to nose. The man with the glove of Titian in the Louvre has evidently inspired Mr. Lawrence, and his picture is so far an imitation ; but what then ? it is better to imitate great things well, than to imitate a simpering barber's dummy, like No. 10,000, let us say, or to perpetrate yonder horror, weak, but oh ! how heavy, smeared, flat, pink and red, grinning, ill-drawn portraits (such as Nos. 99,999 and 99,999^d) which the old Academicians perpetrate. You are right to keep the best picture in the room out of the way, to be sure ; it would sternly frown your simpering unfortunates out of countenance ; but let us have at least a chance of seeing the good picture. Have one room, say, for the Academicians, and another for the clever artists. Diminish your number of exhibited pictures to six, if you like, but give the young men a chance. It is pitiful to see their works pushed out of sight, and to be offered what you give us in exchange.

This does not apply to all the esquires who paint portraits ; but, with regard to the names of the delinquents, it is best to be silent, lest a showing up of them should have a terrible effect on

the otherwise worthy men, and drive them to an untimely desperation. So I shall say little about the portraits, mentioning merely
that Mr. Grant has one or two, a small one especially, of great
beauty and lady-like grace ; and one very bad one, such as that
of Lord Forrester. Mr. Pickersgill has some good heads ; the
little portrait of Mr. Ainsworth by Mr. Maclise is as clever
and like as the artist knows how to make it. Mr. Middleton
has some female heads especially beautiful. Mrs. Carpenter is
one of the most manly painters in the Exhibition ; and if you
walk into the miniature room, you may look at the delicious
little gems from the pencil of Sir William Ross, those still more
graceful and poetical by Mr. Thorburn, and the delightful cox-
combries of Mr. Chalon. I have found out a proper task for that
gentleman, and hereby propose that he should illustrate *Coningsby*.

In the statue-room, Mr. Gibson's classic group attracts attention and deserves praise ; and the busts of Parker, Macdonald,
Behnes, and other well-known portrait sculptors have all their
usual finish, skill and charm.

At the Water-Colour Gallery the pleased spectator lingers as
usual delighted, surrounded by the pleasantest drawings and the
most genteel company. It requires no small courage to walk
through that avenue of plush breeches with which the lobby is
lined, and to pass two files of whiskered men in canes and huge
calves, who contemptuously regard us poor fellows with Bluchers
and gingham umbrellas. But these passed, you are in the best
society. Bishops, I have remarked, frequent this Gallery in
venerable numbers ; likewise dignified clergymen with rosettes ;
Quakeresses, also, in dove-coloured silks meekly changing colour ;
squires and their families from the country ; and it is a fact that
you never can enter the Gallery without seeing a wonderfully
pretty girl. This fact merits to be generally known, and is alone
worth the price of the article.

I suspect that there are some people from the country who
admire Mr. Pont still ; those fresh, honest, unalloyed country
appetites ! There are the Prout Nurembergs and Venices still ;
the awnings, the waterposts, and the red-capped bargemen drawn
with a reed pen ; but we *blasés* young *roués* about London get
tired of these simple dishes, and must have more excitement.
There, too, are Mr. Hill's stags with pink stomachs, his spinach
pastures and mottled farm-houses ; also innumerable windy downs
and heaths by Mr. Copley Fielding ;—in the which breezy flats I
have so often wandered before with burnt-sienna ploughboys, that
the walk is no longer tempting.

Not so, however, the marine pieces of Mr. Bentley. That gentleman, to our thinking, has never painted so well. Witness his 'Indiaman towed up the Thames' (53), his 'Signalling the Pilot' (161), and his admirable view of 'Mount St. Michel' (127), in which the vessel quite dances and falls on the water. He deserves to divide the prize with Mr. Stanfield at the Academy.

All the works of a clever young landscape-painter, Mr. G. A. Fripp, may be looked at with pleasure; they show great talent, no small dexterity and genuine enthusiastic love of nature. Mr. Alfred Fripp, a figure painter, merits likewise very much praise; his works are not complete as yet, but his style is thoughtful, dramatic, and original.

Mr. Hunt's dramas of one or two characters are as entertaining and curious as ever. His 'Outcast' is amazingly fine, and tragic in character. His 'Sick Cigar-boy,' a wonderful delineation of nausea. Look at the picture of the toilette, in which, with the parlour-tongs, Betty, the housemaid, is curling little miss's hair: there is a dish of yellow soap in that drawing, and an old comb and brush, the fidelity of which make the delicate beholder shudder. On one of the screens there are some 'birds' nests,' out of which I am surprised no spectator has yet stolen any of the eggs—you have but to stoop down and take them.

Mr. Taylor's delightful drawings are even more than ordinarily clever. His 'Houseless Wanderers' is worthy of Hogarth in humour; most deliciously coloured and treated. 'The Gleaner' is full of sunshine; the larder quite a curiosity as showing the ease, truth, and dexterity with which the artist washes in his flowing delineations from nature. In his dogs, you don't know which most to admire, the fidelity with which the animals are painted, or the ease with which they are done.

This gift of facility Mr. Cattermole also possesses to an amazing extent. As pieces of effect, his 'Porch' and 'Rook-Shooting' are as wonderful as they are pleasing. His large picture of 'Monks in a Refectory' is very fine; rich, original and sober in colour; excellent in sentiment and general grouping; in individual attitude and drawing not sufficiently correct. As the figures are much smaller than that in the refectory, these faults are less visible in the magnificent 'Battle for the Bridge,' a composition, perhaps, the most complete that the artist has yet produced. The landscape is painted as grandly as Salvator; the sky wonderfully airy, the sunshine shining through the glades of the wood, the huge trees rocking and swaying as the breeze rushes by them; the battling figures are full of hurry, fire and tumult. All these things are rather indicated by the painter than defined by him;

but such hints are enough from such a genius. The charmed and captivated imagination is quite ready to supply what else is wanting.

Mr. Frederick Nash has some unpretending, homely, exquisitely faithful scenes in the Rhine country. 'Boppart,' 'Bacharach,' etc., of which a sojourner in those charming districts will always be glad to have a reminiscence. Mr. Joseph Nash has not some of the cleverest of his mannerism, nor Mr. Lake Price the best of his smart, dandified, utterly unnatural exteriors. By far the best designs of this kind are the Windsor and Buckingham Palace sketches of Mr. Douglas Morison, executed with curious fidelity and skill. There is the dining hall in Buckingham Palace, with all the portraits, all the candles in all the chandeliers ; the China gimcracks over the mantelpiece, the dinner table set out, the napkins folded mitrewise, the round water glasses, the sherry glasses, the champagne ditto, and all in a space not so big as two pages of this Magazine. There is the Queen's own chamber at Windsor, her Majesty's piano, her royal writing table, an *escritoire* with pigeon holes, where the august papers are probably kept ; and very curious, clever, and ugly all these pictures of furniture are too, and will be a model for the avoidance of upholsterers in coming ages.

Mr. John William Wright's sweet female figures must not be passed over ; nor the pleasant Stothard-like drawings of his veteran namesake. The 'Gipsies' of Mr. Oakley will also be looked at with pleasure ; and this gentleman may be complimented as likely to rival the Richmonds and the Chalons 'in another place,' where may be seen a very good full-length portrait drawn by him.

The exhibition of the New Society of Water-Colour Painters has grown to be quite as handsome and agreeable as that of its mamma, the old society in Pall Mall East. Those who remember the first ventures of this little band of painters, to whom the gates of the elder gallery were hopelessly shut, must be glad to see the progress the younger branch had made ; and we have every reason to congratulate ourselves that instead of one pleasant exhibition annually, the amateur can recreate himself now with two. Many of the pictures here are of very great merit.

Mr. Warren's Egyptian pictures are clever, and only need to be agreeable where he takes a pretty subject, such as that of the 'Egyptian Lady' (150) ; his work is pretty sure to be followed by that welcome little ticket of emerald green in the corner, which announces that a purchaser has made his appearance. But the eye is little interested by views of yellow deserts and sheikhs, and woolly-headed warriors with ugly wooden swords.

And yet mere taste, grace, and beauty, won't always succeed ; witness Mr. Absolon's drawings, of which few—far too few— boast the green seal, and which are one and all of them charming. There is one in the first room from *The V-c-r of W-kef-ld* (we are determined not to write that name again), which is delightfully composed, and a fresh happy picture of a country fête. 'The Dartmoor Turf-gatherers' (87) is still better ; the picture is full of air, grace, pretty drawing, and brilliant colour, and yet no green seal. 'A little Sulky,' 'The Devonshire Cottage Door,' 'The Widow on the Stile,' 'The Stocking-knitter,' are all, too, excellent in their way, and bear the artist's *cachet* of gentle and amiable grace. But the drawings, in point of execution, do not go far enough ; they are not sufficiently bright to attract the eyes of that great and respectable body of amateurs who love no end of cobalt, carmine, stippling, and plenty of emerald green, and ver- milion ; they are not made out sufficiently in line to rank as pictures.

Behold how Mr. Corbould can work when he likes—how *he* can work you off the carmine stippling ! In his large piece, 'The Britons deploring the Departure of the Romans,' there is much very fine and extraordinary cleverness of pencil. Witness the draperies of the two women, which are painted with so much cleverness and beauty, that indeed, one regrets that one of them has not got a little drapery more. The same tender regret pervades the bosom while looking at that of Joan of Arc, 'while engaged in the servile offices of her situation as a menial at an inn, ruminating upon the distressing state of France.' Her 'servile situation' seems to be that of an ostler at the establish- ment in question, for she is leading down a couple of animals to drink ; and as for 'the distressing state of France,' it ought not, surely, to affect such a fat little comfortable simple-looking undressed body. Bating the figure of Joan, who looks as pretty as a young lady out of the last novel, bating, I say, baiting Joan, who never rode horses, depend on't, in that genteel way, the picture is exceedingly skilful, and much better in colour than Mr. Corbould's former works.

Mr. Wehnert's great drawing is a failure, but an honourable defeat. It shews great power and mastery over the material with which he works. He has two pretty German figures in the fore-room : 'The Innkeeper's Daughter' (38) and 'Perdita and Florizel' (316). Perhaps he is the author of the pretty arabesques with which the Society have this year ornamented their list of pictures ; he has a German name, and *English* artists can have no need to be copying from the Dusseldorf's embellishments to decorate their catalogues.

Mr. Haghe's great drawing of the 'Death of Zurbarab' is not interesting from any peculiar fineness of expression in the faces of the actors who figure in this gloomy scene ; but it is largely and boldly painted, in deep sombre washes of colours, with none of the niggling prettinesses to which artists in water colours seem forced to resort in order to bring their pictures to a high state of finish. Here the figures and the draperies look as if they were laid down at once with a bold yet careful certainty of hand. The effect of the piece is very fine, the figures grandly grouped. Among all the water-colour painters we know of none who can wield the brush like Mr. Haghe, with his skill, his breadth, and his certainty.

Mr. Jenkins' beautiful female figure in the drawing called 'Love' (123) must be mentioned with especial praise ; it is charming in design colour and sentiment. Another female figure 'The Girl at the Stile,' by the same artist, has not equal finish, roundness, and completeness, but the same sentiment of tender grace and beauty.

Mr. Bright's landscape-drawings are exceedingly clever, but there is too much of the drawing master in the handling, too much dash, skurry, sharp cleverness of execution. Him Mr. Jutsum follows with cleverness not quite equal, and mannerism still greater. After the performance of which the eye reposes gracefully upon some pleasant evening scenes by Mr. Duncan (3, 10) ; and the delightful 'Shady Lane' of Mr. Youngman. Mr. Boys' pictures will be always looked at and admired for the skill and correctness of a hand which, in drawing, is not inferior to that of Canaletti.

As for Suffolk Street, that delicious retreat may or may not be still open. I have been there, but was frightened from the place by the sight of Haydon's Napoleon, with his vast head, his large body, and his little legs, staring out upon the indigo sea, in a grass-green coat. Nervous people avoid that sight, and the Emperor remains in Suffolk Street as lonely as at St. Helena.

PICTURE GOSSIP:

IN A LETTER FROM MICHAEL ANGELO TITMARSH,

ALL' ILLUSTRISSIMO SIGNOR, IL MIO SIGNOR COLENDISSIMO,
AUGUSTO HA ARVÉ, PITTORE IN ROMA.[1]

I AM going to fulfil the promise, my dear Augusto, which I uttered, with a faltering voice and streaming eyes, before I stepped into the jingling old courier's vehicle, which was to bear me from Rome to Florence. Can I forget that night—that parting? Gaunter stood by so affected, that for the last quarter of an hour he did not swear once; Flake's emotion exhibited itself in audible sobs; Jellyson said naught, but thrust a bundle of Torlonia's four baiocchi cigars into the hand of the departing friend; and you yourself were so deeply agitated by the event, that you took four glasses of absinthe to string up your nerves for the fatal moment. Strange vision of past days!—for vision it seems to me now. And have I been in Rome really and truly? Have I seen the great works of my Christian namesake of the Buonarroti family, and the light arcades of the Vatican? Have I seen the glorious Apollo, and that other divine fiddle-player whom Raphael painted? Yes —and the English dandies swaggering on the Pincian Hill! Yes —and have eaten woodcocks and drank Ovieto hard by the huge, broad-shouldered Pantheon Portico, in the comfortable parlours of the Falcone. Do you recollect that speech I made at Bertini's in proposing the health of the Pope of Rome on Christmas Day?—do you remember it? *I* don't. But his Holiness, no doubt, heard of the oration, and was flattered by the compliment of the illustrious English traveller.

I went to the exhibition of the Royal Academy lately, and all these reminiscences rushed back on a sudden with affecting volubility; not that there was anything in or out of the gallery which put me specially in mind of sumptuous and Liberal Rome; but in the great room was a picture of a fellow in a broad Roman hat, in a velvet Roman coat, and large yellow moustachios, and

[1] [*Fraser's Magazine*, June. 1845.]

that prodigious scowl which young artists assume when sitting for their portraits—he was one of our set at Rome ; and the scenes of the winter came back pathetically to my mind, and all the friends of that season,—Orifice and his sentimental songs ; Father Giraldo and his poodle, and MacBrick, the trump of bankers. Hence the determination to write this letter ; but the hand is crabbed, and the postage is dear, and instead of despatching it by the mail, I shall send it to you by means of the printer, knowing well that *Fraser's Magazine* is eagerly read at Rome, and not (on account of its morality) excluded in the *Index Expurgatorius.*

And it will be doubly agreeable to me to write to you regarding the fine arts in England, because I know, my dear Augusto, that you have a thorough contempt for my opinion—indeed, for that of all persons, excepting, of course, one whose name is already written in this sentence. Such, however, is not the feeling respecting my critical powers in this country ; *here* they know the merit of Michael Angelo Titmarsh better, and they say, ' He paints so badly, that, hang it ! he *must* be a good judge ; ' in the latter part of which opinion, of course, I agree.

You should have seen the consternation of the fellows at my arrival !—of our dear brethren who thought I was safe at Rome for the season, and that their works exhibited in May would be spared the dreadful ordeal of my ferocious eye. When I entered the club-room in St. Martin's Lane, and called for a glass of brandy-and-water like a bombshell, you should have seen the terror of some of the artists assembled ! They knew that the frightful projectile just launched into their club-room must *burst* in the natural course of things. Who would be struck down by the explosion ? was the thought of every one. Some of the hypocrites welcomed me meanly back, some of the timid trembled, some of the savage and guilty muttered curses at my arrival. You should have seen the ferocious looks of Daggerly, for example, as he scowled at me from the supper-table, and clutched the trenchant weapon with which he was dissevering his toasted cheese.

From the period of my arrival until that of the opening of the various galleries, I maintained with the artists every proper affability, but still was not too familiar. It is the custom of their friends before their pictures are sent in to the exhibition, to visit the painter's works at their private studios, and there encourage them by saying ' Bravo, Jones (I don't mean Jones, R.A., for I defy any man to say "bravo" to *him*, but Jones in general) ! ' ' Tomkins, this is your greatest work ! ' ' Smith, my boy, they must elect you an Associate for this ! ' and so forth. These harmless banalities of compliment pass between the painters and their friends on such occasions. I, myself, have uttered many such civil phrases in former years under like circumstances. But it is different now. Fame has its privileges as well as its pleasures. The friend may see his companions in private, but the JUDGE must not pay visits to his clients. I stayed away from the *ateliers* of all the artists (at least I only visited one, kindly telling him that he didn't count as an artist at all), would only see their pictures in the public galleries, and judge them in the fair race with their neighbours. This announcement and conduct of mine filled all the Berners Street and Fitzroy Square district with terror.

As I am writing this after having had my fill of their works, so publicly exhibited in the country, at a distance from catalogues, my only book of reference being an orchard whereof the trees are now bursting into full blossom,—it is probable that my remarks will be rather general than particular, that I shall only discourse about those pictures which I especially remember, or, indeed, upon any other point suitable to my honour and your delectation.

I went round the galleries with a young friend of mine, who, like yourself at present, has been a student of 'High Art' at Rome. He had been a pupil of Monsieur Ingres, at Paris. He could draw rude figures of eight feet high to a nicety, and had produced many heroic compositions of that pleasing class and size, to the great profit of the paper-stretchers both in Paris and Rome. He came back from the latter place a year since, with his beard and moustachios of course. He could find no room in all Newman Street and Soho big enough to hold him and his genius, and was turned out of a decent house because, for the purposes of art, he wished to batter down the partition-wall between the two drawing rooms he had. His great cartoon last year (whether it was 'Car-actacus before Claudius,' or a scene from *The Vicar of Wakefield*, I won't say) failed somehow. He was a good deal cut up by the defeat, and went into the country to his relations, from whom he returned after a while, with his moustachios shaved, clean linen, and other signs of depression. He said (with a hollow laugh) he should not commence on his great canvas this year, and so gave up the completion of his composition of 'Boadicea addressing the Iceni:' quite a novel subject, which, with that ingenuity and profound reading which distinguishes his brethren, he had deter-mined to take up.

Well, sir, this youth and I went to the exhibitions together, and I watched his behaviour before the pictures. At the tragic, swaggering, theatrical, historical pictures, he yawned ; before some of the grand, flashy landscapes, he stood without the least emotion ; but before some quiet scenes of humour or pathos, or some easy little copy of nature, the youth stood in pleased contemplation, the nails of his high-lows seemed to be screwed into the floor there, and his face dimpled over with grins.

'These little pictures,' said he, on being questioned, 'are worth a hundred times more than the big ones. In the latter you see signs of ignorance of every kind, weakness of hand, poverty of invention, carelessness of drawing, lamentable imbecility of thought. Their heroism is borrowed from the theatre, their sentiment is so maudlin that it makes you sick. I see no symptoms of thought or of minds strong and genuine enough to cope with elevated subjects. No individuality, no novelty, the decencies of costume (my friend did not mean that the figures we were looking at were naked, like Mr. Etty's, but that they were dressed out of all historical propriety) are disregarded; the people are striking attitudes, as at the Coburg. There is something painful to me in this *naïve* exhibition of incompetency, this imbecility that is so unconscious of its own failure. If, however, the aspiring men don't succeed, the modest do; and what they have really seen or experienced, our artist can depict with successful accuracy and delightful skill. 'Hence,' says he, 'I would sooner have So-and-so's little sketch ("A Donkey on a Common") than What-d'ye-call-'em's enormous picture ("Sir Walter Manny and the Crusaders discovering Nova Scotia"), and prefer yonder unpretending sketch, "Shrimp Catchers, Morning," (how exquisitely the long and level sands are touched off! how beautifully the morning light touches the countenances of the fishermen, and illumines the rosy features of the shrimps!) to yonder pretentious illustration from Spenser, "Sir Botibol rescues Una from Sir Uglimore in the Cave of the Enchantress Ichthyosaura."'

I am only mentioning another's opinion of these pictures, and would not of course, for my own part, wish to give pain by provoking comparisons that must be disagreeable to some persons. But I could not help agreeing with my young friend, and saying, 'Well, then, in the name of goodness, my dear fellow, if you only like what is real, and natural, and unaffected—if upon such works you gaze with delight, while from more pretentious performers you turn away with weariness, why the deuce must *you* be in the heroic vein? Why don't you *do* what you like?' The young man turned round on the iron heel of his high-lows, and walked downstairs clinking them sulkily.

There are a variety of classes and divisions into which the works of our geniuses may be separated. There are the heroic pictures, the theatrical-heroic, the religious, the historical-sentimental, the historical-familiar, the namby-pamby, and so forth.

Among the heroic pictures of course Mr. Haydon's ranks the first, its size and pretensions call for that place. It roars out to you as it were with a Titanic voice from among all the competition to public favour, 'Come and look at me.' A broad-shouldered, swaggering, hulking archangel, with those rolling eyes and distending nostrils which belong to the species of sublime caricature, stands scowling on a sphere from which the devil is just descending bound earthwards. Planets, comets, and other astronomical phenomena roll and blaze round the pair and flame in the new blue sky. There is something burly and bold in this resolute genius which will attack only enormous subjects, which will deal with nothing but the epic, something respectable even in the defeats of such characters. I was looking the other day at Southampton at a stout gentleman in a green coat and white hat, who a year or two since fully believed that he could walk upon the water, and set off in the presence of a great concourse of people upon his supermarine journey. There is no need to tell you that the poor fellow got a wetting and sank amidst the jeers of all his beholders. I think somehow they should not have laughed at that honest ducked gentleman, they should have respected the faith and simplicity which led him unhesitatingly to venture upon that watery experiment; and so, instead of laughing at Haydon, which you and I were just about to do, let us check our jocularity, and give him credit for his great earnestness of purpose. I begin to find the world growing more pathetic daily, and laugh less every year of my life. Why laugh at idle hopes, or vain purposes, or utter blundering self-confidence? Let us be gentle with them henceforth, who knows whether there may not be something of the sort *chez nous?* But I am wandering from Haydon and his big picture. Let us hope somebody will buy. Who, I cannot tell; it will not do for a chapel; it is too big for a house: I have it—it might answer to hang up over a caravan at a fair, if a travelling orrery were exhibited inside.

This may be sheer impertinence and error, the picture may suit some tastes, it does *The Times* for instance, which pronounces it to be a noble work of the highest art; whereas the *Post* won't believe a bit, and passes it by with scorn. What a comfort it is that there are different tastes then, and that almost all artists have thus a chance of getting a livelihood somehow! There is Martin, for another instance, with his brace of pictures about Adam and Eve, which I would venture to place in the theatrical-heroic class. One looks at those strange pieces and wonders how people can be found to admire, and yet they do. Grave old people, with chains and seals, look dumb-foundered into those vast perspectives, and think the apex of the sublime is reached there. In one of Sir Bulwer Lytton's novels there is a passage to that effect. I forget where, but there is a new edition of them coming out in single volumes, and am positive you will find the sentiment somewhere; they come up to his conceptions of the sublime, they answer his ideas of beauty of the Beautiful as he writes with a large B. He is himself an artist and a man of genius. What right have we poor devils to question such an authority? Do you recollect how we used to laugh in the Capitol at the Domenichino Sybil which this same author praises so enthusiastically? a wooden, pink-faced, goggle-eyed, ogling creature, we said it was, with no more beauty or sentiment than a wax doll. But this was our conceit, dear Augusto; on subjects of art, perhaps, there is no reasoning after all: or who can tell why children have a passion for lollypops, and this man worships beef while t'other adores mutton? To the child lollypops may be the truthful and beautiful, and why should not some men find Martin's pictures as much to their taste as Milton?

Another instance of the blessed variety of tastes may be mentioned here advantageously; while, as you have seen, *The Times* awards the palm to Haydon, and Sir Lytton exalts Martin as the greatest painter of the English school, *The Chronicle*, quite as well informed, no doubt, says that Mr. Eddis is the great genius of the present season, and that his picture of Moses's mother parting with him before leaving him in the bulrushes is a great and noble composition.

This critic must have a taste for the neat and agreeable, that is clear. Mr. Eddis's picture is nicely coloured; the figures in fine clean draperies, the sky a bright clean colour; Moses's mother is a handsome woman; and as she holds her child to her breast for the last time, and lifts up her fine eyes to heaven, the beholder may be reasonably moved by a decent *bourgeois* compassion; a handsome woman parting from her child is always an object of proper sympathy; but as for the greatness of the picture as a work of art, that is another question of tastes again. This picture seemed to me to be essentially a prose composition, not a poetical one. It tells you no more than you can see. It has no more wonder or poetry about it than a police report or a newspaper paragraph, and should be placed, as I take it, in the historic-sentimental school, which is pretty much followed in England—nay, as close as possible to the namby-pamby quarter.

Of the latter sort there are some illustrious examples; and as it is the fashion for critics to award prizes, I would for my part cheerfully award the prize of a new silver teaspoon to Mr. Redgrave,

that champion of suffering female innocence, for his 'Governess.'
That picture is more decidedly *spoony* than, perhaps, any other of
this present season ; and the subject seems to be a favourite with
the artist. We have had the 'Governess' one year before, or a
variation of her under the name of 'The Teacher,' or *vice versa*.
The Teacher's young pupils are at play in the garden, she sits sadly
in the schoolroom, there she sits, poor dear !—the piano is open
beside her, and (oh, harrowing thought !) 'Home, sweet home !'
is open in the music-book. She sits and thinks of that dear place,
with a sheet of black-edged note-paper in her hand. They have
brought her her tea and bread and butter on a tray. She has
drunk the tea, *she has not tasted the bread and butter !* There is
pathos for you ! there is art ! This is, indeed, a love for lollypops
with a vengeance, a regular babyhood of taste, about which a man
with a manly stomach may be allowed to protest a little peevishly,
and implore the public to give up such puling food.

There is a gentleman in the Octagon Room who, to be sure,
runs Mr. Redgrave rather hard, and should have a silver pap-spoon
at any rate, if the teaspoon is irrevocably awarded to his rival.
The Octagon Room prize is a picture called the 'Arrival of the
Overland Mail.' A lady is in her bed-chamber, a portrait of her
husband, Major Jones (cherished lord of that bridal apartment,
with its drab-curtained bed), hangs on the wainscot in the distance,
and you see his red coat and moustachios gleaming there between
the wardrobe and the washhand-stand. But where is his lady ?
She is on her knees by the bed-side, her face has sunk into the
feather-bed ; her hands are clasped agonisingly together ; a most
tremendous black-edged letter has just arrived by the overland
mail. It is all up with Jones. Well, let us hope she will marry
again, and get over her grief for poor J.

Is not there something *naïve* and simple in this downright way
of exciting compassion ? I saw people looking at this pair of
pictures evidently with yearning hearts. The great geniuses
who invented them have not, you see, toiled in vain. They can
command the sympathies of the public, they have gained Art-
Union prizes, let us hope, as well as those humble imaginary ones
which I have just awarded, and yet my heart is not naturally
hard, though it refuses to be moved by such means as are here
employed.

If the simple statement of a death is to harrow up the feelings,
or to claim the tributary tear, *mon Dieu !* a man ought to howl
every morning over the newspaper obituary. If we are to cry for
every governess who leaves home, what a fund of pathos *The
Times* advertisements would afford daily ; we might weep down

whole columns of close type. I have said before I am growing more inclined to the pathetic daily, but let us in the name of goodness make a stand somewhere, or the namby-pamby of the world will become unendurable; and we shall melt away in a deluge of blubber. This drivelling, hysterical sentimentality, it is surely the critic's duty to grin down, to shake any man roughly by the shoulder who seems dangerously affected by it, and not sparing his feelings in the least, tell him he is a fool for his pains, to have no more respect for those who invent it, but expose their error with all the downrightness that is necessary.

By far the prettiest of the maudlin pictures is Mr. Stone's *Premier Pas*. It is that old pretty, rococo, fantastic Jenny and Jessamy couple, whose loves the painter has been chronicling any time these five years, and whom he has spied out at various wells, porches, etc. The lad is making love with all his might, and the maiden is in a pretty confusion—her heart flutters, and she only seems to spin. She drinks in the warm words of the young fellow with a pleasant conviction of the invincibility of her charms. He appeals nervously, and tugs at a pink which is growing up the porch-side. It is that pink, somehow, which has saved the picture from being decidedly namby-pamby. There is something new, fresh, and delicate about the little incident of the flower. It redeems Jenny, and renders that young prig, Jessamy, bearable. The picture is very nicely painted, according to the careful artist's wont. The neck and hands of the girl are especially pretty. The lad's face is effeminate and imbecile, but his velveteen breeches are painted with great vigour and strength.

This artist's picture of the 'Queen and Ophelia' is in a much higher walk of art. There may be doubts about Ophelia. She is too pretty to my taste. Her dress (especially the black bands round her arms) too elaborately conspicuous and coquettish. The queen is a noble dramatic head and attitude. Ophelia seems to be looking at us, the audience, and in a pretty attitude expressly to captivate us. The queen is only thinking about the crazed girl, and Hamlet, and her own gloomy affairs, and has quite forgotten her own noble beauty and superb presence. The colour of the picture struck me as quite new, sedate, but bright and very agreeable; the chequered light and shadow is made cleverly to aid in forming the composition; it is very picturesque and good. It is by far the best of Mr. Stone's works, and in the best line. Good-bye, Jenny and Jessamy; we hope never to see you again—no more rococo rustics, no more namby-pamby: the man who can paint the queen of Hamlet must forsake henceforth such fiddle-faddle company.

R

By the way, has any Shaksperian commentator ever remarked how fond the queen really was of her second husband, the excellent Claudius ? How courteous and kind the latter always was towards her ? So excellent a family man ought to be pardoned a few errors in consideration of his admirable behaviour to his wife. He *did* go a little far, certainly, but then it was to possess a jewel of a woman.

More pictures indicating a fine appreciation of the tragic sentiment are to be found in the Exhibition. Among them may be mentioned specially Mr. Johnson's picture of 'Lord Russell taking the Communion in Prison before Execution.' The story is finely told here, the group large and noble. The figure of the kneeling wife, who looks at her husband meekly engaged in the last sacred office, is very good indeed ; and the little episode of the gaoler, who looks out into the yard indifferent, seems to me to give evidence of a true dramatic genius. In *Hamlet*, how those indifferent remarks of Guildenstern and Rosencrantz, at the end, bring out the main figures and deepen the surrounding gloom of the tragedy !

In Mr. Frith's admirable picture of the 'Good Pastor,' from Goldsmith, there is some sentiment of a very quiet, refined, Sir-Roger-de-Coverley-like-sort—not too much of it—it is indicated rather than expressed. 'Sentiment, sir,' Walker of the *Original* used to say,—'sentiment, sir, is like garlic in made dishes : it should be felt everywhere and seen nowhere.'

Now, I won't say that Mr. Frith's sentiment is like garlic, or provoke any other savoury comparison regarding it ; but say, in a word, this is one of the pictures I would like to have sent abroad to be exhibited at a European congress of painters, to shew what an English artist can do. The young painter seems to me to have had a thorough comprehension of his subject and his own abilities. And what a rare quality is this, to know what you can do ! An ass will go and take the grand historic walk, while, with lowly wisdom, Mr. Frith prefers the lowly path where there are plenty of flowers growing, and children prattling along the walks. This is the sort of picture that is good to paint nowadays—kindly, beautiful, inspiring delicate sympathies, and awakening tender good-humour. It is a comfort to have such a companion as that in a study to look up at when your eyes are tired with work, and to refresh you with its gentle, quiet good-fellowship. I can see it now, as I shut my own eyes, displayed faithfully on the camera obscura of the brain—the dear old parson with his congregation of old and young clustered round him ; the little ones plucking him by the gown, with wondering eyes, half-roguery, half-terror ; the smoke is curling up from the cottage chimneys in a peaceful, Sabbath-sort of way; the three village quidnuncs are chattering together at the churchyard stile; there's a poor girl seated there on a stone, who has been crossed in love evidently, and looks anxiously to the parson for a little doubtful consolation. That's the real sort of sentiment—there's no need of a great, clumsy, black-edged letter to placard her misery, as it were, after Mr. Redgrave's fashion; the sentiment is only the more sincere for being unobtrusive, and the spectator gives his compassion the more readily, because the unfortunate object makes no coarse demands upon his pity.

The painting of this picture is exceedingly clever and dexterous. One or two of the foremost figures are painted with the breadth and pearly delicacy of Greuze. The three village politicians, in the background, might have been touched by Teniers, so neat, brisk, and sharp is the execution of the artist's facile brush.

Mr. Frost (a new name, I think, in the Catalogue) has given us a picture of 'Sabrina,' which is so pretty that I heartily hope it has not been purchased for the collection from Comus, which adorns the Buckingham Palace summer-house. It is worthy of a better place and price than our royal patrons appear to be disposed to give for the works of English Arts. What victims have those poor fellows been of this awful patronage! Great has been the commotion in the pictorial world, dear Augusto, regarding the fate of those frescoes which royalty was pleased to order, which it condescended to purchase at a price that no poor amateur would have the face to offer. Think of the greatest patronage in the world giving forty pounds for pictures worth four hundred—condescending to buy works from humble men who could not refuse, and paying for them below their value! Think of august powers and principalities ordering the works of such a great man as Etty to be hacked out of the palace wall—that was a slap in the face to every artist in England; and I can agree with the conclusion come to by an indignant poet of *Punch's* band, who says, for his part,—

> I will not toil for queen and crown,
> If princely patrons spurn me down;
> I will not ask for royal job—
> Let my Maecenas be A SNOB![1]

This is, however, a delicate, an awful subject, over which loyal subjects like you and I had best mourn in silence; but the fate

---

[1] The indignant poet of *Punch's* band was Thackeray. The lines occur in the verses, *A Painter's Wish* (*Punch*, April 5, 1845), which is reprinted in vol. xviii. of this edition: *Ballads, etc.*

of Etty's noble picture of last year made me tremble lest Frost should be similarly nipped ; and I hope for more genuine patronage for this promising young painter. His picture is like a mixture of very good Hilton and Howard raised to a state of genius. There is sameness in the heads, but great grace and beauty—a fine sweeping movement in the composition of the beautiful fairy figures, undulating gracefully through the stream, while the lilies lie gracefully overhead. There is another submarine picture of 'Nymphs cajoling Young Hylas,' which contains a great deal of very clever imitations of Boucher.

That youthful Goodall, whose early attempts promised so much, is not quite realising those promises, I think, and is cajoled, like Hylas before mentioned, by dangerous beauty. His 'Connemara Girls going to Market' are a vast deal too clean and pretty for such females. They laugh and simper in much too genteel a manner ; they are washing such pretty white feet as I don't think are common about Leenane or Ballynahinch, and would be better at ease in white satin slippers than trudging up Croaghpatrick. There is a luxury of geographical knowledge for you ! I have not done with it yet. Stop till we come to Roberts's 'View of Jerusalem,' and Muller's pictures of 'Rhodes,' and 'Xanthus,' and 'Telmessus.' This artist's sketches are excellent; like nature, and like Decamps, that best of painters of Oriental life and colours. In the pictures the artist forgets the brilliancy of colour which is so conspicuous in his sketches, and 'Telmessus' looks as grey and heavy as Dover in March.

Mr. Pickersgill (not the Acamedician, by any means) deserves great praise for two very poetical pieces ; one from Spenser, I think (Sir Botibol, let us say, as before, with somebody in some hag's cave) ; another called the 'Four Ages,' which has still better grace and sentiment. This artist, too, is evidently one of the disciples of Hilton ; and another, who has also, as it seems to me, studied with advantage that graceful and agreeable English painter, Mr. Hook, whose 'Song of the Olden Time' is hung up in the Octagon Closet, and makes a sunshine in that exceedingly shady place. The female figure is faulty, but charming (many charmers have their little faults, it is said) ; the old bard who is singing the song of the olden time a most venerable, agreeable, and handsome old minstrel. In Alnaschar-like moods a man fancies himself a noble patron, and munificent rewarder of artists ; in which case I should like to possess myself of the works of these two young men, and give them four times as large a price as the —— gave for pictures five times as good as theirs.

I suppose Mr. Eastlake's composition from *Comus* is the

contribution in which *he* has been mulcted, in company with his celebrated brother artists, for the famous Buckingham Palace pavilion. Working for nothing is very well; but to work for a good, honest, remunerating price is, perhaps, the best way, after all. I can't help thinking that the artist's courage has failed him over his *Comus* picture. Time and pains he has given, that is quite evident. The picture is prodigiously laboured, and hatched, and tickled up with a Chinese minuteness; but there is a woeful lack of *vis* in the work. That poor labourer has kept his promise, has worked the given number of hours; but he has had no food all the while, and has executed his job in a somewhat faint manner. The face of the lady is pure and beautiful; but we have seen it at any time these ten years, with its red transparent shadows, its mouth in which butter wouldn't melt, and its beautiful brown madder hair. She is getting rather tedious, that sweet, irreproachable creature, that is the fact. She may be an angel; but sky-blue, my wicked senses tell me, is a feeble sort of drink, and men require stronger nourishment.

Mr. Eastlake's picture is a prim, mystic, cruciform composition. The lady languishes in the middle; an angel is consoling her, and embracing her with an arm out of joint; little rows of cherubs stand on each side the angels and the lady,—wonderful little children, with blue or brown beady eyes, and sweet little flossy curly hair, and no muscles or bones, as becomes such supernatural beings, no doubt. I have seen similar little darlings in the toy-shops in the Lowther Arcade for a shilling, with just such pink cheeks and round eyes, their bodies formed out of cotton-wool, and their extremities veiled in silver paper. Well; it is as well, perhaps, that Etty's jovial nymphs should not come into such a company. Good Lord! how they would astonish the weak nerves of Mr. Eastlake's *precieuse* young lady!

Quite unabashed by the squeamishness exhibited in the highest quarter (as the newspapers call it), Mr. Etty goes on rejoicing in his old fashion. Perhaps he is worse than ever this year, and despises *nec dulces amores nec choraeas*, because certain great personages are offended. Perhaps, this year, his ladies and Cupids *are* a little *hazardes;* his Venuses expand more than ever in the line of Hottentot beauty; his drawing and colouring are still more audacious than they were; patches of red shine on the cheeks of his blowsy nymphs; his idea of form goes to the verge of monstrosity. If you look at the pictures closely (and, considering all things, it requires some courage to do so), the forms disappear; feet and hands are scumbled away, and distances appear to be dabs and blotches of lakes, and brown, and ultramarine. It must be confessed that some of these pictures would *not* be suitable to hang up everywhere—in a young ladies' school, for instance. But, how rich and superb is the colour! Did Titian paint better, or Rubens as well? There is a nymph and child in the left corner of the Great Room, sitting, without the slightest fear of catching cold, in a sort of moonlight, of which the colour appears to me to be as rich and wonderful as Titian's best—'Bacchus and Ariadne,' for instance—and better than Rubens'. There is a little head of a boy in a blue dress (for once in a way) which kills every picture in the room, outstares all the red-coated generals, out-blazes Mrs. Thwaites and her diamonds (who has the place of honour); and has that unmistakable, inestimable, indescribable mark of the GREAT painter about, which makes the soul of a man kindle up as he sees it, and owns that there is Genius. How delightful it is to feel that shock, and how few are the works of art that can give it!

The author of that sybilline book of mystic rhymes, the unrevealed bard of the *Fallacies of Hope*, is as great as usual, vibrating between the absurd and the sublime, until the eye grows dazzled in watching him, and can't really tell in what region he is. If Etty's colour is wild and mysterious, looking here as if smeared with the finger, and there with the palette-knife, what can be said about Turner? Go up and look at one of his pictures, and you laugh at yourself and at him, and at the picture, and that wonderful amateur who is invariably found to give a thousand pounds for it, or more—some sum wild, prodigious, unheard-of, monstrous, like the picture itself. All about the author of the *Fallacies of Hope* is a mysterious extravaganza; price, poem, purchaser, picture. Look at the latter for a little time, and it begins to affect you too,—to mesmerise you. It is revealed to you; and, as it is said in the East, the magicians make children see the sultans, carpet-bearers, tents, etc., in a spot of ink in their hands; so the magician, Joseph Mallord, makes you see what he likes on a board, that to the first view is merely dabbed over with occasionally streaks of yellow, and flicked here and there with vermilion. The vermilion blotches become little boats full of harpooners and gondolas, with a deal of music going on on board. That is not a smear of purple you see yonder, but a beautiful whale, whose tail has just slapped a half dozen whaleboats into perdition; and as for what you fancied to be a few zigzag lines spattered on the canvas at hap-hazard, look! they turn out to be a ship with all her sails; the captain and his crew are clearly visible in the ship's bows; and you may distinctly see the oil-casks getting ready under the superintendence of that man with the red whiskers and the cast in his eye; who is, of course, the chief mate. In a word, I say that Turner is a great and awful mystery to me. I don't like to contemplate him too much, lest I should actually begin to believe in his poetry as well as his paintings, and fancy the *Fallacies of Hope* to be one of the finest poems in the world.

Now Stanfield has no mysticism or oracularity about him. You can see what he means at once. His style is as simple and manly as a seaman's song. One of the most dexterous, he is also one of the most careful of painters. Every year his works are more elaborated, and you are surprised to find a progress in an artist who had seemed to reach his acme before. His battle of frigates this year is a brilliant, sparkling pageant of naval war. His great picture of the 'Mole of Ancona,' fresh, healthy, and bright as breeze and sea can make it. There are better pieces still by this painter, to my mind; one in the first room, especially,—a Dutch landscape, with a warm, sunny tone upon it, worthy of Cuyp and Callcott. Who is G. Stanfield, an exhibitor and evidently a pupil of the Royal Academician? Can it be a son of that gent? If so, the father has a worthy heir to his name and honours. G. Stanfield's Dutch picture may be looked at by the side of his father's.

Roberts has also distinguished himself and advanced in skill, great as his care had been and powerful his effects before. 'The Ruins of Carnac' is the most poetical of this painter's works, I think. A vast and awful scene of gloomy Egyptian ruin! the sun lights up tremendous lines of edifices, which were only parts formerly of the enormous city of the hundred gates; long lines of camels come over the reddening desert, and camps are set by the side of the glowing pools. This is a good picture to gaze at, and to fill your eyes and thoughts with grandiose ideas of Eastern life.

This gentleman's large picture of 'Jerusalem' did not satisfy me so much. It is yet very faithful; anybody who had visited this place must see the careful fidelity with which the artist has mapped the rocks and valleys and laid down the lines of the buildings; but the picture has, to my eyes, too green and trim a look; the mosques and houses look fresh and new, instead of being mouldering, old, sun-baked, edifices of glaring stone rising amidst wretchedness and ruin. There is not, to my mind, that sad, fatal aspect, which the city presents from whatever quarter you view it, and which haunts a man who has seen it ever after with an impression of terror. Perhaps in the spring for a little while, at which season the sketch for this picture was painted, the country round about may look very cheerful. When we saw it in autumn, the mountains that stand round about Jerusalem were not green, but ghastly piles of hot rock, patched here and there with yellow, weedy herbage. A cactus or a few bleak olive-trees made up the vegetation of the wretched, gloomy landscape; whereas in Mr. Roberts's picture the valley of Jehoshaphat looks like a glade in a park, and the hills, up to the gates, are carpeted with verdure.

Being on the subject of Jerusalem, here may be mentioned with praise Mr. Hart's picture of a Jewish ceremony, with a Hebrew name I have forgotten. This piece is exceedingly bright and pleasing in colour, odd and novel as a representation of manners and costume, a striking and agreeable picture. I don't think as much can be said for the same artist's 'Sir Thomas More going to Execution.' Miss More is crying on papa's neck, pa looks up to heaven, halberdiers look fierce, etc. : all the regular adjuncts and property of pictorial tragedy are here brought into play. But nobody cares, that is the fact; and one fancies the designer himself cannot have cared much for the orthodox historical group whose misfortunes he was depicting.

These pictures are like boy's hexameters at school. Every lad of decent parts in the sixth form has a knack of turning out great quantities of respectable verse, without blunders, and with scarce any mental labour; but these verses are not in the least like poetry, any more than the great academical paintings of the artists are like great painting. You want something more than a composition, and a set of costumes and figures decently posed and studied. If these were all, for instance, Mr. Charles Landseer's picture of 'Charles I. before the battle of Edge Hill,' would be a good work of art. Charles stands at a tree before the inn-door, officers are round about, the little princes are playing with a little dog, as becomes their youth and innocence, rows of soldiers appear in red coats, nobody seems to have anything particular to do, except the royal martyr, who is looking at a bone of ham that a girl out of the inn has hold of.

Now this is all very well, but you want something more than this in an historic picture, which should have its parts, characters, varieties, and climax like a drama. You don't want the *Deus intersit* for no other purpose than to look at a knuckle of ham; and here is a piece well composed, and (bating a little want of life in the figures) well drawn, brightly and pleasantly painted, as all this artist's works are, all the parts and accessories studied and executed with care and skill, and yet meaning nothing—the part of Hamlet omitted. The king in this attitude (with the baton in his hand, simpering at the bacon aforesaid) has no more of the heroic in him than the pork he contemplates, and he deserves to lose every battle he fights. I prefer the artist's other still-life pictures to this. He has a couple more, professedly so called, very cleverly executed and capital cabinet pieces.

Strange to say, I have not one picture to remark upon taken from *The Vicar of Wakefield*. Mr. Ward has a very good Hogarthian work, with some little extravagance and caricature, representing Johnson waiting in Lord Chesterfield's ante-chamber, among a crowd of hangers-on and petitioners, who are sulky, or yawning, or neglected, while a pretty Italian singer comes out, having evidently had a very satisfactory interview with his lordship, and who (to lose no time) is arranging another rendezvous with another admirer. This story is very well, coarsely, and humorously told, and is as racy as a chapter out of Smollett. There is a yawning chaplain, whose head is full of humour ; and a pathetic episode of a widow and pretty child, in which the artist has not succeeded so well. There is great delicacy and beauty in Mr. Herbert's picture of ' Pope Gregory teaching Children to Sing.' His Holiness lies on his sofa languidly beating time over his book. He does not look strong enough to use the scourge in his hands, and with which the painter says he used to correct his little choristers. Two ghostly *aides-de-camp* in the shape of worn, handsome, shaven ascetic friars, stand behind the pontiff demurely ; and all the choristers are in full song, with their mouths as wide open as a nest of young birds when the mother comes. The painter seems to me to have acquired the true spirit of the middle-age devotion. All his works have unction ; and the prim, subdued, ascetic race, which forms the charm and mystery of the missal-illuminations, and which has operated to convert some imaginative minds from the new to the old faith.

And, by way of a wonder, behold a devotional picture from Mr. Edwin Landseer, ' A Shepherd praying at a Cross in the Fields.' I suppose the Sabbath church-bells are ringing from the city far away in the plain. Do you remember the beautiful lines of Uhland ?

> *Es ist der Tag des Herrn :*
> *Ich bin allein auf weitern Flur,*
> *Noch eine Morgen-Glocke nur*
> *Und Stille nah und fern.*
>
> *Anbetend knie ich hier.*
> *O süsses Graun, geheimes Wehn,*
> *Als knieten viele ungesehn*
> *Und beteten mit mir.*

Here is a noble and touching pictorial illustration of them—of Sabbath repose and *recueillement*—an almost endless flock of sheep

lies around the pious pastor; the sun shines peacefully over the
vast fertile plain; blue mountains keep watch in the distance;
and the sky above is serenely clear. I think this is the highest
flight of poetry the painter has dared to take yet. The numbers
and variety of attitude and expression in that flock of sheep quite
startle the spectator as he examines them. The picture is a
wonder of skill.

How richly the good pictures cluster at this end of the room!
There is a little Mulready, of which the colour blazes out like
sapphires and rubies; a pair of Leslies—one called the 'Heiress'
—one a scene from Molière—both delightful :—these are flanked
by the magnificent nymphs of Etty, before mentioned. What
school of art in Europe, or what age, can show better painters
than these in their various lines? The young men do well, but
the elders do best still. No wonder the English pictures are
fetching their thousands of guineas at the sales. They deserve
these great prices as well as the best works of the Hollanders.

I am sure that three such pictures as Mr. Webster's 'Dame's
School' ought to entitle the proprietor to pay the income-tax.
There is a little caricature in some of the children's faces; but
the schoolmistress is a perfect figure, most admirably natural,
humorous, and sentimental. The picture is beautifully painted,
full of air, of delightful harmony and tone.

There are works by Creswick that can hardly be praised too
much. One particularly, called 'A Place to be Remembered,'
which no lover of pictures can see and forget. Danby's great
'Evening Scene' has portions which are not surpassed by Cuyp
or Claude; and a noble landscape of Lee's, among several others
—a height with some trees and a great expanse of country
beneath.

From the fine pictures you come to the class which are very
nearly being fine pictures. In this I would enumerate a landscape
or two by Collins. Mr. Leigh's 'Polyphemus,' of which the
landscape part is very good, and only the figure questionable; and
let us say Mr. Elmore's 'Origin of the Guelf and Ghibelline
Factions,' which contains excellent passages, and admirable drawing and dexterity, but fails to strike as a whole somehow. There
is not sufficient purpose in it, or the story is not enough to
interest, or, though the parts are excellent, the whole is somewhat deficient.

There is very little comedy in the Exhibition, most of the
young artists tending to the sentimental rather than the ludicrous.
Leslie's scene from Molière is the best comedy. Collins's 'Fetching the Doctor' is also delightful fun. The greatest farce, how-

ever, is Chalon's picture with an Italian title, ' B. Virgine col,'
etc. Impudence never went beyond this. The infant's hair has
been curled into ringlets, the mother sits on her chair with painted
cheeks and a Haymarket leer. The picture might serve for the
oratory of an opera girl.

Among the portraits, Knight's and Watson Gordon's are the
best. A ' Mr. Pigeon ' by the former hangs in the place of
honour usually devoted to our gracious Prince, and is a fine rich
state picture. Even better are these by Mr. Watson Gordon :
one representing a gentleman in black silk stockings whose name
has escaped the memory of your humble servant ; another, a fine
portrait of Mr. De Quincey, the opium-eater. Mr. Lawrence's
heads, solemn and solidly painted, look out at you from their
frames, though they be ever so high placed, and push out of
sight the works of more flimsy but successful practitioners. A
portrait of great power and richness of colour is that of Mr.
Lopez by Linnell. Mr. Grant is the favourite ; but a very un-
sound painter to my mind, painting like a brilliant and graceful
amateur rather than a serious artist. But there is a quiet refinement and beauty about his female heads, which no other painter
can perhaps give, and charms in spite of many errors. Is it
Count D'Orsay, or is it Mr. Ainsworth, that the former has
painted ? Two peas are not more alike than these two illustrious
characters.

In the miniature-room, Mr. Richmond's drawings are of so
grand and noble a character, that they fill the eye as much as
full-length canvasses. Nothing can be finer than Mrs. Fry and
the grey-haired lady in black velvet. There is a certain severe,
respectable, Exeter Hall look about most of this artist's pictures,
that the observer may compare with the Catholic physiognomies
of Mr. Herbert : see his picture of Mr. Pugin, for instance ; it
tells of chants and cathedrals, as Mr. Richmond's work somehow
does of Clapham Common and the May meetings. The genius
of Mayfair fires the bosom of Chalon, the tea-party, the
quadrille, the hairdresser, the tailor, and the flunkey. All Ross's
miniatures sparkle with his wonderful and minute skill ; Carrick's
are excellent ; Thorburn's almost take the rank of historical
pictures. In his picture of two sisters one has almost the most
beautiful head in the world ; and his picture of Prince Albert,
clothed in red and leaning on a turquoise sabre, has ennobled that
fine head, and given his royal highness's pale features an air of
sunburnt and warlike vigour. Miss Corbaux, too, has painted
one of the loveliest heads ever seen. Perhaps this is the
pleasantest room of the whole, for you are sure to meet your

friends here ; kind faces smile at you from the ivory ; and features
of fair creatures, oh ! how . .

Here the eccentric author breaks into a rhapsody of thirteen
pages regarding No. 2576, Mrs. Major Blogg, who was formerly
Miss Poddy of Cheltenham, whom it appears that Michael Angelo
knew and admired. The feelings of the Poddy family might be
hurt, and the jealousy of Major Blogg aroused, were we to print
Titmarsh's rapturous description of that lady ; nor, indeed, can
we give him any further space, seeing that this is nearly the last
page of the *Magazine*. He concludes by a withering denunciation
of most of the statues in the vault where they are buried ; praising,
however, the children, Paul and Virginia, the head of Bayly's
nymph, and M'Dowall's boy. He remarks the honest character
of the English countenance as exhibited in the busts, and contrasts
it with Louis Philippe's head by Jones, on whom, both as a
sculptor and a singer, he bestows great praise. He indignantly
remonstrates with the committee for putting by far the finest
female bust in the room, No. 1434, by Powers of Florence, in
a situation where it cannot be seen ; and, quitting the gallery
finally, says he must go before he leaves town and give one more
look at Hunt's ' Boy at Prayers,' in the Water-Colour Exhibition,
which he pronounces to be the finest serious work of the year.

SKETCHES AFTER ENGLISH LANDSCAPE PAINTERS.

By L. Marvy.

WITH SHORT NOTICES BY W. M. THACKERAY.

PREFACE.

THE revolutionary storm which raged in France in 1848, drove many peaceful artists, as well as kings, ministers, tribunes, and socialists of state, for refuge to our country ; and amongst the former was Monsieur Louis Marvy, a friend of the present writer, who has passed many happy hours in the French artist's *atelier*, which, with his friends and his family, and its constant cheerfulness and sunshine, the Parisian was obliged to exchange for a dingy parlour and the fog and solitude of London. A fine and skilful landscape painter himself, M. Marvy, during his residence here, made the following series of engravings, after the works of our English landscape painters ; and, amongst other persons, especially and thankfully owes an obligation to my kind friend, Mr. Thomas Baring, for permission to make several sketches after pictures in his rich collection.

The task of describer or narrator for the little exhibition devolved upon myself, without whose introduction the publishers would not hear of M. Marvy's appearance before the English public, and who must bespeak its indulgence for the discharge of a task which was one of no small difficulty. There are no incidents in our show upon which the showman can dilate ; in most cases he has to introduce his audience to the sight of a simple and quiet landscape, over which ideal pleasure is ever the best commentary, and concerning which it is as hard to explain one's own emotions, as to cause another to share in them ; but the promise being made, the pictures engraved, and the publisher peremptory, there is nothing for it but to step forward, make a bow to the audience, and begin the lecture.

SIR AUGUSTUS WALL CALLCOTT.

SIR AUGUSTUS takes the precedence in our series, to which his rank entitles him. The present age seldom witnesses combined excellences in any art or science, but Callcott tried every branch of his, before he finally settled down in landscape. He first began by portrait-painting; he then took to historical subjects, by which he won the mastery which adds so much value and interest to his landscapes of English scenery, or to his Dutch and Italian river or canal borders. By treating the subjects which were before handled by Cuyp and Canaletti, he has laid himself open to the charge of plagiarism, but undeservedly; for a genuine vein of English colouring pervades his works, particularly his smaller works, in which, less hampered by the breadth of effect he was bound and successfully to seek, he devoted his admirable skill in finishing. His house in Kensington was long a focus of all that was eminent in art or criticism, from Flaxman to Waagen. The charms of his dwelling made his works looked upon more as the successful efforts of an amateur, than those of an accomplished painter, to which their sterling merit fully entitles them. That from which the artist, permitted by the kindness of Mr. T. Baring, has been enabled to copy, is one of the best-known of Callcott's works, and can bear to be looked at by the side of the Cuyp in the splendid collection where it hangs.

SIR A. W. CALLCOTT, R.A.   P. 254.

J. M. W. TURNER, R.A.

TURNER.

SOME people cannot understand that prodigious poem the *Fallacies of Hope*, with Delphic sentences, from which the notices of Mr. Turner's pictures are often accompanied in the Academy catalogues. Many cannot comprehend the late pictures themselves, but stand bewildered before those blazing wonders, those blood-red shadows, those whirling gamboge suns—awful hieroglyphics which even the Oxford Graduate, Turner's most faithful priest and wor-shipper, cannot altogether make clear. Nay, who knows whether the priest himself has any distinct idea of the words which break out from him, as he sits whirling on the tripod ; or of what spirits will come up as he waves his wand, and delivers his astounding incantation ? In Mr. Irving's latter days, it was the gift of some to utter, of others to interpret the utterances : and possibly the prophet was as much surprised and edified as anybody else in the congregation, when the interpreter rose and translated his mystic cries. It is not given to all to understand ; but at times we have glimpses of comprehension, and in looking at such pictures as the ' Fighting Téméraire,' for instance, or the ' Star Ship,' we admire (and can scarce find words adequate to express our wonder) the stupendous skill and genius of this astonishing master. If these works which we think we understand are sublime, what are those others which are unintelligible ? Are they sublime too, or have they reached that next and higher step, which by some is denominated ridiculous ? Perhaps we have not arrived at the right period for judging ; and Time, which is proverbial for settling squabbles, is also required for sobering pictures. As we cannot look at the sun but through a blackened glass, it has seemed to us that the most dazzling of Turner's fancies have often been improved by the sobering influence of the graver, and in nothing has his style proved more triumphant than in withstanding this test. There are no clap-trap light or shadows to serve the purpose of effect. This may be owing to his having himself wielded the point. He first exhibited in 1790. He first published his celebrated Liber Studiorum in 1812, those sepia etchings which far surpass Claude's in variety of composition as well as feeling. We are tired by the ever-recurring architecture and clumps of trees of the latter. Turner gleans sublimity from the whole Continent, and when satiated with that, rests in more quiet scenes of our shores, glens, and mountains. They contain the germ of what he hereafter created : his mind has ever been expanding, could not rest confined and cramped to common laws.

The picture before us is of the Master's earlier and more intelligible style, before he spoke oracles, and when he wrote poetry : poetry how grand, how sumptuous, how admirably beautiful and true to nature, any one can say who has looked at the picture painted in 1811, exhibited in 1849 ; at Mr. Grundy's Trossachs ; at Sir John Swinburne's picture ; or at the Carthage in the Master's own gallery ; works which seem to us to give him the very foremost place of the landscape artists ;—epic works, so to speak—the greatest in aim, the greatest in art, the greatest in truth to nature.

But these may be mere outer works, and decorations which anybody can understand—who knows what the adept sees behind the curtain, beyond which (and indeed it is so beautiful that one is content to admire but that) the uninitiated cannot peep ? Admiring the early and comprehensible works of the painter is like admiring the early works of Swedenborg, and saying that he was a man of vast science, and a skilled mathematician—he was all this, but his disciples only know how much beside.

In fine, the *Fallacies of Hope* is a mystery, and a wonder, and a perplexity.

HOLLAND.

MR. HOLLAND is alike skilled in oil and water-colour painting ; and the amateur has long ere this admired, on the walls of our exhibitions, his rich and luminous colouring, his sunny buildings of his favourite Venetian architecture, his clear waters, and his deep Italian skies. This painter claims, as a right, to take his place in any gallery of English landscape ; and we hope that his French imitator has succeeded in giving a faithful translation of the skilful and brilliant master's manner.

J. HOLLAND.

P. 256.

F. DANBY, A.R.A.

P. 257.

DANBY.

THE French artist has given a very successful imitation of the beautiful and poetical sepia drawing of Mr. Danby. We have scarcely ever seen a work by that great painter in which a similar poetical beauty was not conveyed, and in regarding which the spectator does not feel impressed by something of that solemn contemplation, and reverent worship of nature, which seems to pervade the artist's mind and pencil. His pictures are always still. You stand before them alone, and with a hushed admiration, as before a great landscape when it breaks on your view. He describes a scene of natural grandeur and beauty—of darkling forests tinged with the brightening dawn of woods, and calm waters gilded with sunset or fading into twilight ; and, as in reading Wordsworth or the Georgics, the mind submits itself, awe-stricken and delighted, to the majestic repose and splendour of the poet's art, one may say of Mr. Danby that he paints morning and evening odes. His works are vast, polished, elaborate. With other painters, differently constituted, it is as if they trilled a ballad, or sang a sea-song.

As the blind man who said that he supposed the colour of scarlet was like the sound of a trumpet, I suppose most persons called upon to give an account of their sensations with regard to art, must be driven to compare pictures to poems, and poems to pictures. One always feels as if they were the same.

S

CRESWICK.

PERHAPS, more than any landscape painter, ancient or modern, Mr. Creswick has united the perfection of aërial perspective in his distances, with a precision in the foregrounds only equalled by the pictures formed in convex glasses, and, we believe, frequently used by artists, to see how nature is 'done.' He seems to take a secret pleasure in unravelling the mysteries of intricate groves as they overarch the trout stream, of which he renders the evanescent form and colour, with the hand of one who has spent many long summers of careful thought and observation amidst such scenes. Here is everything to admire, and nothing hard to understand. The beholder has a perfect confidence in the painter whose happy gift it is to receive and translate nature with an admirable fidelity and truthfulness. We are as much charmed in watching this artist's work and manner, by the delightful instinct which enables him to perceive the truth of nature, as by the perfect skill with which he renders his perceptions. One can speak of art but by illustration. Creswick is a composer singing his own airs with the most charming fresh voice. Which is the more pleasing? the beautiful organ, or the beautiful theme? With a happy organization, a perfect cultivation, and a still constant variety of incident in an occupation always harmless, interesting, beautiful; surely the landscape painters ought to be amongst the happiest people in the world; and, as one looks at these charming works of Mr. Creswick, one fancies the painter happy in his serene occupation, amidst the beautiful scene; tracing the course of the river, the forms of rocks, the play of the sunshine amidst the leaves.

T. CRESWICK, A.R.A.   P. 258.

W. COLLINS.

P. 259.

COLLINS.

IN the pleasant *Life of Collins* by his son, the writer describes how, when his father was preparing studies for his picture of the 'Skittle Players,' he used to frequent a public garden in the neighbourhood of Bayswater where that amusement was practised, and watch, sketchbook in hand, the performers in the play.   'He made studies unobserved of the individual character, the momentary posture, the accidental arrangement of figures.   He bought skittles, and set them up in his garden.   He risked turning his gardener—a great skittle player, and the model for one of his figures—into a permanent Colossus of Rhodes, by keeping him striding in the action of bowling with all his might, as long as his legs would uphold him, and the result was the production of a picture which will go down to posterity as one of the standard works of the English school.'

The affectionate biographer holds up this as a fair example, to show much care, constancy, ingenuity, and patient previous labour are requisite to enable the painter to work out his design.   The man who set up the honest gardener for his model, may now serve in his turn as a model himself to students in his art, and out of it indeed.   To the very last days of his life he loved his art, and humbly laboured to perfect himself in it ; with what success the delighted spectator knows, who has seen and must recollect his works with a grateful personal kindness ;—something like that which one feels on reading a page of *The Traveller* or *The Deserted Village*, from which one brings away the memory of the beautiful sunny landscape, the pretty groups of figures, and of the charming and gentle poet who portrayed them.

REDGRAVE.

VERY many of our figure painters excel as delineators of landscape. The backgrounds of Mr. Mulready's pictures may be matched with the works of the finest Dutch painters. Whether of lake or mountain scenery, whether of distance or foreground, whether of desert or moorland, what artist can be a more skilful painter than Sir Edwin Landseer? The air and sunshine, the murmuring trees, and rippling waters, in the midst of which Etty's buxom nymphs disport themselves, are painted with a brilliancy of tone which no landscape painter, since the time of Velasquez (another splendid instance of our theory), has caught. And in Mr. Redgrave's works, which are chiefly character pieces of the pathetic and domestic cast, the observer will remark with how much delicacy and truth the landscape portions of the picture are rendered, and with what keen observation and relish this accomplished painter evidently pursues nature. The little picture from which this design is taken, is a happy proof of the artist's faithful taste, and talent; a quiet little piece of chequered shade and sunshine, suggestive of repose and peaceful meditation. Wandering through the Academy rooms every year, the visitor will be pretty sure to catch glimpses in quiet nooks of other such works of the painter's hand :—calm little insights into quiet nooks of nature, and glimpses of the artist's mind at work. The figure painter relieves himself with these prolusions, as he might by rhyming a sonnet, or touching a tune on the piano.

R. REDGRAVE, A.R.A.

P. 260.

F. R. LEE, R.A.

LEE.

IT is refreshing to the eyes of the Londoner, on visiting the
Exhibition of the Royal Academy, to pause before the healthy and
cheerful landscapes of Mr. Lee.   Whilst other painters go abroad in
search of subjects for their easel, more picturesque or romantic than
those which can be found at home ; Mr. Lee has confined himself
to English scenery, we believe, almost entirely—to English plains
and corn-fields, and English rivers, and avenues of English trees,
bright with native air and sunshine.   It is not so much, in our
opinion, the art with which he executes his works as their
admirable fidelity to nature, which renders them always so
pleasant ; they are kindly fresh and homely, as a sonnet by Crabbe.
Not at all of the idealist school, the sight of them yet serves to
please and charm, and the eye gazes delighted in the silvery clouds
and blue distances, the chequered shades and lights of those
favourite lanes in which the artist loves to linger, and the wide
fields and meadows with the clouds and the light overhead.   Those
rustic ploughmen and industrious fishermen who people his landscapes, or throw the fly by his shining river sides, ought all to be
people, as we imagine, of happy temperament and robust constitu-
tion.   For it always seems to us in Mr. Lee's pictures, that there
is cheerfulness in the landscape, and health in the air.

CATTERMOLE.

This is scarcely a favourable specimen of the genius of this
dashing and vigorous painter. The peculiar tastes of the French
artist would lead him to give better imitations of pictures of landscape and woodland scenery, than of those romantic architectural
subjects, vast cathedrals and sombre Gothic dungeons, which Mr.
Cattermole's hand delights to depict.

No man can have examined his works upon the walls of the
Water-Colour Exhibition, which they have adorned for some
twenty years, without having been struck, not merely with the
admirable harmony of colour and tone,—a tone and colour quite
original—which pervades them, but with the profound knowledge
of chiaroscuro which they exhibit. As, in listening to a composer
performing a fine piece of music, one is often led away from one's
admiration of the work itself to astonishment at the skill of the
performer, so, in examining Mr. Cattermole's pictures, one pauses,
breathless almost, before the astonishing dexterity, and the brilliant
feats of hand, which the artist flings over his paper. A few
strokes are sufficient to represent long lines of columns or the most
intricate and delicate Gothic tracery. A few glittering dashes of
the brush, and wonderful cups and salvers, and shining suits of
armour, are represented by this marvellously facile pencil.

Monks, cavaliers, battles, banditti, knightly halls, and awful
enchanted forests in which knights and distressed damsels wander
—the pomp and circumstance of feudal war, are subjects in which
Mr. Cattermole chiefly delights. He is the English Salvator, with
more poetry and equal skill.

This vast facility, which we admire in Mr. Cattermole's works,
was not learned without long and previous preparation. Five
and twenty years back, some of the most elaborate architectural
drawings in Britton's Cathedrals are to be found with the signature
of the young student, who afterwards applied the knowledge, of
which he thus laid the ground-work, in the execution of the
thousand brilliant and beautiful works which we owe to his
abundant genius.

Among the finest of his works, everybody who saw it will
remember the 'Skirmish on the Bridges:' and his Scottish designs,
illustrating the life of Queen Mary, are as remarkable for their
beauty of design and colour as for their poetry, which is gloomy
and grand. Some fine delineations of his favourite Cavaliers, and
Roundheads, are to be found ornamenting his brother's volumes of

G. CATTERMOLE.   P. 262.

W. J. MÜLLER.

P. 263.

the history of the civil wars.   In the present year's exhibition he has taken Shakespeare and Chivalry for his theme.   With what a rapid skill has he delineated the combat of the knights—how magnificent is the drear landscape in which the weird sisters appear before Macbeth, quivering in the air, and about to vanish before him, spreading their bloody tartans to ride away in the storm !

W. J. MÜLLER.

The latter part of Müller's career has, in its eastern splendour, eclipsed his more sober and earlier efforts.   We know him chiefly as the intrepid follower of the Xanthian expedition, indefatigable in material-gathering for future fame, till the thorough exhaustion of a vast stock of paper on the very day he sailed to reap in his native land the noble and short-lived fruits of his industry.

With more elasticity of composition, or may-be an eye better formed to seize the impromptu groupings of nature, he equalled the French Decamps in his colouring ; and in the works of these two painters, the East, in all its magic and splendour, has been for the first time revealed to us.   In the delightful glimpses of Eastern life which they discover, they are not unworthy of siding with the Arabian Nights, the illustration of which by these two masters we can only enjoy in imagination.   Amongst the first results of Müller's sojourn in the East, was his brilliant view of Rhodes.   Exhibition dalliers were amazed by his prolific pencil, but perhaps secretly preferred his less ambitious bits : such a one, it may be recollected, was the Maltese Guard, and his verdigris-coloured culverin.   He was of the city of Chatterton, had a good deal of his poetry and genius, and was, like his brother, nipped early by morbid disappointment.

HARDING.

IF one may find a fault with Mr. Harding's works, it is that one is almost too conscious of the artist in his works. The effects are too palpable, the contrasts between light and dark too self-evident ; and yet the ensemble is always brilliant and rich, and every individual work of the painter sure to command admiration. As a painter, he is skilled in the use of every weapon of his art— paints alike upon canvas, and paper, and stone—and has never been excelled in the breadth, richness, and facility with which he handles every subject which he treats. He designs architecture with the brilliancy and dexterity of Bonnington, and possesses over the trees of the forest and park a mastery of delineation of which no other artist can boast. Some of his lithographic sketches of forest scenery, published in the admirable Elementary books, strike upon the eye as fine pictures.

The completed works of no artist can, perhaps, be measured by his sketches ; but it may be said of Mr. Harding, as a landscape painter, that his sketches are among the very finest which any artist has ever produced. Like others of his fortunate brethren, he has pursued his art into a hundred countries, and brought home delightful reminiscences of Alps and Tyrolese mountains, Italian lakes, and quaint Norman cities, in his rich portfolio.

J. D. HARDING.

P. 264.

NASMYTH.

NASMYTH.

NASMYTH has taken his quiet place amongst our landscape painters, and may rank almost as an English Hobbema. A little more light in his pictures, and perhaps a selection of a better vehicle in which to paint, would have rendered them more agreeable to the amateur's eye, which has been accustomed to brighter attractions than are afforded by the somewhat sombre and Quaker-like tone which these modest works wear. But, on closer examination into the pictures, the admirable care and finish of the details, the various minuteness of foreground, foliage, cottage-wall, and garden-weed, the calm silvery tones of the delicately-painted distance will strike everybody who examines the artist's rather rare works, and will strike us with the more admiration when we remember at what time this artist began to paint, and that he came after the sloven Morland, and the somewhat careless practitioners of the English school of that day.

RICHARD WILSON.

WILSON wanted the force which might have made him an original genius. Had he remained at home, there is no knowing what he would have done. However, he got whirled into the Roman vortex, where two or three living minds swayed those who only went to seek inspiration from its traditions.

Wilson adopted the Vernet themes, and in some respects surpassed the man he admired. This abdication of self was not forgiven in England—the public supported him feebly ; and he was snubbed for his ale-house tastes, by the purist Reynolds. We find him fêted and admired while in Rome by Mengs amongst others, who, wonderful condescension ! has handed down to us Wilson's physiognomy in one of his mild pastels. He dragged a slovenly existence in Covent Garden, till he was enabled by pawning a picture to retreat into Wales and die there miserably. Reynolds has mercilessly dissected the figures in his landscapes, which in-fliction, it must be owned, they deserved, though his views in Italy ought now to be cherished more than ever for their happy accuracy in the anatomy of villas, some of them now destroyed.

We are still proud of Wilson : his classicism makes his name respectable ; though there is little sympathy between his bold stroke and the more careful productions of our day. This, nevertheless, does not apply to all his works, as some of them of exquisite finish turn up now and then oddly at sales.

Amongst his works that are engraved, his pictures in the National Gallery are about the worst ; they are coarse in effect, and leave a sort of impression on the mind that he was not happy in their somewhat theatrical execution, for the pains and delight of a painter in his own work have almost always a winning influence.

He was one of the founders of the Royal Academy. Cunningham relates that he painted with one brush, and standing : it is singular that Mengs has represented him sitting with several brushes in his hand, so much for art anecdote.

RICHARD WILSON.   P. 266.

E. W. COOKE.

E. W. COOKE.

MR. COOKE, we believe, is as skilled with the graver as with the pencil; and this is one of the many of his river scenes, which have earned the artist's reputation.   The showman who has engaged himself to describe his friend's exhibition in truth finds the task to be one of uncommon difficulty; and, as the ingenuous reader has perhaps remarked, is often compelled to speak about anything but the subject in hand, while the scene is passing before the public eye.   We are not here to bawl out that this is the wonderful wonder of wonders, that our giant is the biggest, our dwarf the smallest, or our picture the most beautiful, in the world. Our audience is too knowing to be taken in, were any deception attempted.   Nor is much comment necessary about the quiet little picture which now comes in our series, and merits a place there as a specimen of the work of a very favourite and accomplished English painter.

JOHN CONSTABLE.

JOHN CONSTABLE was intended by nature for a landscape painter; but, by his parents, for the honourable craft of miller. For a while, he served two masters : when grinding corn he still had leisure to examine the fleeting effects of nature, and thus turn the mill into an observatory. This influenced his style ever after, as clouds always occupied the prominent part of his compositions; it was in clouds that he excelled, whether in their transparency and misty appearance, or in their masses of light.

When he returned from a sketching excursion, he used to say, ' I have had a good skying ; ' and when he displayed these sketches, they were found marked with the day, hour, and which way the wind blew.

He resided latterly in Hampstead, and has left innumerable reminiscences of its everlasting heath, that untiring ' sitter.' The amateur will recognise in the accompanying excellent sketch, the ' Cornfield ' of the National Gallery. This beautiful piece of autumn seems to be under the influence of a late shower ; the shrubs, trees, and distance, are saturated with it—what a lover of water that youngster must be, who is filling himself within after he has been wetted to the skin by the rain which has just passed away ! As one looks at this delightful picture one cannot but admire the manner in which the specific character of every object is made out ; the undulations of the ripe corn, the chequered light on the road, the freshness of the banks, the trees and their leafage, the brilliant cloud artfully contrasted against the trees, and here and there broken with azure. Fuseli's standing joke, as he looked at Constable's pictures, was to call for his greatcoat and umbrella. The wit of the Academy showed a better appreciation of the great landscape painter's genius than Chantrey did, who one day took up Constable's palette, and rubbed his picture with a glaze of asphaltum. ' There goes all my dew,' the poor artist said to Leslie, his charming biographer. Is not many another poet's dew, and delightful natural bloom, unseen by dull observers, and rubbed away by coarse patrons ?

Not fairly appreciated during his lifetime, every succeeding year adds to the public appreciation of this great genius. Before he was admired as he deserved to be amongst ourselves, the Parisian painters had greatly and justly appreciated him, and he was as much the originator of the modern French landscape, as Scott was the father of French romance.

JOHN CONSTABLE. P. 268.

P. DE WINT.

P. DE WINT

OUR well-beloved De Wint has gone like one of those calm summer days he used to depict.   He spent his life in one revel of sunshine. He caught well the warm purplish blue of the summer sky.   All artists generally choose morning or evening, as the long sweeping shadows form at once easy pictures, but De Wint was not frightened by the sun in its meridian.

Wilson is said to have aimed at representing the subtle air, in which buzzed the ephemeral insects ; we think De Wint, with the more slender material of water, has better succeeded.   Fuseli, who wanted his umbrella to look at Constable's showers, might have called for a pot of porter at seeing one of De Wint's hay-makings. Distant towns, most unpromising in aspect, became pleasant-looking under his pencil ; large masses of trees grew of intelligent shape : he caught the murmuring undulations of quiet streams ; everything basked lazily with him, and one wondered whether he remained torpid in winter.

There was not much depth in his scheme of manipulation, but the charm was in the instinctive perception of nature's cunning simplicity, the simple means by which so much is brought about, as to make us exclaim ' how is it done ?'   As Rousseau said, ' Ce n'est pas ainsi que l'on invente ; ' if man invents, he plunges into affected mannerism, and it must always be so, unless he follows the complaisant model, which is ever posture-making, for him who takes the trouble to look out.   De Wint was one of these ; it is evident in all his works that he never invented the smallest personage, but followed the wise maxim for landscapists —' always to wait for a figure, which will be sure to appear when wanted.'   And so all faithful painters always awaited patiently the coming man.   De Wint painted freely and without effort, avoiding all modern innovations.   He was married to Hilton's sister, and was his early friend and associate.

DAVID COX.

WALES is Cox's field of battle.   He is said to have invariably
bent his steps towards Llanrwst and Bettws-y-Coed for the last
five and thirty years.   The very stones are christened after him ;
as you wind out of Capel Carig, a little turret, in which a stone
seat is inserted, bulges from the walled road-side, and is known as
Cox's pulpit.   One of the greatest favourites amongst our water-
colour painters, the public and the artists alike admire this veteran
painter.   His drawings have the fresh impromptu look of nature,
and never savour of home-manufacture   His hand would seem to
be rapid, and his eye certain, and the delighted beholder wonders
where the secret is, and how, with strokes so rough, and on such
small spaces of paper, air and distance, storm and sunshine, should
be described so lucidly.

DAVID COX.

P. 270.

GAINSBOROUGH.

GAINSBOROUGH.

THE great name of Gainsborough needs scarce any comment or eulogy here. Comparatively obscure when Reynolds was in the full blaze of his reputation, his works are as familiar among us as those of the great President, and we may say of him, that he is the most *beloved* of English painters. All the works which he has bequeathed to us, whether portraits or landscapes, seem graceful and charming, beautiful and serene. He ennobles everything he approaches; his rustic subjects have an idyllic beauty; he touches his courtly figures with a splendid courtesy, so to speak. In Mr. Baring's gallery, as you look at the charming and famous original from which the accompanying sketch is taken, the picture seems to illuminate the place where it hangs with calm, lambent radiance, and we gaze at its shadowy gloom and soft prismatic flicker of light, with such a pleased hush and tranquillity as a fine sunset inspires.

ROBERTS.

WHAT region of earth is there that does not show signs of the
Englishman's labour? Our painters share the spirit of enterprise
along with the rest of our people, and Mr. Roberts, the author of
the original sketch from which the accompanying engraving has
been taken, has visited at least three of the quarters of the globe,
and brought away likenesses of their cities and people, in his
portfolio. He travelled for years in Spain; he set up his tent
in the Syrian desert; he has sketched the spires of Antwerp, the
peaks of Lebanon, the rocks of Calton Hill, the towers and castles
that rise by the Rhine; the airy Cairo minarets, the solemn
pyramids and vast Theban columns, and the huts under the date
trees, along the banks of the Nile. Can any calling be more
pleasant than that of such an artist? The life is at once thoughtful and adventurous; gives infinite variety and excitement, and
constant opportunity for reflection. As one looks at the multi-
farious works of this brave and hardy painter, whose hand is the
perfect and accomplished slave of his intellect, and ready, like
a genius in an eastern tale, to execute the most wonderful feats
and beautiful works with the most extraordinary rapidity, any man
who loves adventure himself must envy the lucky mortal whose lot
it is to enjoy it in such a way. He reads the magnificent book of
nature for himself, and at first hand: *tibi suavis daedala tellus
submittit flores.* O! happy painter—*tibi rident aequora ponti.*
From the deck of your boat you sketch the sea and the shore: you
moor under the city walls; and mosque and dome, Gothic
cathedral, tower, and ancient fortress rise up with their long
perspectives, and varied outlines, and hues, and solemn shadows,
fantastic and beautiful, built in an hour or two under the magical
strokes of your delightful obedient little genius, the pencil! The
ferry-boat puts off from the stairs, and makes its way across the
river to the grey old town on the bank yonder, where the windows
in the quaint-gabled houses, and the vanes on the towers are still
flaming in the sunset, and reflected in the river beneath. Tower
and town, river and distant hill, boat and ferry, and the steers-
man with his paddle, and the peasants with the grape-baskets
singing in the boat, are all sketched down on the painter's drawing
board before the sun has sunk, and before he returns to his snug
supper at the inn, where the landlord's pretty daughter comes
and peers over the magician's portfolio. Or the Cangia moors,

ROBERTS.

by the bank-side : the Arab crew are cooking their meal and chanting their chant : the camels come down to the water and receive their loads of cotton, and disappear with their shouting drivers under the date trees, to the village with the crumbled wall and minaret, where the grave elders are seated smoking under the gate, and the women pass to and fro, straight and stately, robed in flowing blue robes, bearing pitchers on their graceful heads : the painter sees, and notes them all down, while the light lasts him, and before he smokes his own pipe under the stars on the deck ; after a long day of pleasant labour, and before he closes his eyes which have been so busy and so pleased all day.   Or he is up before dawn upon his mule to see the sun rise over the heights of Sierra ; or he is seated at morning, the Sheikh with his long gun over his shoulder watching, and the Arabs lying round the tent, 'silent upon a peak in Lebanon.'

T

STANFIELD.

MR. STANFIELD and Mr. Roberts, but especially the former, who
has executed more, and more various, works in the scenic depart-
ment than his brilliant coadjutor, have had the means of doing
more towards advancing the taste of the English public for landscape art, than any other living painter. Mr. Stanfield for many
years taught the public from the stage—taught the pit and the
gallery to admire landscape art, and the boxes to become
connoisseurs ; and decorated the theatre with works so beautiful,
that one regrets the frail material of which they were constructed ;
and the necessity for 'new and gorgeous effects' and 'magnificent
novelties,' which caused the artist's works to be carried away.
Mr. Stanfield has created, and afterwards painted out with his
own brush, more scenic masterpieces than any man. Clown and
Pantaloon in his time tumbled over and belaboured one another,
and bawled out their jokes, before the most beautiful and dazzling
pictures which ever were presented to the eyes of the theatre-
goer. How a man could do so much and so well as Mr. Stanfield did
during the time when he was the chief of the Drury Lane scene-
room, was a wonder to everybody ; and it was not the public
only which he delighted, and awakened and educated into
admiration, but the members of his own profession were as
enthusiastic as the rest of the world to recognise and applaud
his magnificent imagination and skill.

All through the painter's life his industry and his genius have
been alike remarkable, and it is curious to note, in his performances of the present time, how the carefulness of the artist seems
to increase with his skill : as if this conscientious man were bent
each day upon improving, on elaborating and polishing his works,
on approaching more nearly to nature. Does not such a progress
seem to tell of more than mere talent ? of honesty, of modesty, of
faithful and cheerful labour, of constant love for truth ? It
seems to me that the pictures of some artists tell of these things
too, and that these are amongst the precious qualities which go
to make a painter.

STANFIELD.

p. 274.

PICTURES OF LIFE AND CHARACTER. BY JOHN LEECH.[1]

WE, who can recall the consulship of Plancus, and quite respectable old fogeyfied times, remember amongst other amusements which we had as children the pictures at which we were permitted to look. There was Boydell's Shakespeare, black and ghastly gallery of murky Opies, glum Northcotes, straddling Fuselis! there were Lear, Oberon, Hamlet, with starting muscles, rolling eyeballs, and long pointing quivering fingers; there was little Prince Arthur (Northcote) crying, in white satin, and bidding good Hubert not put out his eyes; there was Hubert crying; there was little Rutland being run through the poor little body by bloody Clifford; there was Cardinal Beaufort (Reynolds) gnashing his teeth, and grinning and howling demoniacally on his deathbed (a picture frightful to the present day); there was Lady Hamilton (Romney) waving a torch and dancing before a black background —a melancholy museum indeed. Smirke's delightful Seven Ages only fitfully relieved its general gloom. We did not like to inspect it unless the elders were present and plenty of lights and company were in the room.

Cheerful relatives used to treat us to Miss Linwood's. Let the children of the present generation thank their stars *that* tragedy is put out of their way. Miss Linwood's was worsted work. Your grandmother or grand-aunts took you there, and said the pictures were admirable. You saw 'The Woodman' in worsted, with his axe and dog, tramping through the snow; the snow bitter cold to look at, the woodman's pipe wonderful; a gloomy piece, that made you shudder. There were large dingy pictures of woollen martyrs, and scowling warriors with limbs strongly knitted; there was especially, at the end of a long passage, a den of lions that would frighten any boy not born in Africa, or Exeter Change, and accustomed to them.

[1] *Pictures of Life and Character. By John Leech.* London : 1854.

Another exhibition used to be West's Gallery, where the
pleasing figure of Lazarus in his grave-clothes, and Death on the
pale horse, used to impress us children.   The tombs of Westminster Abbey, the vaults at St. Paul's, the men in armour at the
Tower, frowning ferociously out of their helmets, and wielding
their dreadful swords ; that superhuman Queen Elizabeth at the
end of the room, a livid sovereign with glass eyes, a ruff, and a
dirty satin petticoat, riding a horse covered with steel : who does
not remember these sights in London in the consulship of Plancus ?
and the waxwork in Fleet Street, not like that of Madame Tussaud's,
whose chamber of death is gay and brilliant, but a nice old gloomy
waxwork, full of murderers ; and, as a chief attraction, the dead
baby and the Princess Charlotte lying in state.

Our story-books had no pictures in them for the most part.
Frank (dear old Frank !) had none ; nor the Parent's Assistant ;
nor the Evenings at Home ; nor our copy of the *Ami des Enfans ;*
there were just a few at the end of the Spelling-Book ; besides
the allegory at the beginning, of Education leading up Youth to
the temple of Industry, where Dr. Dilworth and Professor
Walkinghame stood with crowns of laurel ; there were, we say,
just a few pictures at the end of the Spelling-Book, little oval
grey woodcuts of Bewick's, mostly of the Wolf and the Lamb, the
Dog and the Shadow, and Brown, Jones, and Robinson with long
ringlets and little tights ; but for pictures, so to speak, what had
we ?   The rough old wood-blocks in the old harlequin-backed fairy
books had served hundreds of years ; before our Plancus, in the
time of Priscus Plancus—in Queen Anne's time, who knows ?   We
were flogged at school ; we were fifty boys in our boarding house,
and had to wash in a leaden trough, under a cistern, with lumps
of fat yellow soap floating about in the ice and water.   Are *our*
sons ever flogged ?   Have they not dressing rooms, hair oil, hip
baths, and Baden towels ?   And what picture-books the' young
villains have !   What have these children done that they should
be so much happier than we were ?

We had the Arabian Nights and Walter Scott, to be sure.
Smirke's illustrations to the former are very fine.   We did not
know how good they were then ; but we doubt whether we did
not prefer the little old Miniature Library Nights with frontis-
pieces by Unwins ; for these books the pictures don't count.
Every boy of imagination does his own pictures to Scott and the
Arabian Nights best.

Of funny pictures there were none especially intended for us
children.   There was Rowlandson's Dr. Syntax ; Dr. Syntax in
a fuzz wig, on a horse with legs like sausages, riding races, making

love, frolicking with rosy exuberant damsels. Those pictures were very funny, and that aqua-tinting and the gay coloured plates were very pleasant to witness ; but if we could not read the poem in those days, could we digest it in this? Nevertheless, apart from the text which we could not master, we remember Dr. Syntax pleasantly, like those cheerful painted hieroglyphics in the Nineveh Court at Sydenham. What matter for the arrow-head, illegible stuff? Give us the placid grinning kings, twanging their jolly bows over their rident horses, wounding those good-humoured enemies, who tumble gaily off the towers, or drown, smiling in the dimpling waters, amidst the anerithmon gelasma of the fish.

After Dr. Syntax, the apparition of Corinthian Tom, Jerry Hawthorne, and the facetious Bob Logic must be recorded—a wondrous history indeed theirs was ! When the future student of our manners comes to look over the pictures and the writing of these queer volumes, what will he think of our society, customs and language in the consulship of Plancus ? We have still in our mind's eye some of the pictures of that sportive gallery ; the white coat, Prussian blue pantaloons, Hessian boots and hooked nose of Corinthian Tom ; Jerry's green cutaway and leather gaiters ; Bob Logic's green spectacles, and high-waisted surtout. ' Corinthian,' it appears, was the phrase applied to men of fashion and *ton* in Plancus's time ; they were the brilliant predecessors of the 'swell' of the present period—brilliant, but somewhat barbarous, it must be confessed. The Corinthians were in the habit of drinking a great deal too much in Tom Cribb's parlour ; they used to go and see 'life' in the gin-shops ; of nights, walking home (as well as they could), they used to knock down ' Charleys,' poor harmless old watchmen with lanterns, guardians of the streets of Rome, Plance Consule. They perpetrated a vast deal of boxing ; they put on the 'mufflers' in Jackson's rooms ; they 'sported their prads' in the Ring in the Park ; they attended cock-fights and were enlightened patrons of dogs and destroyers of rats. Besides these sports, the *delassemens* of gentlemen mixing with the people, our patricians, of course, occasionally enjoyed the society of their own class. What a wonderful picture that used to be of Corinthian Tom dancing with Corinthian Kate at Almack's ! What a prodigious dress Kate wore ! With what graceful abandon the pair flung their arms about as they swept through the mazy quadrille, with all the noblemen standing round in their stars and uniforms ! You may still, doubtless, see the pictures at the British Museum, or find the volumes in the corner of some old country-house library.

You are to suppose that the English Aristocracy of 1820 did dance and caper in that way, and box and drink at Tom Cribb's and knock down watchmen ; and the children of to-day, turning to their elders, may say 'Grandmamma, did you wear such a dress as that when you danced at Almack's ? There was very little of it, grandmamma. Did grandpapa kill many watchmen when he was a young man, and frequent thieves' gin-shops, cock-fights, and the ring before you married him ? Did he use to talk the extraordinary slang and jargon which is printed in this book ? He is very much changed. He seems a gentlemanly old boy enough now.'

In the above-named consulate, when *we* had grandfathers alive, there would be in the old gentleman's library in the country two or three old mottled portfolios or great swollen scrap-books of blue paper, full of the comic prints of grandpapa's time, ere Plancus ever had the fasces borne before him. These prints were signed Gillray, Bunbury, Rowlandson, Woodward, and some actually George Cruikshank—for George is a veteran now, and he took the etching needle in hand as a child. He caricatured 'Boney,' borrowing not a little from Gillray in his first puerile efforts. He drew Louis XVIII. trying on Boney's boots. Before the century was actually in its teens, we believe that George Cruikshank was amusing the public.

In those great coloured prints in our grandfather's portfolios in the library, and in some other apartments of the house, where the caricatures used to be pasted in those days, we found things quite beyond our comprehension. Boney was represented as a fierce dwarf, with goggle eyes, a huge laced hat and tricoloured plume, a crooked sabre, reeking with blood ; a little demon revelling in lust, murder, massacre. John Bull was shown kicking him a good deal : indeed, he was prodigiously kicked all through that series of pictures ; by Sydney Smith and our brave allies the gallant Turks ; by the excellent and patriotic Spaniards ; by the amiable and indignant Russians,—all nations had boots at the service of poor Master Boney ! How Pitt used to defy him ! How good old George, king of Brobdignag, laughed at Gulliver Boney, sailing about in his tank to make sport for their Majesties ! This little fiend, this beggar's brat, cowardly, murderous, and atheistic as he was (we remember in those old portfolios, pictures representing Boney and his family in rags, gnawing raw bones in a Corsican hut; Boney murdering the sick at Jaffa ; Boney with a hookah and a large turban, having adopted the Turkish religion, etc.)—this Corsican monster, nevertheless, had some devoted friends in England, according to the Gillray chronicle—a set of villains who

loved atheism, tyranny, plunder and wickedness in general, like their
French friend.   In the pictures these men were all represented as
dwarfs, like their ally.   The miscreants got into power at one
time, and, if we remember right, were called the Broad-backed
Administration.   One with shaggy eyebrows and a bristly beard,
the hirsute ringleader of the rascals, was, it appears, called Charles
James Fox; another miscreant, with a blotched countenance, was
a certain Sheridan; other imps were hight Erskine, Norfolk (Jockey
of), Moira, Henry Petty.   As in our childish innocence we used to
look at these demons, now sprawling and tipsy in their cups,
now scaling Heaven, from which the angelic Pitt hurled them
down; now cursing the light (their atrocious ringleader Fox was
represented with hairy cloven feet and a tail and horns); now
kissing Boney's boot, but inevitably discomfited by Pitt and the
other good angels, we hated these vicious wretches, as good children
should; we were on the side of Virtue and Pitt and Grandpapa.
But if our sisters wanted to look at the portfolios, the good old
grandfather used to hesitate.   There were some prints among them
very odd indeed; some that girls could not understand; some that
boys, indeed, had best not see.   We swiftly turn over those pro-
hibited pages.   How many of them there were in the wild, coarse,
reckless, ribald, generous book of old English humour !

How savage the satire was—how fierce the assault—what
garbage hurled at opponents—what foul blows were hit—what
language of Billingsgate flung !   Fancy a party in a country house
now looking over Woodward's facetiæ, or some of the Gillray
comicalities, or the slatternly Saturnalia of Rowlandson.   Whilst
we live we must laugh and have folks to make us laugh.   We
cannot afford to lose Satyr, with his pipe and dances and gambols.
But we have washed, combed, clothed, and taught the rogue good
manners; or rather, let us say, he has learned them himself; for
he is of nature soft and kindly, and he has put aside his mad
pranks and tipsy habits; and, frolicsome always, has become gentle
and harmless, smitten into shame by the pure presence of our
women, and the sweet confiding smiles of our children.   Among
the veterans, the old pictorial satirists, we have mentioned the
famous name of one humorous designer who is still alive and at
work.   Did we not see, by his own hand, his own portrait of his
own famous face and whiskers in the *Illustrated London News*
the other day ?   There was a print in that paper of an assemblage
of Teetotallers in Sadler's Wells Theatre, and we straightway
recognised the old Roman hand—the old Roman's of the time of
Plancus—George Cruikshank's.   There were the old bonnets and
droll faces and shoes and short trousers and figures of 1820 sure

enough. And there was George (who has taken to the water
doctrine, as all the world knows) handing some teetotalleresses
over a plank to the table where the pledge was being administered.
How often has George drawn that picture of Cruikshank! Where
haven't we seen it? How fine it was, facing the effigy of Mr.
Ainsworth in *Ainsworth's Magazine* when George illustrated that
periodical! How grand and severe he stands in that design in
G. C.'s 'Omnibus,' where he represents himself tonged like S.
Dunstan, and tweaking a wretch of a publisher by the nose! The
collectors of George's etchings—O the charming etchings! O, the
dear old German popular tales!—the capital 'Points of Humour'
—the delightful Phrenology and scrap-books, of the good time, *our*
time,—Plancus's, in fact!—the collectors of the Georgian etchings,
we say, have at least a hundred pictures of the artist. Why, we
remember him in his favourite Hessian boots in 'Tom and Jerry'
itself; and in woodcuts as far back as the Queen's trial. He has
rather deserted satire and comedy of late years, having turned his
attention to the serious, and war-like, and sublime. Having
confessed our age and prejudices, we prefer the comic and fanciful
to the historic, romantic, and at present didactic George. May
respect, and length of days, and comfortable repose, attend the
brave, honest, kindly, pure-minded artist, humourist, moralist! It
was he first who brought English pictorial humour and children
acquainted. Our young people and their fathers and mothers owe
him many a pleasant hour and harmless laugh. Is there no way
in which the country could acknowledge the long services and
brave career of such a friend and benefactor?

Since George's time humour has been converted. Comus and
his wicked satyrs and leering fauns have disappeared, and fled into
the lowest haunts; and Comus's lady (if she had a taste for
humour, which may be doubted) might take up our funny picture-
books without the slightest precautionary squeamishness. What
can be purer than the charming fancies of Richard Doyle? In all
Mr. Punch's huge galleries can't we walk as safely as through Miss
Pinkerton's school-rooms? And as we look at Mr. Punch's pictures,
at *The Illustrated News* pictures, at all the pictures in the book-
shop windows at this Christmas season, as oldsters, we feel a
certain pang of envy against the youngsters.—They are too well
off. Why hadn't *we* picture-books! Why were we flogged so?
A plague on the lictors and their rods in the time of Plancus!

And now, after this rambling preface, we are arrived at the
subject in hand—Mr. John Leech and his *Pictures of Life and
Character* in the collection of Mr. Punch. This book is better
than plum-cake at Christmas. It is an enduring plum-cake, which

you may eat and which you may slice and deliver to your friends ; and to which, having cut it, you may come again and welcome, from year's end to year's end. In the frontispiece you see Mr. Punch examining the pictures in his Gallery—a portly, well-dressed, middle-aged, respectable gentleman, in a white neck-cloth and a polite evening costume—smiling in a very bland and agreeable manner upon one of his pleasant drawings, taken out of one of his handsome portfolios. Mr. Punch has very good reason to smile at the work and be satisfied with the artist. Mr. Leech, his chief contributor, and some kindred humourists, with pencil and pen have served Mr. Punch admirably. Time was, if we remember Mr. P.'s history rightly, that he did not wear silk stockings nor well-made clothes (the little dorsal irregularity in his figure is almost an ornament now, so excellent a tailor has he). He was of humble beginnings. It is said he kept a ragged little booth, which he put up at corners of streets ; associated with beadles, policemen, his own ugly wife (whom he treated most scandalously) and persons in a low station of life ; earning a precarious livelihood by the cracking of wild jokes, the singing of ribald songs, and half-pence extracted from passers-by. He is the Satyric genius we spoke of anon ; he cracks his jokes still, for Satire must live ; but he is combed, washed, neatly clothed, and perfectly presentable. He goes into the very best company ; he keeps a stud at Melton ; he has a moor in Scotland ; he rides in the Park ; has his stall at the Opera ; is constantly dining out at clubs and in private society ; and goes every night in the season to balls and parties, where you see the most beautiful women possible. He is welcomed among his new friends, the great ; though, like the good old English gentleman of the song, he does not forget the small. He pats the heads of street boys and girls ; relishes the jokes of Jack the costermonger and Bob the dustman ; good-naturedly spies out Molly the cook flirting with policeman X, or Mary the nursemaid as she listens to the fascinating guardsman. He used rather to laugh at guardsmen, 'plungers' and other military men ; and was until latter days very contemptuous in his behaviour towards Frenchmen. He has a natural antipathy to pomp and swagger and fierce demeanour. But now that the guardsmen are gone to war, and the dandies of ' The Rag '—dandies no more—are battling like heroes at Balaklava and Inkermann by the side of their heroic allies, Mr. Punch's laughter is changed to hearty respect and en-thusiasm. It is not against courage and honour he wars : but this great moralist—must it be owned ?—has some popular British prejudices, and these led him in peace time to laugh at soldiers and Frenchmen. If those hulking footmen who accompanied the carriages to the opening of Parliament the other day, would form a plush brigade, wear only gun-powder in their hair, and strike with their great canes on the enemy, Mr. Punch would leave off laughing at 'Jeames,' who meanwhile remains amongst us, to all outward appearance regardless of satire, and calmly consuming his five meals *per diem*. Against lawyers, beadles, bishops and clergy, and authorities, Mr. Punch is still rather bitter. At the time of the Papal aggression he was prodigiously angry; and one of the chief misfortunes which happened to him at that period was that, through the violent opinions which he expressed regarding the Roman Catholic hierarchy, he lost the invaluable services, the graceful pencil, the harmless wit, the charming fancy of Mr. Doyle. Another member of Mr. Punch's cabinet, the biographer of Jeames, the author of the Snob papers, resigned his functions on account of Mr. Punch's assaults upon the present Emperor of the French nation, whose anger Jeames thought it was unpatriotic to arouse. Mr. Punch parted with these contributors: he filled their places with others as good. The boys at the rail-road stations cried *Punch* just as cheerily, and sold just as many numbers, after these events, as before.

There is no blinking the fact that in Mr. Punch's cabinet John Leech is the right-hand man. Fancy a number of *Punch* without Leech's pictures! What would you give for it? The learned gentlemen who write the work must feel that, without him, it were as well left alone. Look at the rivals whom the popularity of *Punch* has brought into the field; the direct imitators of Mr. Leech's manner—the artists with a manner of their own—how inferior their pencils are to his in humour, in depicting the public manners, in arresting, amusing the nation. The truth, the strength, the free vigour, the kind humour, the John Bull pluck and spirit of that hand are approached by no competitor. With what dexterity he draws a horse, a woman, a child! He feels them all, so to speak, like a man. What plump young beauties are those with which Mr. Punch's chief contributor supplies the old gentleman's pictorial harem! What famous thews and sinews Mr. Punch's horses have, and how Briggs, on the back of them, scampers across country! You see youth, strength, enjoyment, manliness in those drawings, and in none more so, to our thinking, than in the hundred pictures of children which this artist loves to design. Like a brave, hearty, good-natured Briton, he becomes quite soft and tender with the little creatures, pats gently their little golden heads and watches with unfailing pleasure their ways, their sports, their jokes, laughter, caresses. *Enfans terribles* come home from Eton; young Miss practising her first flirtation ; poor little ragged Polly making dirt pies in the gutter, or staggering under the weight of Jacky, her nurse-child, who is as big as herself—all these little ones, patrician and plebeian, meet with kindness from this kind heart, and are watched with curious nicety by this amiable observer.

We remember, in one of those ancient Gillray portfolios, a print which used to cause a sort of terror in us youthful spectators, and in which the Prince of Wales (His Royal Highness was a Foxite then) was represented as sitting alone in a magnificent hall after a voluptuous meal, and using a great steel fork in the guise of a toothpick. Fancy the first young gentleman living employing such a weapon in such a way ! The most elegant Prince of Europe engaged with a two-pronged iron fork—the heir of Britannia with a *bident !* The man of genius who drew that picture saw little of the society which he satirised and amused. Gillray watched public characters as they walked by the shop in St. James's Street, or passed through the lobby of the House of Commons. His studio was a garret, or little better ; his place of amusement, a tavern parlour where his club held its nightly sittings over their pipes and sanded floor. You could not have society represented by men to whom it was not familiar. When Gavarni came to England a few years since—one of the wittiest of men, one of the most brilliant and dexterous of draughtsmen—he published a book of *Les Anglais,* and his *Anglais* were all Frenchmen. The eye, so keen and so long practised to observe Parisian life, could not perceive English character. A social painter must be of the world which he depicts, and native to the manners which he portrays.

Now, any one who looks over Mr. Leech's portfolio must see that the social pictures which he gives us are authentic. What comfortable little drawing-rooms and dining-rooms, what snug libraries we enter, what fine young gentlemanly wags they are, those beautiful little dandies who wake up gouty old grandpapa to ring the bell ; who decline aunt's pudding and custards, saying that they will reserve themselves for an anchovy toast with the claret ; who talk together in ball-room doors, where Fred whispers Charley—pointing to a dear little partner seven years old—'My dear Charley, she has very much gone off; you should have seen that girl last season !' Look well at everything appertaining to the economy of the famous Mr. Briggs ; how snug, quiet, appropriate all the appointments are ! What a comfortable, neat, clean, middle-class house Briggs' is (in the Bayswater suburb of London, we should guess from the sketches of the surrounding scenery) ! What a good stable he has, with a loose box for those celebrated hunters which he rides ! How pleasant, clean, and warm his breakfast table looks ! What a trim little maid brings in the top-boots which horrify Mrs. B. ! What a snug dressing-room he has, complete in all its appointments, and in which he appears trying on the delightful hunting-cap which Mrs. B. flings into the fire ! How cosy all the Briggs party seem in their dining-room, Briggs reading a Treatise on Dog-breaking by a lamp; Mamma and Grannie with their respective needleworks ; the children clustering round a great book of prints—a great book of prints such as this before us, which, at this season, must make thousands of children happy by as many firesides ! The inner life of all these people is represented ; Leech draws them as naturally as Teniers depicts Dutch boors, or Morland pigs and stables. It is your house and mine ; we are looking at everybody's family circle. Our boys, coming from school, give themselves such airs, the young scape-graces ! our girls, going to parties, are so tricked out by fond mammas—a social history of London in the middle of the nineteenth century. As such future students—lucky they to have a book so pleasant—will regard these pages ; even the mutations of fashion they may follow here if they be so inclined. Mr. Leech has as fine an eye for tailory and millinery as for horse-flesh. How they change those cloaks and bonnets ! How we have to pay milliners' bills from year to year ! Where are those prodigious chatelaines of 1850 which no lady could be without ? Where are those charming waistcoats, those 'stunning' waistcoats which our young girls used to wear a few brief seasons back, and which cause Gus, in the sweet little sketch of 'La Mode,' to ask Ellen for her tailor's address ! Gus is a young warrior by this time, very likely facing the enemy at Inkermann, and pretty Ellen, and that love of a sister of hers, are married and happy, let us hope, superintending one of those delightful nursery scenes which our artist depicts with such tender humour. Fortunate artist, indeed ! You see he must have been bred at a good public school ; that he has ridden many a good horse in his day ; paid, no doubt, out of his own purse for the originals of some of those lovely caps and bonnets ; and watched paternally the ways, smiles, frolics, and slumbers of his favourite little people.

As you look at the drawings, secrets come out of them—private jokes, as it were, imparted to you by the author for your special delectation. How remarkably for instance, has Mr. Leech observed the hair-dresser of the present age ! Look at 'Mr. Tongs,' whom that hideous old bald woman, who ties on her bonnet at the glass, informs that 'she has used the whole bottle of Balm of California, but her hair comes off yet.' You can see the bear's grease, not only on Tongs' head but on his hands, which he is clapping clammily together. Remark him who is telling his client 'there is cholera in the hair,' and that lucky rogue whom the young lady bids to cut off 'a long thick piece' for somebody, doubtless. All these men are different, and delightfully natural and absurd. Why should hair-dressing be an absurd profession?

The amateur will remark what an excellent part hands play in Mr. Leech's pictures; his admirable actors use them with perfect naturalness. Look at Betty, putting the urn down; at cook, laying her hands on the kitchen table whilst her policeman grumbles at the cold meat. They are cook's and housemaid's hands without mistake, and not without a certain beauty too. The bald old lady who is tying her bonnet at Tongs', has hands which you see are trembling. Watch the fingers of the two old harridans who are talking scandal; for what long years past they have pointed out holes in their neighbours' dresses and mud on their flounces. 'Here's a go! I've lost my diamond ring!' As the dustman utters this pathetic cry and looks at his hand, you burst out laughing. These are among the little points of humour. One could indicate hundreds of such as one turns over the pleasant pages.

There is a little snob or gent, whom we all of us know, who wears little tufts on his little chin, outrageous pins and pantaloons, smokes cigars on tobacconists' counters, sucks his cane in the streets, struts about with Mrs. Snob and the baby (the latter an immense woman whom Snob nevertheless bullies), who is a favourite abomination of Leech's and pursued by that savage humourist into a thousand of his haunts. There he is, choosing waistcoats at the tailors—such waistcoats! Yonder he is giving a shilling to the sweeper who calls him 'capting'; now he is offering a paletot to a huge giant who is going out in the rain. They don't know their own pictures, very likely; if they did, they would have a meeting, and thirty or forty of them would be deputed to thrash Mr. Leech. One feels a pity for the poor little bucks. In a minute or two, when we close this discourse and walk the streets, we shall see a dozen such.

Ere we shut the desk up, just one word to point out to the unwary specially to note the backgrounds of landscapes in Leech's drawings—homely drawings of moor and wood and sea-shore and London streets — the scenes of his little dramas. They are as excellently true to nature as the actors themselves; our respect for the genius and humour which invented both increase as we look again and again at the design. May we have more of them; more pleasant Christmas volumes, over which we and our children can laugh together. Can we have too much of truth, and fun, and beauty and kindness?

CRUIKSHANK'S GALLERY.[1]

IN a quiet little room in Exeter Hall a veteran lecturer is holding forth all day upon a subject which moves his heart very strongly. His text, on which he has preached before in many places, is still ' The Bottle.' He divides his sermon into many hundreds of heads, and preaches with the most prodigious emphasis and grotesque variety. He is for no half measures. He will have no compromise with the odious god Bacchus ; the wicked idol is smashed like Bel and Dagon. He will empty into the gutter all Master Bacchus's pipes, his barrels, quarter-casks, demijohns, gallons, quarts, pints, gills, down to your very smallest liqueur glasses of spirits or wine. He will show you how the church, the bar, the army, the universities, the genteel world, the country gentleman in his polite circle, the humble artisan in his, the rustic ploughman in the fields, the misguided washerwoman over her suds and tubs—how all ranks and conditions of men are deteriorated and corrupted by the use of that abominable strong liquor : he will have patience with it no longer. For upwards of half-a-century, he says, he has employed pencil and pen against the vice of drunkenness, and in the vain attempt to shut up drinking shops and to establish *moderate drinking as a universal rule;* but for seventeen years he has discovered that teetotalism, or the total abstaining from all intoxicating liquors, was the only real remedy for the entire abolition of intemperance. His thoughts working in this direction, one day this subject ' The Worship of Bacchus ' flashed across his mind, and hence the origin of a work of art measuring 13 ft. 4 in. by 7 ft. 8 in., which has occupied the author no less than a year and a half.

This sermon has the advantage over others that you can take a chapter at a time, as it were, and return and resume the good homilist's discourse at your leisure. What is your calling in life ? In some part of this vast *tableau* you will find it is *de te fabula.* In this compartment the soldiers are drinking and fighting ; in

[1] [*The Times*, Friday, May 15th, 1863.]

the next the parsons are drinking 'Healths to the young Christian.'
Here are the publicans, filthily intoxicated with their own horrible
liquors ; yonder is a masquerade supper, 'where drunken masquerade fiends drag down columbines to drunkenness and ruin.'
Near them are 'the public singers chanting forth the praises of
the "God of Wine."' 'Is it not marvellous to think,' says Mr.
Cruikshank in a little pamphlet, containing a speech by him
which is quite as original as the picture on which it comments,
—'Is it not marvellous what highly talented poetry and what
harmonious musical compositions have been produced from time
to time in praise of this imaginative, slippery, deceitful, dangerous
myth ?' This 'myth' the spectator may follow all through this
most wonderful and labyrinthine picture. In the nursery the
Doctor is handing a pot of beer to mamma ; the nurse is drinking
beer ; the little boy is crying for beer ; and the papa is drawing a
cork so that 'he and the doctor may have a drop.' Here you
have a group of women, victims of intemperance, 'tearing, biting,
and mutilating one another.' Yonder are two of the police
carrying away a drunken policeman. Does not the mind reel and
stagger at the idea of this cumulated horror ? And what is the
wine which yonder clergyman holds in his hand but the same
kind of stuff which has made the mother in the christening scene
above 'so tipsy that she has let her child fall out of her lap, while
her idiotic husband points to his helpless wife, and exclaims, "Ha,
ha ; she's dr—unk"'?

As with pauperibus so with locupletibus. If they drink, rich
and poor are all bad together. A friend of Mr. Cruikshank's
(a physician) assured him that he knew 'a young gentleman of
fortune who got so drunk on his coming of age that he died the
next day !' Fancy the maddened feelings of the next heir to the
property ! It is on some dismal occasion of this sort that our
stern moralist draws a son consoling his mother 'with a glass of
wine, the daughter being also consoled with a glass, and the
granddaughter likewise.'

This is indeed horror on horror's head. We have an excited
daughter, an intoxicated mother, a vinous grandmother—a ghastly
picture of three generations in liquor ! From another part of the
picture the tutors and young gentlemen of the universities may
take a hint which may do them good. Ten or a dozen of them in
their caps and gowns (and it is to be feared those caps only fit
too well) are represented at 'one of their wine-parties, ruining
themselves for life with the strong ale sold at the Colleges.' Mr.
Cruikshank remarks that 'the ale brewed at Jesus College,
Cambridge, commonly called Jesus ale, used to be thought most

excellent, but the Trinity ale—aye, that's the stuff—is the strongest ale brewed in the whole country.' We may all see there is no mincing the matter here. Wine, beer, gin, the lady's liqueur, the midwife's dram, the divine's festive libation, the policeman's lawless excess—all are depicted with features not, perhaps, un-exaggerated, in colours too dismally true. Have you ever drunk a glass of wine? It is one too many. Half-a-dozen glasses make a pint (nay, two at some taverns). Two pints make a quart, four quarts a gallon; and so on. Fling away pint pots, quart pots, pottle pots, and the rest. Let tea, coffee, cocoa, and ginger-beer, which possibly cheers, but certainly not inebriates, be your tipple. This is the moral of Mr. Cruikshank's great sermon at Exeter Hall, where preachers of all sorts and sects are accustomed to hold forth.

Forty years ago, in Sweetings Alley, near the Royal Exchange, and in a court leading from Ludgate Hill, there used to be two delightful exhibitions of Cruikshank's works which London boys could enjoy *gratis* at the shop window. The 'monstrosities' of the fashion were here ridiculed by the satirical George, who depicted bagging Petersham trousers, the tall collars, the high waists of bygone bucks, the grandfathers of the present youth. You may see here ladies with high waists and very slight upper garments, and young fellows in wondrous pantaloons and pumps, grinning and capering through that newly-invented and elegant dance the quadrille. Do these 'monstrosities' of 1816, 1819, and 1820 actually resemble the garments which we or our ancestors wore? In 1816 the hoops represented in Hogarth's pictures were considered as monstrous and barbarous, and yet they covered no more ground than the trains and dresses with which our ladies in 1863 think fit to sweep the floors of the Exhibition. The intelligent guardian of the Cruikshank Gallery walks round with the visitors and gives comments upon the great temperance tableau, and afterwards on the smaller etchings in detail.

Why, a professor might lecture his class for hours upon these droll pages of bygone manners and social history. When did high waists descend? When did *gigot* sleeves come in and go out? When was the last of the 'Charleys' knocked down? When did the Prince Regent leave off hair-powder? Recount a few of the adventures of Corinthian Tom, Jeremiah Hawthorn, and Robert Logic, Esquires; and, if alive, state what is their present age? Corinthian Tom must be seventy-five, if he is a day old. No doubt, he has lived to laugh over the adventures of Mr. Briggs, of Messrs. Brown, Jones, and Robinson, and of those athletic young Volunteers whose boots, beards, pipes, and tunics Mr. Keene depicts so amusingly. With what vigour, courage, good-humour, honesty, cheerfulness, have this busy hand and needle plied for more than fifty years!

From 1799, 'when about eight or nine years of age,' until yesterday the artist has never taken rest. When you think he might desire quiet, behold he starts up lively as ever, and arms himself to do battle with the demon drunkenness.

With voice and paint-brush, with steel-plate and wood-block, he assails 'that deceitful, slippery, dangerous myth!' To wage war against some wrong has been his chief calling; and in lighter moments to waken laughter, wonder, or sympathy. To elderly lovers of fun, who can remember this century in its teens and its twenties, the benefactions of this great humourist are as pleasant and well remembered as Papa's or Uncle's 'tips' when they came to see the boys at school. The sovereign then administered bought delights not to be purchased by sovereigns of later coinage, tarts of incomparable sweetness which are never to be equalled in these times, sausages whose savour is still fragrant in the memory, books containing beautiful prints (sometimes ravishingly coloured) signed with the magic initials of the incomparable 'G. Ck.' No doubt, the young people of the present day have younger artists to charm them, and many hundred thousand boys and girls are admiring Mr. Leech, and will be grateful to him forty years hence, when their heads are grey. These will not care for the Cruikshank drawings and etchings as men do whose boyhood was delighted by them; but the moderns can study the manners of the early century in the Cruikshank etchings, as of the French Revolution period in Gillray, Woodward, Bunbury. Imitations of the manner of the first-named master one can see in George Cruikshank's early works. Very soon he adopted a manner of his own, which lovers of the art can admire and study from its commencement to its development in the admirable *Points of Humour*, the charming vignettes for the *German Popular Tales*, and *Peter Schlemihl*, in 'Scrap Books,' 'Sketch Books,' 'Omnibuses,' innumerable, in the *Boz* illustrations, in the brilliant etchings of *The Comic Almanac*, and in the plates for the famous Ainsworth's romances, the grim *Tower of London*, the awful *Guy Fawkes*, the much-persecuted, much-read *Jack Sheppard!* Cruikshank found comic art free and unscrupulous, and made it modest and pure. It may be young people do not clamber round the portfolios as they used in days gone by, and laugh and wonder delighted over the fun, the fancy, the *naïveté* of the artist himself. Now is the time for all *aquæ potoribus* to rally round their champion.

U

Is not the sect numbered by millions ? Now is the time for elderly persons to review the amusements, the scenes, the dresses, the boxing-matches, the coaches, the short waists, tall neck-cloths, narrow skirts which in good old days seemed so killing ; and now youth pursuing the study of history may see how their fathers were habited, amused, occupied—their fathers ?—their grand-fathers, who have been depicted by the indefatigable veteran who still cheerfully labours in the public service.

STUBBS'S CALENDAR

OR

THE FATAL BOOTS

JANUARY—THE BIRTH OF THE YEAR.

JANUARY—THE BIRTH OF THE YEAR

Some poet has observed that if any man would write down what has really happened to him in this mortal life he would be sure to make a good book, though he never had met with a single adventure from his birth to his burial. How much more, then, must I, who *have* had adventures most singular, pathetic, and unparalleled, be able to compile an instructive and entertaining volume for the use of the public.

I don't mean to say that I have killed lions, or seen the wonders of travel in the deserts of Arabia or Persia; or that I have been a very fashionable character, living with dukes and peeresses, and writing my recollections of them, as the way now is. I never left this my native isle, nor spoke to a lord (except an Irish one, who had rooms in our house, and forgot to pay three weeks' lodging and extras); but, as our immortal bard observes, I have in the course of my existence been so eaten up by the slugs and harrows of outrageous fortune, and have been the object of such continual and extraordinary ill-luck, that I believe it would melt the heart of a milestone to read of it—that is, if a milestone had a heart of anything but stone.

Twelve of my adventures (one for every month in the calendar) are here presented to the public. They contain a part of the history of a great and, confidently I may say, a *good* man. I was not a spendthrift like other men. I never wronged any man of a shilling, though I am as sharp a fellow at a bargain as any in Europe. I never injured a fellow-creature; on the contrary, on several occasions, when injured myself, have shown the most wonderful forbearance. I come of a tolerably good family, and yet—born to wealth, of an inoffensive disposition, careful of the money that I had, and eager to get more—I have been going down hill ever since my journey of life began, and have been pursued by a complication of misfortunes such as surely never happened to any man but the unhappy Bob Stubbs!

Bob Stubbs is my name; and I haven't got a shilling. I have borne the commission of lieutenant in the service of King George, and am *now*—but never mind what I am now, for the public will know in a few pages more. My father was of the Suffolk Stubbses—a well-to-do gentleman of Bungay. My grandfather had been a respected attorney in that town, and left my papa a pretty little fortune. I was thus the inheritor of competence, and ought to be at this moment a gentleman.

My misfortunes may be said to have commenced about a year before my birth, when my papa, a young fellow pretending to study the law in London, fell madly in love with Miss Smith, the daughter of a tradesman, who did not give her a sixpence, and afterwards became bankrupt. My papa married this Miss Smith, and carried her off to the country, where I was born in an evil hour for me.

Were I to attempt to describe my early years, you would laugh at me as an impostor ; but the following letter from mamma to a friend, after her marriage, will pretty well show you what a poor, foolish creature she was, and what a reckless, extravagant fellow was my other unfortunate parent :—

'To MISS ELIZA HICKS, IN GRACECHURCH STREET, LONDON

'Oh, Eliza! your Susan is the happiest girl under heaven! My Thomas is an angel! not a tall, grenadier-like looking fellow, such as I always vowed I would marry. On the contrary, he is what the world would call dumpy, and I hesitate not to confess that his eyes have a cast in them. But what then? when one of his eyes is fixed on me and one on my babe, they are lighted up with an affection which my pen cannot describe, and which certainly was never bestowed upon any woman so strongly as upon your happy Susan Stubbs.

'When he comes home from shooting or the farm, if you *could* see dear Thomas with me and our dear little Bob, as I sit on one knee and baby on the other, and, as he dances us both about, I often wish that we had Sir Joshua, or some great painter, to depict the group ; for sure it is the prettiest picture in the whole world to see three such loving, merry people.

'Dear baby is the most lovely little creature that *can possibly be*—the very *image* of papa. He is cutting his teeth, and the

delight of *everybody*. Nurse says that when he is older he will
get rid of his squint, and his hair will get a *great deal* less red.
Doctor Bates is as kind and skilful and attentive as we could
desire. Think what a blessing to have had him! Ever since
poor baby's birth it has never had a day of quiet, and he has been
obliged to give it from three to four doses every week. How
thankful ought we to be that the *dear thing* is as well as it is!
It got through the measles wonderfully; then it had a little rash,
and then a nasty whooping-cough, and then a fever, and continual
pains in its poor little stomach, crying, poor, dear child, from
morning till night.

'But dear Tom is an excellent nurse, and many and many a
night has he had no sleep, dear man! in consequence of the poor
little baby. He walks up and down with it *for hours*, singing a
kind of song (dear fellow, he has no more voice than a tea-kettle),
and bobbing his head backwards and forwards, and looking, in his
night-cap and dressing-gown, *so droll*. Oh, Eliza! how you
would laugh to see him.

'We have one of the best nursemaids *in the world*, an Irish-
woman, who is as fond of baby almost as his mother (but that
can *never be*). She takes it to walk in the park for hours together,
and I really don't know why Thomas dislikes her. He says she
is tipsy very often, and slovenly, which I cannot conceive. To be
sure, the nurse is sadly dirty, and sometimes smells very strong
of gin.

'But what of that? These little drawbacks only make home
more pleasant. When one thinks how many mothers have *no*
nursemaids, how many poor, dear children have *no* doctors, ought
we not to be thankful for Mary Malowney, and that Doctor
Bates's bill is forty-seven pounds? How ill must dear baby have
been to require so much physic!

'But they are a sad expense, these dear babies, after all.
Fancy, Eliza, how much this Mary Malowney costs us. Ten
shillings every week; a glass of brandy or gin at dinner, three
pint-bottles of Mr. Thrale's best porter every day—making twenty-
one in a week, and nine hundred and ninety in the eleven months
she has been with us. Then, for baby, there is Doctor Bates's
bill of forty-five guineas, two guineas for christening, twenty for
a grand christening supper and ball (rich Uncle John mortally
offended because he was made godfather, and had to give baby a
silver cup: he has struck Thomas out of his will; and old Mr.
Firkin quite as much hurt because he was *not* asked: he will not
speak to me or Thomas in consequence); twenty guineas for
flannels, laces, little gowns, caps, napkins, and such baby's ware;

George Cruikshank

FEBRUARY—CUTTING WEATHER.

P. 296.

and all this out of three hundred pounds a year ! But Thomas expects to make *a great deal* by his farm.

'We have got the most charming country-house *you can imagine ;* it is *quite shut in* by trees, and so retired that, though only thirty miles from London, the post comes to us but once a week. The roads, it must be confessed, are execrable. It is winter now, and we are up to our knees in mud and snow. But oh, Eliza, how happy we are ! With Thomas (he has had a sad attack of rheumatism, dear man !) and little Bobby, and our kind friend Doctor Bates, who comes so far to see us, I leave you to fancy that we have a charming, merry party, and do not care for all the gaieties of Ranelah.

'Adieu ! dear baby is crying for his mamma. A thousand kisses from your affectionate   SUSAN STUBBS.'

There it is. Doctor's bills, gentleman-farming, twenty-one pints of porter a week ; in this way my unnatural parents were already robbing me of my property.

FEBRUARY—CUTTING WEATHER

I HAVE called this chapter 'cutting weather,' partly in compliment to the month of February, and partly in respect of my own misfortunes, which you are going to read about. For I have often thought that January (which is mostly twelfth-cake and holiday time) is like the first four or five years of a little boy's life ; then comes dismal February, and the working days with it, when chaps begin to look out for themselves, after the Christmas and the New Year's hey-day and merry-making are over, which our infancy may well be said to be. Well can I recollect that bitter first of February, when I first launched out into the world and appeared at Doctor Swishtail's academy.

I began at school that life of prudence and economy which I have carried on ever since. My mother gave me eighteenpence on setting out, poor soul ! I thought her heart would break as she kissed me, and bade God bless me ; and, besides, I had a small capital of my own, which I had amassed for a year previous. I'll tell you what I used to do. Wherever I saw six halfpence I took one. If it was asked for, I said I had taken it, and gave it back ; —if it was not missed, I said nothing about it, as why should I ?— those who don't miss their money, don't lose their money. So I had a little private fortune of three shillings, besides mother's eighteenpence. At school they called me the Copper Merchant, I had such lots of it.

Now, even at a preparatory school, a well-regulated boy may better himself; and I can tell you I did. I never was in any quarrels; I never was very high in the class, or very low; but there was no chap so much respected—and why? *I'd always money*. The other boys spent all theirs in the first day or two, and they gave me plenty of cakes and barley-sugar then, I can tell you. I'd no need to spend my own money, for they would insist upon treating me. Well, in a week, when theirs was gone, and they had but their threepence a week to look to for the rest of the half-year, what did I do? Why, I am proud to say that three-halfpence out of the threepence a week of almost all the young gentlemen at Doctor Swishtail's came into my pocket. Suppose, for instance, Tom Hicks wanted a slice of gingerbread,—who had the money? Little Bob Stubbs, to be sure. 'Hicks,' I used to say, '*I'll* buy you three-halfp'orth of gingerbread, if you'll give me threepence next Saturday;' and he agreed; and next Saturday came, and he very often could not pay me more than three-halfpence, then there was the threepence I was to have *the next* Saturday. I'll tell you what I did for a whole half-year: I lent a chap, by the name of Dick Bunting, three-halfpence the first Saturday for threepence the next; he could not pay me more than half when Saturday come, and I'm blest if I did not make him pay me three-halfpence *for three-and-twenty weeks running*, making two shillings and tenpence-halfpenny. But he was a sad dishonourable fellow, Dick Bunting; for, after I'd been so kind to him, and let him off for three-and-twenty weeks the money he owed me, holidays came, and threepence he owed me still. Well, according to the common principles of practice, after six weeks' holidays, he ought to have paid me exactly sixteen shillings which was my due. For the

First week the 3d. would be			.	.	6d.
Second week	.	.	.	.	1s.
Third week	.	.	.	.	2s.
Fourth week	.	.	.	.	4s.
Fifth week	.	.	.	.	8s.
Sixth week	.	.	.	.	16s.

Nothing could be more just; and yet, will it be believed?—when Bunting came back he offered me *three-halfpence!* the mean, dishonest scoundrel.

However, I was even with him, I can tell you. He spent all his money in a fortnight, and *then* I screwed him down! I made him, besides giving me a penny for a penny, pay me a quarter of his bread-and-butter at breakfast, and a quarter of his cheese at supper ; and before the half-year was out, I got from him a silver fruit-knife, a box of compasses, and a very pretty silver-laced waist-coat, in which I went home as proud as a king ; and, what's more, I had no less than three golden guineas in the pocket of it, besides fifteen shillings, the knife, and a brass bottle-screw, which I got from another chap. It wasn't bad interest for twelve shillings, which was all the money I'd had in the year, was it ? Heigho ! I've often wished that I could get such a chance again in this wicked world ; but men are more avaricious now than they used to be in those dear early days.

Well, I went home in my new waistcoat as fine as a peacock ; and when I gave the bottle-screw to my father, begging him to take it as a token of my affection for him, my dear mother burst into such a fit of tears as I never saw, and kissed and hugged me fit to smother me. ' Bless him, bless him ! ' says she, ' to think of his old father. And where did you purchase it, Bob ? '—' Why, mother,' says I, ' I purchased it out of my savings ' (which was as true as the gospel). When I said this, mother looked round to father, smiling, although she had tears in her eyes, and she took his hand, and with her other hand drew me to her. ' Is he not a noble boy ? ' says she to my father : ' and only nine years old ! ' ' Faith,' says my father, ' he *is* a good lad, Susan. Thank thee, my boy ; and here is a crown piece in return for thy bottle-screw ; it shall open us a bottle of the very best, too,' says my father ; and he kept his word. I always was fond of good wine (though never, from a motive of proper self-denial, having any in my cellar) ; and, by Jupiter ! on this night I had my little skinful,—for there was no stinting, so pleased were my dear parents with the bottle-screw. The best of it was it only cost me threepence originally, which a chap could not pay me.

Seeing this game was such a good one, I became very generous towards my parents ; and a capital way it is to encourage liberality in children. I gave mamma a very neat brass thimble, and she gave me a half-guinea piece. Then I gave her a very pretty needle-book, which I made myself with an ace of spades from a new pack of cards we had, and I got Sally, our maid, to cover it with a bit of pink satin her mistress had given her ; and I made the leaves of the book, which I vandyked very nicely, out of a piece of flannel I had had round my neck for a sore throat. It smelt a little of hartshorn, but it was a beautiful needlebook ; and mamma was so delighted with it, that she went into town and bought me a gold-laced hat. Then I bought papa a pretty china tobacco-stopper ;

but I am sorry to say of my dear father that he was not so generous as my mamma or myself, for he only burst out laughing, and did not give me so much as a half-crown piece, which was the least I expected from him. 'I shan't give you anything, Bob, this time,' says he ; 'and I wish, my boy, you would not make any more such presents—for, really, they are too expensive.' Expensive, indeed ! I hate meanness,—even in a father.

I must tell you about the silver-edged waistcoat which Bunting gave me. Mamma asked me about it, and I told her the truth,— that it was a present from one of the boys for my kindness to him. Well, what does she do but writes back to Doctor Swishtail, when I went to school, thanking him for his attention to her dear son, and sending a shilling to the good and grateful little boy who had given me the waistcoat !

'What waistcoat is it,' says the Doctor to me, 'and who gave it to you ?'

'Bunting gave it me, Sir,' says I.

'Call Bunting !' And up the little ungrateful chap came. Would you believe it ?—he burst into tears, told that the waistcoat had been given him by his mother, and that he had been forced to give it for a debt to Copper Merchant, as the nasty little black-guard called me. He then said how, for three-halfpence, he had been compelled to pay me three shillings (the sneak ! as if he had been *obliged* to borrow the three-halfpence !)—how all the other boys had been swindled (swindled !) by me in like manner,—and how, with only twelve shillings, I had managed to scrape together four guineas. . . .

My courage almost fails me as I describe the shameful scene that followed. The boys were called in, my own little account-book was dragged out of my cupboard, to prove how much I had received from each, and every farthing of my money was paid back to them. The tyrant took the thirty shillings that my dear parents had given me, and said he should put them into the poor-box at church ; and, after having made a long discourse to the boys about meanness and usury, he said, 'Take off your coat, Mr. Stubbs, and restore Bunting his waistcoat.' I did, and stood without coat and waistcoat in the midst of the nasty grinning boys. I was going to put on my coat,—

'Stop !' says he. 'TAKE DOWN HIS BREECHES !'

Ruthless brutal villain ! Sam Hopkins, the biggest boy, took them down—horsed me—and *I was flogged, sir ;* yes, flogged ! Oh revenge ! I, Robert Stubbs, who had done nothing but what was right, was brutally flogged at ten years of age !—Though February was the shortest month, I remembered it long.

MARCH—SHOWERY

WHEN my mamma heard of the treatment of her darling she was for bringing an action against the schoolmaster, or else for tearing his eyes out (when, dear soul! she would not have torn the eyes out of a flea, had it been her own injury), and, at the very least, for having me removed from the school where I had been so shamefully treated. But papa was stern for once, and vowed that I had been served quite right, declared that I should not be removed from the school, and sent old Swishtail a brace of pheasants for what he called his kindness to me. Of these the old gentleman invited me to partake, and made a very queer speech at dinner, as he was cutting them up, about the excellence of my parents, and his own determination to be *kinder still* to me if ever I ventured on such practices again. So I was obliged to give up my old trade of lending: for the Doctor declared that any boy who borrowed should be flogged, and any one who *paid* should be flogged twice as much. There was no standing against such a prohibition as this, and my little commerce was ruined.

I was not very high in the school: not having been able to get farther than that dreadful *Propria quæ maribus* in the Latin grammar, of which, though I have it by heart even now, I never could understand a syllable: but, on account of my size, my age, and the prayers of my mother, was allowed to have the privilege of the bigger boys, and on holidays to walk about in the town. Great dandies we were, too, when we thus went out. I recollect my costume very well: a thunder-and-lightning coat, a white waistcoat embroidered neatly at the pockets, a lace frill, a pair of knee-breeches, and elegant white cotton or silk stockings. This did very well, but still I was dissatisfied. I wanted *a pair of boots.* Three boys in the school had boots—I was mad to have them too.

But my papa, when I wrote to him, would not hear of it; and three pounds, the price of a pair, was too large a sum for my mother to take from the housekeeping, or for me to pay, in the present impoverished state of my exchequer; but the desire for the boots was so strong, that have them I must at any rate.

There was a German bootmaker who had just set up in our town in those days, who afterwards made his fortune in London. I determined to have the boots from him, and did not despair, before the end of a year or two, either to leave the school, when I should not mind his dunning me, or to screw the money from mamma, and so pay him.

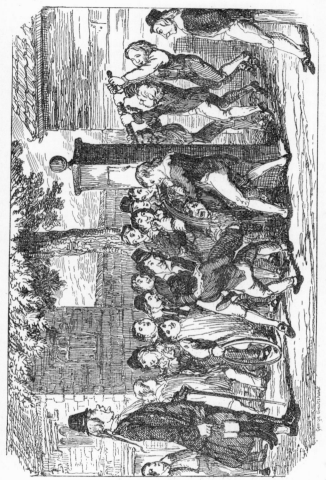

MARCH—SHOWERY.

So I called upon this man—Stiffelkind was his name—and he took my measure for a pair.

'You are a vary yong gentleman to wear dop-boots,' said the shoemaker.

'I suppose, fellow,' says I, 'that is my business and not yours. Either make the boots or not—but when you speak to a man of my rank, speak respectfully!' And I poured out a number of oaths, in order to impress him with a notion of my respectability.

They had the desired effect. 'Stay, sir,' says he. 'I have a nice littel pair of dop-boots, dat I tink will jost do for you.' And he produced, sure enough, the most elegant things I ever saw. 'Dey were made,' said he, 'for de Honourable Mr. Stiffney, of de Gards, but were too small.'

'Ah, indeed!' said I. 'Stiffney is a relation of mine. And what, you scoundrel, will you have the impudence to ask for these things?' He replied, 'Three pounds.'

'Well,' said I, 'they are confoundedly dear; but, as you will have a long time to wait for your money, why, I shall have my revenge, you see.' The man looked alarmed, and began a speech: 'Sare,—I cannot let dem go vidout——' but a bright thought struck me, and I interrupted—'Sir! don't sir me. Take off the boots, fellow, and, hark ye, when you speak to a nobleman, don't say Sir.'

'A hundert tousand pardons, my Lort,' says he: 'if I had known you were a lort, I vood never have called you Sir. Vat name shall I put down in my books?'

'Name?—Oh! why, LORD CORNWALLIS, to be sure,' said I, as I walked off in the boots.

'And vat shall I do with my Lort's shoes?'

'Keep them until I send for them,' said I. And giving him a patronising bow, I walked out of the shop, as the German tied up my shoes in paper.

This story I would not have told, but that my whole life turned upon these accursed boots. I walked back to school as proud as a peacock, and easily succeeded in satisfying the boys as to the manner in which I came by my new ornaments.

Well, one fatal Monday morning—the blackest of all black Mondays that ever I knew—as we were all of us playing between school-hours, I saw a posse of boys round a stranger, who seemed to be looking out for one of us. A sudden trembling seized me —I knew it was Stiffelkind. What had brought him here? He talked loud and seemed angry. So I rushed into the schoolroom, and, burying my head between by hands, began reading for dear life.

'I vant Lort Cornvallis,' said the horrid bootmaker. 'His Lortship belongs, I know, to dis honourable school, for I saw him vid de boys at chorch yesterday.'

'Lord who?'

'Vy Lort Cornvallis to be sure—a very fat young nobleman, vid red hair: he squints a little, and svears dreadfully.'

'There's no Lord Cornwallis here,' said one; and there was a pause.

'Stop! I have it,' says that odious Bunting. '*It must be Stubbs!*' 'And Stubbs! Stubbs!' every one cried out, while I was so busy at my book as not to hear a word.

At last, two of the biggest chaps rushed into the schoolroom, and, seizing each an arm, ran me into the playground—bolt up against the shoemaker.

'Dis is my man. I beg your Lortship's pardon,' says he, 'I have brought your Lortship's shoes, vich you left. See dey have been in dis parcel ever since you vent avay in my boots.'

'Shoes, fellow!' says I; 'I never saw your face before'—for I knew there was nothing for it but brazening it out. 'Upon the honour of a gentleman!' said I, turning round to the boys. They hesitated; and if the trick had turned in my favour, fifty of them would have seized hold of Stiffelkind and drubbed him soundly.

'Stop!' says Bunting (hang him!). 'Let's see the shoes. If they fit him, why then the cobbler's right.' They did fit me; and not only that, but the name of STUBBS was written in them at full length.

'Vat!' said Stiffelkind. 'Is he not a lort? So help me Himmel, I never did vonce tink of looking at de shoes, which have been lying ever since in dis piece of brown paper.' And then, gathering anger as he went on, he thundered out so much of his abuse of me, in his German-English, that the boys roared with laughter. Swishtail came in in the midst of the disturbance, and asked what the noise meant.

'It's only Lord Cornwallis, sir,' said the boys, 'battling with his shoemaker about the price of a pair of top-boots.'

'Oh, sir,' said I, 'it was only in fun that I called myself Lord Cornwallis.'

'In fun!—Where are the boots? And you, sir, give me your bill.' My beautiful boots were brought; and Stiffelkind produced his bill. 'Lord Cornwallis to Samuel Stiffelkind, for a pair of boots—four guineas.'

'You have been fool enough, sir,' says the Doctor, looking very stern, 'to let this boy impose on you as a lord ; and knave enough to charge him double the value of the article you sold him. Take back the boots, sir ! I won't pay a penny of your bill; nor can you get a penny. As for you, sir, you miserable swindler and cheat, I shall not flog you as I did before, but I shall send you home : you are not fit to be the companion of honest boys.'

'*Suppose we duck him* before he goes ?' piped out a very small voice. The Doctor grinned significantly, and left the schoolroom ; and the boys knew by this they might have their will. They seized me and carried me to the playground pump : they pumped upon me until I was half dead ; and the monster, Stiffelkind, stood looking on for the half-hour the operation lasted.

I suppose the Doctor, at last, thought I had had pumping enough, for he rang the school-bell, and the boys were obliged to leave me. As I got out of the trough, Stiffelkind was alone with me. 'Vell my Lort,' says he, 'you have paid *something* for dese boots, but not all. By Jubider, *you shall never hear de end of dem.*' And I didn't.

APRIL—FOOLING

AFTER this, as you may fancy, I left this disgusting establishment, and lived for some time along with pa and mamma at home. My education was finished, at least mamma and I agreed that it was : and from boyhood until hobbadyhoyhood (which I take to be about the sixteenth year of the life of a young man, and may be likened to the month of April when spring begins to bloom) from fourteen until seventeen, I say, I remained at home, doing nothing, for which I ever since have had a great taste, the idol of my mamma, who took part in all my quarrels with father, and used regularly to rob the weekly expenses in order to find me in pocket-money. Poor soul ! many and many is the guinea I have had from her in that way ; and so she enabled me to cut a very pretty figure.

Papa was for having me at this time articled to a merchant, or put to some profession ; but mamma and I agreed that I was born to be a gentleman, and not a tradesman, and the army was the only place for me. Everybody was a soldier in those times, for the French war had just begun, and the whole country was swarming with militia regiments. 'We'll get him a commission in a marching regiment,' said my father ; 'as we have no money

X

George Cruikshank

APRIL—FOOLING.

to purchase him up, he'll *fight* his way, I make no doubt ;'—and papa looked at me with a kind of air of contempt, as much as to say he doubted whether I should be very eager for such a dangerous way of bettering myself.

I wish you could have heard mamma's screech, when he talked so coolly of my going out to fight. 'What, send him abroad ! across the horrid, horrid sea — to be wrecked, and, perhaps, drowned, and only to land for the purpose of fighting the wicked Frenchmen, — to be wounded, and perhaps kick—kick—killed ! Oh Thomas, Thomas ! would you murder me and your boy ?' There was a regular scene ;—however, it ended, as it always did, in mother's getting the better, and it was settled that I should go into the militia. And why not ? The uniform is just as handsome, and the danger not half so great. I don't think in the course of my whole military experience I ever fought anything, except an old woman, who had the impudence to hollo out, 'Heads up, lobster !'—Well, I joined the North Bungays, and was fairly launched into the world.

I was not a handsome man, I know ; but there was *something* about me — that's very evident ; for the girls always laughed when they talked to me, and the men, though they affected to call me a poor little creature, squint-eyes, knock-knees, red-head, and so on, were evidently annoyed by my success, for they hated me so confoundedly. Even at the present time they go on, though I have given up gallivanting, as I call it. But in the April of my existence,—that is, in anno domini 1791, or so— it was a different case ; and having nothing else to do, and being bent upon bettering my condition, I did some very pretty things in that way. But I was not hot-headed and imprudent, like most young fellows. Don't fancy I looked for beauty ! — Pish ! I wasn't such a fool. Nor for temper ; I don't care about a bad temper : I could break any woman's heart in two years. What I wanted was to get on in the world. Of course I didn't *prefer* an ugly woman, or a shrew ; and, when the choice offered, would certainly put up with a handsome, good-humoured girl, with plenty of money, as any honest man would.

Now there were two tolerably rich girls in our parts : Miss Magdalen Crutty, with twelve thousand pounds (and, to do her justice, as plain a girl as ever I saw) and Miss Mary Waters, a fine, tall, plump, smiling, peach-cheeked, golden-haired, white-skinned lass, with only ten. Mary Waters lived with her uncle, the Doctor, who had helped me into the world, and who was trusted with this little orphan charge very soon after. My mother, as you have heard, was so fond of Bates, and Bates so fond of little Mary, that both, at first, were almost always in our house ; and I used to call her my little wife, as soon as I could speak, and before she could walk almost. It was beautiful to see us, the neighbours said.

Well, when her brother, the lieutenant of an India ship, came to be captain, and actually gave Mary five thousand pounds when she was about ten years old, and promised her five thousand more, there was a great talking, and bobbing, and smiling between the Doctor and my parents, and Mary and I were left together more than ever, and she was told to call me her little husband ; and she did ; and it was considered a settled thing from that day. She was really amazingly fond of me.

Can any one call me mercenary after that ? Though Miss Crutty had twelve thousand, and Mary only ten (five in hand, and five in the bush), I stuck faithfully to Mary. As a matter of course, Miss Crutty hated Miss Waters. The fact was, Mary had all the country dangling after her, and not a soul would come to Magdalen, for all her twelve thousand pounds. I used to be attentive to her, though (as it's always useful to be) ; and Mary would sometimes laugh and sometimes cry at my flirting with Magdalen. This I thought proper very quickly to check. 'Mary,' said I, 'you know that my love for you is disinterested,—for I am faithful to you, though Miss Crutty is richer than you. Don't fly into a rage, then, because I pay her attentions, when you know that my heart and my promise are engaged to you.'

The fact is, to tell a little bit of a secret, there is nothing like the having two strings to your bow. Who knows ?' thought I. 'Mary may die ; and then where are my ten thousand pounds ?' So I used to be very kind indeed to Miss Crutty ; and well it was that I was so ; for when I was twenty and Mary eighteen, I'm blest if news did not arrive that Captain Waters, who was coming home to England with all his money in rupees, had been taken-— ship, rupees, self and all—by a French privateer ! and Mary, instead of ten thousand pounds, had only five thousand, making a difference of no less than three hundred and fifty pounds per annum betwixt her and Miss Crutty.

I had just joined my regiment (the famous North Bungay Fencibles, Colonel Craw commanding) when this news reached me ; and you may fancy how a young man, in an expensive regiment and mess, having uniforms and what not to pay for, and a figure to cut in the world, felt at hearing such news ! 'My dearest Robert,' wrote Miss Waters, 'will deplore my dear brother's loss ; but not, I am sure, the money which that kind and generous soul had promised me. I have still five thousand pounds, and with this and your own little fortune (I had one thousand pounds in the five per cents.) we shall be as happy and contented as possible.'

Happy and contented indeed! Didn't I know how my father got on with his three hundred pounds a year, and how it was all he could do out of it to add a hundred a year to my narrow income, and live himself? My mind was made up—I instantly mounted the coach and flew to our village,—to Mr. Crutty's, of course. It was next door to Dr. Bates's; but I had no business there.

I found Magdalen in the garden. 'Heavens, Mr. Stubbs!' said she, as in my new uniform I appeared before her, 'I really did never—such a handsome officer—expect to see you;' and she made as if she would blush, and began to tremble violently. I led her to a garden-seat. I seized her hand—it was not withdrawn. I pressed it;—I thought the pressure was returned. I flung myself on my knees, and then I poured into her ear a little speech which I had made on the top of the coach. 'Divine Miss Crutty,' said I; 'idol of my soul! It was but to catch one glimpse of you that I passed through this garden. I never intended to breathe the secret passion' (oh no! of course not) 'which was wearing my life away. You know my unfortunate pre-engagement,—it is broken, and *for ever!* I am free;—free, but to be your slave,—your humblest, fondest, truest slave!' and so on. . . .

'Oh, Mr. Stubbs,' said she, as I imprinted a kiss upon her cheek, 'I can't refuse you; but I fear you are a sad naughty man. . . .'

. . . . .

Absorbed in the delicious reverie which was caused by the dear creature's confusion, we were both silent for a while, and should have remained so for hours, perhaps, so lost were we in happiness, had I not been suddenly roused by a voice exclaiming from behind us—

'*Don't cry, Mary; he is a swindling, sneaking scoundrel, and you are well rid of him!*'

I turned round! Oh, Heaven! there stood Mary, weeping on Doctor Bates's arm, while that miserable apothecary was looking at me with the utmost scorn. The gardener, who had let me in, had told them of my arrival, and now stood grinning behind them. 'Imperence!' was my Magdalen's only exclamation, as she flounced by with the utmost self-possession, while I, glancing daggers at *the spies*, followed her. We retired to the parlour, where she repeated to me the strongest assurances of her love.

I thought I was a made man. Alas! I was only an APRIL FOOL!

George Cruikshank

MAY—RESTORATION DAY.

MAY—RESTORATION DAY

As the month of May is considered, by poets and other philosophers, to be devoted by nature to the great purpose of love-making, I may as well take advantage of that season, and acquaint you with the result of *my* amours.

Young, gay, fascinating, and an ensign—I had completely won the heart of young Magdalen; and as for Miss Waters and her nasty uncle the Doctor, there was a complete split between us, as you may fancy; Miss pretending, forsooth, that she was glad I had broken off the match, though she would have given her eyes, the little minx, to have had it on again. But this was out of the question. My father, who had all sorts of queer notions, said I had acted like a rascal in the business; my mother took my part in course, and declared I acted rightly, as I always did; and I got leave of absence from the regiment in order to press my beloved Magdalen to marry me out of hand—knowing, from reading and experience, the extraordinary mutability of human affairs.

Besides, as the dear girl was seventeen years older than myself, and as bad in health as she was in temper, how was I to know that the grim king of terrors might not carry her off before she became mine? With the tenderest warmth, then, and most delicate ardour, I continued to press my suit. The happy day was fixed— the ever-memorable 10th of May 1792; the wedding-clothes were ordered; and, to make things secure, I penned a little paragraph for the county paper to this effect :—'Marriage in High Life. We understand that Ensign Stubbs, of the North Bungay Fencibles, and son of Thomas Stubbs, of Sloffemsquiggle, Esquire, is about to lead to the hymeneal altar the lovely and accomplished daughter of Solomon Crutty, Esquire, of the same place. A fortune of twenty thousand pounds is, we hear, the lady's portion. "None but the brave deserve the fair."'

    .   .   .

'Have you informed your relatives, my beloved?' said I to Magdalen one day, after sending the above notice; 'will any of them attend at your marriage?'

'Uncle Sam will, I dare say,' said Miss Crutty, 'dear mamma's brother.'

'And who *was* your dear mamma?' said I: for Miss Crutty's respected parent had been long since dead, and I never heard her name mentioned in the family.

Magdalen blushed, and cast down her eyes to the ground—
'Mamma was a foreigner,' at last she said.

'And of what country?'

'A German; papa married her when she was very young; she
was not of a very good family,' said Miss Crutty hesitating.

'And what care I for family, my love!' said I, tenderly kissing
the knuckles of the hand which I held. 'She must have been an
angel who gave birth to you.'

'She was a shoemaker's daughter.'

A German shoemaker! Hang 'em! thought I, I have had
enough of them; and so I broke up this conversation, which did
not somehow please me.

* * * * *

Well, the day was drawing near; the clothes were ordered;
the banns were read. My dear mamma had built a cake about the
size of a washing-tub; and I was only waiting for a week to pass
to put me in possession of twelve thousand pounds in the *five*
per cents., as they were in those days, Heaven bless 'em! Little
did I know the storm that was brewing, and the disappointment
which was to fall upon a young man who really did his best to get
a fortune.

* * * * *

'Oh, Robert!' said my Magdalen to me, two days before the
match was to come off, 'I have *such* a kind letter from Uncle Sam
in London. I wrote to him as you wished. He says that he is
coming down to-morrow; that he has heard of you often, and knows
your character very well; and that he has got a *very handsome
present* for us! What can it be, I wonder?'

'Is he rich, my soul's adored?' says I.

'He is a bachelor, with a fine trade, and nobody to leave his
money to.'

'His present can't be less than a thousand pounds?' says I.

'Or, perhaps, a silver tea-set, and some corner-dishes,' says she.

But we could not agree to this, it was too little—too mean for
a man of her uncle's wealth; and we both determined it must be
the thousand pounds.

'Dear good uncle! he's to be here by the coach,' says Magdalen.
'Let us ask a little party to meet him.' And so we did, and so
they came. My father and mother, old Crutty in his best wig, and
the parson who was to marry us the next day. The coach was to
come in at six. And there was the tea-table, and there was the
punch-bowl, and everybody ready and smiling to receive our dear
uncle from London.

Six o'clock came, and the coach, and the man from the 'Green Dragon' with a portmanteau, and a fat old gentleman walking behind, of whom I just caught a glimpse—a venerable old gentleman—I thought I'd seen him before.

Then there was a ring at the bell; then a scuffling and bumping at the passage; then old Crutty rushed out, and a great laughing and talking, and 'How are you?' and so on, was heard at the door; and then the parlour-door was flung open, and Crutty cried out with a loud voice—

'Good people all! my brother-in-law, Mr. STIFFELKIND!'

Mr. Stiffelkind!—I trembled as I heard the name!

Miss Crutty kissed him, mamma made him a curtsey, and papa made him a bow; and Doctor Snorter, the parson, seized his hand and shook it most warmly. Then came my turn!

'Vat!' says he. 'It is my dear, goot yong frend from Doctor Schvis'hentail's! Is dis the yong gentleman's honorable moder' (mamma smiled, and made a curtsey), 'and dis his fader? Sare and madam, you should be broud of soch a sonn. And you, my niece, if you have him for a husband, you vil be locky, dat is all. Vat dink you, broder Crotty, and Madame Stobbs, I 'ave made your sonn's boots! Ha! ha!'

My mamma laughed, and said, 'I did not know it; but I am sure, sir, he has as pretty a leg for a boot as any in the whole county.'

Old Stiffelkind roared louder. 'A very nice leg, ma'am, and a very *sheap boot, too.* Vat! you did not know I make his boots! Perhaps you did not know something else too—p'raps you did not know' (and here the monster clapped his hand on the table and made the punch-ladle tremble in the bowl), 'p'raps you did not know as dat young man, dat Stobbs, dat sneaking, baltry, squinting fellow, is as vicked as he is ugly. He bot a pair of boots from me and never paid for dem. Dat is noting,—nobody never pays; but he bought a pair of boots, and called himself Lord Cornvallis; and I was fool enough to believe him vonce. But look you, niece Magdalen, I 'ave got five tousand pounds,—if you marry him I vil not give you a benny; but look you, what I will gif you. I promised you a bresent, and I will give you DESE!'

And the old monster produced THOSE VERY BOOTS which Swishtail had made him take back.

I *didn't* marry Miss Crutty: I am not sorry for it, though. She was a nasty, ugly, ill-tempered wretch, and I've always said so ever since.

George Cruikshank

JUNE—MARROW BONES AND CLEAVERS.

P 314.

And all this arose from those infernal boots, and that unlucky paragraph in the county paper. I'll tell you how.

In the first place, it was taken up as a quiz by one of the wicked, profligate, unprincipled organs of the London press, who chose to be very facetious about the 'Marriage in High Life,' and made all sorts of jokes about me and my dear Miss Crutty.

Secondly, it was read in this London paper by my mortal enemy, Bunting, who had been introduced to old Stiffelkind's acquaintance by my adventure with him, and had his shoes made regularly by that foreign upstart.

Thirdly, he happened to want a pair of shoes made at this particular period, and as he was measured by the disgusting old High-Dutch cobbler, he told him his old friend Stubbs was going to be married.

'And to whom?' said old Stiffelkind.   'To a woman wit gelt, I vill take my oath.'

'Yes,' says Bunting, 'a country girl—a Miss Magdalen Carotty or Crotty, at a place called Sloffemsquiggle.'

'*Schloffemschwiegel !*' bursts out the dreadful bootmaker, 'Mein Gott ! mein Gott ! das geht nicht ! I tell you, sare, it is no go. Miss Crotty is my niece. I vill go down myself. I vill never let her marry dat goot-for-noting schwindler and teif.' *Such* was the language that the scoundrel ventured to use regarding me !

JUNE—MARROWBONES AND CLEAVERS

WAS there ever such confounded ill-luck? My whole life has been a tissue of ill-luck; although I have laboured, perhaps, harder than any man to make a fortune, something always tumbled it down. In love and in war I was not like others. In my marriages, I had an eye to the main chance; and you see how some unlucky blow would come and throw them over. In the army I was just as prudent, and just as unfortunate. What with judicious betting, and horse-swapping, good luck at billiards, and economy, I do believe I put by my pay every year,—and that is what few can say who have but an allowance of a hundred a year.

I'll tell you how it was. I used to be very kind to the young men ; I chose their horses for them, and their wine, and showed them how to play billiards or ecarté, of long mornings, when there was nothing better to do. I didn't cheat—I'd rather die than cheat ; but if fellows *will* play, I wasn't the man to say no,—why

should I ? There was one young chap in our regiment of whom I
really think I cleared three hundred a year.

His name was Dobble. He was a tailor's son, and wanted to
be a gentleman. A poor, weak, young creature ; easy to be made
tipsy, easy to be cheated, and easy to be frightened. It was a
blessing for him that I found him ; for if anybody else had, they
would have plucked him of every shilling.

Ensign Dobble and I were sworn friends. I rode his horses for
him, and chose his champagne ; and did everything, in fact, that
a superior mind does for an inferior—when the inferior has got the
money. We were inseparables, hunting everywhere in couples.
We even managed to fall in love with two sisters, as young soldiers
will do, you know ; for the dogs fall in love with every change of
quarters.

Well, once, in the year 1793 (it was just when the French
had chopped poor Louis's head off), Dobble and I, gay young chaps
as ever wore sword by side, had cast our eyes upon two young
ladies, by the name of Brisket, daughters of a butcher in the town
where we were quartered. The dear girls fell in love with us, of
course. And many a pleasant walk in the country, many a treat
to a tea-garden, many a smart ribband and brooch used Dobble and
I (for his father allowed him six hundred pounds, and our purses
were in common) present to these young ladies. One day, fancy
our pleasure at receiving a note couched thus :—

' DEER CAPTING STUBBS AND DOBBLE,—Miss Briskets presents
their compliments, and it is probble that our papa will be till
twelve at the corprayshun dinner, we request the pleasure of their
company to tea.'

Didn't we go ! Punctually at six we were in the little back-
parlour ; we quaffed more Bohea, and made more love, than half-a-
dozen ordinary men could. At nine, a little punch-bowl succeeded
to the little tea-pot ; and, bless the girls ! a nice fresh steak was
frizzling on the gridiron for our supper. Butchers were butchers
then, and their parlour was their kitchen, too ; at least old Brisket's
was—one door leading into the shop, and one into the yard, on
the other side of which was the slaughter-house.

Fancy, then, our horror when, just at this critical time, we
heard the shop-door open, a heavy staggering step on the flags,
and a loud husky voice from the shop, shouting—' Hallo, Susan !
hallo, Betsy ! show a light !' Dobble turned as white as a sheet ;
the two girls each as red as a lobster ; I alone preserved my
presence of mind. ' The back-door,' says I.—' The dog's in the

court,' say they. 'He's not so bad as the man,' says I. 'Stop!' cries Susan, flinging open the door, and rushing to the fire; 'take *this*, and perhaps it will quiet him.'

What do you think *this* was? I'm blest if it was not the *steak!*

She pushed us out, patted and hushed the dog, and was in again in a minute. The moon was shining on the court, and on the slaughter-house, where there hung a couple of white, ghastly-looking carcasses of a couple of sheep; a great gutter ran down the court —a gutter of *blood!* The dog was devouring his beef-steak (*our* beef-steak) in silence: and we could see through the little window the girls bustling about to pack up the supper-things, and presently the shop-door opened, old Brisket entered, staggering, angry, and drunk. What's more, we could see, perched on a high stool, and nodding politely, as if to salute old Brisket, the *feather of Dobble's cocked hat!* When Dobble saw it, he turned white, and deadly sick; and the poor fellow, in an agony of fright, sank shivering down upon one of the butcher's cutting blocks, which was in the yard.

We saw old Brisket look steadily (as steadily as he could) at the confounded impudent, pert, waggling feather; and then an idea began to dawn upon his mind that there was a head to the hat; and then he slowly rose up,—he was a man of six feet, and fifteen stone,—he rose up, put on his apron and sleeves, and *took down his cleaver.*

'Betsy,' says he, open the yard door.' But the poor girls screamed, and flung on their knees, and begged, and wept, and did their very best to prevent him. 'OPEN THE YARD DOOR!' says he, with a thundering, loud voice; and the great bulldog, hearing it, started up, and uttered a yell which sent me flying to the other end of the court. Dobble couldn't move; he was sitting on the block blubbering like a baby.

The door opened, and out Mr. Brisket came.

'*To him, Jowler!*' says he. '*Keep him, Jowler!*'—and the horrid dog flew at me, and I flew back into the corner, and drew my sword, determining to sell my life dearly.

'That's it,' says Brisket. 'Keep him there—good dog—good dog! And now, sir,' says he, turning round to Dobble, 'is this your hat?

'Yes,' says Dobble, fit to choke with fright.

'Well, then,' says Brisket, 'it's my—(hick)—my painful duty to—(hick)—to tell you, that as I've got your hat, I must have your head;—it's painful, but it must be done. You'd better— (hick)—settle yourself com—comfumarably against that—(hick)

—that block, and I'll chop it off before you can say Jack—(hick)
—no, I mean Jack Robinson.'

Dobble went down on his knees, and shrieked out, ' I'm an
only son, Mr. Brisket! I'll marry her, sir; I will, upon my
honour, sir. Consider my mother, sir! consider my mother!'

'That's it, sir,' says Brisket; 'that's a good—(hick)—a good
boy. Just put your head down quietly—and I'll have it off—
yes, off—as if you were Louis the Six—the Sixtix—the Sixtickle-
teenth. I'll chop the other *chap afterwards.*'

When I heard this, I made a sudden bound back, and gave
such a cry as any man might who was in such a way. The
ferocious Jowler, thinking I was going to escape, flew at my
throat; screaming furious, I flung out my arms in a kind of
desperation,—and, to my wonder, down fell the dog, dead, and run
through the body !

. . . . .

At this moment a posse of people rushed in upon old Brisket
—one of his daughters had had the sense to summon them—and
Dobble's head was saved. And when they saw the dog lying
dead at my feet, my ghastly look, my bloody sword, they gave me
no small credit for my bravery. ' A terrible fellow that Stubbs,'
said they ; and so the mess said the next day.

I didn't tell them that the dog had committed *suicide*—why
should I ? And I didn't say a word about Dobble's cowardice.
I said he was a brave fellow, and fought like a tiger ; and this
prevented *him* from telling tales. I had the dogskin made into a
pair of pistol-holsters, and looked so fierce, and got such a name
for courage in our regiment that, when we had to meet the
regulars, Bob Stubbs was always the man put forward to support
the honour of the corps. The women, you know, adore courage ;
and such was my reputation at this time that I might have had
my pick out of half-a-dozen, with three, four, or five thousand
pounds apiece, who were dying for love of me and my red coat.
But I wasn't such a fool. I had been twice on the point of
marriage, and twice disappointed ; and I vowed by all the saints
to have a wife, and a rich one. Depend upon this, as an infallible
maxim to guide you through life—*It's as easy to get a rich wife
as a poor one.* The same bait that will hook a trout will hook a
salmon.

JULY—SUMMARY PROCEEDINGS

DOBBLE'S reputation for courage was not increased by the butcher's-dog adventure, but mine stood very high; little Stubbs was voted the boldest chap of all the bold North Bungays. And though I must confess, what was proved by subsequent circumstances, that nature has *not* endowed me with a large or even, I may say, an average share of bravery, yet a man is very willing to flatter himself of the contrary; and after a little time I got to believe that my killing the dog was an action of undaunted courage, and that I was as gallant as any one of the hundred thousand heroes of our army. I always had a military taste—it's only the brutal part of the profession, the horrid fighting and blood, that I don't like.

I suppose the regiment was not very brave itself, being only militia; but certain it was that Stubbs was considered a most terrible fellow, and I swore so much, and looked so fierce, that you would have fancied I had made half a hundred campaigns. I was second in several duels; the umpire in all disputes; and such a crack shot myself, that fellows were shy of insulting me. As for Dobble, I took him under my protection, and he became so attached to me that we ate, drank, and rode together every day. His father didn't care for money so long as his son was in good company—and what so good as that of the celebrated Stubbs? Heigho! I *was* good company in those days, and a brave fellow too, as I should have remained but for—what I shall tell the public immediately.

It happened, in the fatal year ninety-six, that the brave North Bungays were quartered at Portsmouth, a maritime place, which I need not describe, and which I wish I had never seen. I might have been a general now, or, at least, a rich man.

The red-coats carried everything before them in those days, and I, such a crack character as I was in my regiment, was very well received by the townspeople. Many dinners I had; many tea-parties; many lovely young ladies did I lead down the pleasant country dances.

Well, although I had had the two former rebuffs in love, which I have described, my heart was still young; and the fact was, knowing that a girl with a fortune was my only chance, I made love here as furiously as ever. I shan't describe the lovely creatures on whom I fixed whilst at Portsmouth. I tried more than one—several; and it is a singular fact, which I have never

George Cruikshank

JULY—SUMMARY PROCEEDINGS.

been able to account for, that, successful as I was with ladies of maturer age, by the young ones I was refused regular.

But 'faint heart never won fair lady ;' and so I went on and on, until I had really got a Miss Clopper, a tolerably rich navy-contractor's daughter, into such a way that I really don't think she could have refused me. Her brother, Captain Clopper, was in a line regiment, and helped me as much as ever he could ; he swore I was such a brave fellow.

As I had received a number of attentions from Clopper, I determined to invite him to dinner, which I could do without any sacrifice of my principle upon this point ; for the fact is, Dobble lived at an inn, and as he sent all his bills to his father, I made no scruple to use his table. We dined in the coffee-room, Dobble bringing his friend ; and so we made a party *carry*, as the French say. Some naval officers were occupied in a similar way at a table next to ours.

Well—I didn't spare the bottle either for myself or my friends, and we grew very talkative and very affectionate as the drinking went on. Each man told stories of his gallantry in the field, or amongst the ladies, as officers will after dinner. Clopper confided to the company his wish that I should marry his sister, and vowed that he thought me the best fellow in Christendom.

Ensign Dobble assented to this. 'But let Miss Clopper beware,' says he, 'for Stubbs is a sad fellow ; he has had I don't know how many *liaisons* already, and he has been engaged to I don't know how many women.'

'Indeed !' says Clopper ; 'come, Stubbs, tell us your adventures.'

'Psha !' said I, modestly, 'there is nothing, indeed, to tell. I have been in love, my dear boy—who has not ?—and I have been jilted—who has not ?'

Clopper swore that he would blow his sister's brains out if ever *she* served me so.

'Tell him about Miss Crutty,' said Dobble. 'He ! he ! Stubbs served *that* woman out, anyhow ; she didn't *jilt* him, I'll be sworn.'

'Really, Dobble, you are too bad, and should not mention names. The fact is, the girl was desperately in love with me, and had money—sixty thousand pounds, upon my reputation. Well, everything was arranged, when who should come down from London but a relation.'

'Well, did he prevent the match ?'

'Prevent it—yes, sir, I believe you, he did ; though not in the sense that *you* mean. He would have given his eyes—ay, and ten

Y

thousand pounds more—if I would have accepted the girl, but I would not.'

'Why, in the name of goodness ?'

'Sir, her uncle was a *shoemaker*. I never would debase myself by marrying into such a family.'

'Of course not,' said Dobble ; 'he couldn't, you know. Well, now—tell him about the other girl, Mary Waters, you know.'

'Hush, Dobble, hush ! don't you see one of those naval officers has turned round and heard you ? My dear Clopper, it was a mere childish bagatelle.'

'Well, but let's have it,' said Clopper—'let's have it. I won't tell my sister, you know.' And he put his hand to his nose and looked monstrous wise.

'Nothing of that sort, Clopper—no, no—'pon honour—little Bob Stubbs is no *libertine;* and the story is simple. You see that my father has a small place, merely a few hundred acres, at Sloffemsquiggle. Isn't it a funny name ? Hang it, there's the naval gentleman staring again,'—I looked terribly fierce as I returned this officer's stare, and continued in a loud careless voice. 'Well, at this Sloffemsquiggle there lived a girl, a Miss Waters, the niece of some blackguard apothecary in the neighbourhood ; but my mother took a fancy to the girl, and had her up to the park and petted her. We were both young—and—and—the girl fell in love with me, that's the fact. I was obliged to repel some rather warm advances that she made me ; and here, upon my honour as a gentleman, you have all the story about which that silly Dobble makes such a noise.'

Just as I finished this sentence, I found myself suddenly taken by the nose, and a voice shouting out—

'Mr. Stubbs, you are a LIAR AND A SCOUNDREL ! Take this, sir,—and this, for daring to meddle with the name of an innocent lady.'

I turned round as well as I could—for the ruffian had pulled me out of my chair—and beheld a great marine monster, six feet high, who was occupied in beating and kicking me, in the most ungentlemanly manner, on my cheeks, my ribs, and between the tails of my coat. 'He is a liar, gentlemen, and a scoundrel ! The bootmaker had detected him in swindling, and so his niece refused him. Miss Waters was engaged to him from childhood, and he deserted her for the bootmaker's niece, who was richer.'—And then sticking a card between my stock and my coat-collar, in what is called the scruff of my neck, the disgusting brute gave me another blow behind my back, and left the coffee-room with his friends.

Dobble raised me up ; and taking the card from my neck, read,

CAPTAIN WATERS. Clopper poured me out a glass of water, and said in my ear, 'If this is true, you are an infernal scoundrel, Stubbs; and must fight me, after Captain Waters;' and he flounced out of the room.

I had but one course to pursue. I sent the Captain a short and contemptuous note, saying that he was beneath my anger. As for Clopper, I did not condescend to notice his remark; but in order to get rid of the troublesome society of these low blackguards, I determined to gratify an inclination I had long entertained, and make a little tour. I applied for leave of absence, and set off *that very night.* I can fancy the disappointment of the brutal Waters, on coming, as he did, the next morning to my quarters and finding me *gone*—ha! ha!

After this adventure I became sick of a military life—at least the life of my own regiment, where the officers, such was their unaccountable meanness and prejudice against me, absolutely refused to see me at mess. Colonel Craw sent me a letter to this effect, which I treated as it deserved.—I never once alluded to it in any way, and have since never spoken a single word to any man in the North Bungays.

AUGUST—DOGS HAVE THEIR DAYS

SEE, now, what life is; I have had ill-luck on ill-luck from that day to this. I have sunk in the world, and, instead of riding my horse and drinking my wine, as a real gentleman should, have hardly enough now to buy a pint of ale;—ay, and am very glad when anybody will treat me to one. Why, why was I born to undergo such unmerited misfortunes?

You must know that very soon after my adventure with Miss Crutty, and that cowardly ruffian, Captain Waters—(he sailed the day after his insult to me, or I should most certainly have blown his brains out; *now* he is living in England, and is my relation; but, of course, I cut the fellow)—very soon after these painful events another happened, which ended, too, in a sad disappointment. My dear papa died, and, instead of leaving five thousand pounds, as I expected, at the very least, left only his estate, which was worth but two. The land and house were left to me; to mamma and my sisters he left, to be sure, a sum of two thousand pounds in the hands of that eminent firm Messrs. Pump, Aldgate, and Co., which failed within six months after his demise, and paid

George Cruikshank.

AUGUST—DOGS HAVE THEIR DAYS.

in five years about one shilling and ninepence in the pound; which really was all my dear mother and sisters had to live upon.

The poor creatures were quite unused to money matters; and, would you believe it?—when the news came of Pump and Aldgate's failure, mamma only smiled, and threw her eyes up to heaven, and said—'Blessed be God, that we have still wherewithal to live! There are tens of thousands in this world, dear children, who would count our poverty riches.'   And with this she kissed my two sisters, who began to blubber, as girls always will do, and threw their arms round her neck, and then round my neck, until I was half stifled with their embraces, and slobbered all over with their tears.

'Dearest mamma,' said I, 'I am very glad to see the noble manner in which you bear your loss; and more still to know that you are so rich as to be able to put up with it.'   The fact was, I really thought the old lady had got a private hoard of her own, as many of them have—a thousand pounds or so in a stocking.   Had she put by thirty pounds a year, as well she might, for the thirty years of her marriage, there would have been nine hundred pounds clear, and no mistake.   But still I was angry to think that any such paltry concealment had been practised—concealment, too, of *my* money; so I turned on her pretty sharply, and continued my speech—'You say, ma'am, that you are rich, and that Pump and Aldgate's failure has no effect upon you.   I am very happy to hear you say so, ma'am—very happy that you *are* rich; and I should like to know where your property, my father's property, for you had none of your own,—I should like to know where this money lies—*where you have concealed it*, ma'am; and, permit me to say, that when I agreed to board you and my two sisters for eighty pounds a year, I did not know that you had *other* resources than those mentioned in my blessed father's will.'

This I said to her because I hated the meanness of concealment, not because I lost by the bargain of boarding them, for the three poor things did not eat much more than sparrows; and I've often since calculated that I had a clear twenty pounds a year profit out of them.

Mamma and the girls looked quite astonished when I made the speech.   'What does he mean?' said Lucy to Eliza.

Mamma repeated the question.   'My beloved Robert, what concealment are you talking of?'

'I am talking of concealed property, ma'am,' says I sternly.

'And do you—what—can you—do you really suppose that I have concealed—any of that blessed sa-a-a-aint's prop-op-op-operty?' screams out mamma.   'Robert,' says she, 'Bob, my own darling boy—my fondest, best beloved, now *he* is gone' (meaning my late governor—more tears), 'you don't, you cannot fancy that your own mother, who bore you, and nursed you, and wept for you, and would give her all to save you from a moment's harm—you don't suppose that she would che-e-e-eat you!' And here she gave a louder screech than ever, and flung back on the sofa, and one of my sisters went and tumbled into her arms, and t'other went round, and the kissing and slobbering scene went on again, only I was left out, thank goodness; I hate such sentimentality.

'*Che-e-e-eat me,*' says I, mocking her. 'What do you mean, then, by saying you're so rich. Say, have you got money, or have you not?' (And I rapped out a good number of oaths, too, which I don't put in here; but I was in a dreadful fury, that's the fact.)

'So help me, Heaven,' says mamma, in answer, going down on her knees and smacking her two hands; 'I have but a Queen Anne's guinea in the whole of this wicked world.'

'Then what, madam, induces you to tell these absurd stories to me, and to talk about your riches, when you know that you and your daughters are beggars, ma'am, *beggars?*'

'My dearest boy, have we not got the house, and the furniture, and a hundred a year still; and have you not great talents, which will make all our fortunes?' says Mrs. Stubbs, getting up off her knees, and making believe to smile as she clawed hold of my hand and kissed it.

This was *too* cool. '*You* have got a hundred a year, ma'am,' says I—'*you* got a house! Upon my soul and honour this is the first I ever heard of it, and I'll tell you what, ma'am,' says I (and it cut her *pretty sharply* too), 'As you've got it, *you'd better go and live in it*. I've got quite enough to do with my own house, and every penny of my own income.'

Upon this speech the old lady said nothing, but she gave a screech loud enough to be heard from here to York, and down she fell—kicking and struggling, in a regular fit.

. . . . .

I did not see Mrs. Stubbs for some days after this, and the girls used to come down to meals, and never speak; going up again and stopping with their mother. At last, one day, both of them came in very solemn to my study, and Eliza, the eldest, said, 'Robert, mamma has paid you our board up to Michaelmas.'

'She has,' says I; for I always took precious good care to have it in advance.

'She says, Robert, that on Michaelmas-day—we'll—we'll go away, Robert.'

'Oh, she's going to her own house, is she, Lizzy? Very good;

she'll want the furniture, I suppose, and that she may have too, for I'm going to sell the place myself;' and so *that* matter was settled.

On Michaelmas-day, and during these two months I hadn't, I do believe, seen my mother twice (once, about two o'clock in the morning, I woke and found her sobbing over my bed)—on Michaelmas-day morning, Eliza comes to me and says, '*Robert, they will come and fetch us at six this evening.*' Well, as this was the last day, I went and got the best goose I could find (I don't think I ever saw a primer, or ate more hearty myself), and had it roasted at three, with a good pudding afterwards ; and a glorious bowl of punch. 'Here's a health to you, dear girls,' says I, 'and you, Ma, and good luck to all three ; and as you've not eaten a morsel, I hope you won't object to a glass of punch. It's the old stuff, you know, ma'am, that Waters sent to my father fifteen years ago.'

Six o'clock came, and with it came a fine barouche. As I live! Captain Waters was on the box (it was his coach) ; that old thief, Bates, jumped out, entered my house, and before I could say Jack Robinson, whipped off mamma to the carriage, and bowed her into it as if she had been a countess. The girls followed, just giving me a hasty shake of the hand ; and as mamma was helped in, Mary Waters, who was sitting inside, flung her arms round her, and then round the girls, and the Doctor, who acted footman, jumped on the box, and off they went ; taking no more notice of *me* than if I'd been a nonentity.

The whole business would make a picture. Fancy mamma and Miss Waters sitting kissing each other in the carriage, with the two girls in the back seat ; Waters is driving (a precious bad driver he is too) ; and fancy me, standing at the garden door, and whistling. You can't see Mary Malowney—the old fool—is crying behind the garden gate ; she went off next day along with the furniture ; and I was left to get into that precious scrape which I shall mention in the next chapter.

SEPTEMBER—PLUCKING A GOOSE

AFTER my papa's death, as he left me no money, and only a little land, I put my estate into an auctioneer's hands, and determined to amuse my solitude with a trip to some of our fashionable watering-places. My house was now a desert to me. I need not say how the departure of my dear parent, and her children, left me sad and lonely.

SEPTEMBER—PLUCKING A GOOSE.

Well, I had a little ready money, and, for the estate, expected a couple of thousand pounds. I had a good military-looking person ; for though I had absolutely cut the old North Bungays (indeed, after my affair with Waters, Colonel Craw hinted to me, in the most friendly manner, that I had better resign)—though I had left the army, I still retained the rank of Captain ; knowing the advantages attendant upon that title in a watering-place tour.

Captain Stubbs became a great dandy at Cheltenham, Harrogate, Bath, Leamington, and other places. I was a good whist and billiard player ; so much so, that in many of these towns, the people used to refuse, at last, to play with me, knowing how far I was their superior. Fancy my surprise, about five years after the Portsmouth affair, when strolling one day up the High Street, in Leamington, my eyes lighted upon a young man, whom I remembered in a certain butcher's yard, and elsewhere—no other, in fact, than Dobble. He, too, was dressed *en militaire*, with a frogged coat and spurs ; and was walking with a showy-looking, Jewish-faced, black-haired lady, glittering with chains and rings, with a green bonnet and a bird of Paradise—a lilac shawl, a yellow gown, pink silk stockings, and light-blue shoes. Three children, and a handsome footman, were walking behind her, and the party, not seeing me, entered the ' Royal Hotel ' together.

I was known myself at the ' Royal,' and calling one of the waiters, learned the names of the lady and gentleman. He was Captain Dobble, the son of the rich army-clothier, Dobble, Hobble & Co., of Pall Mall ;—the lady was a Mrs. Manasseh, widow of an American Jew, living quietly at Leamington with her children, but possessed of an immense property. There's no use to give one's self out to be an absolute pauper ; so the fact is, that I myself went everywhere with the character of a man of very large means. My father had died leaving me immense sums of money and landed estates. Ah ! I was the gentleman then, the real gentleman, and everybody was too happy to have me at table.

Well, I came the next day and left a card for Dobble, with a note. He neither returned my visit nor answered my note. The day after, however, I met him with the widow, as before ; and going up to him, very kindly seized him by the hand, and swore I was—as really was the case—charmed to see him. Dobble hung back, to my surprise, and I do believe the creature would have cut me if he dared ; but I gave him a frown, and said —

' What, Dobble my boy, don't you recollect old Stubbs, and our adventure with the butcher's daughters—ha ?'

Dobble gave a sickly kind of grin, and said, ' Oh ! ah ! yes ! It is—yes ! it is, I believe, Captain Stubbs.'

'An old comrade, madam, of Captain Dobble's, and one who has heard so much, and seen so much of your ladyship, that he must take the liberty of begging his friend to introduce him.'

Dobble was obliged to take the hint; and Captain Stubbs was duly presented to Mrs. Manasseh. The lady was as gracious as possible; and when, at the end of the walk, we parted, she said 'she hoped Captain Dobble would bring me to her apartments that evening, where she expected a few friends.' Everybody, you see, knows everybody at Leamington; and I, for my part, was well known as a retired officer of the army, who, on his father's death had come into seven thousand a year. Dobble's arrival had been subsequent to mine; but putting up as he did at the 'Royal Hotel,' and dining at the ordinary there with the widow, he had made her acquaintance before I had. I saw, however, that if I allowed him to talk about me, as he could, I should be compelled to give up all my hopes and pleasures at Leamington; and so I determined to be short with him. As soon as the lady had gone into the hotel, my friend Dobble was for leaving me likewise; but I stopped him, and said, 'Mr. Dobble, I saw what you meant just now: you wanted to cut me, because, forsooth, I did not choose to fight a duel at Portsmouth. Now look you, Dobble, I am no hero, but I am not such a coward as you—and you know it. You are a very different man to deal with from Waters; and *I will* fight this time.'

Not perhaps that I would; but after the business of the butcher, I knew Dobble to be as great a coward as ever lived; and there never was any harm in threatening, for you know you are not obliged to stick to it afterwards. My words had their effect upon Dobble, who stuttered and looked red, and then declared he never had the slightest intention of passing me by; so we became friends, and his mouth was stopped.

He was very thick with the widow, but that lady had a very capacious heart, and there were a number of other gentlemen who seemed equally smitten with her. 'Look at that Mrs. Manasseh,' said a gentleman (it was droll, *he* was a Jew, too) sitting at dinner by me. 'She is old, and ugly, and yet, because she has money, all the men are flinging themselves at her.'

'She has money, has she?'

'Eighty thousand pounds, and twenty thousand for each of her children. I know it *for a fact*,' said the strange gentleman. 'I am in the law, and we of our faith, you know, know pretty well what the great families amongst us are worth.'

'Who was Mr. Manasseh?' said I.

'A man of enormous wealth—a tobacco merchant—West

Indies ; a fellow of no birth, however ; and who, between ourselves, married a woman that is not much better than she should be.   My dear sir,' whispered he, ' she is always in love.   Now it is with that Captain Dobble ; last week it was somebody else—and it may be you next week, if—ha ! ha ! ha !—if you are disposed to enter the lists.'

' I wouldn't, for *my* part, have the woman with twice her money.'

What did it matter to me whether the woman was good or not, provided she was rich ?   My course was quite clear.   I told Dobble all that this gentleman had informed me, and being a pretty good hand at making a story, I made the widow appear *so* bad, that the poor fellow was quite frightened, and fairly quitted the field.   Ha ! ha ! I'm dashed if I did not make him believe that Mrs. Manasseh had *murdered* her last husband.

I played my game so well, thanks to the information that my friend the lawyer had given me, that in a month I had got the widow to show a most decided partiality for me.   I sat by her at dinner, I drank with her at the Wells—I rode with her, I danced with her ; and at a picnic to Kenilworth, where we drank a good deal of champagne, I actually popped the question, and was accepted.   In another month, Robert Stubbs, Esquire, led to the altar, Leah, widow of the late Z. Manasseh, Esquire, of St. Kitts !

We drove up to London in her comfortable chariot : the children and servants following in a post-chaise.   I paid, of course, for everything ; and until our house in Berkeley Square was painted, we stopped at ' Stevens's Hotel.'

My own estate had been sold, and the money was lying at a bank in the City.   About three days after our arrival, as we took our breakfast in the hotel, previous to a visit to Mrs. Stubbs's banker, where certain little transfers were to be made, a gentleman was introduced, who, I saw at a glance, was of my wife's persuasion.

He looked at Mrs. Stubbs, and made a bow.   ' Perhaps it will be convenient to you to pay this little bill, one hundred and fifty-two poundsh.'

' My love,' says she, ' will you pay this ?—it is a trifle which I had really forgotten.'   My soul !' said I, I have really not the money in the house.'

' Vell, denn, Captain Shtubbsh,' says he, ' I must do my duty —and arrest you—here is the writ !   Tom, keep the door !'—My wife fainted—the children screamed, and I—fancy my condition, as I was obliged to march off to a spunging-house along with a horrid sheriff's officer !

George Cruikshank

OCTOBER—MARS AND VENUS IN OPPOSITION.

OCTOBER—MARS AND VENUS IN OPPOSITION

I SHALL not describe my feelings when I found myself in a cage
in Cursitor Street, instead of that fine house in Berkeley Square,
which was to have been mine as the husband of Mrs. Manasseh.
What a palace !   In an odious, dismal street leading from Chancery
Lane, a hideous Jew boy opened the second of three doors ; and
shut it when Mr. Nabb and I (almost fainting) had entered ; then
he opened the third door, and then I was introduced to a filthy
place called a coffee-room, which I exchanged for the solitary
comfort of a little dingy back-parlour, where I was left for awhile
to brood over my miserable fate.   Fancy the change between this
and Berkeley Square !   Was I, after all my pains, and cleverness,
and perseverance, cheated at last ?   Had this Mrs. Manasseh been
imposing upon me ? and were the words of the wretch I met at the
table-d'hôte at Leamington only meant to mislead me and take me
in ?   I determined to send for my wife, and know the whole truth.
I saw at once that I had been the victim of an infernal plot, and
that the carriage, the house in town, the West India fortune, were
only so many lies which I had blindly believed.   It was true the
debt was but a hundred and fifty pounds, and I had two thousand
at my bankers ; but was the loss of *her* £80,000 nothing ?   Was
the destruction of my hopes nothing ?   The accursed addition to
my family of a Jewish wife and three Jewish children, nothing ?
And all these I was to support out of my two thousand pounds.
I had better have stopped at home with my mamma and sisters,
whom I really did love, and who produced me eighty pounds a
year.

I had a furious interview with Mrs. Stubbs ; and when I charged
her (the base wretch !) with cheating me, like a brazen serpent, as
she was, she flung back the cheat in my teeth, and swore I had
swindled her.   Why did I marry her, when she might have had
twenty others ?   She only took me, she said, because I had twenty
thousand pounds.   I *had* said I possessed that sum ; but in love,
you know, and war, all's fair.

We parted quite as angrily as we met ; and I cordially vowed
that when I had paid the debt into which I had been swindled by
her, I would take my £2000, and depart to some desert island ;
or, at the very least, to America, and never see her more, or any
of her Israelitish brood.   There was no use in remaining in
the spunging-house ; for I knew there were such things as
detainers, and that where Mrs. Stubbs owed a hundred pounds,

she might owe a thousand, so I sent for Mr. Nabb, and tendering him a cheque for £150, and his costs, requested to be let out forthwith. 'Here, fellow,' said I, 'is a cheque on Child's for your paltry sum.'

'It may be a sheck on Shild's,' says Mr. Nabb, 'but I should be a baby to let you out on such a paper as dat.'

'Well,' said I, 'Child's is but a step from this ; you may go and get the cash,—just give me an acknowledgment.'

Nabb drew out the acknowledgment with great punctuality, and set off for the banker's, whilst I prepared myself for departure from this abominable prison.

He smiled as he came in. 'Well,' said I, 'you have touched your money ! and now, I must tell you, that you are the most infernal rogue and extortioner I ever met with.'

'Oh no, Mishter Shtubbsh,' says he, grinning still, 'dere is som greater roag dan me,—mosh greater.'

'Fellow,' says I, 'don't stand grinning before a gentleman ; but give me my hat and cloak, and let me leave your filthy den.'

'Shtop, Shtubbsh,' says he, not even Mistering me this time, 'Here ish a letter, vich you had better read.'

I opened the letter ; something fell to the ground. It was my cheque.

The letter ran thus :—

'Messrs. Child & Co. present their compliments to Captain Stubbs, and regret that they have been obliged to refuse payment of the enclosed, having been served this day with an attachment by Messrs. Solomonson & Co., which compels them to retain Captain Stubbs's balance of £2010 11s. 6d. until the decision of the suit of Solomonson v. Stubbs.

'Fleet Street.'

'You see,' says Mr. Nabb, as I read this dreadful letter, 'you see, Shtubbsh, dere vas two debts,—a littel von and a big von. So dey arrested you for de littel von, and attashed your money for de big von.'

. . . . .

Don't laugh at me for telling this story. If you knew what tears are blotting over the paper as I write it ; if you knew that for weeks after, I was more like a madman than a sane man,—a madman in the Fleet Prison, where I went instead of to the desert island. What had I done to deserve it ? Hadn't I always kept an eye to the main chance ? Hadn't I lived economically, and not like other young men ? Had I ever been known to squander or give away a single penny? No! I can lay my hand on my heart, and, thank Heaven, say, No! Why, why was I punished so?

Let me conclude this miserable history. Seven months (my wife saw me once or twice, and then dropped me altogether) I remained in that fatal place. I wrote to my dear mamma, begging her to sell her furniture, but got no answer. All my old friends turned their backs upon me. My action went against me —I had not a penny to defend it. Solomonson proved my wife's debt, and seized my two thousand pounds. As for the detainer against me, I was obliged to go through the court for the relief of insolvent debtors. I passed through it, and came out a beggar. But fancy the malice of that wicked Stiffelkind; he appeared in court as my creditor for £3, with sixteen years' interest at five per cent., for a PAIR OF TOP-BOOTS. The old thief produced them in court, and told the old story—Lord Cornwallis, the detection, the pumping, and all.

Commissioner Dubobwig was very funny about it. 'So Doctor Swishtail would not pay you for the boots—eh, Mr. Stiffel-kind?'

'No; he said, ven I asked him for payment, dey was ordered by a yong boy, and I ought to have gone to his schoolmaster.'

'What, then you came on a *bootless* errand, eh, sir?' (A laugh.)

'Bootless! no sare, I brought de boots back vid me; how de devil else could I show dem to you?' (Another laugh.)

'You've never *soled* 'em since, Mr. Tickleshins?'

'I never vood sell dem; I svore I never vood, on porpus to be revenged on dat Stobbs.'

'What, your wound has never been *healed*, eh?'

'Vat de you mean vid your bootless errants, and your soling and healing? I tell you I have done vat I svore to do. I have exposed him at school, I have broak off a marriage for him, ven he vould have had tventy tousand pound, and now I have showed him up in a court of justice; dat is vat I 'ave done, and dat's enough.' And then the old wretch went down, whilst everybody was giggling and staring at poor me, as if I was not miserable enough already.

'This seems the dearest pair of boots you ever had in your life, Mr. Stubbs,' said Commissioner Dubobwig, very archly, and then he began to inquire about the rest of my misfortunes.

In the fulness of my heart I told him the whole of them; how Mr. Solomonson the attorney had introduced me to the rich widow, Mrs. Manasseh, who had fifty thousand pounds, and an estate in the West Indies. How I was married, and arrested on coming to

George Cruikshank.

NOVEMBER—A GENERAL POST DELIVERY.

town, and cast in an action for two thousand pounds, brought against me by this very Solomonson for my wife's debts.

'Stop,' says a lawyer in the court. 'Is this woman a showy, black-haired woman with one eye? with three children?—Solomonson—short, with red hair?'

'Exactly so,' says I, with tears in my eyes.

'That woman has married *three men* within the last two years. One in Ireland, and one at Bath. Solomonson is, I believe, her husband, and they both are off for America ten days ago.'

'But why did you not keep your £2000?' said the lawyer.

'Sir, they attached it.'

'Oh! well, we may pass you; you have been unlucky, Mr. Stubbs, but it seems as if the biter had been bit in this affair.'

'No,' said Mr. Dubobwig. 'Mr. Stubbs is the victim of a FATAL ATTACHMENT.'

NOVEMBER—A GENERAL POST DELIVERY

I WAS a free man when I went out of the court; but I was a beggar. I, Captain Stubbs, of the bold North Bungays, did not know where I could get a bed, or a dinner.

As I was marching sadly down Portugal Street, I felt a hand on my shoulder and a rough voice which I knew well.

'Vell, Mr. Stobbs, have I not kept my bromise? I told you dem boots would be your ruin.'

I was much too miserable to reply; and only cast my eyes towards the roofs of the houses, which I could not see for the tears.

'Vat! you begin to gry and blobber like a shild? you vood marry, vood you, and noting vood do for you but a vife vid monny —ha, ha—but you vere de pigeon, and she vas de grow. She has plocked you, too, pretty vell—eh? Ha! ha!'

'Oh, Mr. Stiffelkind,' said I, 'don't laugh at my misery; she has not left me a single shilling under heaven. And I shall starve, I do believe I shall starve.' And I began to cry fit to break my heart.

'Starf! stoff and nonsense! You vil never die of starfing— you vil die of *hanging*, I tink—ho! ho!—and it is moch easier vay too.' I didn't say a word, but cried on, till everybody in the street turned round and stared.

'Come, come,' said Stiffelkind, 'do not gry, Captain Stobbs—

z

it is not goot for a Gaptain to gry—ha ! ha ! Dere—come vid me, and you shall have a dinner, and a bregfast too—vich shall gost you nothing, until you can bay vid your earnings.'

And so this curious old man, who had persecuted me all through my prosperity, grew compassionate towards me in my ill-luck ; and took me home with him as he promised. 'I saw your name among de Insolvents—and I vowed, you know, to make you repent dem boots. Dere now, it is done, and forgotten, look you. Here Betty, Bettchen ! make de spare bed, and put a clean knife and fork ; Lort Cornvallis is come to dine vid me.'

I lived with this strange old man for six weeks. I kept his books, and did what little I could to make myself useful ; carrying about boots and shoes, as if I had never borne His Majesty's commission. He gave me no money, but he fed and lodged me comfortably. The men and boys used to laugh and call me General, and Lord Cornwallis, and all sorts of nicknames ; and old Stiffelkind made a thousand new ones for me.

One day I can recollect—one miserable day, as I was polishing on the trees a pair of boots of Mr. Stiffelkind's manufacture—the old gentleman came into the shop with a lady on his arm.

'Vere is Gaptain Stobbs ?' said he.   'Vere is dat ornament to His Majesty's service ?'

I came in from the back shop, where I was polishing the boots, with one of them in my hand.

'Look, my dear,' says he, 'here is an old friend of yours, His Excellency Lort Cornvallis !—Who would have thought such a nobleman vood turn shoeblack ? Gaptain Stobbs, here is your former flame, my dear niece, Miss Grotty. How could you, Magdalen, ever leaf such a lof of a man ? Shake hands vid her, Gaptain ; dere, never mind de blacking ! ' But Miss drew back.

'I never shake hands with a *shoeblack*,' said she, mighty contemptuous.

'Bah ; my lof, his fingers von't soil you. Don't you know he has just been *vitewashed ?* '

'I wish, uncle,' says she, 'you would not leave me with such low people.'

'Low, because he cleans boots ? De Gaptain prefers *pumps* to boots, I tink—ha ! ha ! '

'Captain indeed ; a nice Captain,' says Miss Crutty, snapping her fingers in my face, and walking away. 'A Captain who has had his nose pulled ! ha ! ha ! ' And how could I help it ? it wasn't by my own *choice* that that ruffian Waters took such liberties with me. Didn't I show how averse I was to all quarrels by refusing altogether his challenge ?—But such is the world.

And thus the people at Stiffelkind's used to tease me, until they drove me almost mad.

At last he came home one day more merry and abusive than ever. 'Gaptain,' says he, 'I have goot news for you—a goot place. Your lortship vil not be able to geep your garridge, but you vil be gomfortable, and serve His Majesty.'

'Serve His Majesty ?' says I. 'Dearest Mr. Stiffelkind, have you got me a place under Government ?'

'Yes, and somting better still—not only a place, but a uniform : yes, Gaptain Stobbs, a *red goat*.'

'A red coat ! I hope you don't think I would demean myself by entering the ranks of the army ? I am a gentleman, Mr. Stiffelkind—I can never—no, I never——'

'No, I know you will never, you are too great a goward, ha ! ha !—though dis is a red goat, and a place where you must give some *hard knocks* too, ha ! ha ! Do you gomprehend ? And you shall be a general instead of a gabdain—ha ! ha !'

'A general in a red coat, Mr. Stiffelkind ?'

'Yes, a GENERAL BOSTMAN ! ha ! ha ! I have been vid your old friend Bunting, and he has an uncle in the Post-Office, and he has got you de place—eighteen shillings a veek, you rogue, and your goat. You must not oben any of de letters, you know.'

And so it was—I, Robert Stubbs, Esquire, became the vile thing he named—a general postman !

. . . .

I was so disgusted with Stiffelkind's brutal jokes, which were now more brutal than ever, that when I got my place in the Post-Office, I never went near the fellow again ; for though he had done me a favour in keeping me from starvation, he certainly had done it in a very rude, disagreeable manner, and showed a low and mean spirit in *pushing* me into such a degraded place as that of postman. But what had I to do ? I submitted to fate, and for three years or more, Robert Stubbs, of the North Bungay Fencibles, was——

I wonder nobody recognised me. I lived in daily fear of the first year ; but, afterwards, grew accustomed to my situation, as all great men will do, and wore my red coat as naturally as if I had been sent into the world only for the purpose of being a letter-carrier.

I was first in the Whitechapel district, where I stayed for nearly three years, when I was transferred to Jermyn Street and Duke Street—famous places for lodgings. I suppose I left a hundred letters at a house in the latter street, where lived some people who must have recognised me had they but once chanced to look at me.

You see that when I left Sloffem, and set out in the gay world, my mamma had written to me a dozen times at least ; but I never

DECEMBER—THE WINTER OF OUR DISCONTENT.

answered her, for I knew she wanted money, and I detest writing. Well, she stopped her letters, finding she could get none from me ; but when I was in the Fleet, as I told you, I wrote repeatedly to my dear mamma, and was not a little nettled at her refusing to notice me in my distress, which is the very time one most wants notice.

Stubbs is not an uncommon name ; and though I saw 'MRS. STUBBS' on a little bright brass plate in Duke Street, and delivered so many letters to the lodgers in her house, I never thought of asking who she was, or whether she was my relation or not.

One day the young woman who took in the letters had not got change, and she called her mistress. An old lady in a poke bonnet came out of the parlour, and put on her spectacles, and looked at the letter, and fumbled in her pocket for eightpence, and apologised to the postman for keeping him waiting ; and when I said, 'Never mind, ma'am, it's no trouble,' the old lady gave a start, and then she pulled off her spectacles, and staggered back ; and then she began muttering, as if about to choke ; and then she gave a great screech, and flung herself into my arms, and roared out, 'MY SON ! MY SON !'

'Lor', mamma,' said I, 'is that you ?' and I sat down on the hall bench with her, and let her kiss me as much as ever she liked. Hearing the whining and crying, down comes another lady from upstairs—it was my sister Eliza ; and down come the lodgers. And the maid gets water and what not, and I was the regular hero of the group. I could not stay long then, having my letters to deliver. But, in the evening, after mail-time, I went back to my mamma and sister ; and over a bottle of prime old port, and a precious good leg of boiled mutton and turnips, made myself pretty comfortable, I can tell you.

DECEMBER—'THE WINTER OF OUR DISCONTENT'

MAMMA had kept the house in Duke Street for more than two years. I recollected some of the chairs and tables from dear old Squiggle, and the bowl in which I had made that famous rum-punch, the evening she went away, which she and my sisters left untouched, and I was obliged to drink after they were gone ; but that's not to the purpose.

Think of my sister Mary's luck ! That chap, Waters, fell in love with her, and married her ; and she now keeps her carriage, and lives in state near Squiggle. I offered to make it up with Waters; but he bears malice, and never will see or speak to me. He had the impudence, too, to say, that he took in all letters for mamma at Squiggle; and that as mine were all begging letters, he burned them, and never said a word to her concerning them. He allowed mamma fifty pounds a year, and, if she were not such a fool, she might have had three times as much; but the old lady was high and mighty, forsooth, and would not be beholden, even to her own daughter, for more than she actually wanted. Even this fifty pounds she was going to refuse ; but when I came to live with her, of course I wanted pocket-money as well as board and lodging, and so I had the fifty pounds for *my* share, and eked out with it as well as I could.

Old Bates and the Captain, between them, gave mamma a hundred pounds when she left me (she had the deuce's own luck, to be sure—much more than ever fell to *me*, I know) ; and as she said she *would* try and work for her living, it was thought best to take a house and let lodgings, which she did. Our first and second floor paid us four guineas a week on an average ; and the front parlour and attic made forty pounds more. Mamma and Eliza used to have the front attic ; but *I* took that, and they slept in the servants' bedroom. Lizzy had a pretty genius for work, and earned a guinea a week that way ; so that we had got nearly two hundred a year over the rent to keep house with,—and we got on pretty well. Besides, women eat nothing ; my women didn't care for meat for days together sometimes,—so that it was only necessary to dress a good steak or so for me.

Mamma would not think of my continuing in the Post-Office. She said her dear Robert, her husband's son, her gallant soldier, and all that, should remain at home, and be a gentleman—which I was, certainly, though I didn't find fifty pounds a year very much to buy clothes and be a gentleman upon ; to be sure, mother found me shirts and linen, so that *that* wasn't in the fifty pounds. She kicked a little at paying the washing too ; but she gave in at last, for I was her dear Robert, you know ; and I'm blest if I could not make her give me the gown off her back. Fancy ! once she cut up a very nice rich black silk scarf, which my sister Waters sent her, and made me a waistcoat and two stocks of it. She was so *very* soft, the old lady !

.   .   .   .   .

I'd lived in this way for five years or more, making myself content with my fifty pounds a year (*perhaps* I'd saved a little out of it ; but that's neither here nor there). From year's end to year's end I remained faithful to my dear mamma, never leaving her except for a month or so in summer, when a bachelor may take a trip to Gravesend or Margate, which would be too expensive for a family. I say a bachelor, for the fact is, I don't know whether I am married or not—never having heard a word since of the scoundrelly Mrs. Stubbs.

I never went to the public-house before meals ; for, with my beggarly fifty pounds, I could not afford to dine away from home ; but there I had my regular seat, and used to come home *pretty glorious*, I can tell you. Then, bed till eleven ; then, breakfast and the newspaper ; then, a stroll in Hyde Park or St. James's ; then, home at half-past three to dinner, when I jollied, as I called it, for the rest of the day. I was my mother's delight ; and thus, with a clear conscience, I managed to live on.

. . . . .

How fond she was of me, to be sure. Being sociable myself, and loving to have my friends about me, we often used to assemble a company of as hearty fellows as you would wish to sit down with, and keep the nights up royally. 'Never mind, my boys,' I used to say, 'send the bottle round—mammy pays for all,' as she did, sure enough ; and sure enough we punished her cellar, too. The good old lady used to wait upon us, as if for all the world she had been my servant, instead of a lady and my mamma. Never used she to repine, though I often, as I must confess, gave her occasion (keeping her up till four o'clock in the morning, because she never could sleep until she saw her 'dear Bob' in bed, and leading her a sad, anxious life). She was of such a sweet temper, the old lady, that I think in the course of five years I never knew her in a passion, except twice ; and then with sister Lizzy, who declared I was ruining the house, and driving the lodgers away one by one. But mamma would not hear of such envious spite on my sister's part. 'Her Bob was always right,' she said. At last Lizzy fairly retreated, and went to the Waterses. I was glad of it, for her temper was dreadful, and we used to be squabbling from morning till night.

Ah, those *were* jolly times ! But ma was obliged to give up the lodging-house at last—for, somehow, things went wrong after my sister's departure — the nasty uncharitable people said, on account of *me* ; because I drove away the lodgers by smoking, and drinking, and kicking up noises in the house ; and because ma gave me so much of her money. So she did ; but if she *would* give it, you know, how could I help it ? Heigho ! I wish I'd *kept* it.

No such luck. The business I thought was to last for ever ; but at the end of two years a smash came—shut up shop—sell off everything. Mamma went to the Waterses; and, will you believe it? the ungrateful wretches would not receive me! That Mary, you see, was so disappointed at not marrying me. Twenty pounds a year they allow, it is true; but what's that for a gentleman? For twenty years I have been struggling manfully to gain an honest livelihood, and, in the course of them, have seen a deal of life, to be sure. I've sold cigars, and pocket-handkerchiefs at the corners of streets; I've been a billiard-marker; I've been a Director (in the panic year) of the Imperial British Consolidated Mangle and Drying-Ground Company. I've been on the stage (for two years as an actor, and about a month as a cad, when I was very low); I've been the means of giving to the police of this empire some very valuable information (about licensed victuallers, gentlemen's carts, and pawnbrokers' names); I've been very nearly an officer again—that is, an assistant to an officer of the Sheriff of Middlesex;—it was my last place.

On the last day of the year 1837, even *that* game was up. It's a thing that has very seldom happened to a gentleman, to be kicked out of a spunging-house; but such was my case. Young Nabbs (who succeeded his father) drove me ignominiously from his door, because I had charged a gentleman in the coffee-rooms seven-and-sixpence for a glass of ale and bread and cheese, the charge of the house being only six shillings. He had the meanness to deduct the eighteenpence from my wages, and, because I blustered a bit, he took me by the shoulders and turned me out— me a gentleman, and, what is more, a poor orphan!

How I did rage and swear at him when I got out in the street! There stood he, the hideous Jew monster, at the double door, writhing under the effect of my language. I had my revenge! Heads were thrust out of every bar of his windows, laughing at him. A crowd gathered round me, as I stood pounding him with my satire, and they evidently enjoyed his discomfiture. I think the mob would have pelted the ruffian to death (one or two of their missiles hit *me*, I can tell you), when a policeman came up, and, in reply to a gentleman, who was asking what was the disturbance, said, — 'Bless you, sir, it's Lord Cornwallis.' 'Move on *Boots*,' said the fellow to me, for, the fact is, my misfortunes and early life are pretty well known—and so the crowd dispersed.

'What could have made that policeman call you Lord Cornwallis and Boots?' said the gentleman, who seemed mightily amused, and had followed me. 'Sir,' says I, 'I am an unfortunate officer of the North Bungay Fencibles, and I'll tell you willingly for a pint of beer.' He told me to follow him to his chambers, at the

Temple, which I did (a five-pair back), and there, sure enough, I had the beer ; and told him this very story you've been reading. You see, he is what is called a literary man—and sold my adventures for me to the booksellers.   He's a strange chap, and says they're *moral.*

.   .   .

I'm blest if *I* can see anything moral in them.   I'm sure I ought to have been more lucky through life, being so very wide awake.   And yet here I am, without a place, or even a friend, starving upon a beggarly twenty pounds a year—not a single six-pence more, upon my *honour.*

BARBER COX,

AND THE CUTTING OF HIS COMB

George Cruikshank

SALOON OF FASHION

GENUINE BEARS GREASE
CURLING FLUID
BONDARE & MACASSAR OIL
CIRCASSIAN CREAM
MAGIC RAZOR STROP
BALM of Columbia

JANUARY—THE ANNOUNCEMENT.

JANUARY—THE ANNOUNCEMENT.

On the first of January, 1838, I was the master of a lovely shop in the neighbourhood of Oxford Market; of a wife, Mrs. Cox; of a business, both in the shaving and cutting line, established three-and-thirty years; of a girl and boy, respectively of the ages of eighteen and thirteen; of a three-windowed front, both to my first and second pair; of a young foreman, my present partner, Mr. Orlando Crump; and of that celebrated mixture for the human hair, invented by my late uncle, and called Cox's Bohemian Balsam of Tokay, sold in pots at two-and-three, and three-and-nine. The balsam, the lodgings, and the old-established cutting and shaving business, brought me in a pretty genteel income. I had had my girl, Jemimarann, at Hackney to school; my dear boy, Tuggeridge, plaited hair already beautifully; my wife at the counter (behind the tray of patent soaps, etc.) cut as handsome a figure as possible; and it was my hope that Orlando and my girl, who were mighty soft upon one another, would, one day, be joined together in Hyming: and, conjointly with my son Tug, carry on the business of hairdressers, when their father was either dead or a gentleman; for a gentleman me and Mrs. C. determined I should be.

Jemima was, you see, a lady herself, and of very high connexions: though her own family had met with crosses, and was rather low. Mr. Tuggeridge, her father, kept the famous tripe-shop near the Pigtail and Sparrow, in the Whitechapel Road; from which place I married her; being myself very fond of the article, and especially when she served it to me — the dear thing!

Jemima's father was not successful in business: and I married her, I am proud to confess it, without a shilling. I had my hands, my house, and my Bohemian balsam to support her!—and we had hopes from her uncle, a mighty rich East India merchant, who, having left this country sixty years ago, as a cabin-boy, had arrived to be the head of a great house in India, and was worth millions, we were told.

Three years after Jemimarann's birth (and two after the death of my lamented father-in-law), Tuggeridge (head of the great house of Budgurow and Co.), retired from the management of it ; handed over his shares to his son, Mr. John Tuggeridge, and came to live in England, at Portland Place, and Tuggeridgeville, Surrey, and enjoy himself.   Soon after, my wife took her daughter in her hand and went, as in duty bound, to visit her uncle ; but whether it was that he was proud and surly, or she somewhat sharp in her way (the dear girl fears nobody, let me have you to know), a desperate quarrel took place between them ; and from that day, to the day of his death, he never set eyes on her.   All that he would condescend to do, was to take a few dozen of lavender-water from us in the course of the year, and to send his servants to be cut and shaved by us.   All the neighbours laughed at this poor ending of our expectations, for Jemmy had bragged not a little ; however, we did not care, for the connexion was always a good one, and we served Mr. Hock, the valet ; Mr. Bar, the coachman ; and Mrs. Breadbasket, the housekeeper, willingly enough.   I used to powder the footman, too, on great days, but never in my life saw old Tuggeridge, except once ; when he said, ' O, the barber ! ' tossed up his nose, and passed on.

One day—one famous day last January—all our Market was thrown into a high state of excitement by the appearance of no less than three vehicles at our establishment.   As me, Jemmy, my daughter, Tug, and Orlando, were sitting in the back-parlour over our dinner (it being Christmas-time, Mr. Crump had treated the ladies to a bottle of port, and was longing that there should be a mistletoe bough ; at which proposal my little Jemimarann looked as red as a glass of negus) : we had just, I say, finished the port, when, all of a sudden, Tug bellows out, ' Law, Pa, here's uncle Tuggeridge's housekeeper in a cab ! '

And Mrs. Breadbasket it was, sure enough—Mrs. Breadbasket in deep mourning, who made her way, bowing and looking very sad, into the back shop.   My wife, who respected Mrs. B. more than anything else in the world, set her a chair, offered her a glass of wine, and vowed it was very kind of her to come.   ' Law, mem,' says Mrs. B., ' I'm sure I'd do anything to serve your family, for the sake of that poor dear Tuck-Tuck-tug-guggeridge, that's gone.'

' That's what ? ' cries my wife.

' What, gone ? ' cried Jemimarann, bursting out crying (as little girls will about anything or nothing) ; and Orlando looking very rueful, and ready to cry too.

' Yes, gaw——.'   Just as she was at this very ' gaw,'

Tug roars out, 'Law, pa! here's Mr. Bar, uncle Tug's coach-man!'

It was Mr. Bar. When she saw him, Mrs. Breadbasket stepped suddenly back into the parlour with my ladies. 'What is it, Mr. Bar?' says I; and, as quick as thought, I had the towel under his chin, Mr. Bar in the chair, and the whole of his face in a beautiful foam of lather. Mr. Bar made some resistance.—'Don't think of it, Mr. Cox,' says he; 'don't trouble yourself, sir.' But I lathered away, and never minded. 'And what's this melancholy event, sir,' says I, 'that has spread desolation in your family's bosoms? I can feel for your loss, sir—I can feel for your loss.'

I said so out of politeness, because I served the family, not because Tuggeridge was my uncle—no, as such I disown him.

Mr. Bar was just about to speak. 'Yes, sir,' says he, 'my master's gaw——': when at the 'gaw,' in walks Mr. Hock, the own man!—the finest gentleman I ever saw.

'What, *you* here, Mr. Bar?' says he.

'Yes, I am, sir; and haven't I a right, sir?'

'A mighty wet day, sir,' says I to Mr. Hock—stepping up and making my bow. 'A sad circumstance too, sir!—and is it a turn of the tongs that you want to-day, sir? Ho, there, Mr. Crump!'

'Turn, Mr. Crump if you please, sir,' said Mr. Hock, making a bow; 'but from you, sir, never, no never, split me!—and I wonder how some fellows can have the *insolence* to allow their MASTERS to shave them!' With this, Mr. Hock flung himself down to be curled: Mr. Bar suddenly opened his mouth in order to reply; but, seeing there was a tiff between the gentlemen, and wanting to prevent a quarrel, I rammed the *Advertiser* into Mr. Hock's hands, and just popped my shaving-brush into Mr. Bar's mouth—a capital way to stop angry answers.

Mr. Bar had hardly been in the chair one second, when whirr comes a hackney-coach to the door, from which springs a gentle-man in a black coat with a bag.

'What, you here?' says the gentleman. I could not help smiling, for it seemed that everybody was to begin by saying, 'What, *you* here?' 'Your name is Cox, sir,' says he; smiling, too, as the very pattern of mine. 'My name, sir, is Sharpus,—Blunt, Hone, and Sharpus, Middle Temple Lane,—and I am proud to salute you, sir; happy,—that is to say, sorry to say, that Mr. Tuggeridge, of Portland Place, is dead, and your lady is heiress, in consequence, to one of the handsomest properties in the kingdom.'

At this I started, and might have sunk to the ground, but for my hold of Mr. Bar's nose ; Orlando seemed putrified to stone, with his irons fixed to Mr. Hock's head ; our respective patients gave a wince out :—Mrs. C., Jemimarann, and Tug, rushed from the back shop, and we formed a splendid tableau which the great Cruikshank has here depicted !

'And Mr. John Tuggeridge, sir ?' says I.

'Why—hee, hee, hee !' says Mr. Sharpus ; 'surely you know that he was only the—hee, hee, hee !—the natural son !'

You now can understand why the servants from Portland Place had been so eager to come to us. One of the housemaids heard Mr. Sharpus say there was no will, and that my wife was heir to the property, and not Mr. John Tuggeridge : this she told in the housekeeper's room ; and off, as soon as they heard it, the whole party set, in order to be the first to bear the news.

We kept them, every one, in their old places ; for, though my wife would have sent them about their business, my dear Jemimarann just hinted, 'Mamma, you know *they* have been used to great houses, and we have not ; had we not better keep them for a little ?'—Keep them, then, we did, to show us how to be gentlefolks.

I handed over the business to Mr. Crump without a single farthing of premium, though Jemmy would have made me take four hundred pounds for it ; but this I was above ; Crump had served me faithfully, and have the shop he should.

FEBRUARY—First Rout.

We were speedily installed in our fine house : but what's a house without friends ? Jemmy made me *cut* all my old acquaintances in the Market, and I was a solitary being, when, luckily, an old acquaintance of ours, Captain Tagrag, was so kind as to promise to introduce us into distinguished society. Tagrag was the son of a baronet, and had done us the honour of lodging with us for two years ; when we lost sight of him, and of his little account, too, by the way. A fortnight after, hearing of our good fortune, he was among us again, however ; and Jemmy was not a little glad to see him, knowing him to be a baronet's son, and very fond of our Jemimarann. Indeed, Orlando (who is as brave as a lion) had, on one occasion, absolutely beaten Mr. Tagrag for being rude to the poor girl ; a clear proof, as Tagrag said afterwards, that he was always fond of her.

George Cruikshank.

FEBRUARY—FIRST ROUT.

P. 353.

Mr. Crump, poor fellow, was not very much pleased by our good fortune, though he did all he could to try, at first; and I told him to come and take his dinner regular, as if nothing had happened. But to this Jemima very soon put a stop, for she came very justly to know her stature, and to look down on Crump, which she bid her daughter to do; and, after a great scene, in which Orlando shewed himself very rude and angry, he was forbidden the house—for ever!

So much for poor Crump. The Captain was now all in all with us. 'You see, sir,' our Jemmy would say, 'we shall have our town and country mansion, and a hundred and thirty thousand pounds in the funds, to leave between our two children; and, with such prospects, they ought surely to have the first society of England.' To this Tagrag agreed, and promised to bring us acquainted with the very pink of the fashion; ay, and what's more, did.

First, he made my wife get an opera-box, and give suppers on Tuesdays and Saturdays. As for me, he made me ride in the park : me and Jemimarann, with two grooms behind us, who used to laugh all the way, and whose very beards I had shaved. As for little Tug, he was sent straight off to the most fashionable school in the kingdom, the Reverend Doctor Pigney's, at Richmond.

Well, the horses, the suppers, the opera-box, the paragraphs in the papers about Mr. Coxe Coxe (that's the way, double your name, and stick an 'e' to the end of it, and you are a gentleman at once), had an effect in a wonderfully short space of time, and we began to get a very pretty society about us. Some of old Tug's friends swore they would do anything for the family, and brought their wives and daughters to see dear Mrs. Coxe and her charming girl; and when, about the first week in February, we announced a grand dinner and ball, for the evening of the twenty-eighth, I assure you there was no want of company; no, nor of titles neither; and it always does my heart good even to hear one mentioned.

Let me see. There was, first, my Lord Dunboozle, an Irish peer, and his seven sons, the Honourable Messieurs Trumper (two only to dinner); there was Count Mace, the celebrated French nobleman, and his Excellency Baron von Punter, from Baden; there was Lady Blanche Bluenose, the eminent literati, author of 'The Distrusted,' 'The Distorted,' 'The Disgusted,' 'The Disreputable One,' and other poems; there was the Dowager Lady Max, and her daughter, the Honourable Miss Adelaide Blueruin; Sir Charles Codshead, from the city; and Field-Marshal Sir Gorman O'Gallagher, K.A., K.B., K.C., K.W., K.X., in the service of the republic of Guatemala : my friend Tagrag, and his fashionable acquaintance, little Tom Tufthunt, made up the party ; and when the doors were flung open, and Mr. Hock, in black, with a white napkin, three footmen, coachman, and a lad, whom Mrs. C. had dressed in sugar-loaf buttons, and called a page, were seen round the dinner-table, all in white gloves, I promise you I felt a thrill of elation, and thought to myself—Sam Cox, Sam Cox, who ever would have expected to see you here ?

After dinner, there was to be, as I said, an evening party ; and to this Messieurs Tagrag and Tufthunt had invited many of the principal nobility that our metropolis had produced. When I mention, among the company to tea, her Grace the Duchess of Zero, her son the Marquis of Fitzurse, and the Ladies North Pole, her daughters ; when I say that there were yet *others*, whose names may be found in the Blue Book, but sha'n't, out of modesty, be mentioned here, I think I've said enough to show that, in our time, No. 96 Portland Place, was the resort of the best of company.

It was our first dinner, and dressed by our new cook, Munseer Cordongblew. I bore it very well, eating, for my share, a *filly dysol allamater dotell*, a cutlet *soubeast*, a *pully bashymall*, and other French dishes ; and, for the frisky sweet wine, with tin tops to the bottles, called Champang, I must say that me and Mrs. Coxe-Tuggeridge Coxe drank a very good share of it (but the Claret and Jonnysberger being sour, we did not much relish) ;—however, the feed, as I say, went off very well, Lady Blanche Bluenose sitting next to me, and being so good as to put me down for six copies of all her poems ; the Count and Baron von Punter engaging Jemimarann for several waltzes, and the Field-Marshal plying my dear Jemmy with Champang until, bless her ! her dear nose became as red as her new crimson satin gown, which, with a blue turban and bird-of-paradise feathers, made her look like an Empress, I warrant.

Well, dinner past, Mrs. C. and the ladies went off :—thunder-under-under came the knocks at the door ; squeedle-eedle-eedle, Mr. Wippert's fiddlers began to strike up ; and, about half-past eleven, me and the gents thought it high time to make our appearance. I felt *a little* squeamish at the thought of meeting a couple of hundred great people ; but Count Mace and Sir Gorman O'Gallagher taking each an arm, we reached, at last, the drawing-room.

The young ones in company were dancing, and the Duchess and the great ladies were all seated, talking to themselves very stately, and working away at the ices and macaroons. I looked

out for my pretty Jemimarann amongst the dancers, and saw her
tearing round the room along with Baron Punter, in what they
call a gallypard ; then I peeped into the circle of the Duchesses,
where, in course, I expected to find Mrs. C. ; but she wasn't
there ! She was seated at the further end of the room, looking
very sulky ; and I went up, and took her arm, and brought her
down to the place where the Duchesses were. ' O, not there ! '
said Jemmy, trying to break away. ' Nonsense, my dear,' says I,
' you are Missis, and this is your place ' :—then, going up to her
Ladyship the Duchess, says I, ' Me and my Missis are most proud
of the honour of seeing of you.'

The Duchess (a tall red-haired grenadier of a woman) did not
speak.

I went on. ' The young ones are all at it, ma'am, you see :
and so we thought we would come and sit down among the old
ones. You and I, ma'am, I think, are too stiff to dance.'

' Sir ! ' says her Grace.

' Ma'am,' says I, ' don't you know me ? My name's Cox—
nobody's introduced me ; but, dash it, it's my own house, and I
may present myself—so give us your hand, ma'am.'

And I shook hers in the kindest way in the world : but, would
you believe it ? the old cat screamed as if my hand had been a
hot 'tater. ' Fitzurse ! Fitzurse ! ' shouted she ; ' help ! help ! '
Up scuffled all the other Dowagers—in rushed the dancers.
' Mamma ! mamma ! ' squeaked Lady Julia North Pole. ' Lead
me to my mother ! ' howled Lady Aurorer ; and both came up and
flung themselves into her arms. ' Wawt's the raw ? ' said Lord
Fitzurse, sauntering up quite stately.

' Protect me from the insults of this man,' says her Grace.
' Where's Tufthunt ? he promised that not a soul in this house
should speak to me.'

' My dear Duchess,' said Tufthunt, very meek.

' Don't Duchess me, sir. Did you not promise they should not
speak ; and hasn't that horrid tipsy wretch offered to embrace
me ? Didn't his monstrous wife sicken me with her odious
familiarities ? Call my people, Tufthunt ! Follow me, my
children ! '

' And my carriage,' ' And mine,' ' And mine ! ' shouted twenty
more voices ; and down they all trooped to the hall : Lady
Blanche Bluenose and Lady Max among the very first ; leaving
only the Field-Marshal and one or two men, who roared with
laughter ready to split.

' O Sam,' said my wife, sobbing, ' why would you take me
back to them ? they had sent me away before ! I only asked the

Duchess whether she didn't like rum-shrub better than all your
Maxarinos and Curasosos: and, would you believe it? all the
company burst out laughing; and the Duchess told me just to
keep off, and not to speak till I was spoken to.   Imperence! I'd
like to tear her eyes out.'

And so I do believe my dearest Jemmy would!

MARCH—A Day with the Surrey Hounds.

Our ball had failed so completely, that Jemmy, who was bent
still upon fashion, caught eagerly at Tagrag's suggestion, and went
down to Tuggeridgeville.   If we had a difficulty to find friends in
town, here there was none; for the whole county came about us,
ate our dinners and suppers, danced at our balls—ay, and spoke
to us too.   We were great people, in fact; I a regular country
gentleman; and, as such, Jemmy insisted that I should be a
sportsman, and join the county hunt.   'But,' says I, 'my love, I
can't ride.'   'Pooh! Mr. C.,' said she, 'you're always making
difficulties; you thought you couldn't dance a quadrille; you
thought you couldn't dine at seven o'clock; you thought you
couldn't lie in bed after six; and haven't you done every one of
these things?   You must and you shall ride!'   And when my
Jemmy said 'must and shall,' I knew very well there was nothing
for it: so I sent down fifty guineas to the hunt, and, out of
compliment to me, the very next week, I received notice that the
meet of the hounds would take place at Squashtail Common, just
outside of my lodge gates.

I didn't know what a meet was; and me and Mrs. C. agreed
that it was most probable the dogs were to be fed there: however,
Tagrag explained this matter to us, and very kindly promised to
sell me a horse, a delightful animal of his own; which, being
desperately pressed for money, he would let me have for a hundred
guineas, he himself having given a hundred and fifty for it.

Well, the Thursday came; the hounds met on Squashtail
Common; Mrs. C. turned out in her barouche to see us throw off;
and, being helped up on my chestnut horse, Trumpeter, by Tagrag
and my head groom, I came presently round to join them.

Tag mounted his own horse; and, as we walked down the
avenue, 'I thought,' he said, 'you told me you knew how to ride;
and that you had ridden once fifty miles on a stretch!'

'And so I did,' says I, 'to Cambridge, and on the box
too.'

' *On the box!* ' says he ; ' but did you ever mount a horse before ? '

' Never,' says I, ' but I find it mighty easy.'

' Well,' says he, ' you're mighty bold for a barber ; and I like you, Coxe, for your spirit ' ; and so we came out of the gate.

As for describing the hunt, I own, fairly, I can't. I've been at a hunt, but what a hunt is—why the horses *will* go among the dogs and ride them down—why the men cry out 'yooooic'—why the dogs go snuffing about in threes and fours, and the huntsman says, 'Good Towler—good Betsy' ; and we all of us, after him, say, 'Good Towler—good Betsy' in course : then, after hearing a yelp here, and a howl there, tow, row, yow, yow, yow! bursts out, all of a sudden, from three or four of them, and the chap in the velvet cap screeches out (with a number of oaths I sha'n't repeat here), 'Hark, to Ringwood!' and then, 'There he goes!' says some one ; and, all of a sudden, helter skelter, skurry hurry, slap bang, hooping, screeching and hurraing, blue coats and red coats, bays and greys, horses, dogs, donkeys, butchers, baro-knights, dustmen, and blackguard boys, go tearing, all together, over the common after two or three of the pack that yowl loudest. Why all this is, I can't say, but it all took place the second Thursday of last March, in my presence.

Up to this, I'd kept my seat as well as the best, for we'd only been trotting gently about the field until the dogs found ; and I managed to stick on very well ; but directly the tow-rowing began, off went Trumpeter like a thunderbolt, and I found myself playing among the dogs like the donkey among the chickens. 'Back, Mr. Coxe,' holloas the huntsman ; and so I pulled very hard, and cried out, 'Wo!' but he wouldn't ; and on I went galloping for the dear life. How I kept on is a wonder ; but I squeezed my knees in very tight, and shoved my feet very hard into the stirrups, and kept stiff hold of the scruff of Trumpeter's neck, and looked betwixt his ears as well as ever I could, and trusted to luck, for I was in a mortal fright, sure enough, as many a better man would be in such a case, let alone a poor hairdresser.

As for the hounds, after my first riding in among them, I tell you, honestly, I never saw so much as the tip of one of their tails ; nothing in this world did I see except Trumpeter's dun-coloured mane, and that I gripped firm : riding, by the blessing of luck, safe through the walking, the trotting, the galloping, and never so much as getting a tumble.

There was a chap at Croydon, very well known as the 'Spicy Dustman,' who, when he could get no horse to ride to the hounds, turned regularly out on his donkey ; and on this occasion made one of us. He generally managed to keep up with the dogs, by trotting quietly through the cross-roads, and knowing the country well. Well, having a good guess where the hounds would find, and the line that sly Reynolds (as they call the fox) would take, the Spicy Dustman turned his animal down the lane from Squashtail to Cutshins Common, across which, sure enough, came the whole hunt. There's a small hedge and a remarkably fine ditch here ; some of the leading chaps took both, in gallant style ; others went round by a gate, and so would I, only I couldn't ; for Trumpeter would have the hedge, and be—hanged to him, and went right for it.

Hoop ! if ever you *did* try a leap ! Out go your legs, out fling your arms, off goes your hat ; and the next thing you feel—that is, *I* did—is a most tremendous thwack across the chest, and my feet jerked out of the stirrups ; me left in the branches of a tree ; Trumpeter gone clean from under me, and walloping and floundering in the ditch underneath. One of the stirrup-leathers had caught in a stake, and the horse couldn't get away ; and neither of us, I thought, ever *would* have got away ; but, all of a sudden, who should come up the lane but the Spicy Dustman !

'Holloa !' says I, 'you gent, just let us down from this here tree !'

'Lor !' says he, 'I'm blest if I didn't take you for a robin.'

'Let's down,' says I ; but he was all the time employed in disengaging Trumpeter, whom he got out of the ditch, trembling and as quiet as possible. 'Let's down,' says I. 'Presently,' says he ; and taking off his coat, he begins whistling and swishing down Trumpeter's sides and saddle ; and when he had finished, what do you think the rascal did ?—he just quietly mounted on Trumpeter's back, and shouts out, 'Git down yourself, old Bearsgrease ; you've only to drop ! *I'll* give your oss a hairing arter them 'ounds ; and you, vy, you may ride back my pony to Tuggeridgeweal !' And with this, I'm blest if he didn't ride away, leaving me holding, as for the dear life, and expecting, every minute, the branch would break.

It *did* break too, and down I came into the slush ; and when I got out of it, I can tell you I didn't look much like the Venuses or the Apollor Belvidearis what I used to dress and titivate up for my shop window, when I was in the hairdressing line, or smell quite so elegant as our rose-oil. Faugh ! what a figure I was ! Look on the other page and you will see.

I had nothing for it but to mount the dustman's donkey (which was very quietly cropping grass in the hedge), and to make my

George Cruikshank.

MARCH—A DAY WITH THE SURREY HOUNDS.

P. 360.

way home; and after a weary, weary journey, I arrived at my own gate.

A whole party was assembled there. Tagrag, who had come back; their Excellencies Mace and Punter, who were on a visit; and a number of horses walking up and down before the whole of the gentlemen of the hunt, who had come in after losing their fox! 'Here's Squire Coxe!' shouted the grooms. Out rushed the servants, out poured the gents of the hunt, and on trotted poor me, digging into the donkey, and everybody dying with laughter at me.

Just as I got up to the door, a horse came galloping up, and passed me; a man jumped down, and, taking off a fantail hat, came up, very gravely, to help me down.

'Squire,' says he, 'how came you by that there hanimal? Jist git down, will you, and give it to its howner.'

'Rascal!' says I, 'didn't you ride off on my horse?'

'Was there ever sich ingratitude?' says the Spicy. 'I found this year oss in a pond, I saves him from drowning, I brings him back to his master, and he calls me a rascal!'

The grooms, the gents, the ladies in the balcony, my own servants, all set up a roar at this; and so would I, only I was so deucedly ashamed, as not to be able to laugh just then.

And so my first day's hunting ended. Tagrag and the rest declared I showed great pluck, and wanted me to try again; but 'No,' says I, 'I *have* been.'

APRIL—The Finishing Touch.

I was always fond of billiards: and, in former days, at Grogram's, in Greek Street, where a few jolly lads of my acquaintance used to meet twice a week for a game, and a snug pipe and beer, I was generally voted the first man of the club; and could take five from John, the marker, himself. I had a genius, in fact, for the game; and now that I was placed in that station of life where I could cultivate my talents, I gave them full play, and improved amazingly. I do say that I think myself as good a hand as any chap in England.

The Count, and his Excellency Baron von Punter, were, I can tell you, astonished by the smartness of my play; the first two or three rubbers Punter beat me, but when I came to know his game, I used to knock him all to sticks; or, at least, win six games to his four: and such was the betting upon me: his

George Cruikshank

APRIL—THE FINISHING TOUCH.

Excellency losing large sums to the Count, who knew what play was, and used to back me. I did not play except for shillings, so my skill was of no great service to me.

One day I entered the billiard-room where these three gentlemen were high in words. 'The thing shall not be done,' I heard Captain Tagrag say, 'I won't stand it.'

'Vat, begause you would have de bird all to yourzelf, hey?' said the Baron.

'You sall not have a single fezare of him, begar,' said the Count, 've vill blow you, M. de Taguerague; *parole d'honneur*, ve vill.'

'What's all this, gents,' says I, stepping in, 'about birds and feathers?'

'O,' says Tagrag, 'we were talking about—about—pigeon-shooting; the Count, here, says he will blow a bird all to pieces at twenty yards, and I said I wouldn't stand it, because it was regular murder.'

'Oh, yase, it was bidgeon-shooting,' cries the Baron: 'and I know no better sbort. Have you been bidgeon-shooting, my dear Squire? De fon is gabidal.'

'No doubt,' says I, 'for the shooters, but mighty bad sport for the *pigeon;*' and this joke set them all a-laughing ready to die. I didn't know then what a good joke it *was*, neither; but I gave Master Baron, that day, a precious good beating, and walked off with no less than fifteen shillings of his money.

As a sporting man, and a man of fashion, I need not say that I took in *The Flare-up*, regularly; ay, and wrote one or two trifles in that celebrated publication (one of my papers, which Tagrag subscribed for me, Philo-pestitiæamicus, on the proper sauce for teal and widgeon; and the other, signed Scru-tatos, on the best means of cultivating the kidney species of that vegetable, made no small noise at the time, and got me in the paper a compliment from the editor). I was a constant reader of the 'Notices to Correspondents,' and, my early education having been rayther neglected, (for I was taken from my studies and set, as is the custom in our trade, to practise on a sheep's-head at the tender age of nine years, before I was allowed to venture on the humane countenance,)—I say, being thus curtailed and cut off in my classical learning, I must confess I managed to pick up a pretty smattering of genteel information from that treasury of all sorts of knowledge; at least sufficient to make me a match in learning for all the noblemen and gentlemen who came to our house. Well, on looking over *The Flare-up* notices to correspondents, I read, one day last April, among the notices, as follows :—

' "Automodon." We do not know the precise age of Mr. Baker of Covent Garden Theatre ; nor are we aware if that celebrated son of Thespis is a married man.

' "Ducks and Green-peas " is informed, that when A plays his rook to B's second Knight's square, and B, moving two squares with his Queen's pawn, gives check to his adversary's Queen, there is no reason why B's Queen should not take A's pawn, if B be so inclined.

' "F. L. S." We have repeatedly answered the question about Madame Vestris : her maiden name was Bartolozzi, and she married the son of Charles Matthews, the celebrated comedian.

' "Fair Play." The best amateur billiard and *écarté* player in England is Coxe Tuggeridge Coxe, Esq., of Portland Place, and Tuggeridgeville : Jonathan, who knows his play, can only give him two in a game of a hundred : and, at the cards, *no* man is his superior. *Verbum sap.*

' "Scipio Americanus " is a blockhead.'

I read this out to the Count and Tagrag, and both of them wondered how the Editor of that tremendous *Flare-up* should get such information ; and both agreed that the Baron, who still piqued himself absurdly on his play, would be vastly annoyed by seeing me preferred thus to himself. We read him the paragraph, and preciously angry he was. ' Id is,' he cried, ' the tables (or " de *dabels*," as he called them), de horrid dabels ; gom viz me to London, and dry a slate-table, and I vill beat you.' We all roared at this ; and the end of the dispute was, that, just to satisfy the fellow, I agreed to play his Excellency at slate-tables, or any tables he chose.

' Gut,' says he, ' gut ; I lif, you know, at Abednego's, in de Quadrant ; his dabels is goot ; ve vill play dere, if you vill ; ' and I said, I would : and it was agreed that, one Saturday night, when Jemmy was at the Opera, we should go to the Baron's rooms, and give him a chance.

We went, and the little Baron had as fine a supper as ever I saw ; lots of champagne (and I didn't mind drinking it), and plenty of laughing and fun. Afterwards, down we went to billiards. ' Is dish Misther Coxsh, de shelebrated player ? ' says Mr. Abednego, who was in the room, with one or two gentlemen of his own persuasion, and several foreign noblemen, dirty, snuffy, and hairy, as them foreigners are. ' Is dish Misther Coxsh ? blesh ma hart, it is a honor to see you, I have heard so much of your play.'

' Come, come,' says I, ' sir ; ' for I'm pretty wide awake ; ' none of your gammon ; you're not going to hook *me*.'

'No, begar, dis fish you not catch,' says Count Mace.

'Dat is gut! haw! haw!' snorted the Baron; 'hook him! *Lieber Himmel*, you might dry and hook me as well. Haw! haw!'

Well, we went to play. 'Five to four on Coxe,' screams out the Count.—'Done and done,' says another nobleman. 'Ponays,' says the Count.—'Done,' says the nobleman. 'I vill take your six crowns to four,' says the Baron.—'Done,' says I; and, in the twinkling of an eye, I beat him;—once making thirteen off the balls without stopping.

We had some more wine after this; and if you could have seen the long faces of the other noblemen, as they pulled out their pencils and wrote I.O.U.'s for the Count. '*Va toujours, mon cher*,' says he to me, 'you have von for me tree hundred pounds.'

'I'll blay you guinease dis time,' says the Baron. 'Zeven to four you must give me though;' and so I did: and in ten minutes *that* game was won, and the Baron handed over his pounds. 'Two hundred and sixty more, my dear, dear Coxe,' says the Count; 'you are *mon ange gardien!*' 'Wot a flat Misther Coxsh is, not to back his luck,' I heard Abednego whisper to one of the foreign noblemen.

'I'll take your seven to four, in tens,' said I to the Baron. 'Give me three,' says he, 'and done.' I gave him three, and lost the game by one. 'Dobbel, or quits,' says he. 'Go it,' says I, up to my mettle; 'Sam Coxe never says no;'—and to it we went. I went in, and scored eighteen to his five. 'Holy Moshesh!' says Abednego, 'dat little Coxsh is a vonder! who'll take odds?'

'I'll give twenty to one,' says I, 'in guineas.'

'Ponays, yase, done;' screams out the Count.

'*Bonies*, done,' roars out the Baron: and, before I could speak, went in, and, would you believe it?—in two minutes he somehow made the game!

.   .   .   .   .

O, what a figure I cut when my dear Jemmy heard of this afterwards!—In vain I swore it was guineas: the Count and the Baron swore to poneys; and when I refused, they both said their honour was concerned, and they must have my life, or their money. So when the Count showed me actually that, in spite of this bet (which had been too good to resist) won from me, he had been a very heavy loser by the night; and brought me the word of honour of Abednego, his Jewish friend, and the foreign noblemen, that ponies had been betted:—why, I paid them one thousand pounds sterling of good and lawful money ;—but I've not played for money since : no, no ; catch me at *that* again if you can.

MAY—A New Drop Scene at the Opera.

No lady is a lady without having a box at the Opera : so my Jemmy, who knew as much about music,—bless her !—as I do about Sanscrit, algebra, or any other foreign language, took a prime box on the second tier. It was what they called a double box ; it really *could* hold two, that is, very comfortably ; and we got it a great bargain—for five hundred a year ! Here, Tuesdays and Saturdays, we used regularly to take our places, Jemmy and Jemimarann sitting in front ; me, behind : but as my dear wife used to wear a large fantail gauze hat, with ostrich feathers, birds of paradise, artificial flowers, and tags of muslin or satin, scattered all over it, I'm blest if she didn't fill the whole of the front of the box ; and it was only by jumping and dodging, three or four times in the course of the night, that I could manage to get a sight of the actors. By kneeling down, and looking steady under my darling Jemmy's sleeve, I *did* contrive, every now and then, to have a peep of Senior Lablash's boots, in the Puritanny, and once actually saw Madame Greasi's crown and head-dress in Annybalony.

What a place that Opera is, to be sure ! and what enjoyments us aristocracy used to have ! Just as you have swallowed down your three courses (three curses I used to call them ;—for so, indeed, they are, causing a deal of heartburns, headaches, doctor's bills, pills, want of sleep, and such like)—just, I say, as you get down your three courses, which I defy any man to enjoy properly unless he has two hours of drink and quiet afterwards, up comes the carriage, in bursts my Jemmy, as fine as a duchess, and scented like our shop. 'Come, my dear,' says she, 'it's Normy to-night' (or Annybalony, or the Nosey di Figaro, or the Gazzylarder, as the case may be) ; Mr. Coster strikes off punctually at eight, and you know it's the fashion to be always present at the very first bar of the aperture ;' and so off we are obliged to budge, to be miserable for five hours, and to have a headache for the next twelve, and all because it's the fashion.

After the aperture, as they call it, comes the opera, which, as I am given to understand, is the Italian for singing. Why they should sing in Italian, I can't conceive ; or why they should do

George Cruikshank

MAY—A NEW DROP SCENE AT THE OPERA.

nothing *but* sing : bless us ! how I used to long for the wooden
magpie, in the Gazzylarder, to fly up to the top of the church-
steeple, with the silver spoons, and see the chaps with the
pitchforks come in and carry off that wicked Don June.   Not
that I don't admire Lablash, and Rubini, and his brother,
Tomrubini, him who has that fine bass voice, I mean, and acts the
Corporal in the first piece, and Don June in the second ; but three
hours is a *little* too much, for you can't sleep on those little rickety
seats in the boxes.

The opera is bad enough ; but what is that to the bally ?   You
should have seen my Jemmy the first night when she stopped to
see it ; and when Madamsalls Fanny and Theresa Hustler came
forward, along with a gentleman, to dance, you should have seen
how Jemmy stared, and our girl blushed, when Madamsall Fanny,
coming forward, stood on the tips of only five of her toes, and
raising up the other five, and the foot belonging to them, almost
to her shoulder, twirled round, and round, and round, like a
teetotum, for a couple of minutes or more ; and as she settled
down, at last, on both feet, in a natural decent posture, you should
have heard how the house roared with applause, the boxes clapping
with all their might, and waving their handkerchiefs ; the pit
shouting, 'Bravo !'   Some people, who, I suppose, were rather
angry at such an exhibition, threw bunches of flowers at her ; and
what do you think she did ? why, hang me, if she did not come
forward, as though nothing had happened, gather up the things
they had thrown at her, smile, press them to her heart, and begin
whirling round again, faster than ever !—Talk about coolness, *I*
never saw such in all *my* born days.

' Nasty thing !' says Jemmy, starting up in a fury ; ' if women
will act so, it serves them right to be treated so.'

' Oh, yes ! she acts beautifully,' says our friend, his Excellency,
who, along with Baron von Punter, and Tagrag, used very seldom
to miss coming to our box.

' She may act very beautifully, Munseer, but she don't dress so ;
and I am very glad they threw that orange-peel and all those
things at her, and that the people waved to her to get off.'

Here his Excellency, and the Baron, and Tag, set up a roar of
laughter.

' My dear Mrs. Coxe,' says Tag, ' those are the most famous
dancers in the world ; and we throw myrtle, geraniums, and lilies,
and roses, at them, in token of our immense admiration !'

' Well, I never !' said my wife ; and poor Jemimarann slunk
behind the curtain, and looked as red as it almost.   After the one
had done, the next begun ; but when, all of a sudden, a somebody

came skipping and bounding in, like an India-rubber ball, flinging itself up, at least six feet from the stage, and there shaking about its legs like mad, we were more astonished than ever !

'That's Anatole,' says one of the gentlemen.

'Anna who ?' says my wife, and she might well be mistaken ; for this person had a hat and feathers, a bare neck and arms, great black ringlets, and a little calico frock, which came down to the knees.

'Anatole ; you would not think he was sixty-three years old, he's as active as a man of twenty.'

'*He !*' shrieked out my wife ; 'what, is that there a man ? For shame ! Munseer. Jemimarann, dear, get your cloak, and come along ; and I'll thank you, my dear, to call our people, and let us go home.'

You wouldn't think, after this, that my Jemmy, who had shown such a horror at the bally, as they call it, should ever grow accustomed to it ; but she liked to hear her name shouted out in the crush-room, and so would stop till the end of everything ; and, law bless you ! in three weeks from that time, she could look at the ballet, as she would at a dancing-dog in the streets, and would bring her double-barrelled opera-glass up to her eyes as coolly as if she had been a born duchess. As for me, I did, at Rome, as Rome does, and precious fun it used to be, sometimes.

My friend, the Baron, insisted, one night, on my going behind the scenes ; where, being a subscriber, he said I had, what they call, my *ontray*. Behind, then, I went ; and such a place you never saw nor heard of ! Fancy lots of young and old gents, of the fashion, crowding round and staring at the actresses practising their steps. Fancy yellow, snuffy foreigners, chattering always, and smelling fearfully of tobacco. Fancy scores of Jews, with hooked noses and black muzzles, covered with rings, chains, sham diamonds, and gold waistcoats. Fancy old men, dressed in old night-gowns, with knock-knees, and dirty flesh-coloured cotton stockings, and dabs of brick dust on their wrinkled old chops, and tow-wigs (such wigs !) for the bald ones, and great tin spears in their hands mayhap, or else shepherds' crooks, and fusty garlands of flowers, made of red and green baize. Fancy troops of girls, giggling, chattering, pushing to and fro, amidst old black canvas, Gothic halls, thrones, pasteboard Cupids, dragons, and such like ; such dirt, darkness, crowd, confusion, and gabble of all conceivable languages, was never known !

If you *could* but have seen Munseer Anatole ! Instead of looking twenty, he looked a thousand. The old man's wig was off, and a barber was giving it a touch with the tongs ; Munseer

2 B

was taking snuff himself, and a boy was standing by, with a pint of beer, from the public-house at the corner of Charles Street.

I met with a little accident during the three-quarters of an hour which they allow for the entertainment of us men of fashion on the stage, before the curtain draws up for the bally, while the ladies in the boxes are gaping, and the people in the pit are drumming with their feet and canes in the rudest manner possible, as though they couldn't wait.

Just at the moment before the little bell rings, and the curtain flies up, and we scuffle off to the sides (for we always stay till the very last moment), I was in the middle of the stage, making myself very affable to the fair *figgerantys* which was spinning and twirling about me, and asking them if they wasn't cold, and such like politeness, in the most condescending way possible, when a bolt was suddenly withdrawn, and down I popped, through a trap in the stage, into the place below. Luckily, I was stopped by a piece of machinery, consisting of a heap of green blankets and a young lady coming up as Venus rising from the sea. If I had not fallen so soft, I don't know what might have been the consequence of the collusion. I never told Mrs. Coxe, for she can't bear to hear of my paying the least attention to the fair sex.

JUNE—Striking a Balance.

Next door to us, in Portland Place, lived the Right Honourable the Earl of Kilblazes, of Kilmacrasy Castle, county Kildare, and his mother, the Dowager Countess. Lady Kilblazes had a daughter, Lady Juliana Matilda Mac Turk, of the exact age of our dear Jemimarann ; and a son, The Honourable Arthur Wellington Anglesea Blucher Bulow Mac Turk, only ten months older than our boy Tug.

My darling Jemmy is a woman of spirit, and, as became her station, made every possible attempt to become acquainted with the Dowager Countess of Kilblazes, which her ladyship (because, forsooth, she was the daughter of the Minister, and Prince of Wales's great friend, the Earl of Portansherry) thought fit to reject. I don't wonder at my Jemmy growing so angry with her, and determining, in every way, to put her ladyship down. The Kilblazes' estate is not so large as the Tuggeridge property, by two thousand a year at least ; and so my wife, when our neighbours kept only two footmen, was quite authorised in having three ;

George Cruikshank

JUNE—STRIKING A BALANCE.

P. 371.

and she made it a point, as soon as ever the Kilblazes' carriage-and-pair came round, to have out her own carriage-and-four.

Well, our box was next to theirs at the Opera; only twice as big. Whatever masters went to lady Juliana, came to my Jemimarann; and what do you think Jemmy did? she got her celebrated governess, Madame de Flicflac, away from the Countess, by offering a double salary. It was quite a treasure, they said, to have Madame Flicflac, she had been (to support her father, the Count, when he emigrated) a *French* dancer at the *Italian* Opera. French dancing, and Italian, therefore, we had at once, and in the best style: it is astonishing how quick and well she used to speak —the French especially.

Master Arthur Mac Turk was at the famous school of the Reverend Clement Coddler, along with a hundred and ten other young fashionables, from the age of three to fifteen; and to this establishment Jemmy sent our Tug, adding forty guineas to the hundred and twenty paid every year for the boarders. I think I found out the dear soul's reason, for, one day, speaking about the school to a mutual acquaintance of ours and the Kilblazes, she whispered to him, that 'she never would have thought of sending her darling boy at the rate which her next-door neighbours paid; *their* lad, she was sure, must be starved! however, poor people: they did the best they could on their income.'

Coddler's, in fact, was the tip-top school, near London; he had been tutor to the Duke of Buckminster, who had set him up in the school, and, as I tell you, all the peerage and respectable commoners came to it. You read in the bill, (the snopsis, I think Coddler called it), after the account of the charges for board, masters, extras, etc.—'Every young nobleman (or gentleman) is expected to bring a knife, fork, spoon, and goblet, of silver (to prevent breakage), which will not be returned; a dressing-gown and slippers; toilet-box, pomatum, curling-irons, etc., etc. The pupil must, on NO ACCOUNT, be allowed to have more than ten guineas of pocket-money, unless his parents particularly desire it, or he be above fifteen years of age. *Wine* will be an extra charge; as are warm, vapour, and *douche* baths; *carriage exercise* will be provided at the rate of fifteen guineas per quarter. It is *earnestly requested* that no young nobleman (or gentleman) be allowed to smoke. In a place devoted to *the cultivation of polite literature*, such an ignoble enjoyment were profane.

'CLEMENT CODDLER, M.A.,

'Chaplain and late tutor to his Grace the
Duke of Buckminster.'

'Mount Parnassus, Richmond, Surrey.'

To this establishment our Tug was sent. ' Recollect, my dear,' said his mamma, ' that you are a Tuggeridge by birth, and that I expect you to beat all the boys in the school, especially that Wellington Mac Turk, who, though he is a lord's son, is nothing to you, who are the heir of Tuggeridgeville.'

Tug was a smart young fellow enough, and could cut and curl as well as any young chap of his age ; he was not a bad hand at a wig either, and could shave, too, very prettily ; but that was in the old time, when we were not great people : when he came to be a gentleman, he had to learn Latin and Greek, and had a deal of lost time to make up for, on going to school.

However, we had no fear ; for the Reverend Mr. Coddler used to send monthly accounts of his pupils' progress, and if Tug was not a wonder of the world, I don't know who was. It was

General behaviour	excellent.
English	very good.
French	*très bien.*
Latin	*optimé.*

And so on :—he possessed all the virtues, and wrote to us every month for money. My dear Jemmy and I determined to go and see him, after he had been at school a quarter ; we went, and were shown by Mr. Coddler, one of the meekest, smilingest little men I ever saw, into the bed-rooms and eating-rooms (the dromitaries and refractories he called them), which were all as comfortable as comfortable might be. ' It is a holiday to-day,' said Mr. Coddler ; and a holiday it seemed to be :—in the dining-room were half a dozen young gentlemen playing at cards ('All tip-top nobility,' observed Mr. Coddler) ;—in the bed-rooms there was only one gent ; he was lying on his bed, reading novels and smoking cigars. ' Extraordinary genius ! ' whispered Coddler ; ' Honourable Tom Fitz-Warter, cousin of Lord Byron's ; smokes all day ; and has written the *sweetest* poems you can imagine. Genius, my dear madam, you know, genius must have its way.' ' Well, *upon* my word,' says Jemmy, ' if that's genius, I had rather that Master Tuggeridge Coxe Tuggeridge remained a dull fellow.'

' Impossible, my dear madam,' said Coddler. ' Mr. Tuggeridge Coxe *couldn't* be stupid if he *tried.*'

Just then up comes Lord Claude Lollypop, third son of the Marquis of Allycompane. We were introduced instantly. ' Lord Claude Lollypop, Mr. and Mrs. Coxe : ' the little lord wagged his head, my wife bowed very low, and so did Mr. Coddler, who, as he saw my lord making for the playground, begged him to show us the way. — ' Come along,' says my lord ; and as he walked before us, whistling, we had leisure to remark the beautiful holes in his jacket, and elsewhere.

About twenty young noblemen (and gentlemen) were gathered round a pastrycook's shop, at the end of the green. 'That's the grub-shop,' said my lord, 'where we young gentlemen wot has money buys our wittles, and them young gentlemen wot has none, goes tick.'

Then we passed a poor red-haired usher, sitting on a bench alone. 'That's Mr. Hicks, the Husher, ma'am,' says my lord. 'We keep him, for he's very useful to throw stones at, and he keeps the chaps' coats when there's a fight, or a game at cricket. —Well, Hicks, how's your mother? what's the row now?' 'I believe, my lord,' said the usher, very meekly, 'there is a pugilistic encounter somewhere on the premises — the Honourable Mr. Mac——'

'O! *come* along,' said Lord Lollypop, 'come along, *this* way, ma'am! Go it, ye cripples!' and my lord pulled my dear Jemmy's gown in the kindest and most familiar way, she trotting on after him, mightily pleased to be so taken notice of, and I after her. A little boy went running across the green. 'Who is it, Petitoes?' screams my lord. 'Turk and the barber,' pipes Petitoes, and runs to the pastrycook's like mad. 'Turk and the ba——,' laughs out my lord, looking at us: 'hurra! *this* way, ma'am;' and, turning round a corner, he opened a door into a court-yard, where a number of boys were collected, and a great noise of shrill voices might be heard. 'Go it, Turk!' says one. 'Go it, barber!' says another. '*Punch hith life out,*' roars another, whose voice was just cracked, and his clothes half a yard too short for him!

Fancy our horror, when, on the crowd making way, we saw Tug pummelling away at the Honourable Master Mac Turk! My dear Jemmy, who don't understand such things, pounced upon the two at once, and, with one hand tearing away Tug, sent him spinning back into the arms of his seconds, while, with the other, she clawed hold of Master Mac Turk's red hair, and, as soon as she got her second hand free, banged it about his face and ears like a good one.

'You nasty—wicked—quarrelsome—aristocratic (each word was a bang)—aristocratic, oh! oh! oh!' Here the words stopped; for what with the agitation, maternal solicitude, and a dreadful kick on the shins which, I am ashamed to say, Master Mac Turk administered, my dear Jemmy could bear it no longer, and sunk, fainting away, in my arms.

JULY—Down at Beulah.

Although there was a regular cut between the next-door people and us, yet Tug and the Honourable Master Mac Turk kept up their acquaintance over the back-garden wall, and in the stables, where they were fighting, making friends, and playing tricks from morning to night, during the holidays. Indeed, it was from young Mac that we first heard of Madame de Flicflac, of whom my Jemmy robbed Lady Kilblazes, as I before have related. When our friend, the Baron, first saw Madame, a very tender greeting passed between them, for they had, as it appeared, been old friends abroad. '*Sapristie*,' said the Baron, in his lingo, '*que fais-tu ici, Aménaïde ?*' '*Et toi, mon pauvre Chicot*,' says she ; '*est-ce qu'on t'a mis a la retraite ? Il parait que tu n'es plus Général chez Franco—*' '*Chut !*' says the Baron, putting his finger to his lips.

'What are they saying, my dear ?' says my wife to Jemimarann, who had a pretty knowledge of the language by this time.

'I don't know what "*Sapristie*" means, mamma ; but the Baron asked Madame what she was doing here ? and Madame said, "And you, Chicot, you are no more a general at Franco."—Have I not translated rightly, Madame ?'

'*Oui, mon chou, mon ange ;* yase, my angel, my cabbage, quite right. Figure yourself, I have known my dear Chicot dis twenty years.'

'Chicot is my name of baptism,' says the Baron ; 'Baron Chicot de Punter is my name.'

'And being a General at Franco,' says Jemmy, 'means, I suppose, being a French General ?'

'Yes, I was,' said he, 'General Baron de Punter, n'est-ce pas, Aménaïde ?'

'O, yes !' said Madame Flicflac, and laughed ; and I and Jemmy laughed out of politeness : and a pretty laughing matter it was, as you shall hear.

About this time my Jemmy became one of the Ladies-Patronesses of that admirable Institution, 'The Washerwoman's-Orphans' Home ;' Lady de Sudley was the great projector of it ; and the manager and chaplain, the excellent and Reverend Sidney Slopper. His salary, as chaplain, and that of Doctor Leitch, the physician (both cousins of her Ladyship's), drew away five hundred pounds from the six subscribed to the Charity : and Lady de Sudley thought a *fête* at Beulah Spa, with the aid of some of the foreign Princes who were in town last year, might bring a little more

JULY—DOWN AT BEULAH.

George Cruikshank

money into its treasury. A tender appeal was accordingly drawn up, and published in all the papers :—

' APPEAL.

' BRITISH WASHERWOMAN'S-ORPHANS' HOME.

' The "Washerwoman's-Orphans' Home" has now been established seven years : and the good which it has effected is, it may be confidently stated, *incalculable*. Ninety-eight orphan children of washerwomen have been lodged within its walls. One hundred and two British washerwomen have been relieved when in the last stage of decay. ONE HUNDRED AND NINETY-EIGHT THOUSAND articles of male and female dress have been washed, mended, buttoned, ironed, and mangled in the Establishment. And, by an arrangement with the governors of the Foundling, it is hoped that THE BABY-LINEN OF THAT HOSPITAL will be confided to the British Washerwoman's Home !

' With such prospects before it, is it not sad, is it not lamentable to think, that the Patronesses of the Society have been compelled to reject the applications of no less than THREE THOUSAND EIGHT HUNDRED AND ONE BRITISH WASHERWOMEN, from lack of means for their support ? Ladies of England ! Mothers of England ! to you we appeal. Is there one of you that will not respond to the cry in behalf of these deserving members of our sex ?

' It has been determined by the Ladies-Patronesses to give a *fête* at Beulah Spa, on Thursday, July 25 ; which will be graced with the first foreign and native TALENT, by the first foreign and native RANK ; and where they beg for the attendance of every WASHERWOMAN'S FRIEND.'

Her Highness the Princess of Schloppenzollernschwigmaringen, the Duke of Sacks-Tubbingen, His Excellency Baron Strumpff, His Excellency Lootf-Allee-Koolee-Bismillah-Mohamed-Rusheed-Allah, the Persian Ambassador, Prince Futtee-Jaw, Envoy from the King of Oude, His Excellency Don Alonzo Di Cachachero-y-Fandango-y-Castañete, the Spanish Ambassador, Count Ravioli, from Milan, the Envoy of the Republic of Topinambo, and a host of other fashionables, promised to honour the festival : and their names made a famous show in the bills. Besides these, we had the celebrated band of Moscow-musiks, the seventy-seven Transylvanian trumpeters, and the famous Bohemian Minnesingers ; with all the leading artists of London, Paris, the Continent, and the rest of Europe.

I leave you to fancy what a splendid triumph for the British

Washerwoman's Home was to come off on that day. A beautiful tent was erected, in which the Ladies-Patronesses were to meet; it was hung round with specimens of the skill of the washer-women's orphans: ninety-six of whom were to be feasted in the gardens, and waited on by the Ladies-Patronesses.

Well, Jemmy and my daughter, Madame de Flicflac, myself, the Count, Baron Punter, Tug, and Tagrag, all went down in the chariot and barouche-and four, quite eclipsing poor Lady Kilblazes and her carriage-and-two.

There was a fine cold collation, to which the friends of the Ladies-Patronesses were admitted; after which, my ladies and their *beaux* went strolling through the walks; Tagrag and the Count having each an arm of Jemmy; the Baron giving an arm apiece to Madame and Jemimarann. Whilst they were walking, whom should they light upon but poor Orlando Crump, my successor in the perfumery and hair-cutting.

' Orlando !' says Jemimarann, blushing as red as a label, and holding out her hand.

' Jemimar !' says he, holding out his, and turning as white as pomatum.

' *Sir !*' says Jemmy, as stately as a duchess.

' What! madam,' says poor Crump, ' don't you remember your shopboy ?'

' Dearest mamma, don't you recollect Orlando ?' whimpers Jemimarann, whose hand he had got hold of.

' Miss Tuggeridge Coxe,' says Jemmy, ' I'm surprised at you. Remember, sir, that our position is altered, and oblige me by no more familiarity.'

' Insolent fellow !' says the Baron, ' vat is dis *canaille ?*'

' Canal yourself, Mounseer,' says Orlando, now grown quite furious; he broke away, quite indignant, and was soon lost in the crowd. Jemimarann, as soon as he was gone, began to look very pale and ill; and her mamma, therefore, took her to a tent, where she left her along with Madame Flicflac and the Baron; going off herself with the other gentlemen, in order to join us.

It appears they had not been seated very long, when Madame Flicflac suddenly sprung up, with an exclamation of joy, and rushed forward to a friend whom she saw pass.

The Baron was left alone with Jemimarann; and, whether it was the champagne, or that my dear girl looked more than commonly pretty, I don't know; but Madame Flicflac had not been gone a minute, when the Baron dropped on his knees, and made her a regular declaration.

Poor Orlando Crump had found me out by this time, and was

standing by my side, listening, as melancholy as possible, to the famous Bohemian Minnesingers, who were singing the celebrated words of the poet Gothy :

> *Ich bin ya hupp lily lee, du bist ya hupp lily lee,*
> *Wir sind doch hupp lily lee, hupp la lily lee.*
> *Chorus—Yodle-odle-odle-odle-odle-odle hupp ! yodle-odle-aw-o-o-o !*

They were standing with their hands in their waistcoats, as usual, and had just come to the ' o-o-o,' at the end of the chorus of the forty-seventh stanza, when Orlando started : ' That's a scream ! ' says he. ' Indeed it is,' says I ; ' and, but for the fashion of the thing, a very ugly scream too : ' when I heard another shrill, ' O ! ' as I thought ; and Orlando bolted off, crying, ' By heavens, it's *her* voice ! ' ' Whose voice ? ' says I.   ' Come and see the row,' says Tag ; and off we went, with a considerable number of people, who saw this strange move on his part.

We came to the tent, and there we found my poor Jemimarann fainting : her mamma holding a smelling-bottle ; the Baron, on the ground, holding a handkerchief to his bleeding nose ; and Orlando squaring at him, and calling on him to fight if he dared.

My Jemmy looked at Crump very fierce.   ' Take that feller away,' says she, ' he has insulted a French nobleman, and deserves transportation, at the least.'

Poor Orlando was carried off.   ' I've no patience with the little minx,' says Jemmy, giving Jemimarann a pinch : ' she might be a Baron's lady ; and she screams out because his Excellency did but squeeze her hand.'

' O, mamma ! mamma ! ' sobs poor Jemimarann, ' but he was t-t-tipsy.'

' T-t-tipsy ! and the more shame for you, you hussy, to be offended with a nobleman who does not know what he is doing.'

AUGUST—A Tournament.

' I say, Tug,' said Mac Turk, one day, soon after our flare-up at Beulah, ' Kilblazes comes of age in October, and then we'll cut you out, as I told you : the old barberess will die of spite when she hears what we are going to do.   What do you think ? we're going to have a tournament ! '   ' What's a tournament ? ' says Tug, and so said his mamma when she heard the news ; and when she knew what a tournament was, I think, really, she *was* as angry as Mac Turk said she would be, and gave us no peace for days together.   ' What ! ' says she, ' dress up in armour, like

George Cruikshank.

AUGUST—A TOURNAMENT.

P. 380.

play-actors, and run at each other with spears? the Kilblazes must be mad!' And so I thought, but I didn't think the Tuggeridges would be mad too, as they were; for, when Jemmy heard that the Kilblazes festival was to be, as yet, a profound secret, what does she do, but send down to *The Morning Post* a flaming account of

'THE PASSAGE OF ARMS AT TUGGERIDGEVILLE!

'The days of chivalry are *not* past. The fair Castellane of T–gg–r–dgeville, whose splendid entertainments have so often been alluded to in this paper, has determined to give one, which shall exceed, in splendour, even the magnificence of the middle ages. We are not at liberty to say more; but a tournament, at which His Ex–l–ncy B–r–n de P–nt–r, and Thomas T–gr–g, Esq., eldest son of Sir Th—s T–gr–g, are to be the knights-defendants against all comers; a *Queen of Beauty*, of whose loveliness every frequenter of fashion has felt the power; a banquet, unexampled in the annals of Gunter; and a ball, in which the recollections of ancient chivalry will blend sweetly with the soft tones of Weippert and Collinet, are among the entertainments which the Ladye of T–gg–ridgeville has prepared for her distinguished guests.'

The Baron was the life of the scheme: he longed to be on horseback, and in the field at Tuggeridgeville, where he, Tagrag, and a number of our friends practised; he was the very best tilter present: he vaulted over his horse, and played such wonderful antics, as never were done except at Ducrow's.

And now—O that I had twenty pages, instead of these miserable two, to describe the wonders of the day!—Twenty-four knights came from Ashley's, at two guineas a head. We were in hopes to have had Miss Woolford, in the character of Joan of Arc, but that lady did not appear. We had a tent for the challengers, at each side of which hung what they called *escoachings* (like hatchments, which they put up when people die), and underneath sat their pages, holding their helmets for the tournament. Tagrag was in brass armour (my city connexions got him that famous suit); his Excellency in polished steel. My wife wore a coronet, modelled exactly after that of Queen Katharine, in Henry V.; a tight gilt jacket, which set off dear Jemmy's figure wonderfully, and a train of at least forty feet. Dear Jemimarann was in white, her hair braided with pearls. Madame de Flicflac appeared as Queen Elizabeth; and Lady Blanche Bluenose as a

Turkish princess. An alderman of London, and his lady; two
magistrates of the county, and the very pink of Croydon; several
Polish noblemen; two Italian Counts (besides *our* Count); one
hundred and ten young officers, from Addiscombe College, in full
uniform, commanded by Major-General Sir Miles Mulligatawney,
K.C.B., and his lady; the Misses Pimminy's Finishing Establishment, and fourteen young ladies, all in white; the Reverend
Doctor Wapshot, and forty-nine young gentlemen, of the first
families, under his charge; were *some* only of the company. I
leave you to fancy that, if my Jemmy did seek for fashion, she
had enough of it on this occasion. They wanted me to have
mounted again, but my hunting-day had been sufficient; besides
I ain't big enough for a real knight: so, as Mrs. Coxe insisted on
my opening the Tournament—and I knew it was in vain to resist
—the Baron and Tagrag had undertaken to arrange so that I
might come off with safety, if I came off at all. They had
procured, from the Strand Theatre, a famous stud of hobby-horses,
which they told me had been trained for the use of the great Lord
Bateman. I did not know exactly what they were till they
arrived; but as they had belonged to a Lord, I thought it was all
right, and consented; and I found it the best sort of riding, after
all, to appear to be on horseback and walk safely a-foot at the
same time, and it was impossible to come down as long as I kept
on my own legs; besides, I could cuff and pull my steed about as
much as I liked, without fear of his biting or kicking in return.
As Lord of the Tournament, they placed in my hands a lance,
ornamented spirally, in blue and gold; I thought of the pole over
my old shop-door, and almost wished myself there again, as I
capered up to the battle in my helmet and breast-plate, with all
the trumpets blowing and drums beating at the time. Captain
Tagrag was my opponent, and preciously we poked each other,
till, prancing about, I put my foot on my horse's petticoat behind,
and down I came, getting a thrust from the Captain, at the same
time, that almost broke my shoulder-bone. 'This was sufficient,'
they said, 'for the laws of chivalry;' and I was glad to get off so.

After that, the gentlemen riders, of whom there were no less
than seven, in complete armour, and the professionals, now ran at
the ring; and the Baron was far, far the most skilful.

'How sweetly the dear Baron rides,' said my wife, who was
always ogling at him, smirking, smiling, and waving her handkerchief to him. 'I say, Sam,' says a professional to one of his
friends, as, after their course, they came cantering up, and ranged
under Jemmy's bower, as she called it;—'I say, Sam, I'm blowed
if that chap in harmer mustn't have been one of hus.' And this

only made Jemmy the more pleased ; for the fact is, the Baron had chosen the best way of winning Jemimarann by courting her mother.

The Baron was declared conqueror at the ring ; and Jemmy awarded him the prize, a wreath of white roses, which she placed on his lance ; he receiving it gracefully, and bowing, until the plumes of his helmet mingled with the mane of his charger, which backed to the other end of the lists, and then, galloping back to the place where Jemimarann was seated, he begged her to place it on his helmet : the poor girl blushed very much, and did so. As all the people were applauding, Tagrag rushed up, and, laying his hand on the Baron's shoulder, whispered something in his ear, which made the other very angry, I suppose, for he shook him off violently. ' *Chacun pour soi*,' says he, ' Monsieur de Taguerague ; '—which means, I am told, ' every man for himself ; ' and then he rode away, throwing his lance in the air, catching it, and making his horse caper and prance, to the admiration of all beholders.

After this came the ' Passage of Arms ; ' Tagrag and the Baron ran courses against the other champions ; ay, and unhorsed two apiece ; whereupon the other three refused to turn out ; and preciously we laughed at them, to be sure !

' Now, it's *our* turn, Mr. *Chicot*,' says Tagrag, shaking his fist at the Baron : ' look to yourself, you infernal mountebank, for, by Jupiter, I'll do my best ; ' and before Jemmy and the rest of us, who were quite bewildered, could say a word, these two friends were charging away, spears in hand, ready to kill each other. In vain Jemmy screamed ; in vain I threw down my truncheon : they had broken two poles before I could say ' Jack Robinson,' and were driving at each other with the two new ones. The Baron had the worst of the first course, for he had almost been carried out of his saddle. ' Hark you, Chicot ! ' screamed out Tagrag, ' next time look to your head : ' and, next time, sure enough, each aimed at the head of the other.

Tagrag's spear hit the right place ; for it carried off the Baron's helmet, plume, rose-wreath and all ; but his Excellency hit truer still—his lance took Tagrag on the neck, and sent him to the ground like a stone.

' He's won ! he's won ! ' says Jemmy, waving her handkerchief ; Jemimarann fainted, Lady Blanche screamed, and I felt so sick that I thought I should drop. All the company were in an uproar : only the Baron looked calm, and bowed very gracefully, and kissed his hand to Jemmy ; when, all of a sudden, a Jewish-looking man, springing over the barrier, and followed by three more, rushed towards the Baron. 'Keep the gate, Bob!' he holloas out. 'Baron, I arrest you, at the suit of Samuel Levison, for——'

But he never said for what; shouting out, 'Aha!' and '*Sapprrrristie!*' and I don't know what, his Excellency drew his sword, dug his spurs into his horse, and was over the poor bailiff, and off before another word. He had threatened to run through one of the bailiff's followers, Mr. Stubbs, only that gentleman made way for him; and when we took up the bailiff, and brought him round by the aid of a little brandy-and-water, he told us all. 'I had a writ againsht him, Mishter Coxsh, but I didn't vant to shpoil shport; and, beshidesh, I didn't know him until dey knocked off his shteel cap!'

Here was a pretty business!

SEPTEMBER—OVER-BOARDED AND UNDER-LODGED.

We had no great reason to brag of our tournament at Tuggeridge-ville: but, after all, it was better than the turn-out at Kilblazes, where poor Lord Heydownderry went about in a black velvet dressing-gown, and the Emperor Napoleon Bonypart appeared in a suit of armour, and silk stockings, like Mr. Pell's friend in *Pickwick;* we, having employed the gentlemen from Astley's Antitheatre, had some decent sport for our money.

We never heard a word from the Baron, who had so distinguished himself by his horsemanship, and had knocked down (and very justly) Mr. Nabb, the bailiff, and Mr. Stubbs his man, who came to lay hands upon him. My sweet Jemmy seemed to be very low in spirits after his departure, and a sad thing it is to see her in low spirits: on days of illness she no more minds giving Jemimarann a box on the ear, or sending a plate of muffins across a table at poor me, than she does taking her tea.

Jemmy, I say, was very low in spirits; but, one day (I remember it was the day after Captain Higgins called, and said he had seen the Baron at Boulogne), she vowed that nothing but change of air would do her good, and declared that she should die unless she went to the sea-side in France. I knew what this meant, and that I might as well attempt to resist her, as to resist Her Gracious Majesty in Parliament assembled; so I told

GEORGE CRUIKSHANK.

SEPTEMBER—OVER-BOARDED AND UNDER-LODGED.

the people to pack up the things, and took four places on board the *Grand Turk* steamer for Boulogne.

The travelling carriage, which, with Jemmy's thirty-seven boxes and my carpet-bag, was pretty well loaded, was sent on board, the night before; and we, after breakfasting in Portland Place (little did I think it was the—but, poh! never mind), went down to the Custom House in the other carriage, followed by a hackney-coach and a cab, with the servants, and fourteen band-boxes and trunks more, which were to be wanted by my dear girl in the journey.

The road down Cheapside and Thames Street need not be described; we saw the Monument, a memento of the wicked Popish massacre of Saint Bartholomew;—why erected here I can't think, as Saint Bartholomew's is in Smithfield;—we had a glimpse of Billingsgate, and of the Mansion House, where we saw the two-and-twenty shilling coal-smoke coming out of the chimneys, and were landed at the Custom House in safety. I felt melancholy, for we were going among a people of swindlers, as all Frenchmen are acknowledged to be; and, besides not being able to speak the language, leaving our own dear country, and honest countrymen.

Fourteen porters came out, and each took a package with the greatest civility; calling Jemmy her ladyship, and me your honour; ay, and your-honouring and my-ladyshipping even my man and the maid in the cab.

I somehow felt all over quite melancholy at going away; 'Here, my fine fellow,' says I to the coachman, who was standing very respectful, holding his hat in one hand and Jemmy's jewel-case in the other; 'here, my fine chap,' says I, 'here's six shillings for you;' for I did not care for the money.

'Six what?' says he.

'Six shillings, fellow,' shrieks Jemmy, 'and twice as much as your fare.'

'Feller, marm!' says this insolent coachman, 'feller yourself, marm; do you think I'm a-going to kill my horses, and break my precious back, and bust my carriage, and carry you, and your kids, and your traps, for six hog?' And with this the monster dropped his hat, with my money in it, and doubling his fist, put it so very near my nose that I really thought he would have made it bleed. 'My fare's heighteen shillings,' says he, 'hain't it?—hask hany of these gentlemen.'

'Why, it ain't more than seventeen and six,' says one of the fourteen porters; 'but, if the gen'l'man *is* a gen'l'man, he can't give no less than a suffering anyhow.'

I wanted to resist, and Jemmy screamed like a Turk; but, 'Holloa!' says one: 'What's the row?' says another: 'Come, dub up!' roars a third; and I don't mind telling you, in confidence, that I was so frightened that I took out the sovereign and gave it. My man and Jemmy's maid had disappeared by this time; they always do when there's a robbery or row going on.

I was going after them. 'Stop, Mr. Ferguson,' pipes a young gentleman of about thirteen, with a red livery waistcoat that reached to his ankles, and every variety of button, pin, string to keep it together: 'Stop, Mr. Heff,' says he, taking a small pipe out of his mouth, 'and don't forgit the cabman.'

'What's your fare, my lad?' says I.

'Why, let's see—yes—ho!—my fare's seven-and-thirty and eightpence eggs—acly.'

The fourteen gentlemen, holding the luggage, here burst out and laughed very rudely indeed; and the only person who seemed disappointed was, I thought, the hackney-coachman. 'Why, *you* rascal!' says Jemmy, laying hold of the boy, 'do you want more than the coachman?'

'Don't rascal *me*, marm!' shrieks the little chap in return. 'What's the coach to me? Vy, you may go in an omlibus for six-pence if you like; vy don't you go and buss it, marm? Vy did you call my cab, marm? Vy am I to come forty mile, from Scarlot Street, Po'tl'nd Street, and not git my fare, marm? Come, give me a suffering and a half, and don't keep my hoss a-vaiting all day.'

This speech, which takes some time to write down, was made in about the fifth part of a second; and, at the end of it, the young gentleman hurled down his pipe, and, advancing towards Jemmy, doubled his fist, and seemed to challenge her to fight. My dearest girl now turned from red to be as pale as white Windsor, and fell into my arms: what was I to do? I called, 'Policeman!' but a policeman won't interfere in Thames Street; robbery is licensed there. What was I to do? Oh! my heart beats with paternal gratitude when I think of what my Tug did!

As soon as this young cab-chap put himself into a fighting attitude, Master Tuggeridge Coxe—who had been standing by, laughing very rudely, I thought—Master Tuggeridge Coxe, I say, flung his jacket suddenly into his mamma's face (the brass buttons made her start, and recovered her a little), and, before we could say a word, was in the ring in which we stood (formed by the porters, nine orangemen and women, I don't know how many newspaper boys, hotel cads, and old clothesmen), and, whirling about two little white fists in the face of the gentleman in the red waistcoat, who brought a great pair of black ones to bear on the enemy, was engaged in an instant.

But, law bless you! Tug hadn't been at Richmond School for nothing; and *milled* away—one, two, right and left—like a little hero as he is, with all his dear mother's spirit in him: first came a crack which sent a long dusky white hat—that looked damp and deep like a well, and had a long black crape rag twisted round it —first came a crack which sent this white hat spinning over the gentleman's cab, and scattered among the crowd a vast number of things which the cabman kept in it,—such as a ball of string, a piece of candle, a comb, a whip-lash, a little warbler, a slice of bacon, etc. etc.

The cabman seemed sadly ashamed of this display, but Tug gave him no time; another blow was planted on his cheek-bone; and a third, which hit him straight on the nose, sent this rude cabman straight down to the ground.

'Brayvo, my lord!' shouted all the people around.

'I won't have no more, thank yer,' said the little cabman, gathering himself up, "give us over my fare, vil yer, and let me git away.'

'What's your fare *now*, you cowardly little thief?' says Tug.

'Vy, then, two and eightpence,' says he. 'Go along—you *know* it is.' And two and eightpence he had; and everybody applauded Tug, and hissed the cab-boy, and asked Tug for something to drink. We heard the packet-bell ringing, and all run down the stairs to be in time.

I now thought our troubles would soon be over; mine were, very nearly so, in one sense at least; for after Mrs. Coxe, and Jemimarann, and Tug, and the maid, and valet, and valuables had been handed across, it came to my turn. I had often heard of people being taken up by a *Plank*, but seldom of their being set down by one. Just as I was going over, the vessel rode off a little, the board slipped, and down I soused into the water. You might have heard Mrs. Coxe's shriek as far as Gravesend; it rung in my ears as I went down, all grieved at the thought of leaving her a disconsolate widder. Well, up I came again, and caught the brim of my beaver hat—though I have heard that drowning men catch at straws:—I floated, and hoped to escape by hook or by crook; and, luckily, just then, I felt myself suddenly jerked by the waist-band of my whites, and found myself hauled up in air at the end of a boat-hook, to the sound of 'Yeho! yeho! yehoi! yehoi!' and so I was dragged aboard. I was put to bed, and had swallowed so much water that it took a very considerable quantity of brandy to bring it to a proper mixture in my inside; in fact, for some hours I was in a very deplorable state.

OCTOBER—Notice To Quit.

Well, we arrived at Boulogne; and Jemmy, after making inquiries, right and left, about the Baron, found no such person was known there; and being bent, I suppose, at all events, on marrying her daughter to a lord, she determined to set off for Paris, where, as he had often said, he possessed a magnificent ——, hotel he called it;—and I remember Jemmy being mightily indignant at the idea; but hotel, we found afterwards, means only a house in French, and this reconciled her. Need I describe the road from Boulogne to Paris? or need I describe that Capitol itself? Suffice it to say, that we made our appearance there, at Murisse's Hotel, as became the family of Coxe Tuggeridge; and saw everything worth seeing in the metropolis in a week. It nearly killed me, to be sure; but, when you're on a pleasure party, in a foreign country, you must not mind a little inconvenience of this sort.

Well, there is, near the city of Paris, a splendid road and row of trees, which, I don't know why, is called the Shandeleezy, or Elysian Fields, in French: others, I have heard, call it the Shandeleery; but mine I know to be the correct pronunciation. In the middle of this Shandeleezy is an open space of ground, and a tent, where, during the summer, Mr. Franconi, the French Ashley, performs with his horses and things. As everybody went there, and we were told it was quite the thing, Jemmy agreed that we should go too; and go we did.

It's just like Ashley's: there's a man just like Mr. Piddicombe, who goes round the ring in a huzzah-dress, cracking a whip; there are a dozen Miss Woolfords, who appear like Polish Princesses, Dihannas, Sultannas, Cachuchas, and heaven knows what! There's the fat man, who comes in with the twenty-three dresses on, and turns out to be the living skeleton! There's the clowns, the sawdust, the white horse that dances a hornpipe, the candles stuck in hoops, just as in our own dear country.

My dear wife, in her very finest clothes, with all the world looking at her, was really enjoying this spectacle (which doesn't require any knowledge of the language, seeing that the dumb animals don't talk it), when there came in, presently, 'the great

George Cruikshank

OCTOBER—NOTICE TO QUIT.

P. 390.

Polish act of the Sarmatian horse-tamer, on eight steeds,' which we were all of us longing to see. The horse-tamer, to music twenty miles an hour, rushed in on four of his horses, leading the other four, and skurried round the ring. You couldn't see him for the sawdust, but everybody was delighted, and applauded like mad. Presently, you saw there were only three horses in front; he had slipped one more between his legs, another followed, and it was clear that the consequences would be fatal, if he admitted any more. The people applauded more than ever; and when, at last, seven and eight were made to go in, not wholly, but sliding dexterously in and out, with the others, so that you did not know which was which, the house, I thought, would come down with applause; and the Sarmatian horse-tamer bowed his great feathers to the ground. At last the music grew slower, and he cantered leisurely round the ring; bending, smirking, seesawing, waving his whip, and laying his hand on his heart, just as we have seen the Ashley's people do. But fancy our astonishment when, suddenly, this Sarmatian horse-tamer, coming round with his four pair at a canter, and being opposite our box, gave a start, and a —hupp! which made all of his horses stop stock-still at an instant!

'Albert!' screamed my dear Jemmy; 'Albert! Bahbahbah— baron!'

The Sarmatian looked at her for a minute; and turning head over heels, three times, bolted suddenly off his horses, and away out of our sight.

It was HIS EXCELLENCY THE BARON DE PUNTER!

Jemmy went off in a fit, as usual, and we never saw the Baron again; but we heard, afterwards, that Punter was an apprentice of Franconi's, and had run away to England, thinking to better himself, and had joined Mr. Richardson's army; but Mr. Richardson, and then London, did not agree with him; and we saw the last of him as he sprung over the barriers at the Tuggeridgeville tournament.

'Well, Jemimarann,' says Jemmy, in a fury, 'you shall marry Tagrag; and if I can't have a baroness for a daughter, at least you shall be a baronet's lady.' Poor Jemimarann only sighed; she knew it was of no use to remonstrate.

Paris grew dull to us after this; and we were more eager than ever to go back to London; for what should we hear, but that that monster, Tuggeridge, of the City—old Tug's black son, forsooth!—was going to contest Jemmy's claim to the property, and had filed I don't know how many bills against us in Chancery. Hearing this, we set off immediately, and we arrived at Boulogne, and set off in that very same *Grand Turk* which had brought us to France.

If you look in the bills, you will see that the steamers leave London on Saturday morning, and Boulogne on Saturday night ; so that there is often not an hour between the time of arrival and departure. Bless us ! bless us ! I pity the poor Captain that, for twenty-four hours at a time, is on a paddle-box, roaring out, 'Ease her ! Stop her !' and the poor servants, who are laying out breakfast, lunch, dinner, tea, supper ;—breakfast, lunch, dinner, tea, supper again ;—for layers upon layers of travellers, as it were ; and, most of all, I pity that unhappy steward, with those unfortunate tin basins that he must always keep an eye over.

Little did we know what a storm was brooding in our absence, and little were we prepared for the awful, awful fate that hung over our Tuggeridgeville property.

Biggs, of the great house of Higgs, Biggs, and Blatherwick, was our man of business : when I arrived in London I heard that he had just set off to Paris after me. So we started down to Tuggeridgeville instead of going to Portland Place. As we came through the lodge-gates, we found a crowd assembled within them ; and there was that horrid Tuggeridge on horseback, with a shabby-looking man, called Mr. Scapgoat, and his man of business, and many more. 'Mr. Scapgoat,' says Tuggeridge, grinning, and handing him over a sealed paper, 'here's the lease ; I leave you in possession, and wish you good morning.'

'In possession of what ?' says the rightful lady of Tuggeridge-ville, leaning out of the carriage-window. She hated black Tuggeridge, as she called him, like poison : the very first week of our coming to Portland Place, when he called to ask restitution of some plate which he said was his private property, she called him a base-born blackamoor, and told him to quit the house. Since then there had been law-squabbles between us without end, and all sorts of writings, meetings, and arbitrations.

'Possession of my estate of Tuggeridgeville, Madam,' roars he, 'left me by my father's will, which you have had notice of these three weeks, and know as well as I do.'

'Old Tug left no will,' shrieked Jemmy ; 'he didn't die to leave his estates to blackamoors—to negroes—to base-born mulatto story-tellers ; if he did, may I be ——'

'O, hush ! dearest mamma,' says Jemimarann.

'Go it again, mother !' says Tug, who is always sniggering.

'What is this business, Mr. Tuggeridge ?' cried Tagrag (who was the only one of our party that had his senses), 'what is this will ?'

'O, it's merely a matter of form,' said the lawyer, riding up. 'For heaven's sake, madam, be peaceable; let my friends, Higgs, Biggs, and Blatherwick, arrange with me. I am surprised that none of their people are here. All that you have to do is to eject us; and the rest will follow, of course.'

'Who has taken possession of this here property?' roars Jemmy, again.

'My friend Mr. Scapgoat,' said the lawyer.—Mr. Scapgoat grinned.

'Mr. Scapgoat,' said my wife, shaking her fist at him (for she is a woman of no small spirit), 'if you don't leave this ground, I'll have you pushed out with pitchforks, I will, you and your beggarly blackamoor yonder;' and, suiting the action to the word, she clapped a stable fork into the hands of one of the gardeners, and called another, armed with a rake, to his help, while young Tug set the dog at their heels, and I hurrahed for joy to see such villainy so properly treated.

'That's sufficient, ain't it?' said Mr. Scapgoat, with the calmest air in the world. 'O, completely,' said the lawyer. 'Mr. Tuggeridge, we've ten miles to dinner, Madam, your very humble servant:' and the whole *posse* of them rode away.

NOVEMBER—Law Life Assurance.

We knew not what this meant, until we received a strange document from Higgs, in London; which begun, 'Middlesex to wit. Samuel Cox, late of Portland Place, in the city of Westminster, in the said county, was attached to answer Samuel Scapgoat, of a plea, wherefore, with force and arms, he entered into one messuage, with the appurtenances, which John Tuggeridge, Esq., demised to the said Samuel Scapgoat, for a term which is not yet expired, and ejected him.' And it went on to say, that 'we, with force of arms, *viz.*, with swords, knives, and staves, had ejected him.' Was there ever such a monstrous falsehood? when we did but stand in defence of our own; and isn't it a sin, that we should have been turned out of our rightful possessions upon such a rascally plea?

Higgs, Biggs, and Blatherwick had, evidently, been bribed; for, would you believe it?—they told us to give up possession at once, as a will was found, and we could not defend the action. My Jemmy refused their proposal with scorn, and laughed at the notion of the will: she pronounced it to be a forgery, a vile

NOVEMBER—LAW LIFE ASSURANCE.

blackamoor forgery; and believes, to this day, that the story of its having been made thirty years ago, in Calcutta, and left there with old Tug's papers, and found there, and brought to England, after a search made, by order of Tuggeridge, junior, is a scandalous falsehood.

Well, the cause was tried. Why need I say anything concerning it? What shall I say of the Lord Chief Justice, but that he ought to be ashamed of the wig he sits in. What of Mr. ——, and Mr. ——, who exerted their eloquence against justice and the poor? On our side, too, was no less a man than Mr. Serjeant Binks, who, ashamed I am, for the honour of the British bar, to say it, seemed to have been bribed too; for he actually threw up his case! Had he behaved like Mr. Mulligan, his junior—and to whom, in this humble way, I offer my thanks—all might have been well. I never knew such an effect produced, as when Mr. Mulligan, appearing for the first time in that court, said, 'Standing here, upon the pidestal of secred Thamis, seeing around me the arnymints of a profission I rispict; having before me a vinnerable Judge, and an elightened Judge, and an elightened Judge—the counthry's glory, the netion's cheap defender, the poor man's priceless palladium—how must I thrimble, my Lard, how must the blush bejew my cheek— (somebody cried out, "O cheeks!" In the court there was a dreadful roar of laughing; and when order was established, Mr. Mulligan, continued)—my Lard, I heed them not; I come from a counthry accustomed to opprission, and as that counthry—yes, my Lard, that Ireland—(do not laugh, I am proud of it)—is ever, in spite of her tyrants, green, and lovely, and beautiful; my client's cause, likewise, will rise shuperior to the malignant imbecility—I repeat, the MALIGNANT IMBECILITY, of those who would thrample it down; and in whose teeth, in my client's name, in my counthry's, ay, and my own, I, with folded arrums, hurl a scarnful and eternal defiance!'

'For heaven's sake, Mr. Milligan'—'MULLIGAN, ME LARD,' cried my defender—'Well, Mulligan, then, be calm, and keep to your brief.'

Mr. Mulligan did; and for three hours and a quarter, in a speech crammed with Latin quotations, and unsurpassed for eloquence, he explained the situation of me and my family; the romantic manner in which Tuggeridge, the elder, gained his fortune, and by which it afterwards came to my wife; the state of Ireland; the original and virtuous poverty of the Coxes—from which he glanced passionately, for a few minutes (until the judge stopped him), to the poverty of his own country; my excellence as a husband, father, landlord; my wife's, as a wife, mother, landlady.   All was in vain—the trial went against us.

I was soon taken in execution for the damages; five hundred pounds of law expenses of my own, and as much more of Tuggeridge's.

He would not pay a farthing, he said, to get me out of a much worse place than the Fleet.

I need not tell you, that along with the land went the house in town, and the money in the funds.   Tuggeridge, he who had thousands before, had it all.

And when I was in prison, who do you think would come and see me?   None of the Barons, nor Counts, nor Foreign Ambassadors, nor Excellencies, who used to fill our house, and eat and drink at our expense,—not even the ungrateful Tagrag!

I could not help now saying to my dear wife, 'See, my love, we have been gentlefolks for exactly a year, and a pretty life we have had of it.   In the first place, my darling, we gave grand dinners, and everybody laughed at us.'

'Yes, and recollect how ill they made you,' cries my daughter.

'We asked great company, and they insulted us.'

'And spoilt mamma's temper,' said Jemimarann.

'Hush!   Miss,' said her mother; 'we don't want *your* advice.'

'Then you must make a country gentleman of me.'

'And send Pa into dunghills,' roared Tug.

'Then you must go to operas, and pick up foreign Barons and Counts.'

'O, thank heaven! dearest papa, that we are rid of them,' cries my little Jemimarann, looking almost happy, and kissing her old pappy.

'And you must make a fine gentleman of Tug there, and send him to a fine school.'

'And I give you my word,' says Tug, 'I'm as ignorant a chap as ever lived.'

'You're an insolent saucebox,' says Jemmy; 'you've learned that at your fine school.'

'I've learned something else, too, ma'am; ask the boys if I haven't,' grumbles Tug.

'You hawk your daughter about, and just escape marrying her to a swindler.'

'And drive off poor Orlando,' whimpered my girl.

'Silence, Miss,' says Jemmy, fiercely.

'You insult the man whose father's property you inherited, and bring me into this prison, without hope of leaving it: for he never can help us after all your bad language.'   I said all this very smartly ; for the fact is, my blood was up at the time, and I determined to rate my dear girl soundly.

'Oh ! Sammy,' said she, sobbing (for the poor thing's spirit was quite broken), 'it's all true ; I've been very, very foolish and vain, and I've punished my dear husband and children by my follies, and I do so, so repent them ! ' Here Jemimarann at once burst out crying, and flung herself into her mamma's arms, and the pair roared and sobbed for ten minutes together. Even Tug looked queer : and as for me, it's a most extraordinary thing, but I'm blest if seeing them so miserable didn't make me quite happy.—I don't think, for the whole twelve months of our good fortune, I had ever felt so gay as in that dismal room, in the Fleet, where I was locked up.

Poor Orlando Crump came to see us every day ; and we, who had never taken the slightest notice of him, in Portland Place, and treated him so cruelly that day at Beulah Spa, were only too glad of his company now. He used to bring books for my girl, and a bottle of sherry for me ; and he used to take home Jemmy's fronts, and dress them for her ; and when locking-up time came, he used to see the ladies home to their little three pair bed-room, in Holborn, where they slept now, Tug and all. 'Can the bird forget its nest ? ' Orlando used to say (he was a romantic young fellow, that's the truth, and blew the flute and read Lord Byron, incessantly, since he was separated from Jemimarann) ; 'can the bird, let loose in eastern climes, forget its home ? Can the rose cease to remember its beloved bulbul ?—Ah, no. Mr. Cox, you made me what I am, and what I hope to die—a hairdresser. I never see a curling-irons before I entered your shop, or knew Naples from brown Windsor. Did you not make over your house, your furniture, your emporium of perfumery, and nine-and-twenty shaving customers, to me ? Are these trifles ? Is Jemimarann a trifle ? if she would allow me to call her so. O, Jemimarann ! your Pa found me in the workhouse, and made me what I am. Conduct me to my grave, and I never, never shall be different ! ' When he had said this, Orlando was so much affected, that he rushed suddenly on his hat, and quitted the room.

Then Jemimarann began to cry too. ' O, Pa ! ' said she, 'isn't he, isn't he a nice young man ? '

'I'm *hanged* if he ain't,' says Tug. 'What do you think of his giving me eighteenpence yesterday, and a bottle of lavender water for Mimarann ? '

' He might as well offer to give you back the shop, at any rate,' says Jemmy.

'What ! to pay Tuggeridge's damages ? My dear, I'd sooner die than give Tuggeridge the chance.'

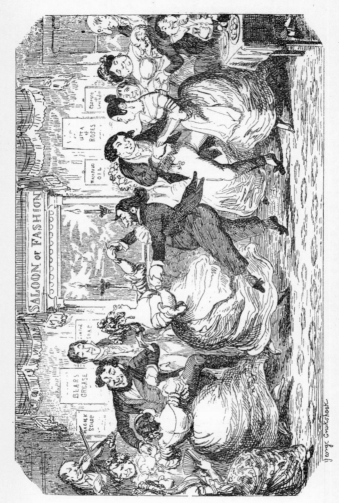

George Cruikshank

DECEMBER—CHRISTMAS BUSTLE.

DECEMBER—Christmas Bustle.

Tuggeridge vowed that I should finish my days there, when he put me in prison. It appears that we both had reason to be ashamed of ourselves; and were, thank God! I learned to be sorry for my bad feelings towards him, and he actually wrote to me to say,—

'Sir,—I think you have suffered enough for faults which, I believe, do not lie with you, so much as your wife; and I have withdrawn my claims which I had against you while you were in wrongful possession of my father's estates. You must remember that when, on examination of my father's papers, no will was found, I yielded up his property, with perfect willingness, to those who I fancied were his legitimate heirs. For this I received all sorts of insults from your wife and yourself (who acquiesced in them); and when the discovery of a will, in India, proved *my* just claims, you must remember how they were met, and the vexatious proceedings with which you sought to oppose them.

'I have discharged your lawyer's bill; and, as I believe you are more fitted for the trade you formerly exercised than for any other, I will give five hundred pounds for the purchase of a stock and shop, when you shall find one to suit you.

'I enclose a draft for twenty pounds, to meet your present expenses. You have, I am told, a son, a boy of some spirit; if he likes to try his fortune abroad, and go on board an Indiaman, I can get him an appointment; and am, Sir, your obedient servant,   John Tuggeridge.'

It was Mrs. Breadbasket, the housekeeper, who brought this letter, and looked mighty contemptuous as she gave it.

'I hope, Breadbasket, that your master will send me my things, at any rate,' cries Jemmy. 'There's seventeen silk and satin dresses, and a whole heap of trinkets, that can be of no earthly use to him.'

'Don't Breadbasket me, mem, if you please, mem. My master says that them things is quite obnoxious to your sphere of life. Breadbasket, indeed!' and so she sailed out.

Jemmy hadn't a word; she had grown mighty quiet since we had been in misfortune; but my daughter looked as happy as a queen; and Tug, when he heard of the ship, gave a jump that nearly knocked down poor Orlando. 'Ah, I suppose you'll forget me now,' says he, with a sigh; and seemed the only unhappy person in company.

'Why, you conceive, Mr. Crump,' says my wife, with a great deal of dignity, 'that connected as we are, a young man born in a work——'

'Woman!' cried I (for once in my life determined to have my own way), 'hold your foolish tongue. Your absurd pride has been the ruin of us, hitherto; and, from this day, I'll have no more of it. Hark ye, Orlando, if you will take Jemimarann, you may have her; and if you'll take five hundred pounds for a half share of the shop, they're yours; and *that's* for you, Mrs. Cox.'

And here we are, back again. And I write this from the old back shop, where we are all waiting to see the new year in. Orlando sits yonder, plaiting a wig for my Lord Chief Justice, as happy as may be; and Jemimarann and her mother have been as busy as you can imagine, all day long, and are just now giving the finishing touches to the bridal dresses; for the wedding is to take place the day after to-morrow. I've cut seventeen heads off (as I say) this very day; and as for Jemmy, I no more mind her than I do the Emperor of China and all his Tambarins. Last night we had a merry meeting of our friends and neighbours, to celebrate our re-appearance among them; and very merry we all were. We had a capital fiddler, and we kept it up till a pretty tidy hour this morning. We begun with quadrills, but I never could do 'em well; and, after that, to please Mr. Crump and his intended, we tried a gallopard, which I found anything but easy; for since I am come back to a life of peace and comfort, it's astonishing how stout I'm getting. So we turned at once to what Jemmy and me excels in—a country dance; which is rather surprising, as we was both brought up to a town life. As for young Tug, he showed off in a sailor's hornpipe; which Mrs. Cox says is very proper for him to learn, now he is intended for the sea. But stop! here comes in the punch-bowls; and if we are not happy, who is? I say I am like the Swish people, for I can't flourish out of my native *hair*.

THE END

Printed by R. & R. Clark, Limited, *Edinburgh*.